Write better with a PC

A publisher's guide to
business and technical writing

Write better with a PC

A publisher's guide to business and technical writing

Mike Murach

Mike Murach & Associates, Inc.
4697 West Jacquelyn Avenue
Fresno, California 93722
(209) 275-3335

Editors

Rebecca Lyles
Judy Taylor
Nancy Johnson

Graphics designer

Steve Ehlers

Desktop publisher

Steve Ehlers

© 1989, Mike Murach & Associates, Inc.
All rights reserved.
Printed in the United States of America.
20 19 18 17 16 15 14 13 12 11 10 9 8 7 6 5 4 3 2

ISBN: 0-911625-51-8

Library of Congress Cataloging-in-Publication Data

Murach, Mike
    Write better with a PC : a publisher's guide to business and technical writing / Mike Murach.
       p. cm.
    Includes index.
    ISBN 0-911625-51-8 (pbk. : alk. paper) : $19.95
    1. Business writing—Data processing. 2. Technical writing—Data processing. 3. English language—Business English.   I. Title.
HF5718.3.M87 1989
070.5'1'0285416—dc20   89-60556
                                                                              CIP

Contents

Introduction vii

Section 1   **How to get the most from your PC** 1

Chapter 1   How 12 types of PC software can help you improve your writing 3

Chapter 2   How a proven writing procedure can help you improve your writing 33

Section 2   **12 easy steps to better writing with a PC** 53

Chapter 3   How to decide what you should write 55

     Step 1:   Define the job 56
     Step 2:   Get the information you need 66
     Step 3:   Select the content 73

Chapter 4   How to plan what you're going to write 85

     Step 4:   Plan the topics and subtopics 86
     Step 5:   Plan the headings and subheadings 101
     Step 6:   Plan the visual aids 118
     Step 7:   Plan the paragraphs 127

Chapter 5   How to write the first draft 133

     Step 8:   Develop the visual aids 134
     Step 9:   Write the text 143

Chapter 6   How to revise a first draft 157

     Step 10:   Analyze and improve the structure of the first draft 158
     Step 11:   Edit and revise the first draft 165
     Step 12:   Proofread and correct the second draft 174

Chapter 7	Six steps for developing a multi-unit document	177
Section 3	**The essential language skills for business and technical writers**	**187**
Chapter 8	How to write effective paragraphs	189
Chapter 9	How to write readable sentences	213
Chapter 10	How to provide continuity in your writing	243
Chapter 11	How to write with an effective tone and style	257
Chapter 12	How to write with manageable sentence structures	281
Chapter 13	How to write with correct grammar and diction	303
Section 4	**Practical presentation skills for PC users**	**331**
Chapter 14	How to use word processing to present your documents	333
Chapter 15	When and how to use desktop publishing to present your documents	349
Appendix A	An effective report in word processing form	373
Appendix B	An effective report in desktop publishing form	387
Appendix C	Writing procedures	399
Appendix D	Writing guidelines	403
Index		407

Introduction

If you want to improve your writing, learning to write with a personal computer (PC) is a good first step. If you have the right skills, a PC can help you improve the structure, readability, tone, and style of your writing. It can also help you double your writing productivity. In short, you should be able to write much better with a PC than you can without one.

The trouble is that most business and technical writers don't have the skills they need to get the most from their PCs. As a result, most writers don't improve the effectiveness of their writing when they start to write with a PC. Similarly, most writers make only marginal improvements in their productivity when they write with a PC.

Fortunately, it's not that difficult to get the maximum benefit from your PC. All you have to do is master the writing and PC skills that I've presented in this book. Once you master them, you'll write with confidence. You'll work with efficiency. Your writing will get the results you want. And you'll never again fear a writing project of any size.

Who this book is for

It should be obvious by now that this book is for people who want to improve their writing. It's also for people who want to use their PCs more effectively as they write. Although this book is especially designed for business and technical writers, it will help you write better with a PC no matter what kind of writing you do.

In our company, for example, we use the skills presented in this book for writing everything from memos to manuscripts. Each year, our writing includes hundreds of memos and letters, dozens of advertisements and direct mail pieces, dozens of reports and proposals, a couple of instructor's guides or procedure manuals, and half a dozen manuscripts for the books we publish.

Although this book is for people who use a PC or are thinking about using one, it doesn't matter what kind of PC you use. This book will help you whether you use an IBM PC (XT or AT), an IBM PS/2, an IBM clone, a Macintosh, or an Apple. It will also help you if you use a minicomputer or mainframe for your writing instead of a PC. In fact, most of the ideas in this book will help you improve your writing even if you don't use a computer. The only assumption this book makes is that you are somewhat familiar with word processing and PCs.

What this book teaches

This book teaches the four types of skills you need for writing with a PC: software skills, procedural skills, language skills, and presentation skills. A description of each follows.

How to use the right PC software at the right time In chapter 1, you'll learn that there are twelve types of software that can be useful to the business or technical writer. In other words, there's a lot more software for the writer than word processing software. The trick is knowing which software products to use and when to use them.

In the other fourteen chapters of this book, you'll get specific advice on how to use the various types of software. In chapter 4, for example, you'll learn how to use word processing or an outline processor to plan what you're going to write. In chapter 5, you'll learn how to use word processing, spreadsheet, or graphics software to prepare visual aids. In chapter 6, you'll learn how to use a writing analyzer for revision, and in chapter 9, you'll learn how to use an analyzer to test readability.

When you finish this book, you'll realize that effective writers don't use just word processing on their PCs. And they don't use word processing just for writing and revision. To get the most from their PCs, successful writers use several different kinds of PC software for their writing assignments.

How to use a writing procedure that prevents "thrashing"
When writers use typewriters, they usually limit themselves to one or two revisions of a document because the entire document has to be retyped for each revision. In contrast, revision on a PC is so easy that many writers prepare several drafts of a single document. Unfortunately, because these extra revisions reduce productivity, many writers are no more productive with PCs than they were when they used manual methods.

When a writer revises a document more than two or three times, we refer to it as "thrashing." Writers thrash when they don't do an effective job of planning what they are going to write before they start writing. As a result, they try to solve content and organizational problems by repeatedly revising what they've written. The trouble is that you usually can't solve significant writing problems that way. The more you try, the more you thrash. But thrashing leads to only marginal writing improvements, even though it seriously decreases writing productivity.

In chapter 2, you'll be introduced to a proven writing procedure that will help you avoid thrashing. Because this procedure emphasizes analysis and planning, it will help you write more effectively than you ever have before. It will also help you write most of your documents with only one revision. Since this procedure is particularly suited for PC users, it will help you get the maximum benefit from your system.

Because a procedure like this is so critical for effective writing, section 2 of this book shows you how to do each of its 12 procedural steps in detail. For each step, you'll learn what software to use and how to use it. Once you master this procedure, you'll never again be overwhelmed by a writing project. No matter how large the project is, you'll always know what to do next and how to do it.

The essential language skills for business and technical writers Whether or not you use a computer, you can't write well unless you know how to write effective paragraphs and readable sentences. Unfortunately, most people graduate from high school and college without ever learning these skills. In addition, most college graduates have never learned how to provide continuity between their paragraphs and between their sentences; how to write with an effective tone and style; or how to write with manageable sentence structures. Some college graduates have never even learned how to write with correct grammar and diction.

In case you've missed any of these skills, section 3 of this book will teach you the ones you must have for business and technical writing. However, in contrast to the way you've been taught these skills in the past, this section presents them in the top-down sequence shown in the table of contents. This sequence starts with paragraphing (chapter 8) and ends with grammar and diction (chapter 13). In our experience, this teaching approach is far more interesting and effective than the traditional bottom-up approach to language skills that starts with grammar and seldom goes much beyond that. So even if you had trouble with these skills when you were in school, I think you'll find you can master them quite easily when you approach them from the top down.

Practical presentation skills for PC users   When you use a PC, you can "present" a document in many different forms. For instance, you can use word processing to present it the same way you would present a typewritten document. Or, you can use word processing to automatically generate a table of contents and index for it. If you have desktop publishing software on your system, you can use it to present your document so it looks as though it was prepared by a magazine or book publisher.

Unfortunately, too many PC users spend too much time on the presentation of their documents. That's why most PC documents look better than they ever did before, even though their contents are as unorganized and unprofessional as ever. To write effectively, though, you need to be more practical than that.

So in section 4, you'll learn practical presentation skills for both word processing and desktop publishing. Here, you'll learn how to present each document in a form that is appropriate for its audience and purpose. If, for example, you're sending a short report to your boss, you can use word processing to do an effective job of presentation in just a few minutes. Chapter 14 will show you how to do that. On the other hand, if you're sending a newsletter to 10,000 customers, you may want to use the full power of desktop publishing. If so, chapter 15 will show you how to do that so the graphics look professional and so you finish the job in a reasonable amount of time.

Why this book practices what it teaches

As I wrote this book, I used all of the skills it teaches. For instance, I wrote the manuscript using WordPerfect on an IBM PC/AT clone. At the appropriate times, I used WordPerfect's spelling checker and thesaurus as well as a writing analyzer, a spreadsheet package, and a graphics package. Occasionally, I used an outline processor. And we produced this entire book using desktop publishing.

As I wrote each chapter, I used the 12-step writing procedure introduced in chapter 2 and presented in detail in section 2. To plan and coordinate the 15 chapters, I used the 6-step procedure presented in chapter 7. As I wrote the paragraphs and sentences, I followed every one of the writing guidelines presented in section 3.

I point this out because I've read many books on writing that don't practice what they teach. I've read chapters on outlining that were completely unorganized. I've read chapters on readability that were unreadable. I've read chapters on clarity that were confusing. And I've read chapters on tone that were pompous. It seems, in fact, that most books on writing don't practice what they teach. Because this book does, you can see for yourself whether the skills it teaches are the ones you want to learn.

How the ideas in this book evolved

As you read this book, you'll learn procedures, principles, and guidelines that are designed to help you improve your writing. As you would hope, these ideas didn't spring to my mind as I wrote this book. They evolved during my 21 years as a writer and publisher. So you'll have confidence in these ideas, let me give you a brief history of how they evolved.

In 1967, I started my writing career as a staff writer with a highly respected, educational publishing company. Since I had worked for IBM and had experience with computers, my first assignment was to write an introductory textbook on data processing. That was a heady assignment for a 28-year-old man with no writing experience.

But that's when I realized that I didn't know how to write. Although I could write a pretty good letter or a short report, the thought of writing an entire chapter overwhelmed me. Apparently, no one had ever taught me how to write anything longer than a page or two...even though I had majored in English at the University of Wisconsin.

Because I was determined to succeed, I began an extensive period of research on writing that continued for the next five years. During that time, I read dozens of books on writing, and I learned all the writing skills presented in section 3 of this book. However, I never did find a book that presented a practical procedure for writing. Worse, no one who worked with me knew of any such procedure, even though most of the managers had doctoral degrees in education.

My boss, for example, said not to worry about a writing procedure. "Writing is an iterative process," he said. "You write; we review; and we repeat the process until you write something we accept." But to me, that was too inefficient. Today, I can identify my boss's writing procedure as an early form of "thrashing."

If books on writing couldn't help me and the people in the publishing industry couldn't either, what was I to do but develop my own procedures for writing? That, of course, is what most professional writers are forced to do when they realize that they never learned how to write when they were in school. So by 1969, I had developed an early version of the writing procedure that's presented in section 2 of this book. Although this procedure was primitive, it helped me start a successful career as a free-lance writer.

By 1972, I was able to start my own publishing company, a small company that has specialized in computer textbooks. As I trained writers and editors for my company, I showed them my writing procedure to see if they would find it useful. All of them did. I also taught them the language skills that are presented in section 3 of this book. As they used the writing procedure and the language skills, my writers and editors had ideas and suggestions that led to continued improvements in both.

By 1980, we started using word processing on a minicomputer for all our writing and editorial work. As a result, we made some refinements to our writing procedure that helped us get the maximum benefit from word processing. By this time, we were using the procedure of section 2 and the skills of section 3 for all our writing. As a direct mail publishing company, our entire business depended on our writing skills, and it was clear that our writing skills were working. We wrote all our books ourselves, we marketed them with ads and direct mail pieces we wrote ourselves, and every book we published was a success.

By 1983, some of our writers started using PCs. That's when we started developing the PC methods we recommend in this book. This also led to some further refinements to our writing procedure so we could get the maximum benefit from our PCs. Today, we have ten writers and editors, and we all use PCs for our writing work. We actively use a dozen or more different software products, and each year we experiment with many others. In chapter 1 and throughout this book, you'll get the recommendations on PC use that have come from these years of experience.

By 1986, we decided to experiment with desktop publishing even though we already had our own graphics and production facilities. For our first project, the book's author also did the desktop publishing. That's when we learned that writers must learn some typographic and design skills before they can make effective use of desktop publishing. Since then, we've produced four more books using desktop publishing (five if you include this one). In section 4 of this book, you'll get the recommendations that come from those experiences.

I relate this history so you'll realize that all of the skills presented in this book have been used successfully for many different projects. These skills have helped one of my writers write books that bring in revenues of more than one million dollars each year. These skills have helped one of my direct marketing writers write the ads and direct mail pieces that bring in sales of over two million dollars each year. These skills have helped my administrative manager write the memos, letters, and reports that keep our company running. If you master these skills, you're going to be able to write well too.

Conclusion

Although many people seem to fear writing, it just isn't that difficult if you break it down into manageable skills. During the last 20 years, I've taught many people how to write, and I think I can teach you too. That's why I wrote this book.

If you have any comments, questions, or criticisms, I would enjoy hearing from you. That's why I've included a postage-paid comment form in the back of this book. If I hear that this book has helped you become a good writer, I'll be delighted. If I hear that this book has helped you double your writing productivity, I'll be doubly delighted. But whether your comments are good or bad, I thank you for reading this book.

Mike Murach
Fresno, California
December 20, 1988

Section 1

How to get
the most from your PC

This section contains two chapters that show you how to get the maximum benefit from your PC when you use it for writing. Chapter 1 introduces you to 12 types of PC software that can help you write better. Chapter 2 introduces you to a 12-step writing procedure that will help you use your PC more efficiently. This procedure will also help you improve your writing. When you complete this section, you can continue with any of the other three sections in this book.

Heading plan for chapter 1

**Six types of PC software
every business writer should use**

    Word processing

    Spelling checkers

    On-line thesauruses

    Writing analyzers

    Electronic spreadsheet software

    Business graphics software

**Six types of PC software
you may not need**

    Desktop publishing software

    Outline or idea processors

    Other graphics software

    Database software

    On-line information services

    Purchased databases

**The benefits you should get
from your PC software**

    Improved writing productivity

    Improved writing effectiveness

**How to get the maximum benefit
from your PC software**

    Recommendation 1:   Learn to type

    Recommendation 2:   Use your computer system whenever it is appropriate for a writing task

    Recommendation 3:   Use the computer system yourself

**Why you won't become
a good writer just by using a PC**

Chapter 1

How 12 types of PC software can help you improve your writing

Just a few years ago, most business writing was tedious work. To start, you usually wrote the first draft of a document in longhand. Then, if you were lucky, someone else would type it for you or enter it into a word processing system. If your document required visual aids, you drew rough drafts by hand, and you frequently drew the final drafts too. As you moved up the organization chart, of course, you got more clerical help for your typing and drawing. But you still did a lot of proofing as you reviewed the several drafts of a typical business document.

Today, thanks to computers, you don't need clerical help for your writing. *Personal computers* (*PC*s), in particular, have changed the way many people in business write. Starting at a cost of about $1500, a modern PC can help you double your writing productivity. It can also help you make dramatic improvements in the effectiveness of your writing.

As I mentioned in the introduction, I'm assuming that you're already familiar with PCs like the Apple II, the Macintosh, the Macintosh II, the IBM PC (including the IBM XT, the IBM AT, and all IBM clones), or the IBM PS/2. If you don't own a PC yourself, you should at least have access to one in your business. That's why I'm not going to take the time to describe the *hardware* of a typical PC (that is, the machine itself).

Instead, I'm going to describe 12 types of *software* that can help you improve your writing. All 12 types are available on Apple systems like the Macintosh as well as on the IBM PC and all of its variations. First, I'll present six types of software every business writer should use. Then, I'll present six more types of software you should be aware

	Software type	Some representative products	Common uses
1	Word processing	*WordPerfect* *Word* *PFS: Professional Write*	Plan your writing Create visual aids Write the first draft Revise your drafts
2	Spelling checker	A *WordPerfect* feature A *Word* feature Pop-up products	Check the spelling of a word, page, or document
3	On-line thesaurus	A *WordPerfect* feature A *Word* feature Pop-up products	Find the appropriate word
4	Writing analyzer	*RightWriter* *Grammatik III*	Check for writing and grammatical problems
5	Electronic spreadsheet	*Lotus 1-2-3* *Quattro*	Organize information Analyze information
6	Business graphics	*Harvard Graphics*	Create visual aids

Figure 1-1 Six types of PC software every business writer should use

of, even though you might not ever need to use them. Last, I'll describe the benefits you can get from using PC software, and I'll explain what you have to do to get these benefits.

Six types of PC software every business writer should use

Figure 1-1 summarizes six types of PC software that can help you improve your writing. I use all six of them. If you don't already use them, I think you'll be delighted to discover how much they can help you.

In column 2 of figure 1-1, you'll see the names of some current software products for each type of software. Although we've used all of these products at our company and all of them are useful, I don't want to imply that I'm recommending them. Because new products come out every day and old products are continually being improved, I just don't feel I can make software recommendations in a book like this.

Word processing   If you're at all familiar with *word processing*, you know that it's the most versatile type of software for a writer. You can use word processing to organize information, to plan what you're going to write, to create visual aids, to write the first draft of a document, and to revise a draft. In this book, you'll learn how to use word processing for all of these purposes and more.

A *word processing package* is the software product that provides the word processing functions. Today, *Microsoft Word* and WordPerfect Corporation's *WordPerfect* are two of the most popular word processing packages, but several others are also widely used. Although all word processing packages provide the same basic functions, the advanced functions vary from one package to another.

In case you're not already using word processing, figure 1-2 illustrates some of the basic functions I used as I entered a report into my PC using *WordPerfect*. Printed at the top of each page is a heading that I entered into the system only once. Within this heading, the date came from the system (I had to enter only two keystrokes to get it), and the pages were automatically numbered. For the document name (PCREC), I used automatic centering. For the report title, I used boldface type. Then, as I reached the end of each line in the text, the *word wrap* function automatically moved the cursor to the start of the next line, so I didn't have to press the return key until I reached the end of a paragraph. If I made a mistake as I entered the copy, I just backspaced and corrected it because nothing was printed until I told the system to print it. Functions like these help you enter a document into a system faster than you can type one.

Word processing packages also provide other basic functions that make it easy for you to enter and revise data. Indent functions let you indent line after line without tabbing each one, and align functions automatically line up numbers in a column by decimal point. If you need to move or copy a sentence, paragraph, or page within a document or from one document to another, you can use the move and copy functions. Change, insert, and delete functions make revision easy, and most systems automatically reformat and repaginate the entire document as revisions are made. When you're done with your document, print functions let you print all or part of it with just a keystroke or two.

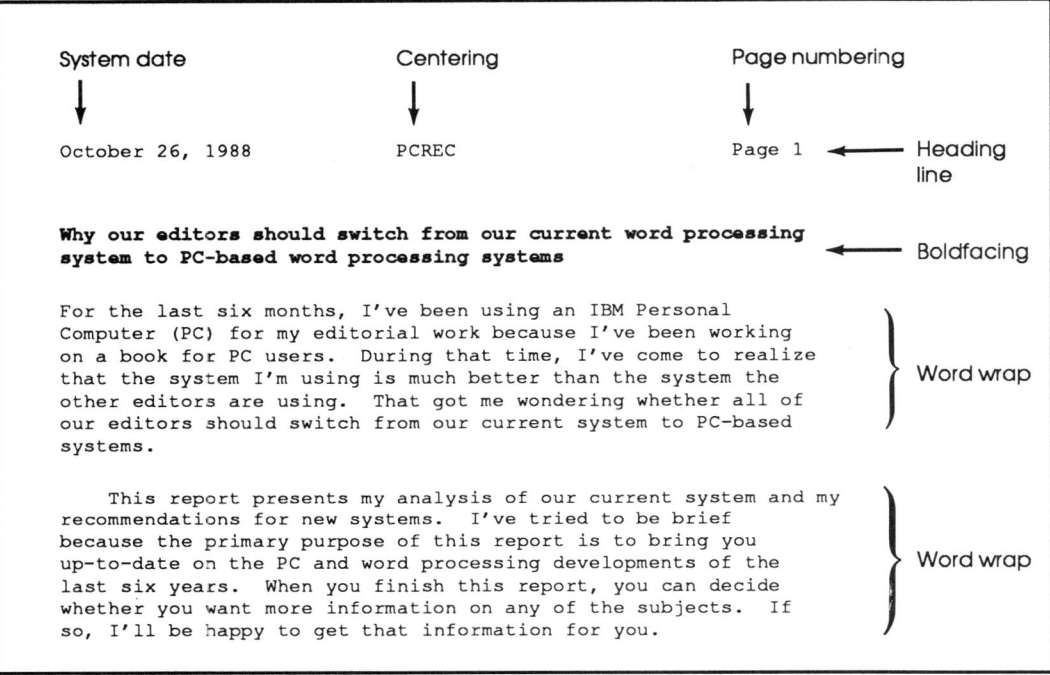

Figure 1-2 Some common word processing functions as illustrated by the first two paragraphs of the report in appendix A

       Today, most word processing packages provide many advanced functions in addition to those I've just described. For instance, *WordPerfect* lets you divide a page into two or more columns so the page prints like a newsletter. It lets you mix typefaces, styles, and sizes within a single document. And it makes it easy for you to use footnotes. In fact, the major word processing packages provide so many advanced functions that most people use only a small percentage of them.

       If writing is an important part of your job, I suggest that you use an advanced word processor like *WordPerfect* or *Word*. I also suggest that you take the time to master its features. Although that may take you a couple of weeks, there's no point in having the advanced features if you don't use them.

       If you write only a couple of hours each week or if you don't need advanced features, you're probably better off with a simple word processing package like *PFS: Professional Write*. Although you can

```
     share the one printer that is located in the department.  They also
     share the minicomputer and its disk drives with 15 other users of the
     system in the administrative and marketing departments.

        Because this is a shared system, the  edittors  experience frequent
     delays when they use the word processing software.  This is
     particularly true between 10 A.M. and 3 P.M. when the system receives
     its heaviest use.  Our editors also experience delays when they go from
     one function like editing to another function like printing.  Because
     the word processing software consists of


     ==================================================================


     A. editors              B. adapters             C. adopters
     D. auditors




     Not Found!  Select Word or Menu Option (0=Continue): 0
     1 Skip Once; 2 Skip; 3 Add Word; 4 Edit; 5 Look Up; 6 Phonetic
```

Figure 1-3 A screen showing a typical display from a spelling checker after it finds an error (*edittors*)

master all of the features of this word processor in just a couple of hours, it is more than adequate for most letters, memos, and reports. Later on, if you find you need more advanced features, the experience you've gained will make it easier for you to master a more complicated word processing package.

Spelling checkers A *spelling checker* checks the spelling of a single word, the words on a page, or the words in an entire document. When I finished the report in appendix A, for example, I pressed three keys, and *WordPerfect*'s spelling checker checked the entire document for spelling errors. When the spelling checker detected an error, it displayed an error screen like the one in figure 1-3. In this example, *edittors* is spelled wrong.

As you can see, the system tried to figure out what I wanted to spell and gave me four possible corrections. When I entered the letter *a* into the system, the spelling checker replaced *edittors* with *editors*.

Then, it continued checking the other words in the document. On my system, the spelling checker runs so quickly that it checked all of the words in this 3700-word document in less than 20 seconds.

To check the spelling of the words in a document, a spelling checker looks up each word in an electronic dictionary. For instance, my system uses a dictionary of 115,000 words. If the word is in the dictionary, the checker assumes it's correct. Otherwise, it assumes it's incorrect. Obviously, then, a spelling checker won't catch all spelling errors. If, for example, you spell *there* as *their*, the checker won't catch the error because both words are in its dictionary. Similarly, if you type *though* when you mean to type *through*, the checker won't catch the error. As a result, you still have to proofread your documents if you want them to be perfect.

Today, almost all word processing packages include spelling checkers. However, if your package doesn't include one or you don't like the way yours works, you can buy a spelling checker as a separate product. Most of these independent products are *pop-up products*. Whenever you want to check a word, page, or document for spelling, you press a special combination of keys and the spelling checker "pops up" onto the screen. When you're done with it, the checker disappears so you can continue with your word processing.

On-line thesauruses An *on-line thesaurus* is a thesaurus that's available to you as you use your word processing system. On my system, for example, if I want to consider using another word for *create*, I can put the cursor on *create* and press two keys to access the thesaurus. For this word, my on-line thesaurus offers words like *develop*, *invent*, and *originate* as shown in figure 1-4. If I want to change to one of the words offered, I enter the letter of the word and the word processor makes the substitution for me.

Although this feature can be useful, you have to know the precise meanings of the words it offers if you're going to use the words correctly. That's why I recommend that you use a dictionary far more often than a thesaurus. Nevertheless, an on-line thesaurus can be a useful feature because it lets you access word alternatives in just a few seconds.

Today, the major word processing packages include an on-line thesaurus. However, if your package doesn't have one, you can get a pop-up thesaurus as a separate product. Or, you can buy a pop-up product that includes both a spelling checker and a thesaurus. Because a pop-up thesaurus is inexpensive, it's worth having one even if you don't use it much.

```
    programs are going to be much use to us, they may come in handy
    for an occasional presentation to the marketing department.  On
    the other hand, the drawing programs would let us create finished
    illustrations instead of the rough drawings that we pass on to the

    create (v)
      1 A .develop                 .make
        B .invent                  .produce
        C .originate
                               create (ant)
      2 D .concoct              6  .destroy
        E .devise
        F .formulate

      3 G .establish
        H .found
        I .institute

      4 J .build
        K .construct
        L .erect

      5 M .beget
        N .generate

    1 Replace Word; 2 View Doc; 3 Look Up Word; 4 Clear Column: 0
```

Figure 1-4   A screen showing a typical display from an on-line thesaurus

Writing analyzers   Today, *writing analyzers* are sold separately from word processing packages. To be useful, a writing analyzer must find certain types of writing flaws and recommend improvements. An analyzer should also measure the readability of your writing. Since some analyzers are able to find certain types of grammatical errors, writing analyzers are sometimes called *grammar checkers*.

Figure 1-5 illustrates one page of the printed output from *Right-Writer* after I used it to analyze the report in appendix A. As you can see, this analyzer raised five questions. To start, it recommended a word like *many* or *several* in place of the words *a number of*, and it recommended the word *now* instead of the phrase *at this time*. I agreed with both of these recommendations. Then, the analyzer questioned the use of the phrase *in case*, questioned whether a sentence should begin with *and*, and said that capital and lowercase letters shouldn't be mixed in a term like *PCs*. Although I agree with those recommendations in general, I didn't agree with them in these specific cases.

```
PC software that can make an editor's job easier

If you just compare PC-based word processing to the word
processing on our current system, you have to be impressed by the
improvements of the last six or eight years. But there's more.
If you use a PC-based system, you have access to a number of

[#Longwinded or wordy       : use "most," "many," "several,"
"some," or "few"]

other programs that can make an editor's job easier. At this
time,

[#Longwinded or wordy       : now]

I'll introduce a few of the most common ones in case

[#Hackneyed, Cliche, or Trite : use "if"]

you're not familiar with them.

Spreadsheet software    I know you've used 1-2-3, so I won't try
to describe what this type of software does. But have you
considered how the editors could use this type of software to
control their projects more effectively? I think spreadsheet
software would be useful for this purpose. And

[#Hackneyed, Cliche, or Trite : use sparingly to begin a
sentence]

it would be available to our editors if they used PCs

[#Capitalization            : don't mix cases]

instead of the minicomputer.
```

Figure 1-5   Two paragraphs of a report after it has been processed by a writing analyzer

Since I changed only two of the five items the analyzer questioned in figure 1-5, you can see the need for judgment when you use one. You can also see the need for a knowledge of grammar. Although the analyzer can identify writing problems and make recommendations based on the rules programmed into it, you have to decide whether the recommendations are correct and appropriate.

Figure 1-6 illustrates the summary page from *RightWriter* after it analyzed the report in appendix A. As you can see, this summary includes a readability index that indicates the reading level of the document. Here, the index is 9.86, so the report is appropriate for

```
              <<** SUMMARY **>>

     OVERALL CRITIQUE FOR: \wp\bc\pcrec

     READABILITY INDEX: 9.86
Readers need a 10th grade level of education to
understand.

        Total Number of Words in Document:3719
        Total Number of Words within Sentences:3644
        Total Number of Sentences: 191
        Total Number of Syllables:5713

     STRENGTH INDEX: 0.30
The writing can be made more direct by using:
                    - the active voice
                    - shorter sentences
                    - fewer weak phrases

     DESCRIPTIVE INDEX: 0.59
The use of adjectives and adverbs is in the normal
range.

     JARGON INDEX: 0.00

SENTENCE STRUCTURE RECOMMENDATIONS:
          1. Most sentences contain multiple clauses.
             Try to use more simple sentences.
         14. Consider using more predicate verbs.
```

Figure 1-6   The summary page from a writing analyzer after it has processed a report

people who read at or above a tenth-grade reading level. You'll learn more about readability measures in chapter 9, but it's worth having a writing analyzer just to get this measurement.

To date, the writing analyzers I've used have been quite limited, and I'm sure we can expect improved versions in the next five years. Nevertheless, I recommend that you start using a writing analyzer now. At first, an analyzer will help you find errors you might overlook otherwise. It will also give you a readability index that indicates the reading ease of your writing. After you use the analyzer for a couple of months, you'll stop making the types of mistakes it detects. Then, it will be clear that the analyzer has helped you improve your writing. When you find that the analyzer no longer finds mistakes of significance and that your documents are at an acceptable level of readability, you can stop using the analyzer. However, you may want to continue to use the analyzer to make sure your writing stays at an acceptable readability level.

Electronic spreadsheet software   *Electronic spreadsheet software* lets you enter data into *cells* that are marked by rows and columns on the screen of your computer. After you've entered your data, you can enter formulas into other cells to perform calculations on the data. Then, the results of the calculations are displayed in the cells that contain the formulas. Among spreadsheet packages today, *Lotus 1-2-3* is the most widely used, but many other programs with similar capabilities are also available.

To illustrate spreadsheet software, figure 1-7 illustrates the use of spreadsheet software for *what-if analysis*. Because the values that result from the formulas are recalculated at electronic speeds whenever you change the data, you can consider many alternatives in a short time once you set up a spreadsheet. For instance, the first spreadsheet in this figure shows the net profits at five levels of sales. Then, I asked "what if" an increase in development cost reduced the cost of sales from 40 percent to 30 percent. To see what the changes would be, I had to enter only the shaded data into the spreadsheet. The ability to do this type of analysis is perhaps the primary reason spreadsheet software has become so popular.

Figure 1-8 illustrates another use for spreadsheet software. It presents a spreadsheet that I used for organizing information when I analyzed four of the best-selling writing texts for college courses. First, I entered the data in the unshaded cells. Then, I entered formulas in the shaded cells. To simplify entry, the spreadsheet software lets me copy formulas from one cell to others, so I had to enter only three unique formulas. As I entered the formulas, the system made the calculations and displayed the results. When I had the spreadsheet in the form I wanted, I printed it.

Spreadsheet software is useful to you as a writer because it helps you analyze and organize the information you get as you prepare to write a document. Later, you may want to use your spreadsheets as visual aids within your document. If your writing projects are extensive, spreadsheet software can also help you schedule them. For these reasons, a business writer should make frequent use of electronic spreadsheet software.

Business graphics software   *Business graphics software* lets you create various types of charts and graphs from data you've entered

```
Assumption 1:  Cost of sales = 40%; development cost= $50,000

An analysis of profit margins                              PFTSTUDY
================================================================
                    % Level 1   Level 2   Level 3   Level 4   Level 5
================================================================
Sales                 100,000   150,000   200,000   250,000   300,000
Cost of sales    40%   40,000    60,000    80,000   100,000   120,000
                      -------------------------------------------------
Gross profit           60,000    90,000   120,000   150,000   180,000
================================================================
Development cost       50,000    50,000    50,000    50,000    50,000
Marketing cost         25,000    25,000    25,000    25,000    25,000
                      -------------------------------------------------
Net profit            (15,000)   15,000    45,000    75,000   105,000
================================================================


Assumption 2:  Cost of sales = 30%; development cost = $75,000

An analysis of profit margins                              PFTSTUDY
================================================================
                    % Level 1   Level 2   Level 3   Level 4   Level 5
================================================================
Sales                 100,000   150,000   200,000   250,000   300,000
Cost of sales    30%   30,000    45,000    60,000    75,000    90,000
                      -------------------------------------------------
Gross profit           70,000   105,000   140,000   175,000   210,000
================================================================
Development cost       75,000    75,000    75,000    75,000    75,000
Marketing cost         25,000    25,000    25,000    25,000    25,000
                      -------------------------------------------------
Net profit            (30,000)    5,000    40,000    75,000   110,000
================================================================

NOTE:  To generate the second spreadsheet from the first, you only have to
       change the shaded fields.
```

Figure 1-7   Two spreadsheets that demonstrate "what if" capabilities

into your PC. Sometimes the graphics software is part of an electronic spreadsheet package such as *Lotus 1-2-3* or *Quattro*. Sometimes the graphics software is a separate product such as *Harvard Graphics*. When you use a separate graphics product, you can sometimes tell it to use data from a spreadsheet you've created.

A typical graphics package will let you create several different types of visual aids. Some of the most common types for use by the business writer are pie charts, line charts, and bar charts. After I

```
To what extent four of the leading textbooks on business            TXTSTUDY
communication deal with the 10 common writing problems
================================================================================
                                    Number of pages on subject      Average
Problem                          Book 1   Book 2   Book 3   Book 4  Pages/Book
================================================================================
Wrong content                       2       14       22       21      14.8

Disorganized content               10        8        8       20      11.5

Improper use of headings            4        1                 1       1.5

Ineffective use of visual aids     22       12       19       16      17.3

Improper paragraphing               6                 1        8       3.8

Failure to support opinions                  2                 3       1.3
with facts

Failure to show relationships       7                 1                2.0
between ideas and thoughts

Confusing sentence structures       7                                  1.8

Confusing language or jargon       37       12        9       18      19.0

Incorrect grammar or diction       27        5       48        6      21.5
================================================================================
Pages dealing with common problems 122      54      108       93      94.3
Pages in book                     680      730      485      522     604.3
================================================================================
Percentage of book dealing with
the common writing problems        18%       7%     22%       18%     16%
================================================================================
NOTE: The shaded fields are calculated by the system.
```

Figure 1-8 A spreadsheet that I used for organizing information

introduce you to each of these, I'm going to tell you about clip art and screenshows.

Figure 1-9 illustrates two kinds of *pie charts*. On the left, you can see a pie chart in the shape of a pie. On the right, you can see a pie chart in a rectangular form. The planning portion of the pie on the left is linked to the entire pie on the right. Both pies are three-dimensional. When you create pie charts on a PC, you have many different options, so I could have created this figure with two round pies, two rectangular pies, two-dimensional pies, unlinked pies, and so on.

12 types of PC software 15

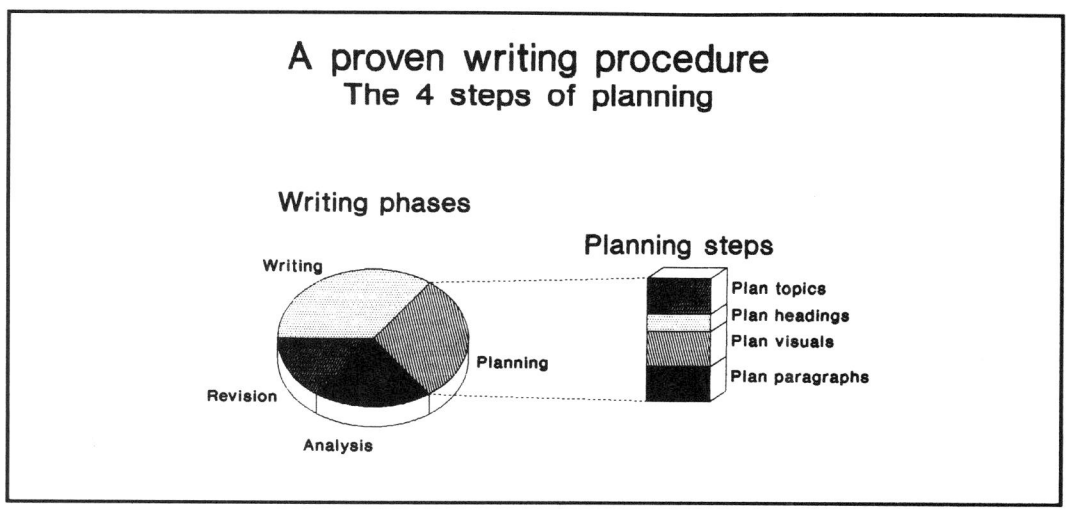

Figure 1-9   Linked pie charts prepared by a graphics package

Figure 1-10 shows a *line chart* and a *bar chart* based on data I extracted from a spreadsheet application. To change from the bar chart to the line chart, you have to change only one option, so it takes just a few seconds. Here again, you have many different options, so you can create stacked bar charts, horizontal charts, two- or three-dimensional charts, and so on.

Figure 1-11 illustrates an item of *clip art* that is available with *Harvard Graphics*. This package provides more than 200 drawings that you can call to the screen. Then, if you want to, you can modify the art or enhance it by adding words, lines, arrows, shadings, and the like to it. For instance, I enhanced the clip art in figure 1-11 by adding the words and lines that identify the four components of a PC system.

Some graphics packages let you create sequential presentations on the screen of your PC so you can review the visual aids you're going to use. Presentations like these are called *screenshows* because they're similar in function to slide shows. When you're writing documents that rely heavily on visual aids, a screenshow can make it easy for you to analyze your presentation or to review it with a colleague. If the screenshow is interesting and illustrates the points you want to make, you can print the visual aids and use them in your written presentation.

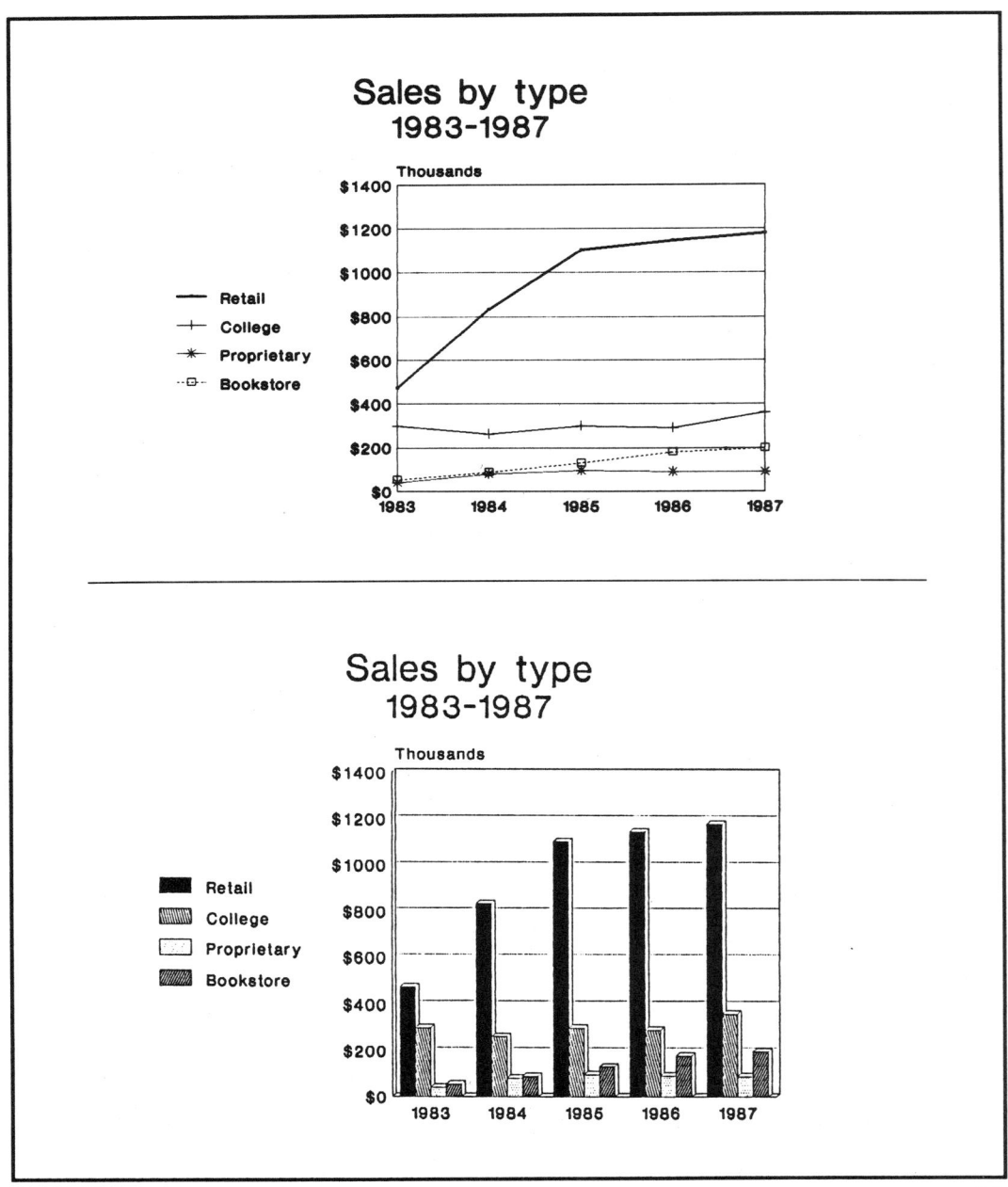

Figure 1-10 A line chart and a bar chart for the same sales data

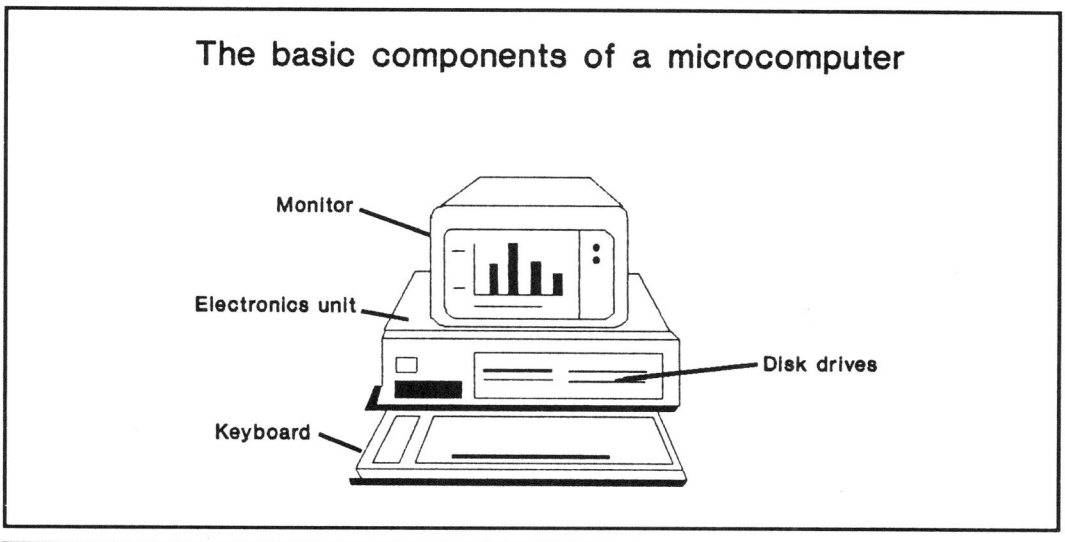

Figure 1-11 Clip art from a graphics package plus enhancements

As one study has shown, business graphics can help you present information 50 percent more effectively in 30 percent less time. That's why graphics software is so important to the business writer. Because business people want to get their information as quickly and as easily as possible, effective visual aids are often critical to the success of a memo, report, or proposal.

Six types of PC software you may not need

Figure 1-12 summarizes six more types of PC software you should be aware of. Although you may need one or more of them at some time during your writing career, you may not need to use any of them. In column 2 of figure 1-12, you'll see the names of some useful products, but here again this doesn't imply that I'm recommending them.

Desktop publishing software *Desktop publishing* software lets you create finished pages that look as if they were done using traditional typesetting and production methods. For instance, we used desktop publishing to prepare this book. To create the pages, we used text from our word processing package and visual aids from word processing, spreadsheet, and business graphics packages. In other

Software type	Some representative products	Common uses
1 Desktop publishing	*Ventura Publisher* *PageMaker*	Present a document in a professionally published form
2 Outline or idea processors	A *Word* feature *Ready!* *GrandView*	Organize information Plan your writing
3 Other graphics software	*Draw* *Freelance Plus* *Macdraw* *Cricket Draw* *Adobe Illustrator* *Designer* *AutoCad*	Create visual aids for use primarily with desktop publishing
4 Database software	A *Lotus 1-2-3* feature *Q & A* *Paradox*	Organize information Extract information
5 On-line information services		Get outside information
6 Purchased databases		Get reference information

Figure 1-12 Six types of PC software you may not need

words, desktop publishing lets you receive input from other software packages as you create the layout for the finished pages.

To print a page produced by desktop publishing software, your PC needs a *laser printer* instead of a traditional business printer. A laser printer prints a full page or more in a single operation with a printing quality that is satisfactory for most business purposes. The quality of laser print is referred to as its *resolution,* and resolution is measured in dots per inch. Today, most laser printers print with 300 dots per inch, but we expect this resolution to increase to 600 dots per inch in the next few years. In contrast, most traditional publishing output has a resolution of from 1200 to 2700 dots per inch.

Today, desktop publishing is used to improve the appearance of many documents formerly prepared by typewriting or word processing. It's also used for many of the jobs formerly done by typesetting equipment. In the future, the print quality of laser printers will improve so desktop publishing will become acceptable for more of the traditional publishing jobs. Even today, though, desktop publishing is acceptable for the production of most books.

Because desktop publishing is *presentation software*, not writing software, most writers don't use it and shouldn't use it. In most companies, the writers write using the six types of software I've already described, and the production people use desktop publishing to present what the writers write. Some writers, though, have jobs that include both writing and production duties, so they use desktop publishing as well as word processing, spreadsheet, and graphics software. If you have mixed duties, chapter 15 of this book will introduce you to the typographic and design skills you need for desktop publishing.

Outline or idea processors An *outline processor* helps you develop outlines or plans. Since outline processors let you arrange your ideas within the structure of an outline or plan, they can also be referred to as *idea processors*. Some word processors like *Word* include an outline processor. Some outline processors like *GrandView* include word processing capabilities.

Some outline processors like *Ready!* are pop-up products, so they're available to you whenever your PC is on. Then, the processor can become an *electronic note pad*. If, for example, you get an idea for some writing project that you're working on while you're using your graphics software, you can pop up your outline processor and add the idea to it. Although you can buy a general-purpose electronic note pad as a separate product, recording ideas is most useful when you add them to an existing structure you've created with an outline processor. Otherwise, you're better off using paper note pads.

One of the benefits of an outline processor is that it encourages you to develop an outline or a plan from the top down and to review the plan one level at a time. Figure 1-13, for example, shows the plan for this chapter at two different levels of detail. If you want to add additional levels or ideas to a plan or if you want to reorganize any of the levels, an outline processor lets you do so with a minimum of

```
The first level of an outline

Six types of PC software every business writer should use
Six types of PC software you may not need
The benefits you should get from your PC software
How to get the maximum benefit from your PC software
Why you won't become a good writer just by using a PC


The first two levels of an outline

Six types of PC software every business writer should use
    Word processing
    Spelling checkers
    On-line thesauruses
    Writing analyzers
    Electronic spreadsheet software
    Business graphics software
Six types of PC software you may not need
    Desktop publishing software
    Outline or idea processors
    Other graphics software
    Database software
    On-line information services
    Purchased databases
The benefits you should get from your PC software
    Improved writing productivity
    Improved writing effectiveness
How to get the maximum benefit from your PC software
    Recommendation 1:  Learn to type
    Recommendation 2:  Use your computer system whenever it is appropriate for a
                       writing task
    Recommendation 3:  Use the computer system yourself
Why you won't become a good writer just by using a PC
```

Figure 1-13 Two different views of an outline prepared by an outline processor

effort. Whenever you want to hide or reveal one or more levels of an outline, you can do so with just a couple of keystrokes.

As you'll learn in chapter 4, an outline processor can help you plan what you're going to write. As you'll learn in chapter 3, an outline processor can also help you organize information as you do the research for a writing project. Beyond that, many managers like to use outline processors for planning and controlling their projects. That's why outline processors are rapidly increasing in popularity.

For writing efficiency, it's best if the outline processor is part of the word processor. That way, you can switch back and forth between outline processing and word processing without any conversion problems. After you finish a writing plan, for example, you can switch to word processing and use the plan as the start of a new document. Similarly, if you decide to modify a plan as you're writing, you can switch back to outline processing and make the modifications. So if your word processor includes an outline processor, by all means learn to use it.

If your word processor doesn't include an outline processor, you probably won't want to buy one just for planning what you're going to write. As you'll learn in chapter 4, you can do an effective job of planning using word processing alone, so you don't need an outline processor just for that purpose. If you're a manager, though, you can probably justify the purchase of an outline processor based on improvements in project planning and control. Then, you can also use the outline processor for your writing projects.

Other graphics software   If you're a business writer, you probably won't need any graphics software other than business graphics software. However, if your writing is more technical, you may need to use other kinds of graphics programs to produce your technical illustrations. In our company, for example, we sometimes use other graphics software to produce the charts and diagrams we require for our computer books.

The most common type of general-purpose graphics program is called a *paint program*. It's also the least useful for business and technical writing. When you use a paint program, you use a "mouse" to create images on your screen. To draw a box, for example, you use the mouse to mark the location of the top left corner of the box. Then, you move the mouse to the location you want for the bottom right corner of the box, thus creating the box. When you finish, though, the paint program doesn't know that you've created a box. It treats the box as a pattern of dots. As a result, you can't easily move the box or change its size. This inflexibility is the primary limitation of a paint program.

In contrast, *object oriented drawing programs* remember the objects that you place in your drawing. If, for example, you draw a box, the drawing program remembers the object type (box), its size and location, and any other attributes you may have assigned to that box (such as the width of the lines used to draw the box and whether or not the box is shaded). As a result, you can easily change the location, size, or other attributes of the box. Because these programs make it easy for you to modify your drawings, they are far more useful than paint programs for business and technical writing.

Draw programs are the easiest object oriented drawing programs to use. These programs let you draw pictures using a modest selection of object types: lines, boxes, circles, arcs, text, and maybe a few others. For instance, we've used a draw program to create the schematic illustrations for several of our technical books. One example is shown in figure 1-14. If you want to create line drawings like that and you're using an IBM PC, you can use a draw program like *Draw* by Micrografx or *Freelance Plus* by Lotus. If you're using a Macintosh, you can use a program like *Macdraw* or *Cricket Draw*.

Beyond the simple paint and draw programs, you can find many other kinds of graphics programs. If you need a more artistic look to your drawings, you can use a program like *Adobe Illustrator* (for Macintosh and IBM systems) or *Designer* by Micrografx (for IBM systems only). These programs let you produce commercial-quality artwork. If you use engineering drawings in your work, you can use a *computer aided design and drafting (CAD) program*. One of the most popular of these is called *AutoCad*. If you use special types of illustrations like data flow diagrams or Gantt charts in your work, you can buy special-purpose software for creating them.

If you frequently use certain types of illustrations for the work you do, you may be able to justify the hardware, software, and training costs associated with one or more graphics programs. However, the training costs alone can be high. That's why you probably shouldn't use any of these graphics programs for your business or technical writing. Instead, you should create occasional illustrations by hand. Or, if your company has an art department, you should draw rough drafts of your illustrations by hand and pass them on to the art department for completion. Then, an artist can decide whether or not a computer should be used to create each illustration.

If you're using desktop publishing to present your document, it's often best to create your visual aids using graphics software. Then, you can use the desktop publishing software to adjust the sizes of the visual aids and to put them in place on the finished pages. If you don't use graphics software, you have to create your visual aids to size and paste them into the finished pages by hand. Here again, though, you shouldn't use the graphics software yourself if you have an artist or desktop publishing specialist in your company who can do this work for you. I'll talk more about this in chapter 15.

Database software *Database software* helps you organize data on your PC in a form called a *database*. Once the database is established, you can extract information from it using other facilities of the

12 types of PC software

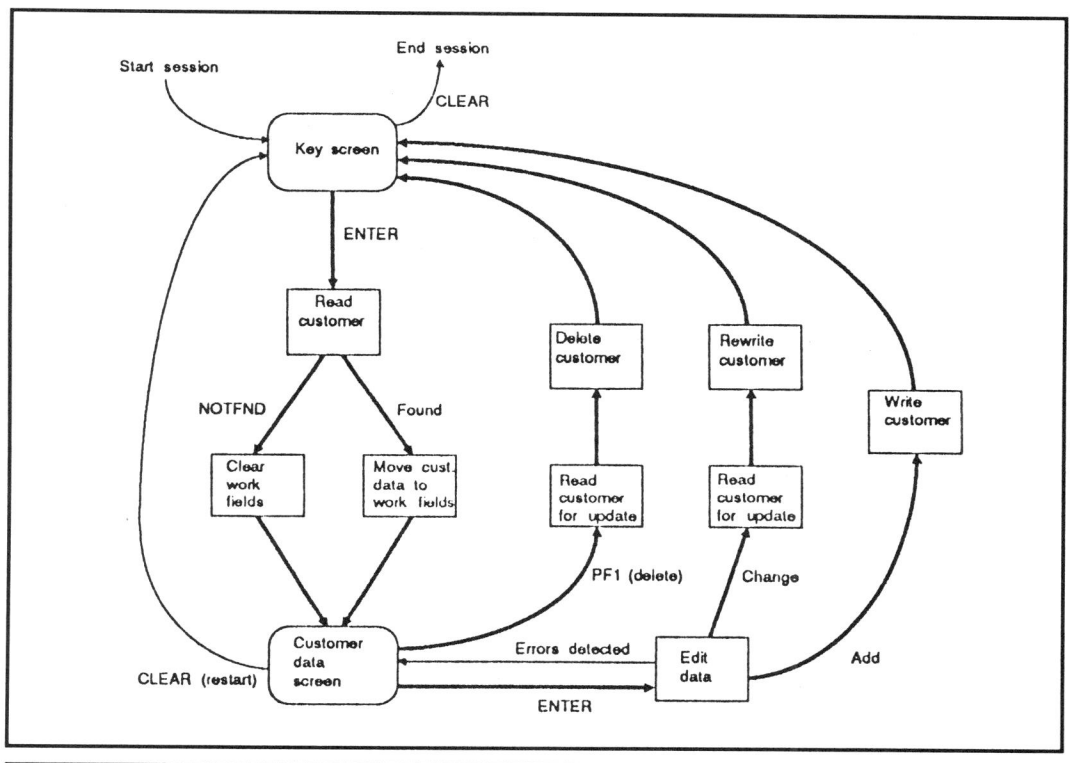

Figure 1-14 A visual aid prepared by a draw program

database software. As a result, database software can be useful during the research phase of a writing project.

Because a database can be simple or complex, database software is available at many different levels of complexity. A simple product like *Q & A* or the database feature of *Lotus 1-2-3* can help you organize data in a simple file such as a file of names and addresses. A more complex product like *Paradox* can help you organize data with several different relationships.

Most writers, however, don't use database software for their writing projects. One reason has been that traditional database software requires the data to be organized in a rigid structure. When you start to get information, though, you don't always know what that structure should be. As a result, you can't define the database in a way that is adequate for the life of your project. In addition, database software is relatively difficult to use, so it's hard to define a database even when you know what its structure should be.

Nevertheless, if you aren't already familiar with database software, it's worth taking the time to learn more about it. If you're looking for an efficient way to keep track of some clearly structured data, one of the traditional database products may be just what you need. And some of the newer products let you organize data in a loosely structured way that is more in keeping with the type of data gathering that writers do.

On-line information services   If your PC has a modem and communications software, you have access to many *on-line information services*. To use these services, you follow a simple dial-up procedure that connects your PC via phone lines to an outside computer system that contains one or more databases. Then, you can use your PC to extract information from the databases. Of course, you pay for the telephone line charges and for the information service, but sometimes these costs are justified by the information you get and the efficiency with which you get it.

Today, you can use your PC to access hundreds of databases throughout the world, and many of these databases are enormous. For instance, the DIALOG service offers more than 250 databases, including book and periodical directories plus abstracts and reviews. The NEXIS service offers the full text of hundreds of magazines, newspapers, and newsletters. And the Dow Jones News/Retrieval Service offers about 35 separate databases that include stock quotations, news briefs, and the full text of *The Wall Street Journal*.

Even if you don't need an information database, you may find it helps to participate in an *on-line forum* that is offered as part of an on-line service. Recently, for example, one of our writers started using an information service so he could participate in several on-line forums for programmers who develop PC software. Since he is working on a series of books for PC users, this service helps him keep up-to-date on technical developments. In a forum, the users converse via their keyboards so anyone who signs onto the system can read all of the recent conversations recorded in the forum's database. Although this is a good way to get practical, firsthand information, this can also be time-consuming and expensive.

One of the problems you have when using an information service is that too much data is available to you. That often makes it both difficult and expensive for you to find the right database and to extract the information you need from it. Nevertheless, if you have a frequent need for the type of information that's available through these services, it's nice to know you can get it through your PC.

When you're doing business and technical writing, though, you usually get the information you need from sources within your own company. That's why you probably won't ever need an on-line information service. For occasional reference, it's usually quicker and easier to call your library than it is to use an on-line service.

Purchased databases   Occasionally, you can buy a database on diskette that provides the information you want. For instance, we subscribe to a service that provides an index to all the articles in *PC Magazine*. Each quarter we receive a diskette that updates this database index. Then, if we want to look up all the articles that have been printed about a PC product, we can get a list of them in just a minute or two.

Today, you can also buy databases on a *CD ROM* with a storage capacity of more than half a billion characters of information. A CD ROM is like an audio CD you buy for a stereo system. To read a CD ROM, you need to add a CD ROM reader to your system at a cost of about $1000, but this gives your system the ability to access huge databases.

Because the CD ROM technology is relatively new, only a few CD ROM databases are available today. One of these products, *Microsoft's Bookshelf*, consists of ten separate databases including *Roget's Thesaurus*, *The World Almanac*, *The Chicago Manual of Style*, and *The American Heritage Dictionary*. Although that should be a useful set of databases for writers, many of the people who have used *Bookshelf* aren't satisfied with it. They say it takes too long to get the information they're looking for so they're better off using reference books. In addition, the cost of the CD ROM reader plus the cost of *Bookshelf* ($295) makes this alternative too expensive for most PC users.

Nevertheless, you can expect to see improved CD ROM products in the future. As they become available, they are likely to reduce the need for on-line information services. If you can get the same information on CD ROM that you can get from an on-line service, the CD ROM product is likely to be less expensive and easier to use.

The benefits you should get from your PC software

In simplest terms, the benefits you should get from PC software are (1) improved writing productivity and (2) improved writing effectiveness. More specifically, PC software should help you double your writing productivity at the same time it helps you improve your writing. If it's not clear how these benefits are derived from PC software, let me explain.

Improved writing productivity   Since word processing is the most important software product for the writer, I'll start by explaining how it helps you increase your productivity. It does so in three primary ways.

First, you can enter a document into a word processing system much faster than you can type it. That's partly because you don't have to worry about paper handling and carriage returns. But I think it's mainly because you don't have to worry about making mistakes. Since you can correct or change anything you want before you print a copy of the document, you can enter data as fast as your fingers will go.

Second, word processing dramatically improves revision speed because you only have to make the changes, insertions, and deletions you require. You don't have to retype the entire document. When I wrote this chapter, for example, it took me about eight hours to enter the first draft. However, it took me less than one hour to revise the draft after I had edited it, even though I made some extensive changes.

Third, word processing improves your productivity because it reduces the need for proofing. When someone makes word processing changes for you (or you make them yourself), you only have to proof the changes. In contrast, when a document is retyped, you should proof the entire document because the typist may have made new errors.

The other types of software can also help you increase your productivity. For instance, an on-line spelling checker and thesaurus can help you look up words in seconds rather than minutes. Spreadsheet and graphics software help you create spreadsheets and charts in a fraction of the time that it would take you to create them manually. And desktop publishing software lets you produce books in weeks rather than months.

Improved writing effectiveness   Although improved productivity is an important benefit of PC software, improved writing effectiveness is even more important. The improvement, of course, starts with word processing.

First, because revisions are easy to make on a word processing system, you won't hesitate to make any changes that will improve a document. In contrast, you hesitate to make even minor changes to a document when you know that you or someone else will have to retype the entire document if you do. Second, because you only have to proof the changed areas of a revised document, there's less chance that an error will slip by you.

Beyond this, word processing helps you improve your writing in subtle ways. If you do your own entry work, you can change a sentence, decide you liked it better the way it was, and restore the first version with just a keystroke or two. You can move a paragraph or group of paragraphs from one portion of a document to another to see how that works with just a few keystrokes. You can copy paragraphs you used successfully in other documents into the document you're working on and revise them so they're appropriate for your new purpose. Until you've used word processing for a while, it may be hard for you to understand how these capabilities will improve your writing, but they will...and the improvements can be dramatic.

The other types of software can also have an important effect on your writing. For instance, writing analyzers can help you correct grammatical and stylistic problems. Electronic spreadsheet software can help you do a better job of analysis so you can develop a solid basis for your conclusions and recommendations. And graphics software can help you create better visual aids.

How to get the maximum benefit from your PC software

Today, business managers who use PCs are in the minority. Many of the old timers, it seems, consider the use of a keyboard to be menial work. They don't realize how much they could improve their writing and their writing productivity if they learned to use the computer system themselves.

Fortunately, the next generation of managers won't have this problem. Most of them have used PCs in college, so they expect to use PCs in business. In fact, they're likely to be disappointed if they don't have access to a PC whenever they want to use one.

Whether you're from the old school or the new, you won't get the maximum benefit from your PC unless you use it properly. And asking someone else to do something on the PC for you isn't using it properly. With that in mind, here are three recommendations for getting the most from your system.

Recommendation 1: Learn to type If you haven't already done so, learn to type and learn to type well. Even today, we occasionally hire a recent college graduate who doesn't know how to type, and I often see people hunting and pecking as they enter data into PCs.

Fortunately, it's easy to learn to type well by using an inexpensive instructional program on the PC itself. If you use a program like this for about two hours a day for five days, you'll improve your typing dramatically. And that ten hours of training will pay for itself many times over during your business career.

Recommendation 2: Use your computer system whenever it is appropriate for a writing task As you'll learn in the next chapter, you can use word processing for every phase of writing: analyzing, planning, writing, and revising. You can use spreadsheet software for organizing information and preparing visual aids. You can use graphics software to prepare visual aids. By using your computer system whenever it is appropriate for the task you're working on, you'll improve your writing and your writing efficiency.

On the other hand, you shouldn't use your PC for every task just because you like working with it. Sometimes, it's more efficient to do a task manually than it is to use the computer system for it. As you learn the writing procedure that's presented in this book, I'll give you specific advice on when to use your PC and when not to use it.

Recommendation 3: Use the computer system yourself The most efficient way for you to get your words and data into a computer system is to enter them yourself. If, for example, you can enter your documents into a system at the rate of 50 words per minute, which most people can do after a few weeks' practice, you can enter a single-spaced page of type into the system in about 10 minutes. That means you can enter a 6-page, or 3000-word, report into a system in about one hour. That's much faster than you can write in longhand. That's also faster than the rate at which most people dictate. Besides that, you can enter your words, data, or visual aids just the way you want them.

With that in mind, it's hard to understand why most business writers don't do their own entry. Of those who do, many write their first draft in longhand before they enter it into the system, a practice that is extremely inefficient. Instead of this, your goal should be to enter your words directly from your mind into the system through the keyboard, the way journalists do. That takes a little practice, but the improvement in efficiency is tremendous.

Before you can use the PC yourself, of course, you have to learn how to use your software. That can take a couple of weeks for word processing software, a week or so for spreadsheet software, and so on. I know because that's how long it took me, even though I've been using computers for over 20 years. If it's frustrating or difficult for you to take the time for this training, just remind yourself that this training will help you double your writing productivity. It will also give you many ideas that will help you use your PC more effectively for analysis and management as well as for writing.

Why you won't become a good writer just by using a PC

If you use a computer as I've just described, your writing efficiency should improve dramatically. In addition, you should have fewer typographical, spelling, and grammatical errors. If you spend more time revising your work than you did using manual methods, you may even make some minor improvements in the structure and clarity of your writing. But that still won't make you a good writer.

No, as I said in the introduction, there's more to writing than using a PC. To become a good writer, you need to use a proven writing procedure like the one that's introduced in the next chapter and presented in detail in section 2. You also need to master the essential language skills that are presented in section 3. So let's get on with it.

Terms

personal computer
PC
hardware
software
word processing
word processing package
word wrap
spelling checker
pop-up product
on-line thesaurus
writing analyzer
grammar checker
electronic spreadsheet software
what-if analysis
business graphics software
pie chart

line chart
bar chart
clip art
screenshow
desktop publishing
laser printer
resolution
presentation software
outline processor
idea processor
electronic note pad
paint program
object oriented drawing program
draw program
computer aided design and drafting program
CAD program
database software
database
on-line information service
on-line forum
CD ROM

Objectives

1. Explain how the first six types of PC software described in this chapter can help you write more efficiently and effectively.

2. Explain how a writer can use the second six types of PC software described in this chapter.

3. List the three requirements for getting the most from your PC software.

Heading plan for chapter 2

What's wrong with your current writing procedure

A 12-step writing procedure

- Step 1: Define the job
- Step 2: Get the information you need
- Step 3: Select the content
- Step 4: Plan the topics and subtopics
- Step 5: Plan the headings and subheadings
- Step 6: Plan the visual aids
- Step 7: Plan the paragraphs
- Step 8: Develop the visual aids
- Step 9: Write the text
- Step 10: Analyze and improve the structure of the first draft
- Step 11: Edit and revise the first draft
- Step 12: Proofread and correct the second draft

The benefits of this writing procedure

You're able to write more efficiently

You're able to write more effectively

How you can adapt this procedure to your writing assignments and your working habits

What ever happened to the outline?

Chapter 2

How a proven writing procedure can help you improve your writing

To start you on your way to improved writing, this chapter introduces you to a 12-step writing procedure. If you're like most business and technical writers, this procedure is far more specific than the writing procedure you have been using. But when you start to use it, you'll quickly see how much this procedure can help you improve your writing efficiency and your writing effectiveness. By the time you complete this chapter, you'll realize that this procedure helps you treat writing as a manageable science instead of an elusive art.

What's wrong with your current writing procedure

Before I present the writing procedure I recommend, I'd like you to think about the procedure you have been using. For instance, what procedure would you use to develop a report like the one in appendix A? Take a few minutes to read this report so you can formulate a reasonable answer to my question.

As you can see, the report in appendix A is thirteen pages long including four visual aids, and it uses twenty-four different headings and subheadings. This report recommends that all the editors in a publishing company switch from the word processing system they have been using to word processing on IBM PCs. That's why I'll refer to this report as the "PC recommendation." You may as well take the time to become familiar with this report now because I'll refer to it throughout this chapter and throughout the first four chapters of the next section.

If you're like most business writers, you won't have an efficient procedure for preparing a report like this. As a result, you won't know when or how to decide what content to present or what visual aids to use. You won't know when or how to decide what headings or subheadings to use. And you won't know when or how to plan the paragraphs you're going to write. Although you may take ten minutes or so to create a general outline for what you're going to write, you'll soon get frustrated by the planning process and decide to start writing.

Then, because you haven't done an adequate job of planning, you'll have trouble doing the writing. You'll spend a lot of time staring at a blank page or a blank PC screen. If you have enough trouble with your writing, you may try to do some more planning. But by the time you finish your first draft, you'll have spent more than twice as much time as necessary writing it, and it still may not be effective.

To make matters worse, if you're like most business writers, you won't know how to analyze and revise your first draft. As a result, you'll spend most of your time making word and sentence changes that won't do much to improve the effectiveness of your document. By the time you finish your revisions, you'll have spent half as much time revising the first draft as writing it. And you still won't have corrected its major weaknesses.

I hope you don't write that way, but if you're like most business writers, you do. That's why most of you can quickly and easily improve your writing. All you have to do is improve your writing procedure.

A 12-step writing procedure

Figure 2-1 presents the writing procedure I recommend. As you can see, it consists of twelve steps in four phases: three steps for the *analysis* phase, four for the *planning* phase, two for the *writing* phase, and three for the *revision* phase. If at first that seems like a lot of steps for a writing procedure, you'll soon see that each step is simple and manageable. After I show you how to apply these steps to all your writing assignments, I'll show you how you can adapt this procedure to your working habits.

Before I tell you more about the twelve steps of this procedure, I want you to realize that this procedure is meant for *documents* that consist of only one *unit*. We call documents like this *one-unit documents*. For instance, memos, letters, and short reports are one-unit documents. Then, in chapter 7, you'll learn how to develop *multi-unit documents* like books or manuals. In this case, each chapter or section is a unit. You use the procedure in figure 2-1 to develop a unit

Analysis

1. Define the job.
2. Get the information you need.
3. Select the content.

Planning

4. Plan the topics and subtopics.
5. Plan the headings and subheadings.
6. Plan the visual aids.
7. Plan the paragraphs.

Writing

8. Develop the visual aids.
9. Write the text.

Revision

10. Analyze and improve the structure of the first draft.
11. Edit and revise the first draft.
12. Proofread and correct the second draft.

Figure 2-1 The 12 steps within the 4 phases of a proven writing procedure

whether you're developing a one-unit document or one unit of a multi-unit document.

Step 1: Define the job In step 1, the first analysis step, you define the job. At the least, that means you define or identify who you're writing the document for and what the purpose of the document is. In this step, you may also decide to write more than one document. For instance, you may decide to write a report along with a cover letter to introduce it. Although defining the job can be a trivial step for some documents like letters and memos, it is a critical step for many business documents. Unless you know who you're writing for and why, you can't do the next analysis steps.

Most of the time, you won't bother to write down your definitions of audience and purpose, you'll just make mental notes. Sometimes,

```
Document to be prepared

A report recommending that the employees in the editorial department switch
from Wang word processing on a Wang VS system to word processing on IBM PC
ATs


Audience

1.  The manager of the editorial department

2.  Other people in the editorial department to whom the managing editor may
    pass the report


Purposes

1.  To convince the manager that the sooner we switch to PCs, the better off
    we'll be

2.  To show the manager that we not only can benefit from the word processing
    software on a PC, but also from other software such as graphics,
    spreadsheet, and desktop publishing software


Related documents

1.  A cover memo that introduces the report to the managing editor
```

Figure 2-2   The job definition for the PC recommendation

though, it helps to write them down. For instance, figure 2-2 shows the *job definition* for the PC recommendation in appendix A. As you can see, a cover memo is going to accompany the report.

Step 2: Get the information you need   In step 2, you get any information you need for the assignment. Since most business and technical writers are pretty good researchers, this step normally isn't a problem. But you can't know what information to get unless you have clear definitions of audience and purpose.

As you get the information you need, you keep notes, make copies of articles or other documents you may want to refer to, and so on. You may also want to use PC software like electronic spreadsheet or database software to help you record and organize the information you get. For some assignments, you may be able to get some of the information you need from an on-line information service or a purchased database.

Step 3: Select the content   In step 3, you select the content for the unit you're writing. For instance, figure 2-3 shows the *contents list* for the PC recommendation. This is my final contents list after I deleted many items I thought were irrelevant to my audience and for my purposes. You can create a list like this manually or by using PC software like word processing or an outline processor. Once you're sure your list includes all the information you need for your purposes, you have finished the analysis phase.

Step 4: Plan the topics and subtopics   In step 4, the first planning step, you create a *topic plan* using word processing or an outline processor on your PC. To create the plan, you arrange the content you've selected into topics and subtopics. For instance, figure 2-4 presents the topic plan for the PC recommendation. Here, the indentation distinguishes subtopics from topics. Although you probably won't create topic plans for most one-page documents like letters and memos, you definitely should do this step for documents that consist of three pages or more.

What you're trying to do in this step is divide a large unmanageable writing assignment (writing the unit) into smaller manageable assignments (writing topics and subtopics). You're also trying to arrange the topics and subtopics in a structure that will make sense to your readers. When the topics or subtopics are so small that you can write them in several paragraphs or less, you've finished this step.

Step 5: Plan the headings and subheadings   In step 5, you convert the topics and subtopics of your topic plan into the headings and subheadings you will use when you write the unit. We call the revised plan a *heading plan*. For instance, figure 2-5 shows the heading plan for the PC recommendation. If you refer again to appendix A, you can see that each line in the heading plan is one heading or subheading in the finished document. The indentation in the heading plan distinguishes subheadings from headings. If you use word processing or an outline processor for your planning, it's easy to derive a heading plan from a topic plan.

In contrast to a topic plan, a heading plan puts the topics and subtopics in terms that are more meaningful and interesting to the

```
The status of our current system

The features of PC word processing
    new functions
    simplified or improved functions
    improved printing capabilities
    improved screen resolution

The benefits of PC word processing
    improved editorial productivity
    improved editorial quality

Costs of new equipment
    hardware
    software
    training materials
    training time

Analysis
    what would it take to justify one system in terms of improved productivity?
    what value could we put on improved editorial quality?

New WP functions
    on-line spelling checker
    on-line thesaurus
    overlapped editing and printing
    two documents active at the same time
    automatic generation of contents lists and indexes
    automatic dating via the system date
    integrated file handling and printing
    flush right
    footnoting

Simplified or improved WP functions
    super/subscript
    search/search & replace
    headings and pagination
    boldface, underlining, centering
    macro creation and use

Other software for PCs
    improved project management via spreadsheet software
    improved illustrations via graphics software
    improved editing via writing analyzers
    desktop publishing

Miscellaneous benefits
    improved employee morale
    preparation for the future
```

Figure 2-3   The contents list for the PC recommendation

```
A proposal for replacing our current word processing system with IBM PC's

Our current word processing system

A modern PC-based word processing system
    Improved system speed
    Improved functions
    New functions
    Improved monitors and printers

Other PC software for editors
    Spreadsheet software
    Writing analyzers
    Graphics software
    Desktop publishing

The benefits of a PC-based system
    Improved editorial productivity
    Improved editorial quality
    Improved project management
    Improved morale
    Preparation for the future

The costs of a PC-based system
    Hardware costs
    Software costs
    Training costs

Analysis and recommendation
```

Figure 2-4   The topic plan for the PC recommendation

reader. As you revise the topic plan with the reader in mind, you may also decide that some organizational changes are needed. If, for example, you compare figure 2-4 with figure 2-5, you can see that I added some subtopics, deleted some, and made some structural changes as I created the heading plan.

The heading plan is the most important planning document. If it has a logical structure and its headings and subheadings are written in terms that are meaningful to your readers, your document has a good chance for success. To write well, you have to plan your topics (headings) and subtopics (subheadings) before you plan your visual aids, plan your paragraphs, or start writing.

Step 6: Plan the visual aids   In step 6, you plan the visual aids you're going to use when you write a document. For short documents with no visual aids, you can skip this step. For longer documents, like

```
Why our editors should switch from our current word processing system to
PC-based word processing systems

What's wrong with our word processing system

What's right about PC-based word processing
    Improved system speed
    Improved functions
    Improved monitors and printers

PC software that can make an editor's job easier
    Spreadsheet software
    Writing analyzers                               figure 1
    Graphics software
    Desktop publishing

The benefits of a PC-based system                   figure 2
    Improved editorial productivity
    Improved editorial quality
    Adaptability to future systems

The costs of a PC-based system                      figure 3
    Hardware costs
    Software costs
    Training costs

Cost/benefit analysis                               figure 4

Recommendations
    What hardware should we buy?
    What software should we buy?
    When and how should we convert?

Conclusion
```

Figure 2-5 The heading plan for the PC recommendation with visual aids indicated

reports and proposals, you usually will need visual aids, so it's important to plan their use carefully.

During this step, you first decide what visual aid or aids you want to use for each heading or subheading in the heading plan. As you decide, you may create rough drafts of them or merely visualize them. Whether or not you create drafts of them, though, you number them and add each number to the heading plan alongside the appropriate heading or subheading. Figure 2-5 shows the heading plan for the PC recommendation after the numbers for the visual aids have been added to it.

Step 7: Plan the paragraphs   In step 7, you plan the paragraphs you're going to use when you write the first draft. We call the document that results from this step a *paragraph plan*. For instance, figure 2-6 presents the first page of the paragraph plan I used for writing the PC recommendation. As you can see, a paragraph plan is an expanded form of a heading plan that shows the paragraphs to be written and the numbers of the visual aids to be used. When you're using word processing or an outline processor on a PC, it's easy to expand your heading plan into a paragraph plan.

By dividing analysis and planning into the seven steps I've just described, you reduce a complex writing project to a series of manageable steps. As a result, you never have to write anything more complicated than a topic or a subtopic that consists of several paragraphs. So you write a lengthy report just as you do a one-page memo. You write one paragraph at a time using your paragraph plan as a guide.

Step 8: Develop the visual aids   In step 8, the first writing step, you create rough or finished drafts of the visual aids you've planned. Whenever appropriate, you'll use PC software like word processing, electronic spreadsheet, or business graphics software to develop the aids. Whether you go on to the next step with rough drafts or finished drafts depends on the type of project you're working on and your own working habits. However, the drafts of the visual aids have to be complete enough for you to refer to specific details as you write the first draft of your document.

Step 9: Write the text   In step 9, you write the *text* using word processing. The text is the written part of the document, as distinguished from the visual aids. The *first draft* of a document includes both the text and the visual aids.

Using a traditional writing procedure, writers spend most of their time on this step. If you use the 12-step writing procedure, though, you should cut your writing time in half. This is still the most time-consuming step in the writing process, but it doesn't have to be nearly as time-consuming as it traditionally has been.

Step 10: Analyze and improve the structure of the first draft
Step 10 is the first of two revision phases the first draft goes through (step 11 is the second phase). In step 10, you analyze and improve the structure of the draft. When I refer to the *structure of a draft*, I mean the arrangement of topics and subtopics within a unit, and the arrangement of paragraphs within the topics and subtopics. If you've

```
    Why our editors should switch from our current word processing
    system to PC-based word processing systems

            introduction
What's wrong with our word processing system
            the antiquated status of system
            limitations of system
What's right about PC-based word processing
            the improvements of the last 10 years
    Improved system speed
            the removal of editing delays
            the removal of interprogram delays
            spooling
    Improved functions
            general improvements in ease of use
            example: pagination
            example: spelling checker
    Improved monitors and printers
            resolution
            printer functions
PC software that can make an editor's job easier
            the availability of other software for PC users
    Spreadsheet software
            the idea and benefits
    Writing analyzers
            the idea and benefits
            example of RightWriter output          figure 1
    Graphics software
            the idea and benefits
    Desktop publishing
            the idea and benefits
The benefits of a PC-based system
            introduction to benefits               figure 2
    Improved editorial productivity
            hard to measure, but it's there
            some idea of degree of improvement
    Improved editorial quality
            impossible to measure, but it's there
            some idea of degree of improvement
    Adaptability to future systems
            differences between minicomputer and PC software
            training for improved products
```

Figure 2-6 The first page of the paragraph plan for the PC recommendation

planned down to the paragraph level, your writing shouldn't have many structural problems. But planning is the most difficult phase of writing, so some structural problems usually slip through. That's why you need to know how to analyze and improve the structure of your documents.

To analyze a document, I recommend that you create a *paragraph analysis*. For instance, figure 2-7 shows the paragraph analysis I created for the first draft of the PC recommendation. As you can see, a paragraph analysis looks like a paragraph plan, but it's created after a document is written, not before. As you create the paragraph analysis, you also analyze the structure of the draft, which means you raise questions about the completeness of the contents, the arrangement of the topics and subtopics, the usefulness of the headings and subheadings, the sequence of the paragraphs, and so on. You can create a paragraph analysis using word processing or an outline processor, but you'll note the changes you're going to make in pencil.

When you complete your analysis, you use word processing to make the changes to the first draft of the document. In figure 2-7, for example, I noted a paragraph that should be two paragraphs; I marked two sets of paragraphs that should be combined into one; I marked one paragraph with an *X* to indicate that it wasn't developed fully; I marked one paragraph for deletion; and I identified two paragraphs that should be added to the draft. When I finished this analysis, I used word processing to make these structural improvements. In all, these improvements involved only nine paragraphs so it didn't take me long to make them.

When you finish making the improvements, you print the improved version of the first draft. Then, you're ready for the next revision step.

Step 11: Edit and revise the first draft   After you analyze and improve the structure of the first draft, you're ready to look at it on a lower level. So in step 11, you edit and revise the structurally improved version of the first draft, thus creating a *second draft* of the document. Since you've corrected any structural problems in the previous step, you can now concentrate on the sentences within the paragraphs as you edit and revise. Here, the term *editing* refers to marking the changes you want to make on the first draft of a document. The term *revising* means making the changes indicated by the editing marks.

To help you edit and revise a draft efficiently, chapter 6 teaches you the editing marks professional editors and writers use. To illus-

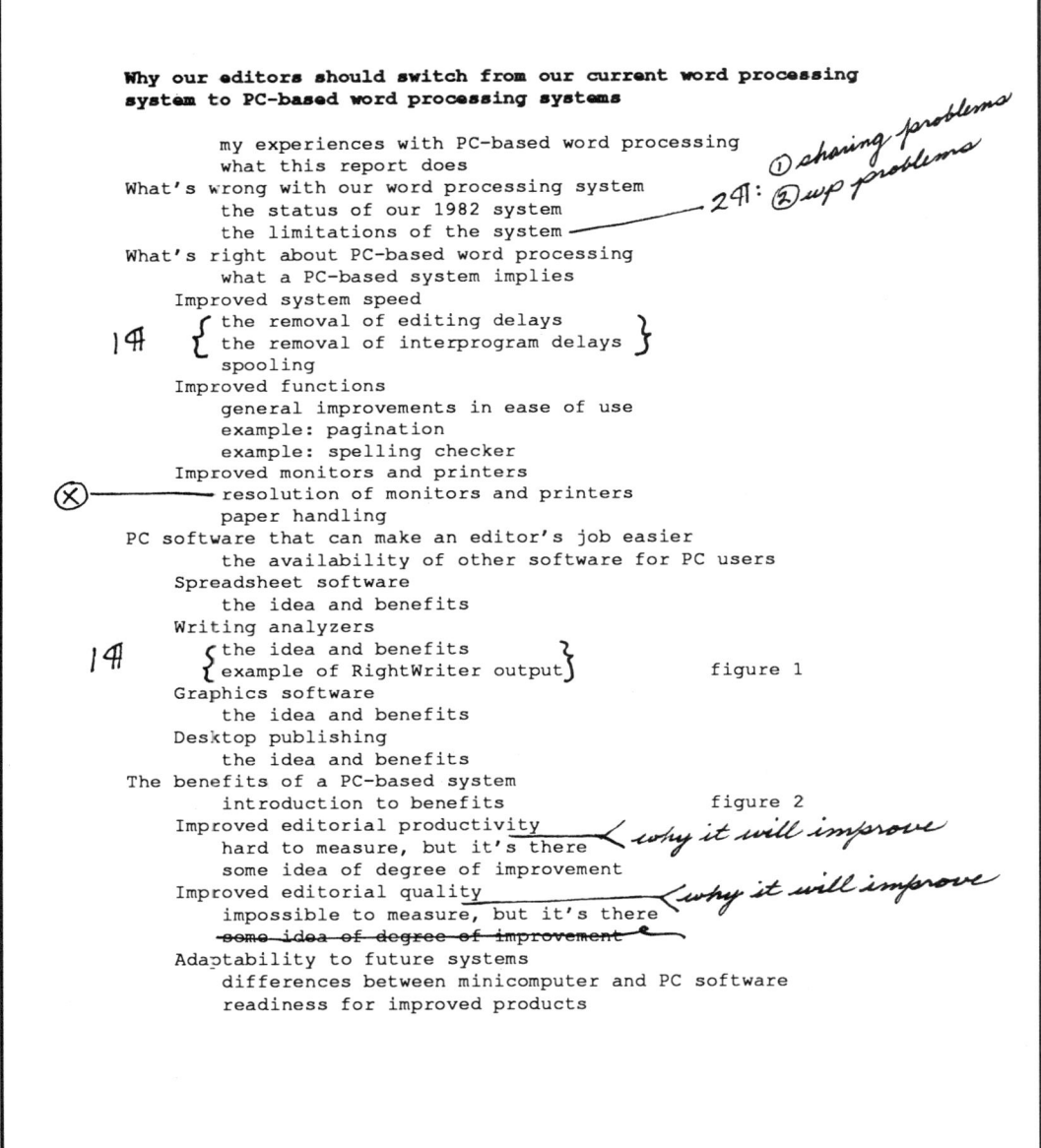

Figure 2-7 The first page of the paragraph analysis for the PC recommendation

trate, figure 2-8 shows the first page of the first draft of the PC recommendation with some typical editing marks. As you'll learn in chapter 6, these marks can be used on single-spaced drafts as in figure 2-8 or on double-spaced drafts.

To revise your draft, you will use your word processing software. If you have a spelling checker and a writing analyzer on your PC, you should also use them as part of this step. The corrections that result are often easy to make on the screen without requiring that you write anything on the printed page. Sometimes, you may even edit and revise at the same time on the PC screen without using the editing marks. In general, I don't recommend this, but chapter 6 gives some guidelines that will help you decide when it's acceptable.

Step 12: Proofread and correct the second draft　　In step 12, you proofread the second draft and, if necessary, correct it to produce a finished document. In the publishing business, this finished document is called a *final draft*, so that's the term I'll use for it throughout this book. When you print the final draft of a business or technical document, it will usually be ready for distribution. Sometimes, though, you may want to improve its presentation by using some of the features of word processing or desktop publishing. These features are presented in chapters 14 and 15.

When you proofread, you use the same editing marks you used in step 11. By this time, though, you should be confident that the structure and text of your draft is effective. As a result, you can just look for trivial errors like misspellings and punctuation mistakes. If the document is short and simple, you may not find any mistakes and the second draft may stand as your final draft. But most documents of any length and complexity require a few small corrections.

In general, when you use the 12-step procedure, your writing should require only three versions: the first draft, the second draft, and the final draft. Occasionally, you'll find so many problems with the second draft that you'll decide to do a third draft before the final draft. But your goal as an efficient writer should be a maximum of three drafts: first, second, and final.

The benefits of this writing procedure

If you use the 12-step writing procedure, you'll write more efficiently than you ever have before. In addition, your documents will be more effective than they have ever been before. But let me be more specific.

Why our editors should switch from our current word processing system to PC-based word processing systems

For the last six months, I've been using an IBM Personal Computer (PC) for my editorial work because I've been working on a book for PC users. During that time, I've come to realize that the system I'm using is much better than the system the other editors are using. That got me wondering whether all of ~~the~~ editors should~~n't~~ switch from our current system to PC-based systems. *our*

This report presents my analysis of our current system and my recommendations for new systems. I've tried to be ~~as~~ brief ~~as possible~~ because the primary purpose of this report is to bring you up-to-date on the PC and word processing developments of the last ~~6 or 8~~ years. When you finish this report, you can decide whether you want more information on any of the subjects. If so, I'll be happy to get that information for you. *six*

What's wrong with our word processing system

We installed our current system in 1982. It is a minicomputer system with one terminal, keyboard and monitor, for each person in the editorial department. The nine people in this department share the one printer that is located in the department. They also share the ~~CPU~~ and its disk drives with 15 other users of the system in the a*d*ministrative and marketing departments. *minicomputer / to*

Because this is a shared system, the editors experience frequent delays when they use the word processing software ~~of the system~~. This is particularly true between 10 A.M. and 3 P.M. when the system receives its heaviest use. Our editors also experience delays when they go from one function like editing to another function like printing. Because the word processing software consists of several programs rather than just one large program, the system must load the next program to be processed when a user changes functions. The delays occur while a program is loaded. *being*

Because the word processing software for this system was developed in the 1970s, it is dated. Although most of our editors don't realize it ~~because they have nothing to compare it to,~~ our word processing system just doesn't compare with a modern word processing package. In particular, it is inefficient when it comes to some of the time-consuming functions like paginating and checking spelling. Although ~~this~~ software was at one time the best word processing software in the industry, it is no longer a competitive product. *current / our*

Figure 2-8 The first page of the first draft of the PC recommendation

You're able to write more efficiently   Many business people have complained to me over the years that they just don't know how to get started when they write something. Sure, they know they should start by planning what they should write, but how do they go about it?

If you use the 12-step procedure in figure 2-1, though, you don't have this problem. You start by defining the job. Next, you get the information you need based on your job definition. Then, you select the content for your document. And so on. You continue like this right on down to proofing the final draft. As a result, you don't spend much time shuffling papers or staring at blank ones because *you always know what to do next*.

Another complaint I often hear from business people is that they get overwhelmed by the writing process. If, for example, they have to write a ten-page report, the planning overwhelms them, so they start writing. Then, because they haven't finished the planning, the writing overwhelms them. But you won't have these problems if you use the 12-step procedure, because each step is small enough to be manageable.

If, for example, you try to plan a large document down to its paragraphs as a single step, you'll probably be overwhelmed. But you can do that quite easily if you first plan the topics, then the subtopics, then the headings and subheadings, then the visual aids, and then the paragraphs. Similarly, if you try to write a large document without a paragraph plan, you're likely to be overwhelmed. With a paragraph plan to guide you, though, writing a long document isn't much harder than writing a one-page letter. In short, you don't get overwhelmed by writing when you use the 12-step procedure because *you are always able to do the next step*.

Because you always know what to do next and you are always able to do it, the 12-step writing procedure will help most writers improve their efficiency dramatically. For instance, it's common today for a businessperson to take an hour or more to write a one-page letter, a day to write a three-page proposal, and a week to write a 10-page report. And this doesn't include the time it takes to do the research for the letter, proposal, or report. By adopting an efficient writing procedure, you can cut these times by 20 to 50 percent, and sometimes even more. In general, the longer your documents are, the more the 12-step procedure will help you improve your efficiency.

You're able to write more effectively   When I speak of effectiveness, I mean the effectiveness of the documents you write. If they achieve their intended purposes, they're effective. If they don't, they're not.

One way the 12-step procedure helps you improve the effectiveness of your documents is by letting you concentrate on one level of writing at a time. It lets you do this because it's a top-down procedure for writing. Once you've defined the job, you can concentrate on getting and selecting appropriate content for the job. Next, you can concentrate on dividing this content into logical topics and subtopics that are identified by understandable headings and subheadings. Then, you can concentrate on the visual aids and paragraphs that will help you get your points across. By the time you start writing, you have a paragraph plan to guide you, so you can concentrate on the relationships between the paragraphs in each topic and the sentences within the paragraphs. You continue working like this, from the top down, right through the editing and proofreading steps.

Another way the 12-step procedure helps you improve the effectiveness of your writing is by forcing you to put structure into your documents. In other words, if you develop a document from the top down as prescribed by the 12-step procedure, your writing will have a logical organization and flow of ideas. Whether your readers notice this or not, it will help them understand what you're presenting. When your writing lacks structure, your readers are left to figure out the relationships between your ideas by themselves. But that's something many readers aren't able to do. As a result, logical, well-structured documents are easier to understand and more likely to achieve their objectives.

How you can adapt this procedure to your writing assignments and your working habits

Figure 2-9 gives you an idea of how you can apply the 12-step procedure to all your writing assignments. It doesn't matter whether you're writing a one-page letter, a three-page memo, or a ten-page report. For larger documents that require visual aids, you should do all twelve steps every time. For shorter documents, you can use the twelve steps as a checklist. Ask yourself: Do I need to divide my document into topics and subtopics? Do I need to use headings and subheadings? Would visual aids improve my document? Should I analyze the structure of my draft to make sure it is satisfactory? By going down the steps of the procedure for every document you write, you can make sure your documents are as effective as you can make them.

A proven writing procedure 49

		1-page letter	3-page memo	10-page report
Analysis				
1.	Define the job.	Yes	Yes	Yes
2.	Get the information you need.	Yes	Yes	Yes
3.	Select the content.	Yes	Yes	Yes
Planning				
4.	Plan the topics and subtopics.	No	Yes	Yes
5.	Plan the headings and subheadings.	No	Yes	Yes
6.	Plan the visual aids.	No	Maybe	Yes
7.	Plan the paragraphs.	Yes	Yes	Yes
Writing				
8.	Develop the visual aids.	No	Maybe	Yes
9.	Write the text.	Yes	Yes	Yes
Revision				
10.	Analyze and improve the structure of the first draft.	No	Maybe	Yes
11.	Edit and revise the first draft.	Yes	Yes	Yes
12.	Proofread and correct the second draft.	Yes	Yes	Yes

Figure 2-9   How the 12-step procedure applies to documents of different lengths

   After you get some experience with this procedure, you can adapt it to your working habits. If, for example, the twelve steps seem to be too tedious and methodical for you when you're writing short reports, you can combine steps 4 and 5. Then, you plan the topics and subtopics at the same time you create your headings and subheadings. If you're confident about the structure of your report after you've written its first draft, you can also skip step 10. When I write short reports, I often use an abbreviated procedure like that.

Before you start modifying the 12-step procedure, though, I recommend that you use it for a while. For each document you write, do each of the twelve steps that apply to that type of document. If you do that long enough, you'll see how each step can improve your writing and your writing efficiency. After you've mastered all twelve steps, you can modify the procedure so it works best for you.

What ever happened to the outline?

You may have noticed that I haven't used the word *outline* in describing the 12-step writing procedure. You know the kind of outline I mean, with Roman numerals (I, II, III), capital letters (A, B, C), Arabic numerals (1, 2, 3), and so on. I haven't mentioned outlines like this because they have been more of a hindrance than a help when it comes to business and technical writing. Although outlining may be all right for taking notes and even for organizing information, it hasn't been effective for planning what you're going to write.

Based on my discussions with business and technical writers during the last 20 years, I know some of you will agree with what I've just said, and some of you won't. For those of you who don't agree, here are four reasons why the traditional practice of outlining has hindered the business writer. There are other reasons, but these are the most obvious ones.

First, most people create their outlines in a way that doesn't correspond to the structure of writing: their Roman numerals don't represent headings; their capital letters don't represent subheadings; and their Arabic numerals don't represent paragraphs. That's why the outline isn't an efficient guide for writing. Second, most people don't create their outlines from the top down: they don't create all Roman numerals first; all capital letters second; and so on. That's why the structure of an outline usually isn't as consistent and logical as it should be for effective writing. Third, most people use language in their outlines that is meaningful to them, not to their readers. That's why outlining doesn't help the writer focus on what the reader needs to know. Fourth, the letters and numbers don't add anything to an outline that the indentation doesn't already show, so putting them in just wastes time.

Because of these problems with the traditional outlining process, I'm not going to present it as a planning method in this book. Instead, you'll learn how to plan more effectively by using the four planning steps in the 12-step writing procedure. Instead of an outline, you'll learn how to create a paragraph plan, an efficient and effective guide for writing.

Terms

analysis
planning
writing
revision
document
unit
one-unit document
multi-unit document
job definition
contents list
topic plan

heading plan
paragraph plan
text
first draft
structure of a draft
paragraph analysis
second draft
editing
revising
final draft

Objectives

1. List and describe the four phases and twelve steps of the 12-step writing procedure.

2. Distinguish between these terms:

   a one-unit document
   a multi-unit document

3. Explain how the 12-step writing procedure can help you improve your writing efficiency.

4. Explain how the 12-step writing procedure can help you improve your writing effectiveness.

Section 2

12 easy steps to better writing with a PC

This section presents a complete writing procedure for the PC user. This procedure will help you treat writing as a manageable science instead of an elusive art. When you use this procedure, you'll have a systematic method for doing each phase of writing. As a result, you'll be able to make dramatic improvements in your writing. You'll also be more productive than you've ever been before. In chapter 7 of this section, you'll learn how to use this 12-step procedure as you develop large, multi-unit documents.

Heading plan for chapter 3

Step 1: Define the job

The procedure for defining a job
1. Define the audience
2. Define your purpose or purposes
3. Consider alternatives to the document you're developing

Other ideas that will help you define a job
How to handle two or more audiences

How to handle two or more unrelated purposes

When and how to review your job definitions with others

Two examples of documents with content problems
A letter that gave the wrong answers

A memo that said too much

Discussion

Step 2: Get the information you need

Sources of information
Primary sources

Secondary sources

Other ideas that will help you get the information you need
How to record information

How to use PC software to organize your information

When to stop getting information

Discussion

Step 3: Select the content

The procedure for selecting the content
1. Create a preliminary contents list
2. Expand the contents list
3. Select the final contents

Other ideas that will help you select the content
When to use PC software for this step

What level of detail should you put in your contents lists

How much will your content change during the planning, writing, and revision phases

When can you combine content selection and the planning steps

Discussion

Chapter 3

How to decide what you should write

This chapter presents the first three steps of the 12-step writing procedure I introduced in chapter 2. In step 1, you define the audience for your document and the purpose or purposes of your document. Then, you consider alternatives for the document you intend to prepare. In step 2, you get the information you need for writing your document based on the definitions you developed in step 1. In step 3, you select the content for your document using the definitions you developed in step 1 and the information you got in step 2.

These steps make up the analysis phase of writing. When you finish this phase, you should know what kind of document you're going to develop, who you're writing it for, and why. You should also know what information you're going to include in your document.

This is an important chapter because content problems are serious problems. If, for example, you don't present the right information in a document, it can't be effective. Similarly, if you don't present enough information in a document, it's not likely to be convincing. And if you present too much information, it's liable to be confusing or boring.

Step 1: Define the job

When I analyze letters that members of my staff write, I find that most of the letters are good. When I do find one I don't like, it's usually not because of the writing. It's because the writer didn't have a clear view of the letter's audience and purpose.

The same holds true for reports, proposals, and manuals. When you read one that you find boring or unconvincing, it's often because the writer didn't start with adequate definitions of audience and purpose. Quite simply, if you don't know who you're writing to or why, you can't write effectively. That's why defining the job is a critical step for many writing assignments.

The procedure for defining a job

To define a writing job, I recommend the procedure in figure 3-1. Perhaps this is more of a checklist than a procedure because it doesn't tell you how to do anything. It just says to make sure you know who your audience is, make sure you know what your purposes are, and make sure you've considered any alternatives that would make your job easier or your document more effective. Even at that, though, this procedure is a useful one. At the least, it gets you thinking about what you're doing and how you can do it better.

1. Define the audience For many business documents, you know right away who your audience is. You're answering a specific customer's inquiry. You're writing to a distributor who wants more information about one of your company's products. You're writing a progress report to your boss describing your progress on your current project. In cases like these, you know from the start who your audience is, so you don't have to define it.

Frequently, though, you have to decide who your document will be distributed to. When you write a memo, should you send it to all employees or only to administrative personnel? When you write a report on the accomplishments of your company in the first quarter of the year, should the audience include everyone from the clerical workers to the chief executive officer? Or would it be better to have one report for clerical people, one for operations and middle managers, and one for top-level managers?

Even if you do know who your document is going to be distributed to, it often helps to define the audience. For most documents, you don't have to write down the definition once you understand what it

---

The procedure for defining a job

1. Define the audience.
2. Define your purpose or purposes.
3. Consider alternatives to the document you're developing.

Figure 3-1 The procedure for defining a writing job

is. But sometimes it helps to jot down a one- or two-sentence definition so you can use it as a guideline for the later development steps.

If there's some doubt about who the audience is or should be, it often helps to develop a more formal definition using word processing so it can be reviewed by your colleagues or manager. For instance, figure 3-2 gives the job definition for the PC recommendation in appendix A. As you can see, I defined a primary audience as well as a secondary audience.

Because you can usually write better if you have a clear view of who your readers are going to be, it is sometimes worth taking the time to develop specific descriptions of your primary and secondary audiences. For instance, figure 3-3 presents expanded descriptions for the audiences defined in figure 3-2. If you know that your primary reader, your boss, is enthusiastic about the productivity gains of modern technology, it may affect the way you write your recommendation. If you know that your secondary readers aren't familiar with the systems you're recommending and they're too busy to care about them, it should affect the way you write your report. In general, the more specific you can be about your audience, the more effective your writing will be.

2. Define your purpose or purposes Although audience and purpose are closely related, it helps to think of them separately. You know you're writing a letter to a customer, but is the purpose to answer the customer's questions, to sell the customer something, or both? You know you're writing a report to your boss on the status of your project, but is the purpose to report the facts or to make a recommendation on how the project should be managed in the future?

As you focus on purpose, you'll sometimes find that you don't have one. Or that the purpose you do have can't be fulfilled in a written document. Each year I get many letters I find difficult to answer because the purposes aren't clear. And years ago, when I

```
Document to be prepared

A report recommending that the employees in the editorial
department switch from Wang word processing on a Wang VS
system to word processing on IBM PC ATs


Audience

1.  The manager of the editorial department

2.  Other people in the editorial department to whom the
    managing editor may pass the report


Purposes

1.  To convince the manager that the sooner we switch to word
    processing on PCs, the better off we'll be

2.  To show the manager that we not only can benefit from the
    word processing software on a PC, but also from other
    software such as graphics, spreadsheet, and desktop
    publishing software


Related documents

1.  A cover memo that introduces the report to the managing
    editor
```

Figure 3-2   The job definition for the PC recommendation

worked in large corporations, I read dozens of memos and reports that had questionable purposes. In general, if you can't define a useful purpose for your document, you should cancel the writing project.

Frequently, as you try to define your purpose, you'll find that you have two or more purposes. For instance, figure 3-2 shows two purposes for the PC recommendation. When the goals are closely related, as they are in figure 3-2, they usually can be handled in a single document. But when you define two or more purposes that are unrelated, it's often best to develop two or more documents to accomplish your purposes. I'll talk more about this in a moment.

For simple documents, you don't need to put your purposes in writing as long as you're sure that you know what they are. For more complicated documents, though, it often helps to write your purposes down in a few short statements on a scratch pad. For some projects,

> **Primary audience**
>
> The managing editor has been using Wang word processing since 1982 and loves it. He frequently recalls how difficult editorial work was in the days of typewriters, and he often has said that he feels that the productivity in the editorial group doubled once we switched from typewriters to Wang word processing.
>
> **Secondary audience**
>
> Most of the editors are unfamiliar with PCs and PC software. They also seem to feel that they already have an excellent word processing system so they have no reason to change. Furthermore, they're so busy that they probably wouldn't want to take the time to learn a new word processing system.

Figure 3-3   A more specific audience definition for the PC recommendation

you may even want to prepare your definitions using word processing so they can be printed and reviewed by others.

3. Consider alternatives to the document you're developing

Sometimes, you intend to write one kind of document, but you realize as you define the job that there may be a better way to handle the communication. Then, you should consider alternatives to the document you're developing.

Recently, for example, a friend asked me for information about two unrelated subjects. To handle his inquiry as quickly as possible, I started to write a letter. As I tried to define my objectives, though, I realized that I had two distinct purposes in writing: (1) to present information about a specific computer he was interested in, and (2) to give him my opinion on whether he should revise one of his books. I then decided that three documents would be better than one. First, I found a report on the computer he was interested in and wrote a short summary of my experiences with it. Second, I wrote a recommendation that answered his question about revising his book. Third, I wrote a cover letter that introduced the documents I was sending him and summarized their conclusions. If I had tried to do everything in a single document, the document would have been more difficult for me to develop and more difficult for my friend to read and use.

My point is that you should think about what you're doing before you go on to the next step of the 12-step writing procedure. Would it be better to prepare two documents instead of one? Is there an existing document you could use to achieve your purpose without writing a new one? Should you send the report or proposal you're developing with a cover letter or memo? If you consider all of the alternatives, it's more likely that you'll achieve your purposes as efficiently as possible.

Other ideas that will help you define a job

Although the procedure for this step is a simple one, it isn't always easy to define a job. So let me present some ideas that may help you do this step more efficiently.

How to handle two or more audiences In general, you should try to avoid writing documents that are intended for more than one type of audience. For instance, you'll have a hard time writing one document that is effective for both teachers and students. Similarly, you'll have a hard time writing a document that is effective for both clerical workers and managers. So when you define two or more types of audiences, you'll probably accomplish your purposes more effectively if you write one document for each audience.

How to handle two or more unrelated purposes Sometimes, when you try to define the purposes of your document, you'll find that you have two or more unrelated ones. If this happens, consider developing one document for each purpose.

That doesn't mean you should always develop one document for each purpose. If, for example, each purpose requires only a paragraph or two, it's reasonable to use one document for several purposes. But if each purpose requires several pages, you probably can do the job more efficiently by writing one document for each purpose.

If you're trying to accomplish two or more purposes *and* you're trying to reach two or more audiences, it's a clear indication that you should consider any reasonable alternatives. By redefining what you're doing, you can usually improve your efficiency as well as the effectiveness of the resulting documents. In general, you'll write most efficiently and most effectively when you define only one audience for each document and keep the purposes closely related.

When and how to review your job definitions with others
Whenever you're working on a writing project that's going to be costly or critical, you should review your definitions with others. If you're a

manager, you should review them with your staff members. If you're a staff member, you should review them with your manager and perhaps with the other members of the staff. If the review leads you to a better job definition, it will usually save you time, and it may help you avoid a serious mistake.

When you prepare your definitions for review, I recommend you use the general form shown in figure 3-2. This form presents the definitions of audience and purpose, and it identifies any related documents that will be used to support the primary document. I also recommend that you use word processing to prepare your definitions so you can easily revise them based on the suggestions you get from your reviewers.

Of course, if a project is costly or critical, you should get reviews at later stages of development too. But this early review will help you get started right. Since mistakes in the analysis phase of writing are usually the most costly ones, you should do whatever you can to avoid them. If you don't define your job correctly, it usually means that your document is going to be ineffective no matter how well you write it.

Two examples of documents with content problems

To show you how critical this step can be, here are two examples of documents that probably weren't defined properly. That's why they didn't have the right content. And that's why they turned out to be expensive mistakes.

A letter that gave the wrong answers Figure 3-4 illustrates an exchange of correspondence between a vice president in one company and a sales correspondent in another. In brief, a vice president of a large retailing company wanted to buy a book for distribution in her company's 560 retail stores, so she wrote a letter inquiring about volume discounts. The sales correspondent replied with a letter saying that they offered 20 percent off the list price.

When the sales manager discovered a copy of the letter several months later, he was furious. What if the retailing company wanted to buy 10 books for each of the 560 stores? Or 20 books for each store? Certainly, for an order of 5000 copies or more they would be willing to give a better discount than 20 percent off list. But when the sales manager called the vice president personally to see if they could still make a deal, it was too late.

Here, you can see that the writer didn't take the time to define the job he was doing. If he had, he would have realized that his purpose was to sell books, not to present his company's standard discount policies.

A memo that said too much Figure 3-5 presents a memo written by the vice president in charge of the Development Division of a company I used to work for. In brief, the vice president had just been appointed to his position, so his memo says that he needs a few more weeks to plan the reorganization of the division. Unfortunately, he says this in a two-page memo that's heavy in figurative speech, but light in meaning. At a time when many employees were concerned about their futures with the company, this memo became the object of jokes and gossip for several days after its distribution.

Did the vice president take the time to define the job before he wrote the memo? I don't think so. If he just wanted to announce that he needed two more weeks for planning, he could have done so in two or three paragraphs. Apparently, though, he also wanted to let people know how important the reorganization was, to encourage them to keep working no matter what happened, to assure them that they wouldn't lose their jobs, and to let them know that it's not easy being a vice president. But when his plans were finally announced, the reorganization itself was trivial, people did lose their jobs, and managers from other companies were hired to replace them. The memo then became written proof that the new boss was something less than honest.

Discussion

Because this step is so critical to the efficiency and effectiveness of your writing, I hope you'll take the time to define your writing jobs. For simple jobs, the procedure should take only a few moments. But you should give this step as much time as it requires no matter what kind of document you're developing. In general, the more important a job is, the more important this step is.

Objectives

1. Describe the procedure for defining a job.

2. Given a writing assignment, prepare a written job definition.

How to decide what you should write 63

An inquiry from a well-known company specializing in retail distribution

Gentlemen:

We're interested in buying one of your books for distribution in our 560 retail outlets. The title of the book is <u>The Least You Should Know About Computing</u>. Your catalog shows its list price as $14.95.

My questions are:

1. Will you sell this book through retail distributors like us or do you only sell through college bookstores?

2. If so, what kind of volume discounts can we get?

          Sincerely,

          Sally Westchester
          Vice-President
          Retail Distribution

The reply from a sales correspondent

Dear Mrs. Westchester:

Thanks for your inquiry about <u>The Least You Should Know About Computing.</u> You'll be pleased to know we offer a discount of 20 percent off the list price for all retail distributors.

If you have any further questions, I'll be happy to answer them.

          Sincerely,

          Richard Garnett
          Sales Correspondent

Figure 3-4   A letter that gave the wrong answers

MEMORANDUM TO: All development personnel

A friend of mine is in the wine business in France and tells me that he can never make Americans understand that a delivery date cannot be committed for good wine. A last minute tasting can suggest that six more months would do a lot of good.

The decision to reorganize the Development Division was made partially because we wanted to revitalize and refresh peoples' outlook. The recent series of circumstances seems to be contributing to frustration, however.

It does seem to make sense to take whatever time seems essential to make the wisest possible decision.

The main purpose of the reorganization is to increase the Development Division's flexibility in planning and building for the immediate and long term future. What we are hoping to achieve is a correction of the over-extension and at the same time provide the framework for rather dramatic growth within the next one to three years.

As I have said to most of you, the only real asset we have is people and our only resource is talent. My responsibility, it seems to me, is to help provide the framework and the context that will permit this talent to be used most effectively.

Obviously, an organizational chart doesn't solve problems, but maybe it can cut red tape. One of the major objectives that I have is to see to it that the dollars in the development budget are in fact spent on editorial development work as opposed to management and administrative functions. Every manager ought to be a "working manager" with his hands and his mind deeply involved in our major editorial business.

At this point in time, the easiest thing to do psychologically, emotionally and practically would be to make a decision, almost any decision, get it out of the way, and get on with the show. I think I feel this pressure even more than you do. I seem to face the dilemma of my French friend in seeing a much better result if we wait a couple more weeks. You face the same dilemma that the American distributors face, namely that you have to trust my sense of taste.

Figure 3-5 A memo that said too much (part 1 of 2)

How to decide what you should write 65

```
Memorandum to Development Personnel
Page 2


The reorganization is not going to affect what most of us do
as a daily activity nor will it affect the supervisory
relationships that exist for most of you.  I sincerely hope
that it will make doing our jobs easier and more exciting
because the administrative chores will have been streamlined
and refined and the clerical burdens eased somewhat.

The decision has been made to capitalize on existing talent
which we have in abundance rather than to bring in outsiders
for any jobs.  The decision has also been made to put to
maximum and efficient use all of the talent currently on
board; I think my phrase has been that everybody should feel
"stimulatingly overworked."  Consequently, the faces you see
around you the day after this fabled ANNOUNCEMENT will be
the same as you see around today.  As I mentioned to most of
you last Friday, I am 100% more encouraged about our
opportunities to launch dramatic new projects and more
convinced than ever that we will continue to have an even
greater impact on what happens in education.  We plan to set
a direction for ourselves that will move us very quickly
into the business of developing sophisticated educational
systems packages.  Our competitors are moving slowly in
these directions, and I think that by mobilizing our current
strengths efficiently we can beat them to the punch and be
there as soon as the market is ready.

If we are to achieve the projected sales growth that we are
planning, we have no alternative but to get deeply involved
in a wide variety of projects.  The reorganization obviously
will put each of you in a position of being completely aware
of all that is happening within the Development Division and
will encourage your contribution and suggestions to any
project that could benefit from them.

In the meantime, I am no longer asking for your patience but
rather that you get on with the jobs at hand with as much
efficiency and speed as possible so that we can clear the
decks and be prepared for next year's effort as soon as
possible.  I promise you that the pressures I mentioned
earlier won't be lifted from me until we can make this
announcement.

Would you believe Thanksgiving..........?
```

Figure 3-5 A memo that said too much (part 2 of 2)

Step 2: Get the information you need

After you define the document you're going to write, you decide whether or not you have the information you need to write it. If you don't have what you need, the next step is to get the required information. If you do have it, you skip this step and go on to the next one.

This is an important step because business requires that you get your information right. To write effectively, you must back up your statements with facts. That means you must know how to get the information you need and how to record it so you can refer to it later.

Fortunately, most business and technical writers are good researchers, so I'll assume that you already use effective techniques for getting information. That's why I won't try to present a procedure for this step. Instead, I'll start by presenting some common sources of business information. Then, I'll present some ideas that may help you improve the way you handle that information.

Sources of information

Your search for information may take many forms. You may have to ask your boss what the company policy is on some issue. You may have to search through files for product data. You may have to find and review a report you know you saw sometime in the last month or two. To get the information for a large document, you may have to read several books or articles. No matter how you get your information, though, your sources can be divided into two categories: primary sources and secondary sources.

Primary sources In business, *primary sources* are sources of information you access directly. This means that you get the information from your own experiences or observations. When you use primary sources, you are doing *primary research*. In figure 3-6, you can see some of the common sources for primary research.

In business, you'll probably write more memos and letters than anything else. For these, you'll get most of your information from primary sources. If, for example, you answer a letter that asks for purchasing information, you may ask the engineering department for product specifications or the sales staff for price quotations. In each instance, you'll get your information directly from the primary sources.

When you write a longer document like a report or proposal, you'll still use primary sources most of the time. You'll get informa-

---

Primary sources

Your boss and your co-workers
People in other departments
People in other companies
Reports from the data processing system
Meetings
Seminars
Speeches
Data from your own experiments
Data from your own research

Secondary sources

Newspapers
Periodicals
Books
Government publications
Encyclopedias
Dictionaries
Almanacs
On-line information services
Purchased databases

Figure 3-6   Sources of information

tion from your boss, co-workers, people in other departments and branches, and people in other companies. You'll get information from meetings, seminars, and speeches you attend. You'll get information from data processing reports, marketing research questionnaires, and experiments. To a large extent, your ability to use your primary sources will determine how efficiently you can get the information you need.

Secondary sources   When you use *secondary sources*, you don't get your information directly as you do from primary sources. Instead, you get it secondhand from published materials like newspapers, periodicals, and books. Then, you are doing *secondary research*. Figure 3-6 lists some of the common sources for secondary research.

When you need secondary sources, a library is a superb resource. Sometimes, though, you'll buy the materials you need at a bookstore or through a direct mail supplier. Occasionally, you may be able to use an on-line information service or a purchased database to get the information you need, but these sources are usually too expensive and time-consuming to be practical.

Since this book isn't intended to teach researching techniques, I won't go any further. But I hope you realize that you can use your library to get information on almost any subject. Too often, business writers don't use the library as much as they should, so they don't get all the information that would help them write more effectively.

**Other ideas
that will help you get the information you need**

As you get the information you need, you must record it. After you record it, you may want to organize it using PC software. Once you're satisfied that you have all the information you need for your writing assignment, you must stop researching and go on to the next step. Here, then, are a few more ideas for getting information as efficiently as possible.

How to record information   When you get information from primary or secondary sources, you often need to record it so you can refer to it later. If, for example, you ask your boss what quantity discounts you should offer a customer, you should record the information and its source. Similarly, when you read a book to get information for a research report, you should record the main ideas and facts so you can refer to them as you select the content for your report. You should also record enough information to identify each of your secondary sources.

When you record information, I recommend that you use standard 8-1/2-by-11 sheets of paper, not 3-by-5 or 4-by-6 cards. That way you'll be able to file your notes easily in a standard-sized folder. For each source, you should record the date on which you got the information along with a description of your source. After that, you can list any ideas or facts that are relevant to the document you're developing. Figure 3-7, for example, presents a source sheet for some research on writing.

Although you can record your information by hand, you can often do so more easily by using your PC. For instance, you can use word processing or an outline processor to record information in the form

How to decide what you should write 69

```
March 19, 1988

Rudolf Flesch.  How to Write, Speak, and Think More
Effectively.  Signet Books, 1946.


Sentence length
    17 words/sentence is standard
    25 words/sentence is difficult

Word length
    avoid affixes
    37/100 words is standard
    46/100 is difficult

Human interest
    6 personal words/100 is standard
    3/100 is difficult

Same rules apply for scientific writing:  pages 78-84
    A reader shouldn't say "A layman like me will never
        understand this."
    He should say, "The author of this can't write."
```

Figure 3-7   Information from one source

shown in figure 3-7. Because you can type faster than you can write, you'll usually record more detail on your PC than you would manually, so your notes will be easier to follow later on. Also, a word or outline processor encourages you to give some structure to your information by using indentation.

How to use PC software to organize your information   If your writing project requires large amounts of information, you may want to organize your information as you get it. Normally, this isn't necessary because you'll be organizing your information in the next three steps of the writing procedure. But there's nothing wrong with taking the time to organize your information during this step. This can be particularly useful if you want to make sure that your information is complete or that you understand your data.

One of the easiest ways to organize your information is to outline it using your word processor or an outline processor. For instance, figure 3-8 presents an information summary that I developed with an outline processor. Note that this outline doesn't include the letters and numbers of a traditional outline because they're unnecessary.

If you're working with large amounts of numerical data, you may want to use electronic spreadsheet software to help you organize it. Sometimes, for example, it helps to summarize the data from several data processing reports in a single spreadsheet. This makes the data easier for you to understand. Once you understand it, you can analyze it using what-if analysis. Later on, you may want to use the spreadsheet or a variation of it as a visual aid.

Business graphics software can also help you understand your data. If the relationships are complex, a chart or a graph may help you see them more clearly. Since you can change the form of a chart or graph with just a few keystrokes, you can experiment until you do see the relationships clearly. Later on, you may want to use some of your charts or graphs as visual aids.

If you gather so much information that you can't seem to control it, you may want to consider the use of database software. This software can be particularly helpful if you're trying to organize many items of information within a predictable structure. Then, after you've developed the database, you can extract the information you need from it. As I said in chapter 1, though, the structural limitations of database software make it impractical for most writing projects. That's why you usually shouldn't bother with it until you've exhausted the organizational possibilities of a word or outline processor and electronic spreadsheet software.

When to stop getting information Some writers have the problem of getting too much information. They may be remembering their college days when the more information they got, the more likely they were to get a good grade. In business and technical writing, though, efficiency is such a serious concern that you have to know when to stop getting information.

Since you have already defined your purposes when you start your research, you should let these definitions guide you. Whenever you think you have enough information to achieve your purposes, it's time to stop getting information.

If you're not sure whether you have enough information, I recommend you stop researching and go on to the next step. If you decide during one of the later steps that you don't have all the information you need, you can always return to this step. In most cases, though, you'll already have what you need.

```
PC software uses for editors and writers
   Word processing packages
      Develop job definition
      Record information
      Organize information
      Select content
      Plan what you're going to write
      Create visual aids
      Write the first draft of the text
      Revise subsequent drafts of the text
   Spelling checkers
      Check spelling during revision phase
   On-line thesauruses
      Find synonyms as you write
      Find synomyms as you revise
   Writing analyzers
      Identify writing weaknesses during revision phase
      Identify grammatical errors during revision phase
      Establish readability index during revision phase
   Electronic spreadsheets
      Organize information
      Analyze information
      Develop visual aids
      Plan and control writing and editorial projects
   Business graphics
      Analyze information
      Develop visual aids
   Outline processors
      Record information
      Organize information
      Plan what you're going to write
      Analyze what you've written
   Database software
      Organize information
      Extract information from an established database
   Other graphics software
      Create visual aids for use with desktop publishing
      Create the types of visual aids that you use
      frequently
   On-line information services
      Get the information you need
   Purchased databases
      Get the information you need
   Desktop publishing
      Present text and visual aids with published quality
```

Figure 3-8 Information that I organized with an outline processor

Discussion

If you refer back to the letter in figure 3-4, you can see that the writer simply didn't get the information he needed for the letter he wrote. Specifically, he didn't check with a primary source like his boss to find out what the company's policy would be for a large order. As a result, the letter probably lost his company thousands of dollars in sales.

That example shows how important this step can be. In business, you have an obligation to get the information you need for every document you write. No one is going to care much for your opinions if they're not based on the *right* facts.

Terms

primary source
primary research
secondary source
secondary research

Objectives

1. Distinguish between primary and secondary sources of information.

2. Explain how you can use PC software to help you record and organize information.

3. After you've defined the job for a writing assignment, get the information you need.

Step 3: Select the content

When you have all the information you need to accomplish the purposes you've defined, you're ready to select the specific items of content you'll use in your document. In most cases, though, you won't use all the information you've gathered. That's why this step is so important. To write effectively, you must make sure your document includes all of the content that will help you achieve your purposes, and none of the content that won't.

The procedure for selecting the content

Figure 3-9 presents the procedure I recommend for selecting the content for a document. First, you create a preliminary contents list. Second, you expand that list so it includes every item of information that could possibly help your document achieve its purposes. Third, you select the specific content items you'll use when you write your document, based on your definitions of audience and purpose.

1. Create a preliminary contents list As you define the job you're doing, you usually have many ideas about what your document should include. Then, as you get the information you need, you have many more ideas about the content for your document. To start creating the contents list, write down all of these ideas.

After you've written down all of the content items that come to mind easily, go through the notes you recorded when you gathered your information. Whenever you come across an item that might be appropriate for your document, add it to your list. When you're finished, you have what we call a *preliminary contents list*.

When you create a preliminary contents list, you shouldn't be too critical about the content items you're listing. Instead, you should put down any items you think might possibly help your document achieve its objectives. Don't try to put your content items in any order, and don't worry about the quality of your items. At this point, it doesn't matter whether a content item represents a topic, a subtopic, a paragraph, or just a thought, fact, or quotation. You just want to get your content items down on paper so you can evaluate them later on.

To illustrate a preliminary contents list, figure 3-10 presents the list for the PC recommendation in appendix A. As you can see, the content items range from topic ideas ("problems with the current system") to paragraph ideas ("signing on and off takes several seconds"). If an item is related or subordinate to another item, I

The procedure for selecting content

1. Create a preliminary contents list.
2. Expand the contents list.
3. Select the final contents.

Figure 3-9 The procedure for selecting content

indented it to show this relationship. Because a preliminary contents list is a working paper that only you will see, you can use whatever style you feel is appropriate.

2. Expand the contents list For short documents like letters and memos, you'll probably be able to list all of the content items you need as you create the preliminary contents list. In other words, the ideas you have in your head and in your notes will be all you'll need to achieve your purposes. If so, you don't have to try to expand your preliminary list.

However, for longer documents like reports and proposals, you'll often wonder whether you're overlooking any critical content items. If so, you can remove any doubts you have by expanding your contents list.

To expand your list, you should review other documents like the one you're preparing. If, for example, you're preparing a sales proposal, review some of the proposals written by other sales representatives or some of the proposals you've written yourself. Maybe they will give you ideas for topics or subtopics that could improve the effectiveness of your proposal. If you're writing a recommendation for equipment purchases, review some of the other recommendations you've written or some of those written by your colleagues. Whenever you see a content item that could improve your document, add it to your preliminary contents list. When you're done, you'll have an *expanded contents list*.

As you expand your contents list, don't be too critical about the items you list. If you list the same idea twice, don't worry about it. At this stage, you want to make sure your list includes *everything* that might possibly be relevant to your audience and your purpose. Since one of the problems in writing is not telling your audience enough,

```
                Costs of new equipment
                    hardware
                    software
                    training materials
                    training time

                Problems with current system
                    the walk to the printer to get output
                    if the system goes down, everybody's down
                    the spelling checker is inefficient
                    pagination is only semi-automatic
                    signing on and off takes several seconds
                    inititiating a printing operation is tedious
                    many functions are inefficient:  e.g. 2 column documents

                The features of PC word processing
                    solve all of the above problems
                    new functions
                    simplified or improved functions
                    printing quality

                The benefits of PC word processing
                    improved editorial productivity
                    improved editorial quality

                Analysis
                    what would it take to justify one system in terms of
                        improved productivity?
                    what value could we put on improved editorial quality?
```

Figure 3-10 The preliminary contents list for the PC recommendation

your efforts to make a complete contents list will help solve that problem.

To illustrate an expanded contents list, figure 3-11 shows the list for the PC recommendation. The items above the line are the ones from the preliminary contents list; those below the line are the ones I added during this step of the procedure. To expand my list, I reviewed the functions available with the current word processing software as well as those available with PC word processing. I also reviewed some of the hardware and software recommendations and cost/benefit analyses done by other employees. Later on, when I selected the content for my document, I used only a few of the ideas I listed during the expansion of my preliminary list. But at least I considered any

```
            Costs of new equipment
                hardware
                software
                training materials
                training time

            Problems with current system
                the walk to the printer to get output
                if the system goes down, everybody's down
                the spelling checker is inefficient
                pagination is only semi-automatic
                signing on and off takes several seconds
                inititiating a printing operation is tedious
                many functions are inefficient:  e.g. 2 column documents

            The features of PC word processing
                solve all of the above problems
                new functions
                simplified or improved functions
                printing quality

            The benefits of PC word processing
                improved editorial productivity
                improved editorial quality

            Analysis
                what would it take to justify one system in terms of
                    improved productivity?
                what value could we put on improved editorial quality?
            - - - - - - - - - - - - - - - - - - - - - - - - - - - - - -
            New WP functions
                on-line spelling checker
                on-line thesaurus
                overlapped editing and printing
                two documents active at the same time
                automatic generation of contents lists and indexes
                system date
                integrated file handling
                integrated printing
                flush right
                footnoting

            Simplified or improved WP functions
                super/subscript
                search, search & replace
                headings
                pagination
                boldface and underlining
                centering
                macro creating and use
```

Figure 3-11 The expanded contents list for the PC recommendation (part 1 of 2)

```
Other software for PCs
    spreadsheet software for managing projects
    graphics software for creating and refining illustrations
    desktop publishing software, the software for the future
    writing analyzers for improving editorial quality
    time and project management software

The benefits of other software
    improved project management
    improved graphics and accuracy in our illustrations
    improved editorial quality

The costs of the current system
    hardware maintenance
    backup costs

Miscellaneous benefits
    improved employee morale
    preparation for the future

Training requirements
    one 3-hour tutorial
    periodic frustrations for about 2 weeks
    improving productivity thereafter

Improved monitor resolution
```

Figure 3-11 The expanded contents list for the PC recommendation (part 2 of 2)

content that even remotely applied to the purposes I had defined for the PC recommendation.

3. Select the final contents After you expand your contents list, you select the actual contents you'll use for your document. You do this by analyzing each item in your list. If you feel that the item is appropriate for your audience and that it will help your document accomplish its purposes, you leave it in the list. Otherwise, you delete it. When you're done, you have what we call the *final contents list*, or just the *contents list*.

For a short list, you can delete any item by drawing a line through it. For a long list, it's often more practical to rewrite your expanded contents list. As you rewrite it, you analyze each item so you can drop out any items that won't contribute to the purpose of your document. You may also want to group lower-level items under topical headings to show their relationships.

Figure 3-12 presents the final contents list I used for the PC recommendation. If you compare it to the expanded list in figure 3-11, you can see that I deleted many items as I rewrote the list. I also rearranged some of the items. When I finished this step, I was confident that my recommendation would be effective if I presented everything in the final contents list. I knew that I had considered all content that could possibly be useful for my purposes and that I had deleted all of the content that was irrelevant.

Deleting items increases your writing productivity because it reduces the amount of work you have to do. Each time you delete an item, it means you don't have to organize the item, you don't have to write it, and you don't have to revise it. If, for example, you reduce the amount of content you're going to present by 10 percent, that will reduce the amount of work you have to do by 10 percent or more.

Other ideas that will help you select the content

As simple as it is, the procedure I've just presented will help you select the right content for any document. Now, let me give you a few more ideas that will help you use this procedure as efficiently as possible.

When to use PC software for this step Most of the time I do this step manually because I find that's just as efficient as using a PC. If I write on a desk pad, I can record all of the content items for a large document on one side of the sheet with plenty of room left over for expanding and revising this list. When I finish this step, I use my handwritten contents list as the input for the next step of the writing procedure. That's when I start to use word processing or an outline processor.

Of course, you can use a word processor or an outline processor for this step if you want to. If you've used your PC to record and organize the information you gathered in step 2, you may be able to use this information as the start of your contents list. If so, you may be able to do this step more efficiently by using your PC.

In general, though, you won't increase your efficiency by using your PC. Because you'll be paging through many notes and other documents as you create your list, this step doesn't lend itself too well to computer entry. Sometimes, in fact, it's easier to keep track of content items on paper just because a PC screen is too small to

```
The status of our current system

The features of PC word processing
    new functions
    simplified or improved functions
    improved printing capabilities
    improved screen resolution

The benefits of PC word processing
    improved editorial productivity
    improved editorial quality

Costs of new equipment
    hardware
    software
    training materials
    training time

Analysis
    what would it take to justify one system in terms of
        improved productivity?
    what value could we put on improved editorial quality?

New WP functions
    on-line spelling checker
    on-line thesaurus
    overlapped editing and printing
    two documents active at the same time
    automatic generation of contents lists and indexes
    automatic dating via the system date
    integrated file handling and printing
    flush right
    footnoting

Simplified or improved WP functions
    super/subscript
    search/search & replace
    headings
    pagination
    boldface, underlining, centering
    macro creation and use

Other software for PCs
    improved project management via spreadsheet software
    improved illustrations via graphics software
    improved editing via writing analyzers

Miscellaneous benefits
    improved employee morale
    preparation for the future
```

Figure 3-12 The final contents list for the PC recommendation

display them all at once. That's why I recommend that you do this step manually, at least until you become familiar with it. After that, you can try doing it on your PC to see if that's efficient for you.

What level of detail should you put in your contents lists   As I said earlier, your contents lists are papers no one else will review. Since they're your working papers, you can list your content items at any level of detail you feel is useful. If you want to list quotations, by all means list them. If you want to list all the ideas you'll use in your paragraphs later on, list them. If you just want to list the topics and subtopics you intend to cover and you know what content they'll include, that's okay too.

To some extent, your level of detail will depend on the length and complexity of the document you're preparing. If, for example, you're preparing a one-page letter, you'll probably list one content item for each paragraph you intend to write. For instance, figure 3-13 presents a contents list for a sales letter that consists of four content items. In this case, the contents list will probably become the paragraph plan because this letter doesn't require topics, subtopics, or visual aids. When the author writes the letter, it will probably contain four paragraphs in the same sequence as the contents list.

If you're working on a large document, many of your content items will probably be at the level of topics or subtopics. However, you may want to list subordinate items beneath these items, and you may also want to list trivial items like facts and quotations so you won't forget them. Here again, you should list your items at the level of detail that is most useful for you.

The level of detail doesn't matter much because your content list *is simply going to be used as a checklist in the subsequent develop*ment steps. When you develop a heading plan or a paragraph plan during the planning phase of writing, you'll use your contents list to make sure your plans include all of the content items you selected. After you write the first draft of a document, you'll use your contents list to make sure the draft includes everything you wanted to include.

How much will your content change during the planning, writing, and revision phases   When you're working on a large document, one that takes several days or more to complete, you'll probably think of additional content items during the planning, writing, or revision phases. You may also decide that some of the items in your final contents list aren't necessary. I don't think there's anything wrong with this, and it doesn't mean you didn't do an

```
            No, we don't offer the book you requested
            Why we don't
            Related products we do offer
            Thanks for your interest
```

Figure 3-13 The contents list for a letter that answers a customer's inquiry

adequate job of selecting content in the first place. When you're working on a difficult assignment, you're bound to improve your ideas as you focus on successively lower levels of detail during the development process.

To illustrate, look again at figure 3-12. If you were to compare this contents list with the contents in the PC recommendation itself, you would discover that I didn't present everything in the list. In particular, I decided that I didn't need to present the new and improved word processing functions in detail. Instead, I presented only two of these functions as examples of improvements.

Fortunately, the development methods presented in this book make it easy for you to improve your content as you plan, write, and revise a document. The methods also force you to keep thinking about the content you're presenting so you'll have many chances to improve it. That doesn't mean you shouldn't try to develop as complete a contents list as possible as you do this step. It just means you'll be able to rethink and improve your content selections throughout the development process.

When can you combine content selection and the planning steps In practice, it's difficult to select the content for a document without ever thinking about how you'll organize it. As a result, you'll often start the planning steps while you're selecting the content for a document. For instance, after you learn how to do the planning steps, you'll start to arrange your content items in logical groupings that will become topics and subtopics in the planning phase. You may also start to list your content items with names that will become headings and subheadings later on. For short documents, you may plan the paragraphs you're going to use as you select the content for a document.

As I see it, there's nothing wrong with combining the analysis and planning steps in this way as long as you make sure you're selecting the right content. But while you're learning, I think it's best to treat each of the steps separately. Once you've mastered these steps, you can combine them in the ways that are appropriate for your working style and for the types of documents you normally develop.

Discussion

If you refer back to the memo in figure 3-5, you can see now that the writer didn't do an adequate job of content selection. If he had, he wouldn't have written such a long memo with so many irrelevant content items. In fact, I don't think the writer made any conscious effort to select the content for the document he was writing. Unfortunately, that's not the right way to develop effective documents.

When you finish selecting the content for your document, you should feel confident that your contents list includes everything that will help you achieve your purposes and nothing that is irrelevant to your purposes. You should also feel confident that your document will be effective if you present everything in the list in an effective manner. Yes, you'll have to organize the content well and you'll have to write it well, but you know at this point that your document is going to have the right content. As a result, you will have eliminated one of the major causes of ineffective writing.

Terms

preliminary contents list
expanded contents list
final contents list
contents list

Objectives

1. Describe the procedure for selecting content.

2. After you've done the first two steps for a writing assignment, prepare an acceptable contents list for the document.

Heading plan for chapter 4

Step 4: Plan the topics and subtopics

The procedure for planning topics and subtopics
1. Group the contents into topics
2. Arrange the topics into a reasonable presentation sequence
3. If necessary, divide the topics into subtopics
4. Try to develop alternative topic plans
5. Select the best plan

Nine organizational methods
- Order of importance
- Order of interest
- Simple-to-complex organization
- Familiar-to-unfamiliar organization
- Procedural organization
- Functional organization
- Chronological organization
- Geographical organization
- Traditional organization

Other ideas that will help you plan topics and subtopics
- How to plan presentation sequences when the organizational methods don't apply
- When to use three levels of topics and subtopics
- How an outline processor can help you do the planning steps
- When to combine content selection with topic planning

Discussion

Step 5: Plan the headings and subheadings

Why headings and subheadings are important

The procedure for planning headings and subheadings
1. Rewrite your topic plan in language that is meaningful to your readers
2. If necessary, improve the structure of your plan

Two guidelines for writing effective headings and subheadings
- Promise a benefit
- Use consistent language structures

Other ideas that will help you plan headings and subheadings
- How to create report titles
- When and how to use introductory headings
- When and how to use concluding headings
- How long should your headings and subheadings be
- How the use of more subheadings can improve your writing
- When to use three levels of headings
- When to combine the first two planning steps

Four examples of heading plans
- A heading plan with meaningless headings
- A heading plan with an ineffective structure
- A heading plan with too much introduction and summarization
- An effective heading plan

Discussion

Heading plan for chapter 4 (continued)

Step 6: Plan the visual aids

The procedure for planning visual aids
1. Identify the visual aids that will improve the effectiveness of the topics and subtopics in your heading plan
2. Develop a legend list, rough drafts, or first drafts for the visual aids you've planned

Other ideas that will help you plan visual aids
How many visual aids should you use

What to call the visual aids

How to number the visual aids

How to write the legends for visual aids

Discussion

Step 7: Plan the paragraphs

The procedure for planning paragraphs
1. Expand your heading plan into a paragraph plan
2. If necessary, check your final contents list against your paragraph plan to make sure your plan provides for all of the content items

When and how to overlap paragraph planning and writing

Discussion

Chapter 4

How to plan what you're going to write

This chapter presents steps 4 through 7 of the 12-step writing procedure. These are the planning steps. When you start step 4, you work from the contents list you developed in step 3. When you finish step 7, you have a paragraph plan that you'll use as a guide for your writing in step 9.

In step 4, you divide the content for a document into topics and subtopics. In step 5, you convert your topic and subtopic names into the headings and subheadings you'll use when you write your document. As a result, you'll do steps 4 and 5 only for documents that require headings and subheadings, usually those two pages or longer. However, you may occasionally want to use headings and subheadings even for one-page documents.

In step 6, you plan the visual aids you're going to use in your document. As a result, you do this step only if your document requires visual aids. Then, in step 7, you plan the paragraphs you'll write for each topic and subtopic in your document. You should do this step for every document you write.

Most business writers don't do an adequate job of planning what they write. To a large extent, that explains why they write inefficiently and why most of their documents are ineffective. In most cases, business writers can make dramatic improvements in their writing just by improving their planning methods. That is why this is one of the most important chapters in this book; it helps you overcome the most common writing problem, poor planning.

Step 4: Plan the topics and subtopics

When you finish step 3 for a document, you have a list of the content items you want to include in it. Then, in step 4, you start the planning phase of writing by dividing the content you've selected into topics and subtopics. What you're trying to do is divide a large, unmanageable writing assignment (writing a document of two or more pages) into smaller manageable assignments (writing topics and subtopics). That makes it easier for you to write your document later on, and it makes it easier for your readers to understand your document.

The procedure for planning topics and subtopics

To organize content into topics and subtopics, I recommend the procedure in figure 4-1. When you finish this step, you should be confident that your document will be effective if it presents the topics and subtopics of your topic plan in the order shown.

1. Group the contents into topics To start, you try to arrange the items on your contents list into groups that will represent *topics* when you write your document. Often, the best way to do this is to rewrite the contents list using your word processor. As you rewrite, you group content items. As you group the items, you give each group a name that indicates what topic the items make up. You can call these names *topic names*, and you can call your new listing a *topic list*.

Figure 4-2, for example, shows the topic list I created for the PC recommendation in appendix A. Here, the content items in each group are indented beneath the topic name for the group. If you compare the list in figure 4-2 with the final contents list in figure 3-12, you can see that the topic list is just a refined version of the contents list. Although I started to group some items when I created the contents list, I did so only when there was an obvious logical relationship. In contrast, when I created the topic list, I tried to place every content item within a topic.

As you group content items, you should keep your readers in mind. Gather the content items into topics you think will be useful and interesting to them. If you come across items on your contents list that you don't think will be useful, delete them from your list. When I finished the topic list in figure 4-2, I felt confident that all of the topics would provide useful information to my readers.

The procedure for planning topics and subtopics

1. Group the contents into topics.
2. Arrange the topics into a reasonable presentation sequence.
3. If necessary, divide the topics into subtopics.
4. Try to develop alternative topic plans.
5. Select the best plan.

Figure 4-1 The procedure for planning topics and subtopics

After you create a topic list for a document, make sure it accounts for all of the content items on your contents list. To do this, go through your contents list and put each item in one of the topic groups you've just created if it's not in one already. If you end up with items that don't fit into any of the groups, you can compose new groups to accommodate them. Or, if a content item represents a topic by itself, you can just give the item an appropriate topic name and leave it as an ungrouped item. For instance, "our current word processing system" in figure 4-2 is a topic name with no subordinate content items.

2. Arrange the topics into a reasonable presentation sequence   After you've grouped all of the content items into topics, you arrange the topics into a reasonable presentation sequence. To do this efficiently, you start a new word processing page or document, and you work with only the topic names. That way you can easily try several different presentation sequences before you decide on one you think will be effective. In a moment, I will present some organizational methods you may want to consider as you plan the sequence of your topics.

To illustrate the end product of this step, figure 4-3 shows my first presentation sequence for the PC recommendation. You can call a list like this a *sequenced topic list*. If you need to know what content items the topic names represent, you can refer back to your topic list for the details.

3. If necessary, divide the topics into subtopics   By this time, you should have some idea how complex your topics are. You can judge this complexity by evaluating the content items listed for a

```
Our current word processing system

A modern PC-based word processing system
    system speed
    new functions
    simplified or improved functions
    improved printing capabilities
    improved screen resolution

The benefits of a PC-based word processing system
    improved editorial productivity
    improved editorial quality

The costs of a PC-based system
    hardware
    software
    training materials
    training time

Analysis
    what would it take to justify one system in terms of
        improved productivity?
    what value could we put on improved editorial quality?

The benefits of other PC software for editors
    improved project management via spreadsheet software
    improved illustrations via graphics software
    improved editing via writing analyzers
    improved employee morale
    preparation for the future

Other PC software for editors
    spreadsheet software
    writing analyzers
    graphics software
    desktop publishing
```

Figure 4-2   The topic list for the PC recommendation

topic on your topic list. Then, if you think you can make the topics more manageable by dividing them into *subtopics,* you do so. The result is your first *topic plan* for the document. In figure 4-4, you can see the first topic plan for the PC recommendation.

If you don't think any of the topics need to be divided, your sequenced topic list becomes your topic plan. If, for example, I had decided that none of the topics needed to be divided into subtopics, the sequenced topic list in figure 4-3 would have been my first topic

```
A proposal for replacing our current word processing system

Our current word processing system

A modern PC-based word processing system

The benefits of a PC-based word processing system

Other PC software for editors

The benefits of other PC software for editors

The costs of a PC-based system

Analysis
```

Figure 4-3 The sequenced topic list for the PC recommendation

plan for this document. For short documents, you will frequently end up with one-level topic plans.

4. Try to develop alternative topic plans The longer a document is, the more alternatives you have when you plan it. That's why you shouldn't always accept the first topic plan you come up with for a document. Frequently, it pays to consider other possibilities.

To develop alternative topic plans, just revise your first topic plan. As you revise, you ask questions like these: Are the topics in the best presentation sequence? Are the subtopics for each topic in the best presentation sequence? Should any topics or subtopics be added to the topic plan to help achieve your purposes? Should any topics or subtopics be deleted from the topic plan because they're irrelevant to your purposes? Can any topics or subtopics be combined to improve the presentation?

As you do this analysis, you should concern yourself with the sequence and structure of your topics and subtopics, not with the names you use for them. If you get the sequence and structure right, your document will have a good chance for success. Then, in step 5 of the 12-step writing procedure, you'll revise your topic and subtopic names so they'll be as meaningful as possible to your readers.

To illustrate the type of alternative plan I'm suggesting, figure 4-5 shows the second topic plan that I created for the PC recommen-

```
Topic plan 1
A proposal for replacing our current word processing system

Our current word processing system

A modern PC-based word processing system
    System speed
    New functions
    Improved functions
    Monitors and printers

The benefits of a PC-based word processing system
    Editorial productivity
    Editorial quality

Other PC software for editors
    Spreadsheet software
    Writing analyzers
    Graphics software
    Desktop publishing

The benefits of other PC software for editors
    Project management
    Editorial quality
    Illustrations
    Preparation for the future
    Morale

The costs of a PC-based system
    Hardware
    Software
    Training

Analysis
```

Figure 4-4   The first topic plan for the PC recommendation

dation. If you compare it with the first plan in figure 4-4, you can see that I combined the two topics on benefits into one. I changed the sequence of two subtopics in the topic on benefits and deleted the subtopic on illustrations from that topic. I also changed the sequence of two subtopics in the topic on PC-based word processing.

5. Select the best plan   For short documents, you may find that only one way of organizing a document seems reasonable. That's particularly true if you decide that you don't need to divide any of your topics into subtopics. When you have six or more topics and

```
Topic plan 2
A proposal for replacing our current word processing system

Our current word processing system

A modern PC-based word processing system
    Improved system speed
    Improved functions
    New functions
    Monitors and printers

Other PC software for editors
    Spreadsheet software
    Writing analyzers
    Graphics software
    Desktop publishing

The benefits of a PC-based system
    Editorial productivity
    Editorial quality
    Project management
    Morale
    Preparation for the future

The costs of a PC-based system
    Hardware
    Software
    Training

Analysis
```

Figure 4-5 The second topic plan for the PC recommendation

subtopics within a document, though, you'll usually realize that there are several different ways to organize your content items. Once you've developed alternative versions, you have to select the one that's best.

Often, one of the plans is clearly the best, and you'll realize that right away. For instance, I realized that my second topic plan for the PC recommendation (figure 4-5) was better than the first one as I developed it. It presented the same information, but it had one less topic and a more effective presentation sequence. As a result, I decided to go on to the next planning step as soon as I finished the second topic plan.

Usually, you will select the plan you feel is going to be the most effective. Sometimes, though, you may select the one you think you can develop most efficiently. In this case, you reason that a small improvement in effectiveness isn't worth the cost of the extra development time. In either case, though, you should feel confident that your document will be effective if you present all of the topics and subtopics of the topic plan in the sequence shown.

Nine organizational methods

Now that you know the general procedure for developing a topic plan, let me describe nine organizational methods you can use within your plans. As you learn about these methods, you should realize that you can use more than one of them in a single document. For instance, you can use one method to organize the topics, another method to organize the subtopics for one topic, a third method to organize the subtopics for another topic, and so on.

Order of importance   When you arrange a document by *order of importance*, you present the most important topic first, the second most important topic second, and so on. To be more specific, this organizational method is sometimes called the order of *decreasing* importance. Newspaper articles are usually organized this way, and this method of organization often works well in memos, letters, and short reports. Figure 4-6 presents the topic plan for a report that is organized this way.

You can also organize a document in the order of *increasing* importance. This means you present items of least importance first and put the most important information last. In general, though, this form of organization isn't effective for business documents. As a result, whenever I refer to the order of importance in this book, I mean the order of decreasing importance.

When you use this organizational method, you sometimes realize that your order of importance may not be the same as your reader's. Then, you have to decide whose order to use. In the topic plan in figure 4-5, for example, I presented the five subtopics under "the benefits of a PC-based system" in what I thought my reader's order of importance was going to be. If I had presented these subtopics in my order of importance, I would have presented editorial quality first and productivity second.

Order of interest   Often, the *order of interest* is the same as the order of importance. Sometimes, though, you have to present a sequence of topics or subtopics that are about equal in importance.

```
A general topic plan for a report

Summary of findings

Details of major findings
    First major finding
    Second major finding

Details of minor findings
    First minor finding
    Second minor finding
    Third minor finding

Miscellaneous findings
```

Figure 4-6 A topic plan in the order of decreasing importance

Then, it makes sense to put them in order from the most interesting to the least interesting. In the topic plan in figure 4-5, I presented the four subtopics under "other PC software for editors" in what I thought would be the order of interest for my reader.

Simple-to-complex organization   When you use *simple-to-complex organization*, you start with the simplest concepts or functions and move on to progressively more difficult concepts or functions. This type of organization is commonly used in instructional materials and technical manuals, but it is useful whenever you're presenting information that ranges in difficulty from the simple to the complex. Figure 4-7 presents the topic plan for a section in a word processing guide that is organized this way.

Familiar-to-unfamiliar organization   When you use *familiar-to-unfamiliar organization*, you start with the topics or subtopics that your readers are most familiar with and you end with those they are least familiar with. This is similar to the simple-to-complex method of organization, but it's not the same. This method is useful in many types of business documents ranging from memos and letters to reports and training materials.

Procedural organization   Whenever you develop a document that shows someone how to do something, you should consider *procedural organization*. This means that your topic plan reflects the order

---

A topic plan for a section in a word processing guide

```
How to print a one-page document
How to print a multi-page document
How to print a one-page document
    with variable information from a second document
```

Figure 4-7 A topic plan that uses simple-to-complex organization

in which a procedure is done. Some people refer to this as *how-to organization*. As you can imagine, many instructional booklets and manuals use procedural organization. Figure 4-8, for example, presents the topic plan for one of the sections in a writing manual that is organized in this way.

Functional organization   When you develop a document that shows someone how to do more than one thing, you should consider *functional organization*. This means that each topic in your topic plan represents one function. When you use this organization, your readers can easily find the functions they want to learn about so they can apply them to their daily tasks.

To illustrate, figure 4-9 presents the topic plan for a section in a manual on office procedures. In this plan, there is one topic for each of the seven functions the staff members are expected to do. If these topics were divided into subtopics, it's likely that the subtopics would have procedural organization.

Chronological organization   When you use *chronological organization*, you present topics in the order they have occurred or should occur in time. If you write the history of your company or the schedule for daily operations, you can use chronological organization. Figure 4-10, for example, presents a topic plan for a company history that is organized in this way.

Geographical organization   When you use *geographical organization*, each topic represents information for a location or place. If you write a summary of your company's branch office operations or review all of your company's locations, you'll use this method of organization. In figure 4-11, you can see a topic plan for a report that is organized this way.

> **A topic plan for a section in a writing manual**
>
> ```
> Step  1: Define the job
> Step  2: Get the information you need
> Step  3: Select the content
> Step  4: Plan the topics and subtopics
> Step  5: Plan the headings and subheadings
> Step  6: Plan the visual aids
> Step  7: Plan the paragraphs
> Step  8: Develop the visual aids
> Step  9: Write the text
> Step 10: Analyze and improve the structure of the first draft
> Step 11: Edit and revise the first draft
> Step 12: Proofread and correct the second draft
> ```

Figure 4-8   A topic plan that uses procedural organization

> **A topic plan for a section in a manual on office procedures**
>
> ```
> Opening and sorting mail
> Handling orders
> Handling payments
> Handling customer inquiries
> Handling customer complaints
> Handling vendor invoices
> Handling vendor correspondence
> ```

Figure 4-9   A topic plan that uses functional organization

Traditional organization   Some subjects in business have traditionally been treated in a certain way. When you present one of these subjects, it often makes sense to treat your topics or subtopics in the sequence that has traditionally been used. When you do this, you're using a *traditional organization*.

Data processing costs, for example, have traditionally been treated in this sequence: hardware costs, software costs, and other costs. That's why I used this sequence for the three subtopics under "the costs of a PC-based system" in the topic plan in figure 4-5. If I had used order of importance, the sequence would have been this: training costs, hardware costs, software costs.

A topic plan for a brief history of MMA

```
1972:  We start our business
1974:  We publish our first product
1980:  IBM adopts our COBOL package
1982:  Our annual sales top $1,000,000 for the first time
1986:  OS JCL becomes our first $1,000,000 book
1987:  Doug Lowe becomes our first $1,000,000/year author
```

Figure 4-10 A topic plan that uses chronological organization

Other ideas that will help you plan topics and subtopics

As simple as it is, the procedure in figure 4-1 will help you develop effective topic plans for any document you create. But now, let me give you some other ideas that will help you do this step.

How to plan presentation sequences when the organizational methods don't apply   Sometimes, when you develop a document, the organizational method is obvious. Other times, it's obvious that a combination of organizational methods will lead to an effective presentation sequence. To present this step, for example, I used procedural organization for the first topic. Then, I used the order of importance for presenting the organizational methods and the other ideas for planning.

Quite often, though, none of the methods I've just presented seems to apply to the topics in your document. Or, one method seems to apply to one set of subtopics; another method seems to apply to a second set of subtopics; but none of the methods seems to apply to the rest of your topics and subtopics. How then do you choose an effective presentation sequence?

To illustrate these complexities, try to apply the organizational methods I've just presented to the four subtopics listed under "a modern PC-based word processing system" in figure 4-5:

    Improved system speed
    Improved functions
    New functions
    Monitors and printers

```
           Marketing report for the first half of the year
     The East
         Sales up 8.5%
         Outstanding trainee award
     The South
         Sales up 13%
         Merchandising award
     The Midwest
         Sales up 9%
     The West
         Sales up 22%
         Outstanding manager award
```

Figure 4-11   A topic plan that uses geographical organization

For these topics, I considered the order of importance, simple-to-complex, and familiar-to-unfamiliar, but none of these sequences by itself satisfied me. So I used a combination of two of them. Since the ideas on monitors and printers were least important, I put this subtopic last. Then, I moved from the familiar to the unfamiliar as I presented system speed, improved functions, and new functions.

When the organizational methods don't apply to what you're trying to do, my only advice is to depend on your own logic and creativity. Sometimes, you'll be able to use a combination of methods. Sometimes, you'll have to develop your own organizational method. No matter how you decide upon your presentation sequence, though, make sure that it's reasonable. That means you should always be able to explain why you decided upon your presentation sequences. If you want to write effectively, nothing should be left to chance.

When to use three levels of topics and subtopics   When you plan a business document, you shouldn't often require subdivisions below subtopics. In other words, your documents should consist only of topics and subtopics.

Occasionally, though, you may write complicated documents that require another level of structure. For a document like this, you can use a three-level topic plan. For example, figure 4-12 presents a three-level topic plan for one chapter in a technical manual on the use of COBOL. Here, the chapter is divided into four topics; the first three topics are divided into subtopics; and some of the subtopics are divided down one more level.

```
The topic plan for a chapter in a technical manual on COBOL

Sequential processing
    The SELECT statement
    FILE STATUS codes
    Procedure Division statements
        The OPEN statement
        The START statement
        The READ statement
        The REWRITE statement
        The DELETE statement
    Two illustrative programs
        A file creation program
        A sequential update program
Random processing
    The SELECT statement
    Procedure Division statements
        The OPEN statement
        The READ statement
        The WRITE, REWRITE, and DELETE statements
    A random update program
Dynamic processing
    A report preparation program that uses dynamic access
    The report preparation program without dynamic access
Discussion
```

Figure 4-12   A three-level topic plan for a technical presentation

Although three-level topic plans are used quite frequently for technical documents, I recommend that you avoid them for most business writing. When you use a third level, your document is more difficult to create, and it's likely to be more difficult for your reader to follow. Besides that, you can usually create an effective topic plan without going to a third level. As a result, I recommend that you use a third level only when you're sure you can't develop an acceptable topic plan for your document using two levels.

How an outline processor can help you do the planning steps
An outline processor is specifically designed for creating indented plans like topic plans, heading plans, and paragraph plans. That's why an outline processor can make it easier for you to do this step and the planning steps that follow.

When you use an outline processor, you can "collapse" and "expand" headings with just a keystroke or two. When you're doing this step, for example, you can collapse the subtopic names in a topic plan like the one in figure 4-4 so your PC screen looks like the sequenced topic list of figure 4-3. Then, you can rearrange the topic names to start an alternative topic plan. As you move a topic name, all of its subtopics come with it even though you don't see them. After you're satisfied with the new sequence of topics, you can expand the plan so the subtopic names show.

Similarly, you can use an outline processor to revise your topic plan into a heading plan in the next step of this procedure. Then, you can add another level to the plan as you develop a paragraph plan in step 7 of the procedure. Whenever you want, you can collapse one or more levels of your plan so you can concentrate on one level or one portion of a plan at a time. You can also print just the levels or portions of a plan that you want to print.

If you frequently develop lengthy documents, it's worth getting an outline processor if you don't already have one. Then, you can use it for planning in steps 4, 5, and 7 as well as for organizing data in step 2 or for selecting content in step 3. Keep in mind, though, that you can do these steps quite efficiently using word processing. So you should only expect minor improvements in efficiency from your outline processor.

When to combine content selection with topic planning As I started to explain in the last chapter, it's difficult to select the content for a document without thinking about how you'll organize it. As a result, you'll often start thinking about topics and subtopics as you select the content. In fact, for short, simple documents, it's natural to treat step 3 and step 4 in the 12-step procedure as a single step.

As long as you make sure you're selecting the right content, there's nothing wrong with combining content selection and topic planning in this way. However, when you're learning to use the 12-step writing procedure, I think it's best to treat each of these steps separately. When you do step 3, you should be asking yourself which content items will help you achieve your purpose. When you do step 4, you should be asking yourself how you can organize the content into a logical structure of topics and subtopics that will make sense to your readers.

Discussion

This is the most critical of the planning steps. If you do it well, your topic plan will represent a logical structure of topics and subtopics. Then, if you follow that structure as you write the document, you'll write more efficiently. That structure will also make your document more effective because it will make your document easier for your readers to read, understand, and refer to.

Terms

topic
topic name
topic list
sequenced topic list
subtopic
topic plan
order of importance
order of decreasing importance
order of increasing importance

order of interest
simple-to-complex organization
familiar-to-unfamiliar organization
procedural organization
how-to organization
functional organization
chronological organization
geographical organization
traditional organization

Objectives

1. Describe the procedure for planning the topics and subtopics of a document.

2. Explain the concept behind each of the following organizational methods:

   order of importance
   order of interest
   simple-to-complex organization
   familiar-to-unfamiliar organization
   procedural organization
   functional organization
   chronological organization
   geographical organization
   traditional organization

3. After you've done the first three steps for a writing assignment, develop an effective topic plan for the document.

Step 5: Plan the headings and subheadings

When you finish step 4, you have a topic plan for the document you're going to write. Then, in step 5, you revise this plan so its topic and subtopic names become the *headings* and *subheadings* you'll use when you write your document. These headings and subheadings will guide your readers through your document.

Why headings and subheadings are important

Before I describe the procedure you should use when you plan your headings and subheadings, I want to explain why you need headings and subheadings in your writing. If you understand their importance, you'll take more time to develop them. In general, headings and subheadings can improve the effectiveness of your documents in four ways.

First, good headings and subheadings provoke curiosity and make your readers want to read your documents. Did you ever start a chapter in a book and wonder if you should bother reading it? If so, did you page through the chapter reading the headings? Many people approach their reading in this fashion. So if your headings are interesting, they'll entice your readers to read the rest of your document.

Second, good headings show your readers the structure of your document. As your readers move from one heading to another, they should be able to anticipate what they're going to read about next and see how it relates to what they've already read. Headings and subheadings should identify topics and subtopics within a unit and show your readers how the subtopics relate to the main topics. If your headings do this, your readers will read and understand your material more easily because they'll see the relationships between your ideas.

Third, headings make it possible for your readers to read selectively. Often, some topics within a document interest a reader, and some don't. Then, if your headings and subheadings clearly identify your topics and subtopics, your readers can read those that interest them and skip the ones they already know about.

Fourth, headings help your readers use your documents for later reference. Where is the lot description in the Jefferson report? What was Steve's recommendation on the alternative collection procedure? If your headings properly identify the topics and subtopics of your documents, your readers will be able to find what they're looking for easily. In contrast, if you use headings poorly (or not at all), it's diffi-

---

The procedure for planning headings and subheadings

1. Rewrite your topic plan in language that is meaningful to your readers.
2. If necessary, improve the structure of your plan.

Figure 4-13 The procedure for planning headings and subheadings

cult to use your documents for later reference. Just think how this can affect the efficiency of a business organization.

The procedure for planning headings and subheadings

If you want your headings and subheadings to provide the four benefits I've just described, you can't develop them after you've created the first draft of a document. Instead, you must develop them as part of your planning process so each heading represents one topic and each subheading represents one subtopic. Since you've planned the topics and subtopics for your document in step 4, all you have to do in step 5 is convert the topic and subtopic names to headings and subheadings.

Figure 4-13 presents a procedure for this step. First, you rewrite your topic plan in language that is meaningful to your readers. The new plan is called a *heading plan*. Second, you try to improve the structure of your heading plan now that your headings show how the plan relates to your readers.

1. Rewrite your topic plan in language that is meaningful to your readers   To start, you use your word or outline processor to convert the topic and subtopic names in your topic plan to heading and subheading names that you think will be meaningful to your readers. To be meaningful, a heading should give a reader a good indication of what a topic is about; a subheading should give a good indication of what a subtopic is about.

To illustrate, figure 4-14 shows the heading plan I developed from the topic plan in figure 4-5. Although the structure in figure 4-14 is the same as it is in figure 4-5, the names in figure 4-14 are more meaningful to the reader. If you look at each heading and subheading in figure 4-14, you should have a good idea of what each topic and subtopic is going to be about.

```
Why our editors should switch from our current word
processing system to PC-based word processing systems

What's wrong with our word processing system

What's right about PC-based word processing
    Improved system speed
    Improved functions
    New functions
    Improved monitors and printers

PC software that can make an editor's job easier
    Spreadsheet software
    Writing analyzers
    Graphics software
    Desktop publishing

The benefits of a PC-based system
    Improved editorial productivity
    Improved editorial quality
    Improved project management
    Improved morale
    Adaptability to future systems

The costs of a PC-based system
    Hardware costs
    Software costs
    Training costs

Cost/benefit analysis
```

Figure 4-14 The first heading plan for the PC recommendation

To make it easy for you to compare the topic plan for the PC recommendation with the heading plan, figure 4-15 shows all of the topic and subtopic names that were changed during this first part of step 5. Instead of "our current word processing system," the heading plan says "what's wrong with our word processing system." Doesn't that give a better indication of what the topic is about? Instead of "preparation for the future," the heading plan says "adaptability to future systems." Won't that mean more to the reader? Instead of "analysis," the heading plan says "cost/benefit analysis" because that's the type of analysis the topic is going to do and the readers should be familiar with that term.

Language in topic plan	Language in heading plan
Our current word processing system	What's wrong with our word processing system
A modern PC-based word processing system	What's right about PC-based word processing
Monitors and printers	Improved monitors and printers
Other PC software for editors	PC software that can make an editor's job easier
Editorial productivity	Improved editorial productivity
Editorial quality	Improved editorial quality
Project management	Improved project management
Morale	Improved morale
Preparation for the future	Adaptability to future systems
Hardware	Hardware costs
Software	Software costs
Training	Training costs
Analysis	Cost/benefit analysis

Figure 4-15 Rewriting the topic and subtopic names of a topic plan into headings and subheadings that will be meaningful to the reader

2. If necessary, improve the structure of your plan After you've changed the topic plan into a heading plan, you should take another look at its structure. Now that the plan is written in terms that are meaningful to the reader, you'll often get ideas about how you can improve the structure of the plan. You'll realize that some topics or subtopics are too trivial to be included in the plan. You'll realize that you ought to add a topic or subtopic to the plan. You'll realize that you should switch the order of some of the headings or subheadings. Or you'll realize that you can combine two or more of the subheadings. If you decide that improvements are necessary, you use your word or outline processor to make the changes.

To illustrate the type of improvement you might make, figure 4-16 presents the heading plan in figure 4-14 after I improved its structure. Specifically, I decided to present "new functions" along with "improved functions," so I dropped "new functions" from the heading plan. I also dropped "improved project management" and "improved morale" as subheadings under the topic on benefits because I didn't think they were important enough to be treated as subtopics. Finally, I added a topic and three subtopics on "recommendations" because I thought I should present some specific recommendations along with my analysis of costs and benefits.

When you complete this step, you should feel confident that your document will be effective if you present the topics and subtopics represented by the headings and subheadings. You should feel that the structure of the heading plan is complete and logical. You should feel that each of the headings and subheadings will be meaningful to your readers.

Two guidelines for writing effective headings and subheadings

To make it easier for your readers to read, understand, and refer to your documents, you should write your headings so they're meaningful to your readers. In addition, you should try to write your headings so they promise a benefit and so they use consistent language structures.

Promise a benefit When you study the effectiveness of printed advertising, you learn that the most effective headlines are those that *promise a benefit*. For instance, "why these tires can save your life" will probably be a more effective headline for an ad than "new tires are now available." When you promise a benefit in a headline, you try to appeal to the reader's self-interest.

If you apply this guideline to the headings and subheadings you use, your headings will help motivate your readers to read what you've written. That in turn will mean that your documents will be

```
Why our editors should switch from our current word
processing system to PC-based word processing systems

What's wrong with our word processing system

What's right about PC-based word processing
    Improved system speed
    Improved functions
    Improved monitors and printers

PC software that can make an editor's job easier
    Spreadsheet software
    Writing analyzers
    Graphics software
    Desktop publishing

The benefits of a PC-based system
    Improved editorial productivity
    Improved editorial quality
    Adaptability to future systems

The costs of a PC-based system
    Hardware costs
    Software costs
    Training costs

Cost/benefit analysis

Recommendations
    What hardware should we buy
    What software should we buy
    When and how should we convert
```

Figure 4-16 The heading plan for the PC recommendation after its structure has been improved

more effective. Although you can't always write your headings and subheadings so they promise a benefit, you can do it often enough to improve the effectiveness of your documents.

Unlike advertising headlines, most of your headings and subheadings will offer the benefit of new information. For instance, headings like "what's wrong with our word processing system" and "what hardware should we buy" simply promise that you'll learn something of value. Sometimes, though, your headings and subheadings can offer benefits that go beyond the information itself. For instance, "improved editorial productivity" and "improved edito-

Topic name	Rewritten as headings
New accounts	How to open a new account
	Two ways to open a new account
Form 127	Form 127: Documenting a customer's complaint
	How to document a customer's complaint using form 127
Organizational methods	Proven organizational methods
	Ten ways to organize a document

Figure 4-17 Write headings that promise a benefit

rial quality" are effective subheadings in the PC recommendation because they promise benefits that go beyond the information itself.

Figure 4-17 shows you how you can apply this guideline to topic names when you create your heading plans. Here, the topic names are not meaningful to the reader, so they don't promise benefits. However, the rewritten versions are meaningful headings that do promise the benefit of new information.

Use consistent language structures   As you create your heading plans, you should try to keep your language consistent. Whenever you are able to do this, your readers are more likely to recognize the structure of your writing. Then, they will get the maximum benefit from your headings and subheadings.

"Consistent language structures" means the words in the headings or subheadings should agree in form. To illustrate, figure 4-18 presents three headings that are written with inconsistent language structures. Then, it shows three ways to rewrite these headings so they are consistent. If your headings and subheadings are inconsistent, your readers may not recognize the relationships between them no matter how logical their structure is.

```
Inconsistent heading language

Writing with specifics
How to use the active voice
Avoid figurative language

Consistent language using the same verb form

Be specific
Use the active voice
Avoid figurative language

Consistent language using verbal phrases

Writing with specifics
Using the active voice
Avoiding figurative language

Consistent language using how-to structures

How to be convincing by being more specific
How to improve your style by using the active voice
How to avoid confusion by avoiding figurative language
```

Figure 4-18   Use consistent language structures in your headings

Other ideas that will help you plan headings and subheadings

By now, you should be able to develop effective heading plans for your documents. But here are some related ideas that will help you develop even better heading plans.

How to create report titles   When you write a report like the PC recommendation, you should give it a title. You can create this title when you develop your heading plan, or you can create it later on in the 12-step writing procedure. However, since titles aren't difficult to create, you may as well create your title as you create your heading plan.

When you write a report title, you should use language that is meaningful to your readers and that promises a benefit. If you look at the title at the top of the heading plan for the PC recommendation in

figure 4-16, you can see that the title promises the benefit of new information: "Why our editors should switch from our current word processing system to PC-based word processing systems."
Sometimes, though, you can write your report titles so they promise benefits beyond the information itself. For instance, I could have used titles like these for the PC recommendation:

> How we can get a 71% return on our investment by converting from our current word processing system to PC-based systems

> How we can improve editorial productivity by 20% by replacing our current word processing system with an improved system

Titles like these can be effective, but they can also be misleading. So try to keep them as honest as possible. Don't use them to overstate a benefit or to imply a benefit that isn't there.
Figure 4-19 illustrates some weak report titles along with some improvements. All of the improved titles are in language that is meaningful to the reader, and all promise the benefit of information. As you can see, none of the improved titles overstates the benefit that the reader will get from reading the report.

When and how to use introductory headings Most reports start with a short introduction, but you usually don't need a heading to identify this introduction. To illustrate, look at the PC recommendation in appendix A. It starts with a two-paragraph introduction, but no heading identifies that introduction. Furthermore, I never included a heading for this introduction on any of my planning documents like topic plans or heading plans. I just assumed that I would write an introduction, and I knew that it would come immediately after my report title. That's the standard way we write reports in our company.
On the other hand, you can use an introductory heading if you want to. Then, your first heading will start right after the report title. You can also include this heading in your planning documents. For example, figure 4-20 presents two general plans for a report arranged in order of decreasing importance. Both plans include an introductory heading.
If you do use an introductory heading, I recommend that you avoid general headings like "introduction" or "preview." Instead, you

Weak titles	Revised titles
A PC proposal	A re-evaluation of our word processing system
	Why our editors should switch from our current word processing system to PC based word processing systems
Collection policies	Three recommendations for improving our collection policies
	How we can improve our collection policies
Our commission structure	What's wrong with our commission structure
	Is our commission structure working?

Figure 4-19 Write meaningful report titles that promise a benefit

should consider a more specific heading that promises a benefit like "Why this report is important." The second heading plan in figure 4-20 shows how a heading like this can provoke interest and help get your report read.

When and how to use concluding headings In general when you're asked to write a report, you're not only expected to present the facts, but you're also expected to interpret them and give your opinions. The right place for these interpretations and opinions is often in a concluding topic identified by an appropriate heading.

Here again, we recommend that you think twice before you use a general heading, like "conclusion" or "summary," to identify your concluding thoughts. Instead, you should try to identify your concluding thoughts with a meaningful heading that promises a benefit. If you want to give your own interpretations of the facts after you've tried to be completely objective, use a heading like "My inter-

---

Heading plan 1: General headings for the introductory and concluding topics

```
Introduction
Summary of findings
Details of major findings
    First major finding
    Second major finding
Details of minor findings
    First minor finding
    Second minor finding
    Third minor finding
Miscellaneous findings
Conclusion
```

Heading plan 2: Specific headings for the introductory and concluding topics

```
Why this report is important
Summary of findings
Details of major findings
    First major finding
    Second major finding
Details of minor findings
    First minor finding
    Second minor finding
    Third minor finding
Miscellaneous findings
My recommendations for action
```

Figure 4-20 Two heading plans for a report with introductory and concluding headings

pretation of the facts." If you want to urge management to get started on your plan, try a heading like "Why it's important that we act quickly." Use a general heading only when one is appropriate.

Figure 4-20 illustrates the use of both general and specific headings for a concluding topic in a report. In the first heading plan, the concluding topic is called the "conclusion." That's okay if this topic draws some conclusions that differ from those in the "summary of findings." Otherwise, why have it at all? In the second heading plan, the concluding topic is called "my recommendations for action." If that's what the concluding topic is about, this more specific title is better than "conclusion."

How long should your headings and subheadings be It seems that most business writers try to keep their headings short. But short headings often aren't as meaningful as they should be, and they usually don't promise a benefit. So don't worry about keeping your headings short. Write them so they're as long as they need to be.

This idea is corroborated by research in advertising that tells us that long headlines are frequently more effective than short headlines. The determining factor isn't the length of the headline; it's the content. In particular, the determining factor is whether or not the headline promises a benefit.

How the use of more subheadings can improve your writing
As I've already said, subheadings can improve the effectiveness of your writing in several ways. They can provoke curiosity, show your readers the structure of your documents, allow your readers to read selectively, and make it easy for your readers to refer to your documents later on. So don't hesitate to use subheadings whenever you think they can improve the effectiveness of your documents.

To illustrate, figure 4-21 presents two heading plans for a memo to all the employees of a company. The original one is taken from a nine-page memo that was actually sent to more than 10,000 employees. The revised version includes four subheadings for each topic. These subheadings allow the employees to read only those subtopics that apply to them. Can you imagine how many hours of reading and reference the use of subheadings could have saved the employees of the company?

When to use three levels of headings When I showed you how to create topic plans, I recommended that you avoid three-level topic plans like the one in figure 4-12 for most business documents. That, of course, applies to your heading plans too. In general, you should use a third level of headings only when you're writing a technical document. Otherwise, it's usually quite easy to avoid using them by revising the structure of your topic plan.

When to combine the first two planning steps Once you get used to working with heading plans, it's natural to combine step 4 (topic planning) and step 5 (heading planning). In other words, you start using heading and subheading names as you create your topic plans. Then, if all of the topics and subtopics have meaningful names, your topic plan becomes your heading plan with little or no revision.

```
Original heading plan

Vacations
Compensatory time
Medical plan


Revised heading plan

Improved vacation benefits
    More days for employees of 5 years or more
    More days for employees of 10 years or more
    More days for employees of 20 years or more
    More freedom on vacation carryover from one year to the next
Improved policies for compensatory time
    New policy on recording overtime
    New policy for applying for compensatory time
    New limits on maximum amount of compensatory time per
        calendar year
Improved medical benefits
    Increased surgical payments for most operations
    Decreased deductible on major medical payments
    Stricter control of double coverage
    Extended eligibility for terminated employees
```

Figure 4-21 How the use of subheadings can improve the efficiency and effectiveness of your writing

As I said earlier, there's nothing wrong with combining some of the development steps in this way. This is particularly true when you're planning short documents. Just make sure that you've developed an acceptable structure for your headings and subheadings and that you've also created meaningful headings and subheadings.

Four examples of heading plans

If you analyze the heading plans for a sampling of business documents, you'll quickly see that most of them have major flaws. Many of them have weak or inadequate structures. Many have headings that aren't meaningful. To show you what I mean, here are four examples of heading plans I've taken from actual business documents: three of them are ineffective; one is effective even though it has considerable room for improvement.

```
┌─────────────────────────────────────────────────────────┐
│                                                         │
│      The executive's guide to better business equipment │
│                                                         │
│      Treating the disease, not the symptoms             │
│                                                         │
│           The operation was successful, but the patient died │
│           Far-sighted problems, short-sighted solutions │
│           The old rabbit-out-of-the-hat trick           │
│           Why put off 'till tomorrow what you can have today │
│                                                         │
│      We didn't get where we are by magic                │
│                                                         │
│           Your office and the 80-20 phenomenon          │
│           Bringing our rivals to their knees            │
│           New medicines for old diseases                │
│           David takes a crack at Goliath                │
│                                                         │
└─────────────────────────────────────────────────────────┘
```

Figure 4-22 A heading plan with meaningless headings

A heading plan with meaningless headings Figure 4-22 presents the heading plan for a sales brochure on business equipment. Here, the writer has used cute headings, not meaningful ones. As a result, it's impossible to see the logic of the document's structure, to read the document selectively, or to refer to it later on. At best, the headings and subheadings provoke some curiosity, but not enough to get me to start reading the brochure or to keep reading it.

A heading plan with an ineffective structure Figure 4-23 presents the heading plan for a tutorial report on advertising effectiveness. The primary problem with this plan is that it has an ineffective structure. In fact, because all of its 21 headings are at the same level, you could say that it doesn't have any structure at all. To provide a guide to its content, the major headings should be divided into subheadings so the reader can see the structure of the document.

A secondary problem is that only some of the headings are meaningful to the reader, and the language of the headings is so inconsistent that it's impossible to see any relationships. To improve this plan, you'd have to start by improving its structure. Then you'd have to improve the language of its headings.

A heading plan with too much introduction and summarization Figure 4-24 presents a heading plan that has too much introduction and summarization. If you were to review this four-page docu-

How to plan what you're going to write 115

```
How to sell advertising to management

A look at the challenge
Advertising:  Salesman's competitor or servant?
The power of understatement
Show correlation between advertising and sales
How advertising sells in depth
Time is limited
Ads reach key men
$128 for 850 sales calls!
Advertising reduces the cost of selling
Misuses are cataloged
Cost of a sales call:  $42.92
There must be enough
Advertising vs. sales expense
How a top pro documents advertising's contribution
What interests top management
Entire picture defined
Media analysis and schedule
Proof of results
Questionnaire revealing
What your dollars buy
Summary
```

Figure 4-23 A heading plan with an ineffective structure

ment, you would find a one-paragraph overview; a one-page background topic; half a page of broad conclusions; three one-paragraph topics on productivity gains, ease of use, and ease of training; and a half-page summary. In all, more than half the document consists of introductory or summarization topics. I present this example because it typifies what's wrong with many business documents today: too much filler, too much repetition, too much summary, and not enough facts.

An effective heading plan   Figure 4-25 presents a heading plan for a report on the art of delegation just as it was published in one of the business magazines. Although this plan isn't perfect, it is effective. It has an understandable structure, and most of its headings and subheadings are meaningful. Incidentally, it is a three-level heading plan since some of its subheadings are further divided to a third level.

```
Executive summary for a report on the benefits of PCs

Overview
Background
Broad conclusions
Productivity gains
Ease of use
Ease of training
Summary
```

Figure 4-24 A heading plan with too much introduction and summarization

```
The art of delegation

Benefits of an effective delegation
The delegation process
    Overcoming the reluctance to delegate
    Deciding what to delegate
    Selecting the right person
    Delegate the whole
    Transferring responsibility and authority
        Responsibility
        Authority
    Accountability
    Put it in writing
        Job descriptions
    Review results, not methods
        Freedom
        Controls
    Evaluate results
Conclusion
```

Figure 4-25 An effective heading plan

Discussion

This step can have a dramatic effect on your writing. If you convert your topic and subtopic names into headings and subheadings that guide the reader, your document will be more effective. These headings and subheadings also help the reader use the document more efficiently, and that can have a positive effect on a company's communications.

Once you've established an effective heading plan, the next two steps are easy. That's why the heading plan is the most important planning document. In step 6, you'll enhance your heading plan as you plan the visual aids for your document. In step 7, you'll enhance your heading plan as you plan the paragraphs for your document.

Terms

heading
subheading
heading plan
promising a benefit

Objectives

1. Describe the procedure for planning the headings and subheadings of a document.

2. Explain what it means to (1) promise a benefit and (2) use consistent language structures as you create your headings and subheadings.

3. After you've done the first four steps for a writing assignment, develop an effective heading plan for the document.

Step 6: Plan the visual aids

When you finish step 5, you have a heading plan for the document you're going to write. Then, in this step, you plan the visual aids you'll use when you write your document. Sometimes, of course, you'll decide that you don't need any visual aids for the document you're writing. That will be true for most letters and memos. Frequently, though, you can improve the effectiveness of a document by using one or more visual aids. That's particularly true for longer documents like reports, proposals, and tutorial presentations.

When you use visual aids, you can improve the effectiveness of your document in three ways. First, visual aids can increase comprehension. In other words, they can help your readers understand your ideas more completely. Second, visual aids can improve efficiency by helping your readers get your ideas more quickly. Third, visual aids can be effective reference materials in themselves. Readers can glance through them to review important points or to find specific information when referring to your document later on.

The procedure for planning visual aids

To plan the visual aids for a document, I recommend the procedure in figure 4-26. First, you identify those visual aids that can improve the effectiveness of your document. Second, you develop a better idea of what those aids are going to look like.

1. Identify the visual aids that will improve the effectiveness of the topics and subtopics in your heading plan To start, you go through your heading plan to identify those topics or subtopics that could be improved by the use of one or more visual aids. The best way to do this is to go from the top down, one heading or subheading at a time. For each heading or subheading, you ask this question: Will the use of one or more visual aids make this topic or subtopic more efficient or effective?

If you decide that a topic or subtopic would be improved by the use of visual aids, you decide what the contents of the visual aid or aids should be. Then, you annotate your heading plan to indicate the visual aids you've planned for that topic or subtopic. You can do that by writing a short description of what each visual aid will be next to the heading or subheading that the aid applies to. Remember that your heading plan is a private working paper, so you can use what-

> **The procedure for planning visual aids**
>
> 1. Identify the visual aids that will improve the effectiveness of the topics and subtopics in your heading plan.
> 2. Develop a legend list, rough drafts, or first drafts for the visual aids you've planned.

Figure 4-26 The procedure for planning visual aids

ever notation you want to remind yourself what visual aids you're going to use and where you're going to use them.

Sometimes, you will already have developed some visual aids by the time you do this step. For instance, you may have developed summaries of information that are appropriate as visual aids. Or, you may have copies of tables or charts from other sources that are appropriate as visual aids. Don't use them, though, just because you already have them. Make sure that they will improve the effectiveness of your document.

As you decide what visual aids to use, you should keep three general uses in mind. First, you can use visual aids to give examples or illustrations of what you're presenting in the text. Second, you can use visual aids to summarize detailed information you're presenting in the text. Third, you can use visual aids to illustrate ideas, concepts, or relationships that are difficult to present using words alone.

To illustrate the end product of this step, figure 4-27 shows the heading plan for the PC recommendation in appendix A after I identified the visual aids I thought it needed. To develop this plan, I went down the heading plan to identify the topics or subtopics that could be improved by visual aids. When I got to "writing analyzers," I decided that an example of the output from a writing analyzer would improve the effectiveness of this subtopic. When I got to "the benefits of a PC-based system," I decided that a summary of the benefits would make this topic easier to follow. When I got to "the costs of a PC-based system," I decided that a summary of the costs would improve this topic. When I got to "cost/benefit analysis," I decided that a summary of the analytical calculations would improve this topic. As I went along, I annotated the heading plan to show where I would use these visual aids and what they would be.

```
Why our editors should switch from our current word
processing system to PC-based word processing systems

What's wrong with our word processing system

What's right about PC-based word processing
    Improved system speed
    Improved functions
    Improved monitors and printers

PC software that can make an editor's job easier
    Spreadsheet software
    Writing analyzers                            1-Example of RW output
    Graphics software
    Desktop publishing

The benefits of a PC-based system                2-Summary
    Improved editorial productivity
    Improved editorial quality
    Improved adaptability to future systems

The costs of a PC-based system                   3-Summary
    Hardware costs
    Software costs
    Training costs

Cost/benefit analysis                            4-Summary

Recommendations
    What hardware should we buy
    What software should we buy
    When and how should we convert
```

Figure 4-27 The final heading plan for the PC recommendation showing the planned visual aids

2. Develop a legend list, rough drafts, or first drafts for the visual aids you've planned When you plan the visual aids, you usually have only a hazy notion of what they're going to look like. So now, you try to get a better idea of what they're going to be. Although it's still too early to develop final drafts of your visual aids, you should at least develop a legend list, rough drafts, or first drafts. What you develop depends on how clearly you have envisioned the visual aids you intend to use.

Occasionally, you have a clear view of what your visual aids are going to be when you plan them. Then, you may decide that you don't

How to plan what you're going to write 121

```
Figure 1    The summary page from RightWriter when run on the
            first draft of this report
Figure 2    The benefits of a PC-based system
Figure 3    Typical costs of a PC-based system
Figure 4    Payback and return-on-investment (ROI) possibilities
            based on productivity improvements only
```

Figure 4-28 The legend list for the PC recommendation

need to develop rough drafts or first drafts before you go on to the next step of the 12-step procedure. Instead, you may only want to develop a *legend list* for the visual aids. A *legend* is the title that identifies a visual aid. In figure 4-28, for example, you can see the legend list that I developed for the PC recommendation. As you can see, it gives more information about the planned visual aids than my notations on the heading plan. In this case, the legends clearly defined the visual aids I intended to use, so I went on to the next step without developing rough drafts or first drafts for any of the visual aids.

If you want to give yourself a better idea of what your visual aids are going to look like, you can develop rough drafts for them instead of a legend list. For instance, figure 4-29 presents a rough draft of the cost summary I used in the PC recommendation. In this case, I used word processing to prepare the rough draft, but you can draw rough drafts by hand as sketchily as you want. Their purpose is just to give you a clear vision of what they're going to look like in their final form. You should, however, include complete legends with your rough drafts so you won't need to develop a separate legend list for them.

When you develop a rough draft, you should assure yourself that the visual aid will actually improve the effectiveness of the topic or subtopic it applies to. If the rough draft doesn't give you this assurance, you may decide *not* to use it as one of your visual aids. Then, you can modify the notations on your heading plan.

If you want to develop finished drafts instead of rough drafts during this planning step, that's all right too. For instance, figure 4-30 presents a finished draft of the cost summary I used in the PC recommendation. When you develop finished drafts, you know exactly what your visual aids will look like when you go on to the next step.

```
Hardware

IBM AT clone                        $2,500
Printer                                500
                                    _____
                                    $3,000

Software costs

WP                                  $  400
Spreadsheet software                   100
Writing analyzer                        50
                                    _____
                                    $  550

Training costs

Training materials                  $   50
1/52 of $30,000                        600
                                    _____
                                    $  650

Total cost

Hardware                            $3,000
Software                               550
Training                               650
                                    _____
                                    $4,200


Figure 3  Typical costs of a PC-based system
```

Figure 4-29 A rough draft of figure 3 of the PC recommendation

You should realize, though, that you may want to modify some of your visual aids as you do the later development steps. That's why you should think of your drafts as first drafts, even if you've developed them into what you think will be their final form.

With a PC, you can use word processing to create and revise your legend list. You can also use word processing, spreadsheet, business graphics, or other graphics packages to create first drafts of many of your visual aids. When you use these packages, you can often create the first drafts of your visual aids faster than you can draw rough drafts of them by hand. It's also easy to revise your first drafts once

```
Hardware costs

An AT clone with color monitor        $2,500
    and 40-megabyte hard disk
Printer                                  500
                                      -------
                                      $3,000

Software costs

Word processing package               $  400
Spreadsheet software                     100
Writing analyzer                          50
                                      -------
                                      $  550

Training costs

Training and reference materials      $   50
One week of $30,000 salary               600
                                      -------
                                      $  650

Total cost

Hardware                              $3,000
Software                                 550
Training                                 650
                                      -------
                                      $4,200

Figure 3   Typical costs of a PC-based system
```

Figure 4-30   A finished draft of figure 3 of the PC recommendation

they're stored in your PC. In short, the use of PC software can have a major impact on your efficiency as you do this step and subsequent steps related to the use of visual aids.

Other ideas that will help you plan visual aids

Although the two-part procedure for planning visual aids is a simple one, it's not always easy to decide when and how you should use visual aids. So let me give you some ideas to help you make these decisions.

How many visual aids should you use If you're developing a document that presents complex or detailed information, you should try to identify at least one visual aid for each major topic in your heading plan. These visual aids should present examples, summarize the information of the text, or present information in a visual form that is easier to understand than a textual form. If you force yourself to use a visual aid to support every major topic, your documents should be more effective.

On the other hand, it takes time to develop visual aids, so you don't want to overdo your use of them. If you use unnecessary visual aids, you decrease your efficiency as a writer without improving the effectiveness of your writing. Unnecessary visual aids also make it more difficult for your readers to get through your documents. You have an obligation, then, to make sure that every one of your visual aids contributes to the effectiveness of your document. If a visual aid isn't going to help your document accomplish its purpose, you should drop it from your plan.

To see an illustration of this decision-making process, refer back to the planned visual aids for the heading plan in figure 4-27. If I decided that an example of RightWriter output would improve the effectiveness of the subtopic on writing analyzers, why didn't I use an example or two of spreadsheet, graphics, or desktop publishing output? If I decided that summaries of benefits, costs, and cost/benefit analysis would improve the effectiveness of the document, why didn't I include summaries of the problems of the old word processing system, the features of PC-based systems, or my recommendations for change? You can see from this that judgment is demanded when you plan your visual aids.

To answer the questions I've just raised, I didn't use other examples of PC output because I knew my reader was already familiar with spreadsheet, graphics, and desktop publishing software. As a result, I didn't think visual aids would improve the effectiveness of these subtopics. On the other hand, I felt that my reader was both unfamiliar with and resistant to the use of writing analyzers, so I thought an output example could quickly demonstrate the significance of this type of software. Similarly, I didn't include more summaries because I didn't think they would improve the effectiveness of any of the other topics. In contrast, the ones I did include summarized a considerable amount of detailed information that I knew would be more difficult to present as text.

In general, then, you should use a visual aid whenever you're confident that it will help a document achieve its purposes. If you're in doubt about a visual aid or if you expect only a trivial improvement in effectiveness from it, you should drop the visual aid from your plan. Because it takes time to develop visual aids, you should only use them when they clearly make a difference.

What to call the visual aids   In the books our company publishes, we refer to all of the visual aids as *figures*. It's a general term we recommend because it can apply to charts, tables, conceptual drawings, or whatever else you set off as a visual aid. If you prefer, though, you can call your visual aids by some other name like *illustrations* or *visual aids*.

What you shouldn't do is refer to one type of visual aid by one name, such as "chart," and to another type by another name, such as "table." When you do this, you have to have two different numbering systems for your visual aids, which just complicates the development process.

How to number the visual aids   If you're writing a one-unit document, you should number your visual aids sequentially: 1, 2, 3, and so on. If you're writing a multi-unit document, we suggest that you number the visual aids sequentially within each unit: 1-1, 1-2, 1-3 for the first unit; 2-1, 2-2, 2-3 for the second unit; and so on.

As obvious as this may seem, I've often come across documents that use figure numbers like A-10 or 3-C so the reader has a hard time relating the numbers to the units. Even worse, some documents use no numbers at all for the visual aids. Then, the text has no way to refer to a visual aid. But, as I'll explain in the next chapter, the text should always refer to a visual aid.

How to write the legends for visual aids   When you write the legend for a visual aid, you should try to give a full description of what the visual aid is. Then, your readers should be able to understand the purposes of your visual aids without referring to the text. If you refer back to figure 4-28, you can see that I've tried to write the legends for the PC recommendation so they give a full description of what the aids are. Research in advertising has shown that descriptive legends improve the effectiveness of your visual aids.

From a practical point of view, though, you should keep your legends to a reasonable length. If your legends are too long, they become difficult to read and refer to. As a rule of thumb, you should be able to write an adequate legend in three lines or less, and most of your legends should require only one line.

Discussion

Visual aids can have a significant effect on how well your readers understand your documents and how efficiently they can read and refer to them. When you plan your visual aids in step 6 of the 12-step writing procedure, you decide which visual aids will help you improve the effectiveness of your documents and which ones won't. Once you've planned your visual aids, you've done the most difficult task related to their use.

Terms

legend list
legend

Objectives

1. Describe the procedure for planning the visual aids of a document.

2. After you've done the first five steps for a writing assignment, plan the visual aids for the document.

Step 7: Plan the paragraphs

When you finish step 6, you have a heading plan for the document you're going to write, and you know what visual aids you're going to use for each of the topics and subtopics in the plan. Then, in this last planning step, you plan the paragraphs you're going to write for each topic and subtopic. When you finish this step, you're ready to start writing the first draft of your document.

The procedure for planning paragraphs

To plan the paragraphs for a document, I recommend the procedure in figure 4-31. First, you expand your heading plan into a *paragraph plan* by writing the idea for each paragraph you intend to write under each heading or subheading. Second, you check your final contents plan against your paragraph plan to make sure your plan provides for all of the content items you selected for the document in step 3.

1. Expand your heading plan into a paragraph plan To expand your heading plan into a paragraph plan, you go through your heading plan from the top down, one topic or subtopic at a time. For each topic or subtopic, you list your paragraph ideas in the sequence you intend to present them in.

To illustrate, figure 4-32 presents the paragraph plan I created for the first three topics of the PC recommendation in appendix A. Before the first heading in the heading plan, I listed just one paragraph idea, "introduction to report." At this point, I didn't know quite how I would introduce the report, but I knew that my first paragraph would be introductory. Below the first heading, I listed three paragraph ideas: one on the antiquated status of the current system, one on the problems of a shared system like the one we had, and one on the word processing limitations of the current system. I continued listing paragraph ideas in this way until the paragraph plan was complete.

When you read chapter 8, you'll learn some principles that will help you plan your paragraphs. In particular, you'll learn what an effective paragraph should consist of. Then, you'll know what types of ideas you should be listing as you plan your paragraphs. Because a paragraph plan is a private working paper, you can use any language that makes sense to you when you record your paragraph ideas.

Since you shouldn't have to plan more than half a dozen paragraphs for most of your topics and subtopics, you shouldn't have

> **The procedure for planning paragraphs**
>
> 1. Expand your heading plan into a paragraph plan.
> 2. If necessary, check your final contents list against your paragraph plan to make sure your plan provides for all of the content items.

Figure 4-31   The procedure for planning paragraphs

much trouble creating a paragraph plan. Using word processing or an outline processor to expand your heading plan, you just try to write down the ideas you intend to present for each topic and subtopic. Then, if necessary, you can rearrange them into a logical presentation sequence. Often, though, the ideas will come to you in a logical sequence so you won't have to rearrange them.

2. If necessary, check your final contents list against your paragraph plan to make sure your plan provides for all of the content items   When you finish your paragraph plan, you should feel confident that your document will be effective if you present all of its ideas in your final draft. Sometimes, though, you wonder whether your planned paragraphs provide for all of the content you selected for your document back in step 3 of the 12-step writing procedure. If you have any doubts, you should check your final contents list against your paragraph plan to make sure your plan provides for everything.

To do this, you go through your contents list, one item at a time. Since you've just developed your paragraph plan, you should be able to remember whether you've provided for each content item without much trouble (though if you can't remember, you can refer to your paragraph plan). Most of the time, then, you can do this step about as fast as you can read the items on your contents list.

If your paragraph plan doesn't provide for a content item, you have two choices. First, you can add one or more paragraphs to your plan to provide for the content item. Second, you can drop the content item from your document. Often, if you haven't already provided for an item, it isn't that significant so it can probably be dropped. Sometimes, though, you'll find that you've forgotten an important item.

```
Why our editors should switch from our current word
processing system to PC-based word processing systems

        introduction to report
What's wrong with our word processing system
        antiquated status of system
        problems of shared system
        limitations of word processing software
What's right about PC-based word processing
        introduction to PC-based word processing
    Improved system speed
        the removal of delays
        print spooling
    Improved functions
        general improvements in ease of use
        example: pagination
        example: spelling checker
    Improved monitors and printers
        resolution of monitors and printing
        printer functions
PC software that can make an editor's job easier
        the availability of other software for PC users
    Spreadsheet software
        the idea and benefits
    Writing analyzers
        the idea and benefits
        example of RightWriter output                    figure 1
    Graphics software
        the idea and benefits
    Desktop publishing
        the idea and benefits
```

Figure 4-32 The paragraph plan for the first three topics of the PC recommendation

When and how to overlap paragraph planning and writing

If you're working on a relatively long document, it's tedious to plan all of its paragraphs at once. Often, you're so anxious to start writing that planning paragraphs becomes frustrating. Fortunately, it's relatively easy to overlap paragraph planning and writing with little or no loss in writing efficiency.

To overlap these steps, you work on a document one topic or a few topics at a time. To illustrate, figure 4-33 shows you how to overlap these steps when preparing a three-topic document. You start by planning the paragraphs for the introduction, developing the figures for

```
Plan introduction
Develop figures for the introduction (if any)
Write first draft of introduction

Plan first topic
Develop figures for this topic (if any)
Write first draft of this topic

Plan second topic
Develop figures for this topic (if any)
Write first draft of this topic

Plan third topic
Develop figures for this topic (if any)
Write first draft of this topic
```

Figure 4-33 How to overlap paragraph planning and writing as you develop a three-topic document

the introduction, and writing the introduction. Next, you plan the paragraphs, develop the figures, and write the first draft of the first topic. You continue in this way with the next two topics to complete the first draft of the document. Often, it's more satisfying to work in this way, so your writing actually improves when you overlap these steps.

Discussion

When you finish this step, you have a paragraph plan that's an effective guide for writing your document. This plan tells you what headings and subheadings you'll use as you write. It tells you what visual aids or figures you're going to refer to as you write. And it guides you through the paragraphs that you're going to write. As a result, your paragraph plan will help you write more efficiently than you have ever written before.

Terms

paragraph plan

How to plan what you're going to write 131

Objectives

1. Describe the procedure for planning the paragraphs of a document.

2. After you've done the first six steps for a writing assignment, develop a paragraph plan for the document.

Heading plan for chapter 5

Step 8: Develop the visual aids

Five guidelines for developing visual aids
- Keep your visual aids simple
- Keep your visual aids honest
- Make your visual aids as complete as possible
- Make sure your visual aids serve your purpose
- Make sure your visual aids justify their development expense

Other ideas that will help you develop visual aids
- How to manage your visual aids during development
- How you can use your visual aids to preview your presentation
- How you can overlap the development of visual aids with writing

Discussion

Step 9: Write the text

Five guidelines for writing a first draft
- Visualize your readers as you write
- Show the structure of your document
- Let your headings and subheadings do their job
- Coordinate your text with your visual aids
- Concentrate on writing effective paragraphs

Other ideas that will help you write the text of your first draft
- How to use your heading plan as the start of your word processing document
- How to start writing
- How to keep going
- How to type two levels of headings
- How to type three levels of headings
- When to use inline visual aids

Discussion

Chapter 5

How to write
the first draft

This chapter presents steps 8 and 9 of the 12-step writing procedure. In step 8, you develop the visual aids that you planned in step 6. In step 9, you write the first draft of the text of your document. These are usually the most time-consuming steps of the 12-step procedure.

Step 8: Develop the visual aids

When you finish step 6, you know what visual aids you're going to use in your document. You also have a legend list, rough drafts, or first drafts of these aids. Now, in step 8, you develop a complete set of first drafts for the visual aids you've planned.

To develop your visual aids, you will frequently use PC software such as spreadsheet or business graphics software. You can also use word processing to prepare tables and other types of summarized information. For instance, I prepared three of the four visual aids in the PC recommendation in appendix A by using word processing.

Five guidelines for developing visual aids

In this chapter, I'm not going to try to show you how to develop visual aids because each field in business has its own types of visual aids and its own software for preparing them. Instead, I'm going to present five guidelines that you should follow no matter what kind of visual aid you're developing. These guidelines will help you develop effective visual aids as efficiently as possible.

Keep your visual aids simple Business writers traditionally have used visual aids that were more complicated than they needed to be. Today, using PCs, it's easier than ever to develop visual aids that are overly detailed and complex. When your visual aids are too complicated, though, your readers won't take the time to figure them out. That's why you should keep your visual aids simple if you want them to be effective.

To illustrate this point, figure 5-1 present two computer-generated bar charts that present the same data. The first one is a one-dimensional chart that is an effective visual presentation. The second one is a three-dimensional bar chart with more grid marks and tick marks than are necessary. If you study these charts, you can see that the simple chart is more effective than the complicated one. In the three-dimensional chart, for example, it's difficult to tell what the college, proprietary, and bookstore sales were in 1986 and 1987. Also, for 1984 and 1985, it looks like proprietary sales were greater than bookstore sales when the opposite is true.

Keep your visual aids honest You can misrepresent data in many different ways when you present it visually. If someone recognizes deception in one or more of your visual aids, it damages your

How to write the first draft

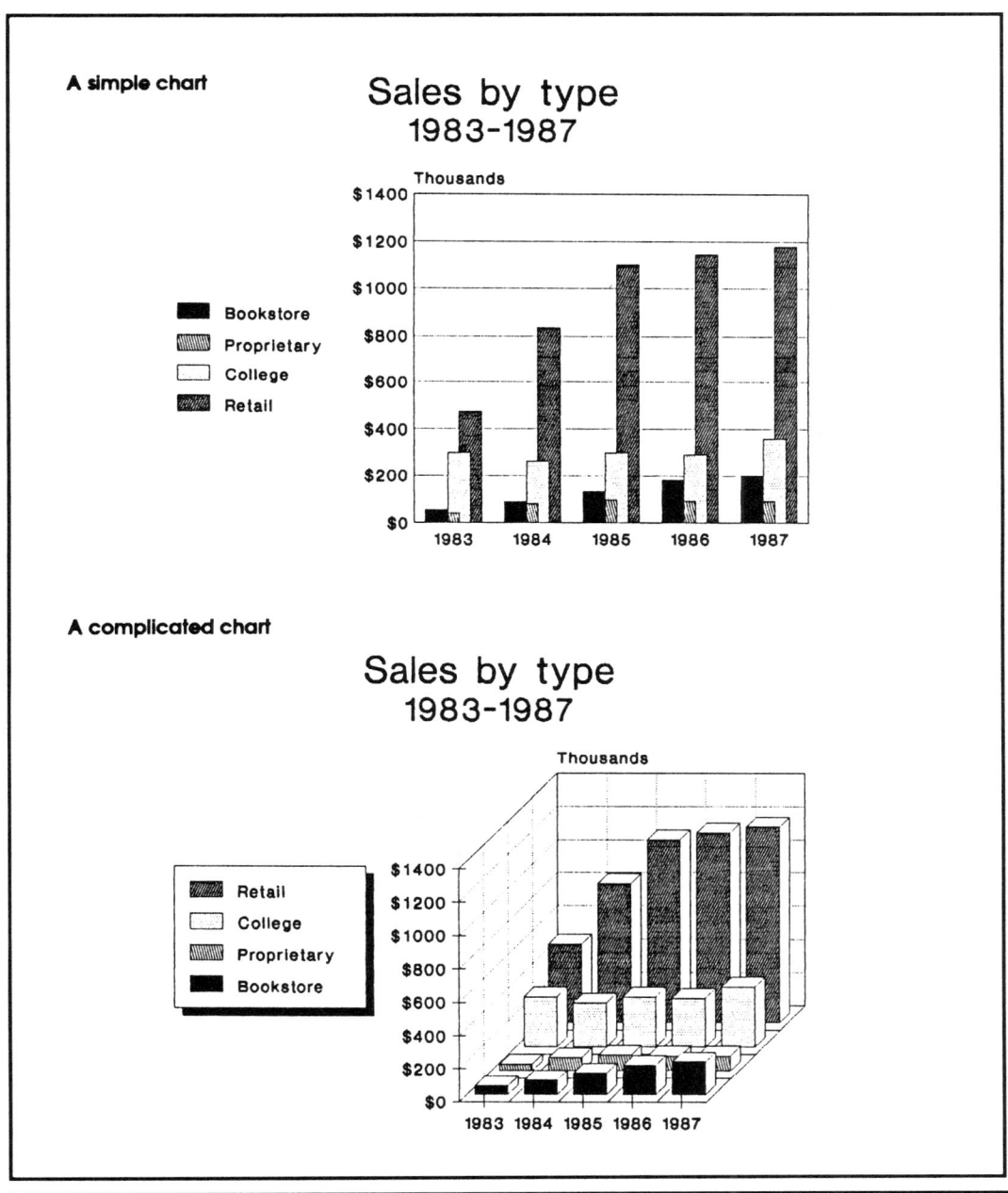

Figure 5-1 Keep your visual aids simple

credibility and limits your ability to persuade. So make sure your visual aids are honest.

To illustrate this point, figure 5-2 presents two line charts that present the same data. The first one shows a company's sales over an eight-year period. Although sales have always gone up from one year to the next, the growth rate has been slow, and the chart shows this. The second chart has a much steeper growth line, even though the data is the same. This chart is misleading because the y-axis starts with a value of .9 (or $900,000 in sales) instead of zero. It should be obvious that the first chart is more honest, and thus more effective, than the second chart.

To keep a series of charts or graphs honest, you should set the axis values for each chart or graph so they all have the same ranges. Unfortunately, if you accept the defaults of your PC software, the charts or graphs are likely to have different ranges. So you have to be careful not to create a series of visual aids that will be misleading. With few exceptions, the minimum value for any axis in any chart or graph should be zero.

Make your visual aids as complete as possible   Although you should try to keep your visual aids simple, you should also try to make them as complete as possible. In other words, each visual aid should tell a complete story. If you obey this guideline, each of your visual aids should make sense without the text. If you write your legends so they are as descriptive as possible, you help make your visual aids complete.

To illustrate this point, figure 5-3 shows two charts that present the same data, test results from two different computer systems. If you read the first one, it should make sense to you because it is complete. The performance standard is a two-second response time, which system B meets when the system has from one to four users and which system A meets when the system has from one to seven users.

In contrast, the second chart in figure 5-3 isn't complete. You can't tell whether the X-axis represents the results for eight different users or the average results when from one to eight users use the system. You can't tell that the Y-axis represents the average response time in seconds. You can't even tell that the line with a value of 2 represents the performance standard. If you analyze some typical business documents, you'll find many examples of visual aids that are ineffective because they're incomplete.

How to write the first draft 137

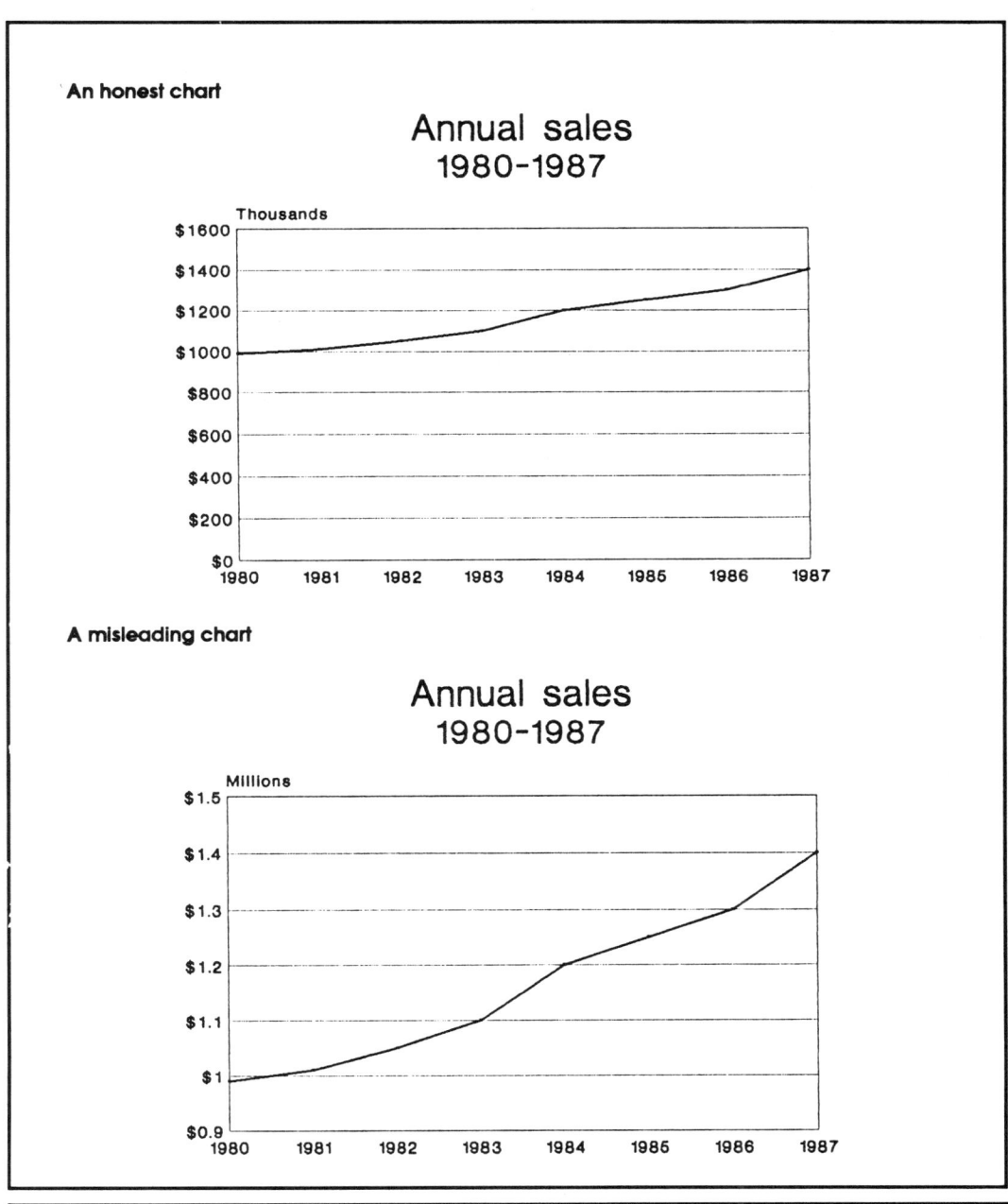

Figure 5-2 Keep your visual aids honest

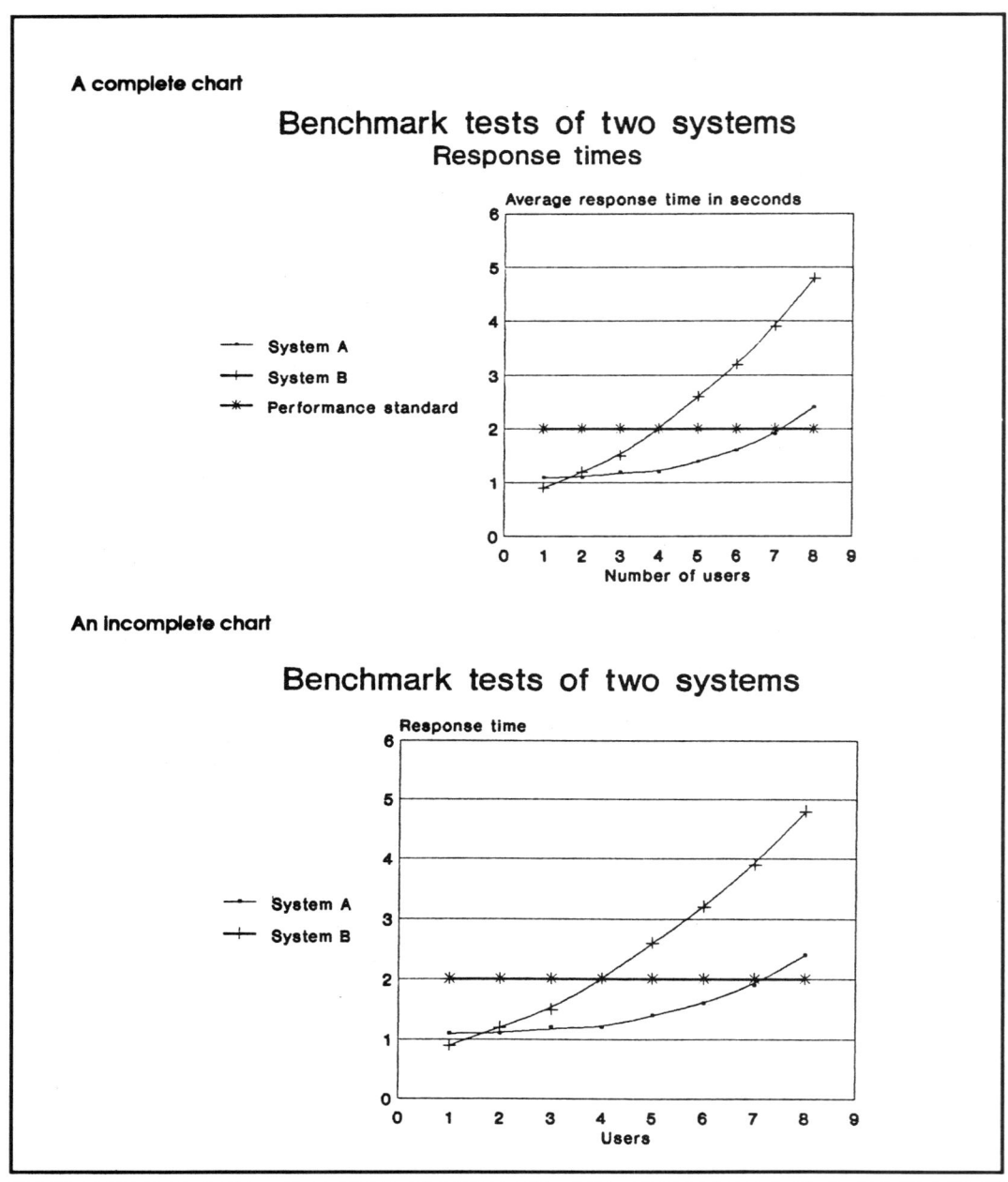

Figure 5-3 Make your visual aids as complete as possible

How to write the first draft   139

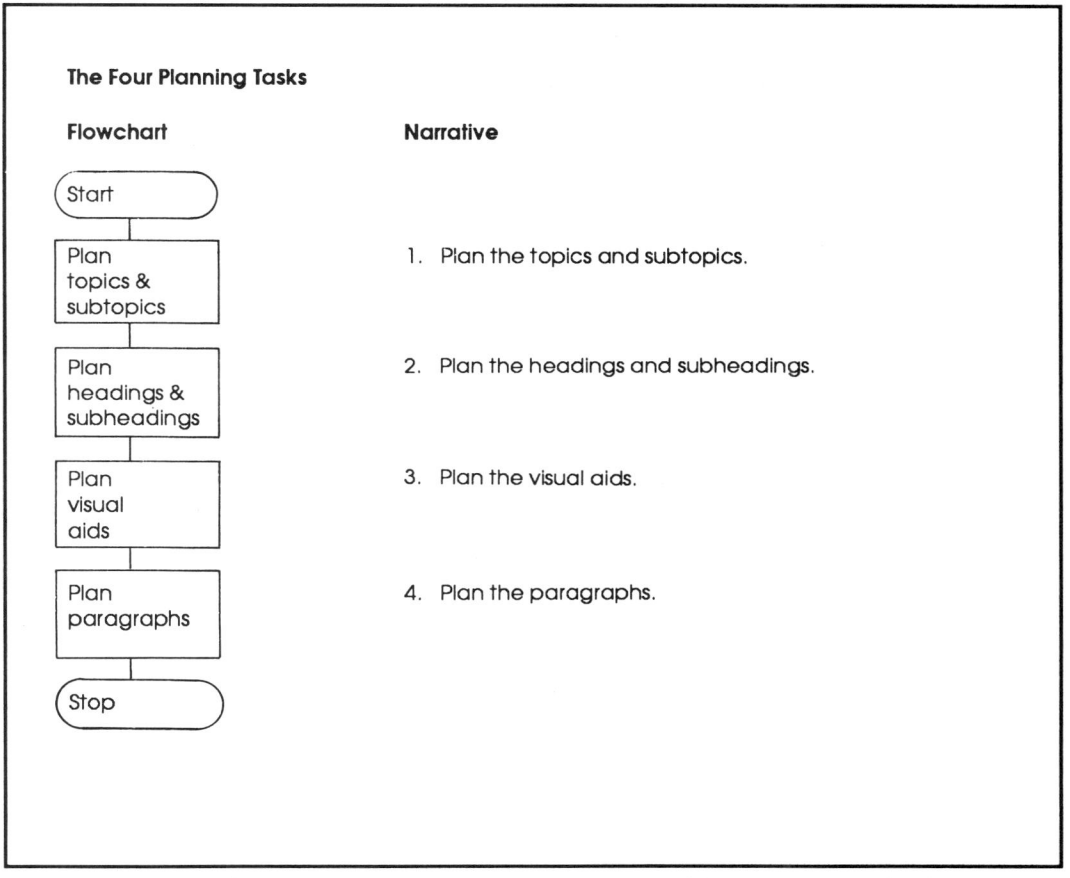

Figure 5-4   A flowchart that doesn't improve upon the effectiveness of the narrative

Make sure your visual aids serve your purpose   Sometimes, when you plan your visual aids in step 6, you plan a few that don't turn out the way you envisioned them. Then, in step 8, you can re-evaluate each one to make sure it's going to serve the purpose of your document. If you start working on one that you realize isn't going to improve your document, you can drop it from your plan.

To illustrate, figure 5-4 shows a flowchart that isn't any more effective than the narrative alongside it. In fact, a flowchart like this is often less effective than a narrative because the size of the boxes limits what you can write in them. But if a visual aid doesn't accomplish something you can't accomplish in words, it doesn't serve your purpose and should be deleted.

Often, when you take visual aids from another source instead of developing them yourself, they don't quite serve your purposes. Then, you should either modify them so they do or drop them from your plans. For this reason, you're sometimes better off developing a visual aid from scratch. If you develop a visual aid yourself, you know it will serve your purpose.

Make sure your visual aids justify their development expense
Whenever you develop a visual aid, it adds to your development time for the document. As a result, each visual aid adds to the cost of the writing project. If you want to work as productively as possible, you must make sure that each visual aid justifies its development cost by increasing the effectiveness of your document.

If a visual aid isn't effective, of course, it doesn't justify its development cost. That's true for the flowchart in figure 5-4. Similarly, a visual aid often doesn't justify its development cost if it makes only a trivial improvement in effectiveness or if it takes an excessive amount of time to develop.

To illustrate, figure 5-5 presents a visual aid that I could have used in the PC recommendation in appendix A. It shows the relationship between an improvement in editorial productivity and the return-on-investment for PC purchases. However, this relationship is trivial, so this visual aid won't do much to improve the effectiveness of the PC recommendation. In addition, it takes at least 15 minutes to develop a chart like this, even on a PC. As a result, I didn't develop a chart like this for the PC recommendation because I didn't think its development expense would be justified.

Other ideas that will help you develop visual aids

If you follow the five guidelines I've just presented, you should develop and use visual aids effectively. But here are a couple of other ideas that will help you develop them.

How to manage your visual aids during development   When you develop visual aids, I recommend that you put only one on each sheet of paper. That way, you can easily add another visual aid to your document later on, and you can easily delete one. If you decide that you want to combine some of the smaller visual aids on a single sheet of paper when you present the final draft, that's okay. But keep

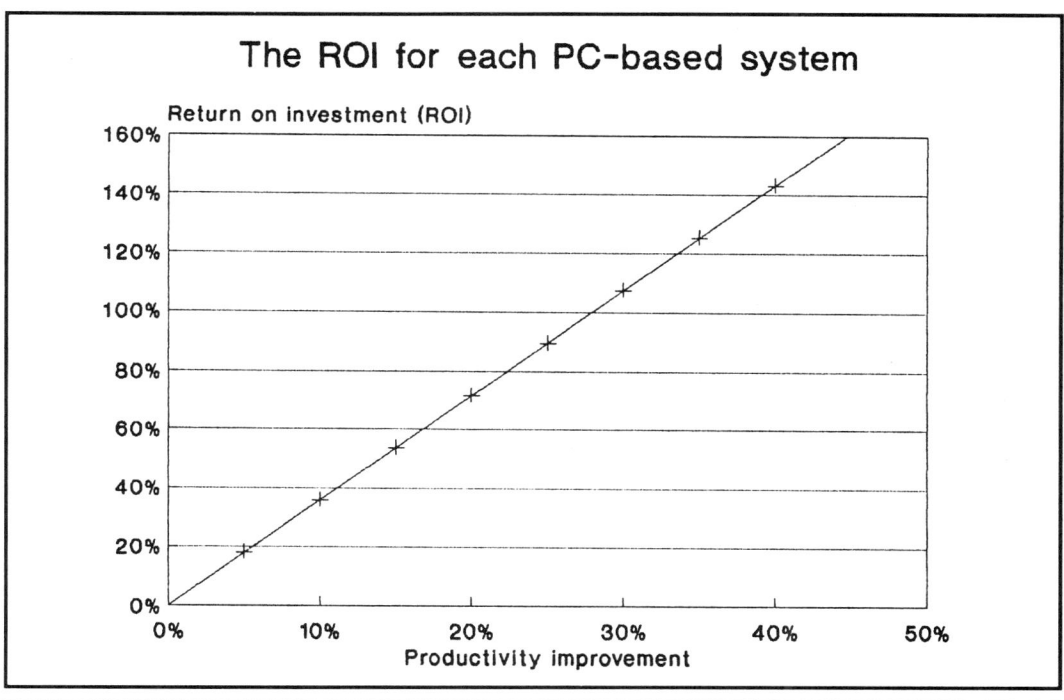

Figure 5-5   A chart that doesn't justify its development expense

each visual aid on its own page until then. I'll talk more about presentation in chapters 14 and 15.

I also recommend that you keep your visual aids separate from your text during development. When we develop reports at our company, for example, we keep the visual aids together at the end of the text pages. When we develop a book manuscript, we keep the visual aids for a chapter in one folder, the text in another.

How you can use your visual aids to preview your presentation   If you're preparing a document with several visual aids, you can use them to preview your presentation as a final check that you've done your planning right. This is particularly useful when you are developing instructional materials, but it's also useful for other types of documents. Since each visual aid should present one complete idea, you can preview the sequence and content of your document by paging through your visual aids, from the first to the last. If you've developed your visual aids using business graphics on a PC, you can use a screenshow to preview them before you print them.

Often, when you preview your document in this way, you'll get some ideas. Sometimes, you'll decide that another visual aid would improve your presentation or that one of the visual aids should be modified to improve its effectiveness. Sometimes, you'll decide that you should modify your heading plan so it's more consistent with the visual aids. Modifications like these take only a few moments, but they help refine the final document.

How you can overlap the development of visual aids with writing If you're working on a long document with several topics and many visual aids, you may get tired of developing all of the visual aids at once. If so, you can overlap the development of visual aids with writing. To do so, you work on one or two topics at a time. After you develop the visual aids for the first topic or two, you write the text for these topics. Then, you go on to the next topic or two. You continue in this way until you have developed all the visual aids and written all the text for the entire document.

Discussion

Effective visual aids usually go right along with good writing. When I evaluate instructional materials, for example, I often start by evaluating the visual aids. If the visual aids are effective, the writing usually is too.

Unfortunately, the visual aids in many business documents aren't effective. So remember to keep your visual aids simple, honest, and complete. Remember too that your visual aids must help your documents achieve their purposes and they must justify their development expenses. If they don't, you're better off without them.

Objectives

1. Describe the five guidelines for developing visual aids.

2. Develop effective visual aids for any document you've planned.

Step 9: Write the text

When you finish step 8, you have everything you need for writing the first draft of your document as efficiently and as effectively as possible. You have a paragraph plan you will use as a guide to your writing. You have first drafts for all of the visual aids you will refer to as you write your first draft.

In step 9, you write the first draft of your document using word processing on your PC. To do this well, you need to know how to write effective paragraphs and readable sentences. You also need to know how to write with an effective tone and style. However, section 3 of this book teaches you those writing skills, so I'm not going to duplicate any of that information now.

Instead, I'm going to focus on the mechanical aspects of writing the first draft. I'll start by presenting five guidelines you should keep in mind as you write your first draft. I'll finish by presenting some ideas that will help you write your first drafts.

Five guidelines for writing a first draft

You can't think of everything as you write a first draft. For instance, you can't think of all the writing guidelines presented in section 3 as you write your first draft, particularly if many of these skills are new to you. What, then, should you be thinking of? The five guidelines that follow will help answer that question.

Visualize your readers as you write   Back in step 1, you defined the audience for your document. Now, as you write your first draft, you should try to visualize your readers. Often, if your document is going to be distributed to more than one reader, it helps to keep one particular reader in mind, a reader who typifies your intended audience.

If you keep your readers in mind, it will help you adapt your writing to your readers' knowledge. What do your readers know and what don't they know? What terms must you define and what terms do your readers already know? By visualizing your readers, you'll write more effectively.

Show the structure of your document   During the four planning steps, you've created an effective structure for your document. In particular, you've created a heading plan with logical relationships between the headings and subheadings. Now, as you write the first

---

> As I mentioned in the introduction, I'm assuming that you're already familiar with PCs like the Apple II, the Macintosh, the IBM PC (including the IBM XT, the IBM AT, and all IBM clones), or the IBM PS/2. If you don't own a PC yourself, you should at least have access to one in your business. That's why I'm not going to take the time to describe the <u>hardware</u> of a typical PC.
>
> Instead, I'm going to describe twelve types of <u>software</u> that can help you improve your writing. First, I'll present six types of software that every business writer should use. Then, I'll present six more types of software that you should be aware of, even though you probably won't ever need to use them. After that, I'll describe the benefits that you can get from using PC software, and I'll explain what you have to do to get these benefits.
>
> **Six types of PC software that every business writer should use**
>
> Figure 1-1 summarizes six types of PC software that can help you improve your writing. I use all six of them. If you don't already use them, I think you'll be delighted to discover how much they can help you.

Figure 5-6   A first draft that shows its structure

draft, don't be afraid to show that structure. If your readers understand the structure, they'll get your ideas more easily.

How do you show this structure to your readers? By giving them previews of the topics and subtopics to come and by summarizing the relationships between the topics and subtopics you've already presented. Of the two, previewing is more important than summarizing because it shows your readers the structure in advance so they'll recognize it when they encounter it.

To illustrate, figure 5-6 presents three paragraphs taken from the first draft of chapter 1. Here, the second paragraph introduces the main topics of the chapter. Then, after the first heading identifies the first of these topics, the third paragraph introduces the six types of software that will be treated as subtopics. By introducing the topics and subtopics in this way, I've shown you the structure for the whole chapter and for the first topic.

Sometimes, though, the structure of your document is obvious. This can happen when your document has only a few headings or subheadings or when the document moves logically and easily from one topic or subtopic to another. Then, you don't have to try to show the structure of your document. For instance, the PC recommendation in appendix A seemed to move quite easily from one topic to the next, so I made no special efforts to show its structure.

In general, I recommend that you show the structure of a document whenever you think your readers will have any trouble recognizing it. As a result, you should consider introductory paragraphs that show structure near the start of each document and near the start of each topic. These paragraphs are easy to write, and they can only improve the effectiveness of your documents.

Let your headings and subheadings do their job   The main purpose of a heading or subheading is to show where a topic or subtopic starts. If you have written your headings and subheadings so they are meaningful to your readers, they also tell what your topics and subtopics are about. As a result, you don't have to write sentences to do these functions. Instead, you should let your headings and subheadings do these jobs by themselves.

To illustrate, figure 5-7 presents two paragraphs from the PC recommendation in appendix A written in two different ways. In the first example, the heading "what's wrong with our word processing system" is left to do its job. It marks the start of a topic and tells what the topic is going to be about.

In the second example in figure 5-7, the writer didn't let the heading do its job. Instead, the last sentence in the paragraph before the heading introduces the topic to come. This sentence, though, detracts from the strength of the paragraph because it's unrelated to the idea of the paragraph. In addition, this sentence is redundant because it says the same thing as the heading that follows.

If you let your headings and subheadings do their work, you'll write more efficiently. Instead of worrying about the transitions between topics or subtopics, you write each topic so it's independent of the other topics; you write each subtopic so it's independent of the other subtopics. Yes, you write an occasional introductory paragraph that shows the structure of your topics and subtopics, but otherwise you let the headings and subheadings do their work.

Coordinate your text with your visual aids   In step 8, you try to develop visual aids that are as complete and understandable as possible. Now, to get the maximum benefit from your visual aids, you should write your text so your readers don't miss them. To do this,

Text that lets the heading do its job

This report presents my analysis of our current system and
my recommendations for new systems. I've tried to be brief
because the primary purpose of this report is to bring you
up-to-date on the PC and word processing developments of the
last six years. When you finish this report, you can decide
whether you want more information on any of the subjects.
If so, I'll be happy to get that information for you.

What's wrong with our word processing system

We installed our current system in 1982. It is a
minicomputer system with one terminal (keyboard and monitor)
for each person in the editorial department. The nine
people in this department share the one printer that is
located in the department. They also share the minicomputer
and its disk drives with 15 other users of the system in the
administrative and marketing departments.

Text that duplicates the work of the heading

This report presents my analysis of our current system and
my recommendations for new systems. I've tried to be brief
because the primary purpose of this report is to bring you
up-to-date on the PC and word processing developments of the
last six years. When you finish this report, you can decide
whether you want more information on any of the subjects.
**I'll start this report by explaining what's wrong with our
word processing system.**

What's wrong with our word processing system

We installed our current system in 1982. It is a
minicomputer system with one terminal (keyboard and monitor)
for each person in the editorial department. The nine
people in this department share the one printer that is
located in the department. They also share the minicomputer
and its disk drives with 15 other users of the system in the
administrative and marketing departments.

Figure 5-7 Let your headings and subheadings do their job

How to write the first draft 147

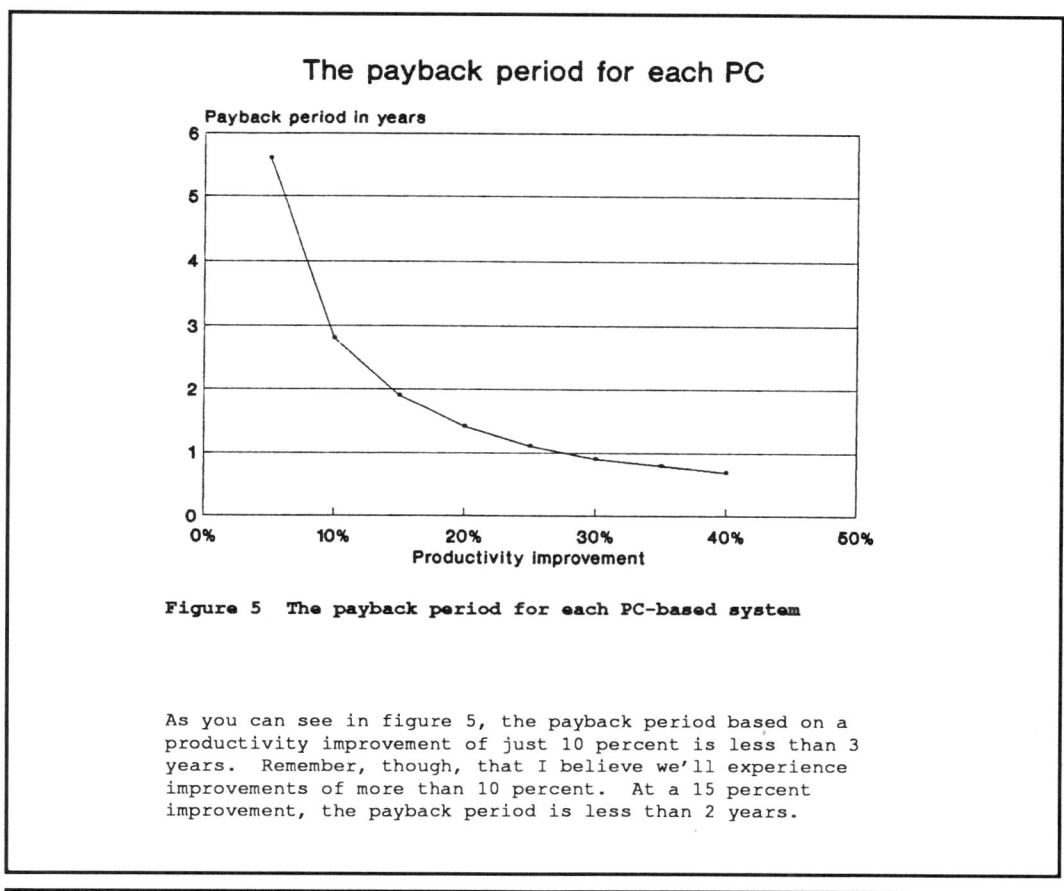

Figure 5-8 Get the maximum benefit from your visual aids

make sure your text at least refers to each visual aid. In addition, your text should explain anything that isn't obvious in a visual aid, and it should point out any highlights or relationships in the visual aids that are critical to their meaning.

To illustrate what's required, figure 5-8 presents a visual aid I could have added to the PC recommendation along with a paragraph that refers to it. The first phrase in the first sentence of the paragraph, "as you can see in figure 5," refers the reader to the figure. Then, the text points out two relationships in the figure so the reader is encouraged to focus on them.

Concentrate on writing effective paragraphs   As you write your first draft, you can't think about all of the writing principles and guidelines covered in section 3 of this book at once. Instead, you should just try to write effective paragraphs. You can do this by following your paragraph plan and by obeying the principles of paragraphing that are presented in chapter 8 of this book. Then, in step 11 of the 12-step writing procedure, you can revise your sentences to improve their readability, tone, and style.

**Other ideas
that will help you write the text of your first draft**

If you follow the guidelines I've just presented, you should be able to write the text of your first draft without too much trouble. But here are some other ideas that will help you.

How to use your heading plan as the start of your word processing document   If you've created your heading plan using word processing, you should start your first draft with your heading plan. That way, you don't have to re-enter the headings and subheadings into your system. As you write, you insert the paragraphs you've planned beneath the appropriate headings and subheadings that are already in your word processing document.

If you've used an outline processor to develop your heading plan, you can still start your word processing document with the plan. If your outline processor is designed for compatibility with your word processing package, this is a simple procedure. If not, you can copy your heading plan from your outline processor to your word processor as a text file. That's a bit more complicated, but you should still be able to do it in just a minute or two.

How to start writing   Usually, the first few paragraphs of a document are the hardest to write. So the best advice is to write them and forget about them, no matter how bad or inappropriate you may feel they are. Remember that you can always revise or rewrite those paragraphs after you've finished your document. *But you can't improve on a blank page.*

One reason it's tough to write the first few paragraphs is that they're introductory paragraphs. As a result, you don't have a clear idea of what these paragraphs should say. To compound the problem, many business writers want to say something clever or provocative in their opening paragraphs. Then, they end up staring at a blank page or screen waiting for a clever approach to enter their minds.

Perhaps the easiest way to get started is to tell the reader what your document is trying to do and to present the overall structure of your document. That's how most of the chapters in this book start. Generally speaking, that's also how the PC recommendation in appendix A starts. If you begin your documents in this straightforward fashion, you'll probably get started more easily. Later on, if you can think of a better way to write your opening paragraphs, you can revise or rewrite them.

How to keep going   Even if you get off to a good start, it's sometimes tough to keep going. You get an awful feeling that what you're writing isn't going to be effective. You feel that your choice of words is bad, your sentences are awkward, and maybe you didn't plan your document the right way...maybe you should have planned it another way altogether.

The main point here is to trust your planning. If you took the time to do the analysis and planning steps right, have confidence in what you've done. As long as you put down the right content within a logical structure of headings and subheadings, it won't be hard to revise what you've written. So keep on writing. Once you get the first draft done, the rest will be easy.

How to type two levels of headings   In the last chapter, I showed you how to create heading plans that have both headings and subheadings. You can say that a plan like this provides for two levels of headings. The headings can be called *level-1 headings*; the subheadings can be called *level-2 headings*. Now, as you prepare your first draft, you may wonder how these levels should be typed or entered into word processing.

Figure 5-9 shows two ways to prepare documents that contain two levels of headings. In both styles, you capitalize only the first letter of a heading or subheading because studies have shown that lowercase letters are easier to read than capital letters. In style 1, you center level-1 headings, start level-2 headings in the left margin, and skip a line before and after both levels of headings. In style 2, you type a level-1 heading starting in the left margin, and you skip a line before and after the heading. In contrast, the level-2 headings are *run-in headings*. In either style, you use boldface for all headings if that's easy to do on your PC; otherwise, you underline all headings. In our company, we use style 2 for all of our documents, but some

> **Headings for style 1**
>
> You center headings in this style. For efficiency and readability, you capitalize only the first letter of the first word in the heading, plus any letters or words that require capitalization. To set off the heading from the text, you skip one line before and after the heading.
>
> If it's easy for you to use boldface on your word processing system, you should use it for both headings and subheadings (as I've done in this example). If it isn't easy to use boldface, you should underline headings and subheadings. Notice that the first paragraph after a heading starts at the left margin, but subsequent paragraphs are indented.
>
> **Subheadings for style 1**
>
> You start subheadings in this style at the left margin. For efficiency and readability, you capitalize only the first letter of the first word in the subheading. To set off the subheading from the text, you skip one line before and after the subheading. The first paragraph after this style of subheading starts at the left margin, but subsequent paragraphs are indented.
>
> ---
>
> **Headings for style 2**
>
> You start headings in this style at the left margin. For efficiency and readability, you capitalize only the first letter of the first word in the heading, plus any letters or words that require capitalization. To set off the heading from the text, you skip one line before and after the heading.
>
> If it's easy for you to use boldface on your word processing system, you should use it for both headings and subheadings (as I've done in this example). If it isn't easy to use boldface, you should underline headings and subheadings. Notice that the first paragraph after a heading starts at the left margin, but subsequent paragraphs are indented.
>
> **Subheadings for style 2**   You start subheadings in this style at the left margin. For efficiency and readability, you capitalize only the first letter of the first word in the subheading. To set off the subheading from the text, you skip one line before the subheading and four spaces after it. This type of subheading is called a <u>run-in subheading</u>.

Figure 5-9   Two ways to type two levels of headings

```
                    Level-1 Headings

    You center headings in this style.  To emphasize that this
    is a level-1 heading, you can capitalize all the letters in
    the heading or the first letter of each word in the heading
    (as shown here).  To set off level-1 headings from the text,
    you skip one line before and after the heading.

        If it's easy for you to use boldface on your word processing
    system, you should use boldface for both headings and
    subheadings (as I've done in this example).  If it isn't
    easy, you should underline all three levels of headings.
    Notice that the first paragraph after a level-1 heading
    starts at the left margin, but subsequent paragraphs are
    indented.

    Level-2 headings

    You start level-2 headings in this style at the left margin.
    For efficiency and readability, you capitalize only the
    first letter of the first word in the subheading.  To set
    off level-2 headings from the text, you skip one line before
    and after the heading.  The first paragraph after a level-2
    heading starts at the left margin, but subsequent paragraphs
    are indented.

    Level-3 headings    You start level-3 headings in this style
    at the left margin.  For efficiency and readability, you
    capitalize only the first letter of the first word in the
    heading.  To set off the heading from the text, you skip one
    line before the heading and four spaces after it.  This type
    of heading is called a run-in heading.
```

Figure 5-10   One way to type three levels of headings

people prefer the headings in style 1 because they are a little more obvious to the readers.

How to type three levels of headings   Although you won't use three levels of headings in many of your documents, figure 5-10 shows one way to type them if you do. This style is similar to style 1 in figure 5-9, but it provides for *level-3 headings*, which are run-in headings. To emphasize the level-1 headings, you can type them as all capitals or with the first letter of every significant word capitalized. Remember, though, that people don't read capital letters as easily as they read lowercase letters, so you should keep your capitalization to a minimum.

When to use inline visual aids   In steps 6 and 8, you planned your visual aids and developed the first drafts for them. These visual aids should be developed separately from the text, and they should be presented separately in the final draft of your document.

Sometimes, though, as you prepare your first draft of the text, you'll wonder whether you should present a visual aid as part of the text. A visual aid like this can be referred to as an *inline visual aid*. An inline visual aid is developed along with the text and is presented within the paragraph that refers to it.

To illustrate the use of inline visual aids, figure 5-11 presents two examples of them. In the first example, the paragraph refers to the function symbol for flowcharting and gives an example of one. Since this symbol doesn't represent a complete visual aid, it's acceptable to treat the symbol as an inline visual aid.

In the second example, the paragraph contains a complete table showing changes in accounts receivable. It's better to present a table like this as a separate visual aid, though. Then, if you need to refer to the table from other paragraphs in the text, you can do so just by using its figure number. And you don't have to deal with page breaks coming in the middle of the table...a problem that often occurs when you use long inline figures.

To decide whether an inline visual aid should be treated separately, you should consider three factors. First, how large is the visual aid? If it's more than six lines long, it's easier to present it separately. Second, how important is the visual aid? If it's important, you should treat it separately so your readers can refer to it easily after they've read your document. Third, how many times will you refer to the visual aid? If the answer is more than once, you should treat the visual aid separately so you can refer to it by figure number.

Discussion

For most documents, this is the most time-consuming step of writing, and it's the step that requires the most concentration. Even when you're working from a detailed paragraph plan, you have to recall or refer to all of the facts that support the ideas of your paragraphs. Then, you have to present these ideas and facts as understandably as possible in fully developed paragraphs. To do all of this well requires

How to write the first draft 153

An acceptable use of an inline visual aid

```
The symbol that follows can be used for any function in a
flowchart:
```

```
When you use it, you should write a brief description of the
function within the symbol.  Also, you should draw lines to
and from this symbol showing the sequence of the functions.
```

An inline table that should be a separate visual aid

```
    The table that follows shows how our accounts receivable
have increased relative to our sales:
```

Year	Monthly Sales	Receivables	Ratio (R/S)
1984	$48,525	$ 64,221	1.32
1985	59,977	121,440	2.02
1986	75,456	165,422	2.19
1987	91,200	211,990	2.32

```
Since the industry standard is a ratio of 1.5, you can see
that we have had a problem for three years now.  And it's
getting worse.
```

Figure 5-11 When to use inline visual aids

several different skills, so this step routinely requires all your mental strength and energy.

By using the 12-step writing procedure, though, you simplify the job of writing a first draft. By the time you start writing, you've already decided what content you're going to present and what paragraphs you're going to put it in. That leaves you free to concentrate on your writing. In particular, you can concentrate on writing fully developed paragraphs as explained in chapter 8. Then, in step 10, you can concentrate on correcting any content, structure, or paragraphing problems. In step 11, you can concentrate on improving the readability and tone of your writing. By dividing the mental steps of writing in this way, you'll write your first draft more efficiently than you ever have before.

Terms

level-1 heading
level-2 heading
run-in heading
level-3 heading
inline visual aid

Objectives

1. Describe the five guidelines for writing a first draft.

2. When you write documents with headings and subheadings, use one of the two styles presented in this book for typing two levels of headings.

3. Describe the three criteria for deciding when it's okay to use inline visual aids.

Heading plan for chapter 6

Step 10: Analyze and improve the structure of the first draft

The procedure for analyzing and improving the structure of a draft

1. Develop a paragraph analysis
2. Identify any structural problems
3. Plan the structural improvements
4. Revise the draft to correct its structural problems

Other ideas that will help you analyze and improve the structure of a draft

How much editing should you do while you analyze a document

How a paragraph analysis can help you analyze the work of others

Discussion

Step 11: Edit and revise the first draft

The procedure for editing and revising a draft

1. Edit the draft
2. Revise the draft
3. Run your spelling checker and correct any misspellings
4. If necessary, run your writing analyzer and revise based on its suggestions

Four major guidelines for editing a draft

Edit for readability

Edit for continuity

Edit for tone

Edit for grammar

Other ideas that will help you edit and revise

When to edit and revise on your PC

When to prepare a third draft

When to stop editing

Discussion

Step 12: Proofread and correct the second draft

The procedure for proofreading and correcting a draft

1. Proofread the draft
2. Correct the draft

Discussion

Chapter 6

How to revise a first draft

This chapter presents the three revision steps of the 12-step writing procedure. In step 10, you analyze and improve the structure of your first draft. In step 11, you edit and revise your draft. In step 12, you proofread and correct the second draft.

Why are there three steps for revision? So you can concentrate on three different types of problems as you revise. In step 10, you concentrate on content and structure. In step 11, you concentrate on readability, continuity, tone, and style. In step 12, you concentrate on spelling and punctuation.

Step 10: Analyze and improve the structure of the first draft

When you finish your first draft, you sometimes feel confident about its content, structure, and paragraphing. That's often true when you create a short document. If that's the way you feel, you can omit this step.

Sometimes, though, you feel anything but confident when you finish your first draft. After all, if you've taken my advice for step 9, you've written the draft without being too critical of yourself. So it's natural that you should have some doubts about it. But by doing this step, you can remove those doubts and correct any structural problems your first draft might have.

The procedure for analyzing and improving the structure of a draft

Figure 6-1 presents the procedure I recommend for doing this step. You can usually do this step in just a little more time than it takes to read your draft.

1. Develop a paragraph analysis A *paragraph analysis* looks like a paragraph plan, but you develop it after you write your draft, not before. For example, figure 6-2 presents the first page of my paragraph analysis for the PC recommendation in appendix A. Here, the lines below each heading and subheading represent the main ideas for the paragraphs that support those headings and subheadings.

Because a paragraph analysis is a private working paper, you can create and annotate yours in whatever way you think is most efficient. Although I usually prepare my paragraph analyses by hand, some people in our company prepare theirs using word processing or an outline processor. You can use whatever method you prefer.

Theoretically, of course, your paragraph analysis should be exactly like your paragraph plan. In practice, though, your first draft usually doesn't come out exactly the way you've planned it. As you write, you may realize that you need more paragraphs than you've planned, that a paragraph or two isn't necessary, or that a few paragraphs need to be rearranged. You may even realize that some of the topics need to be rearranged. That's why this step is worth doing. It lets you analyze what you wrote, not what you planned.

The procedure for analyzing and improving the structure of a draft

1. Develop a paragraph analysis.
2. Identify any structural problems.
3. Plan the structural improvements.
4. Revise the draft to correct its structural problems.

Figure 6-1 The procedure for analyzing and improving the structure of a draft

2. Identify any structural problems   As you read your manuscript and create the paragraph analysis, you try to identify any structural problems the draft has. When I say "structural problems," I mean any type of problem related to content, heading structure, or paragraphing. Those are the problems that are most critical to the effectiveness of your document, so those are the problems you should try to identify and correct first. When you identify a problem, you should make a manual notation about it on the paragraph analysis as I've done in figure 6-2.

If you developed an effective heading plan for your document before you started writing, you shouldn't identify any serious problems during this step. Figure 6-3 presents six of the most common problems you're likely to find, and none of them is serious. As you can see, the first three are paragraphing problems. If you haven't read chapter 8 yet, you'll learn more about these problems when you do. The last three problems have to do with content that should be added to the document, deleted from the document, or rearranged.

In figure 6-2, you can see that I identified only some minor problems when I did this step for the PC recommendation. Specifically, I identified two sets of paragraphs that should be combined and one paragraph that should be made into two paragraphs. I also marked one paragraph for deletion and indicated that two paragraphs should be added to the document. Next to one of the paragraphs, I marked an X and circled it; that's my notation for a paragraph that needs to be expanded because it isn't fully developed.

3. Plan the structural improvements   After you've identified all of the possible problems, you decide how to correct them. If the problems are minor, you can often plan the improvements as you identify the problems. In fact, that's how I planned the improvements that

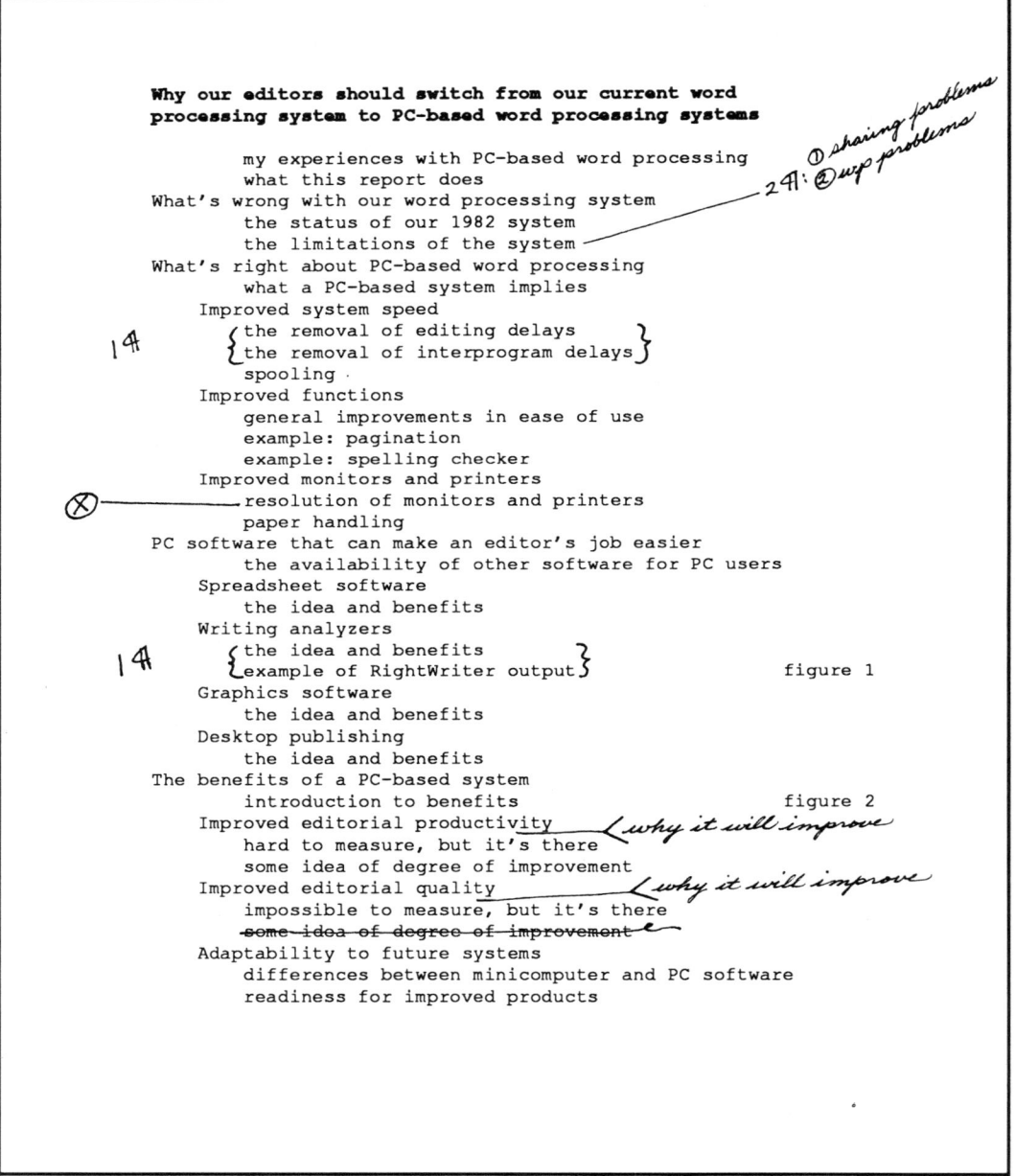

Figure 6-2 The first page of the paragraph analysis for the PC recommendation

---

Six common structural problems

1. Paragraphs that aren't fully developed
2. Paragraphs that present more than one idea
3. Paragraphs that should be combined
4. Paragraphs or topics that should be added to the document
5. Paragraphs or topics that should be deleted from the document
6. Paragraphs or topics that are out of place

Figure 6-3   Six common structural problems

I've marked in figure 6-2. When the problems are serious, though, you sometimes have to finish your analysis before you can plan the improvements.

4. Revise the draft to correct its structural problems   In this step, you make the changes you planned. Since your changes shouldn't be extensive, you can usually make them in a short time using word processing. Usually, you'll just be adding, deleting, combining, rearranging, or expanding paragraphs.

To complete this step, you print the modified version of your first draft. I think of this intermediate draft as either a structurally improved version of the first draft or the start of the second draft. Either way you think of it, the first draft has been revised to correct its structural problems, but it hasn't yet been revised to improve its language (step 11). When that's done, you have the second draft of your document.

Other ideas that will help you analyze and improve the structure of a draft

You shouldn't have much trouble using the procedure in figure 6-1 because it's consistent with the top-down approach you used for planning your document. Here, though, are a couple of other ideas that will help you do this step.

How much editing should you do while you analyze a document   When you do this step, you're often tempted to do some editing. You see a word misspelled. You read a word you want to change. You see a punctuation error. Should you delay marking these changes until you have analyzed your draft?

My advice is to make minor changes like those I've just described, but to resist making any extensive changes. The more you edit, the more you're distracted from your analytical work. Then, it's more likely that you'll overlook a structural change that should be made.

How a paragraph analysis can help you analyze the work of others If you ever have to analyze the work of others, you can usually do it best by using a paragraph analysis. This is particularly true when you read a document and feel that it's ineffective. When you finish your paragraph analysis, you won't have to say: "I don't quite know what's wrong with your report, but I just don't like it." Instead, you'll be able to identify specific problems of significance.

Figure 6-4, for example, presents a paragraph analysis I prepared for the first section of a manual on employee training. The manual was published by a large publishing company, so I'm sure someone spent several weeks editing it. Nevertheless, in its first 29 paragraphs, I identified 5 sets of paragraphs that should be combined, 3 out-of-place paragraphs, 2 or 3 paragraphs that weren't necessary, and a couple of paragraphs that were downright foolish. I also realized about halfway through my analysis that the headings talk about learning curves, training, and skill deterioration, but the paragraphs are trying to present the benefits of training.

When you analyze a draft with that many problems, you can't plan the improvements at the same time that you identify the problems. Then, you must use the procedure in figure 6-1 just as it's shown. In the second step, you make notations on the paragraph analysis to indicate the problems. In the third step, you try to make notations that indicate the required improvements. In figure 6-4, however, the problems are so serious that it's hard to determine what all of the improvements should be. From a practical point of view, the author probably should start the document over from the beginning of the 12-step writing procedure.

Why didn't the editor identify the problems? Probably, because the editor didn't have a method for analyzing them. If the editor had analyzed this section using a paragraph analysis, most of the problems would have been obvious.

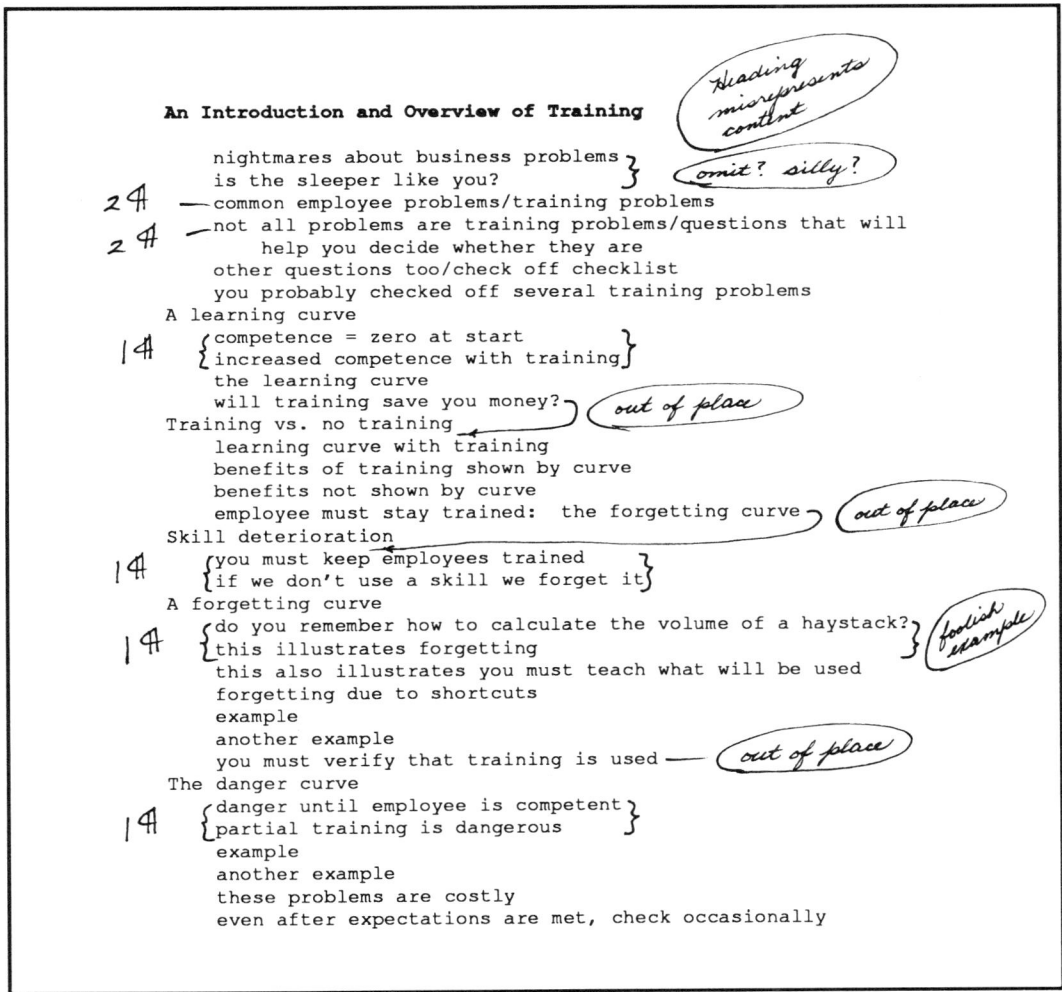

Figure 6-4 The first page of a paragraph analysis for a manual on training

Discussion

This is the most important step in the revision phase of writing because it helps you identify and correct the most critical writing problems. Once you're confident that the content, structure, and paragraphing of your draft are okay, you're ready to edit and revise the sentences within your paragraphs.

Terms

paragraph analysis

Objectives

1. Describe the procedure for analyzing and improving the structure of a draft.

2. After you've done the first nine steps for a document, analyze and improve its structure.

Step 11: Edit and revise the first draft

After you analyze and improve the structure of your first draft, you should feel confident that your document will be effective if your writing is acceptable. So in this step, you revise your sentences with the goal of improving them. For most documents, there should be considerable room for improvement.

The procedure for editing and revising a draft

Figure 6-5 presents the procedure for this revision step. First, you edit your draft. Second, you revise it. Third, you use your spelling checker to help you correct any misspellings. Fourth, you use your writing analyzer to help you make any final revisions that will help you improve your document's readability.

1. Edit the draft When you *edit* a draft, you mark any changes you want to make on the draft itself. For example, figure 6-6 shows an edited version of the first two paragraphs of the PC recommendation.

If you expect to make many changes to a draft, it's best to prepare a double-spaced copy like the one in figure 6-6. If you expect only a few changes, you can edit the draft in single-spaced form as shown in figure 6-7. When you use word processing, you can usually switch from single- to double-spacing with just a keystroke or two, so it's easy to print your document in the most appropriate form.

Figure 6-8 summarizes most of the *editing marks* that professional editors use. Although you can use any editorial marks that make sense to you (or whoever is going to prepare your next draft), I recommend that you use the ones in figure 6-8 because they will improve your efficiency. You use these editing marks whether you're editing a single- or a double-spaced draft.

Figure 6-9 presents the symbols for *special characters* (characters other than letters and numbers). I recommend that you use these symbols because they will prevent confusion. For instance, it's often hard to tell a handwritten period from a handwritten comma. If you circle the period, though, there's less chance for confusion.

If you study the examples in figures 6-6 and 6-7, you should see how you can use the editing marks and symbols when you edit a draft. When you're working on a double-spaced draft, you just mark your changes wherever they apply. When you're working on a single-spaced draft, you put the editing marks within the text and the

---

The procedure for editing and revising a draft

1. Edit the draft.
2. Revise the draft.
3. Run your spelling checker and correct any misspellings.
4. If necessary, run your writing analyzer and revise based on its suggestions.

Figure 6-5 The procedure for editing and revising a draft

changes in the margins. For instance, the first change in figure 6-7 means to insert a comma after the word *months*. The change for the fourth line of the first paragraph means to transpose the letters *t* and *s* in the word *system*.

When you're working on a single-spaced draft, you can write the changes in both the left and right margins with the leftmost change applying to the leftmost mark, then moving from left to right on a one-to-one basis. If you write more than one change for a line in one margin, you separate the changes with a slash (/) as illustrated by the third set of changes in the right margin in figure 6-7. In this line, the marks mean that the word *the* is replaced by the word *our*, and the last three characters in the word *shouldn't* are deleted.

When you edit a draft, you edit both the text and the visual aids. So if you find things that you want to change on the visual aids, you use the editing marks on them too. Usually, though, you won't want to change your visual aids much so you won't spend much time editing them.

2. Revise the draft   Once you've marked your changes, you *revise* your draft so you end up with a new draft. If you've made editing marks on any of your visual aids, you should revise them first using whatever software is appropriate. Then, you should make all the changes you've marked on the text using word processing. However, you don't reprint the revised version of the text until you've run your spelling checker.

3. Run your spelling checker and correct any misspellings
If you have a spelling checker on your system, you should use it after you've made all of your revisions to the text. Then, after you've

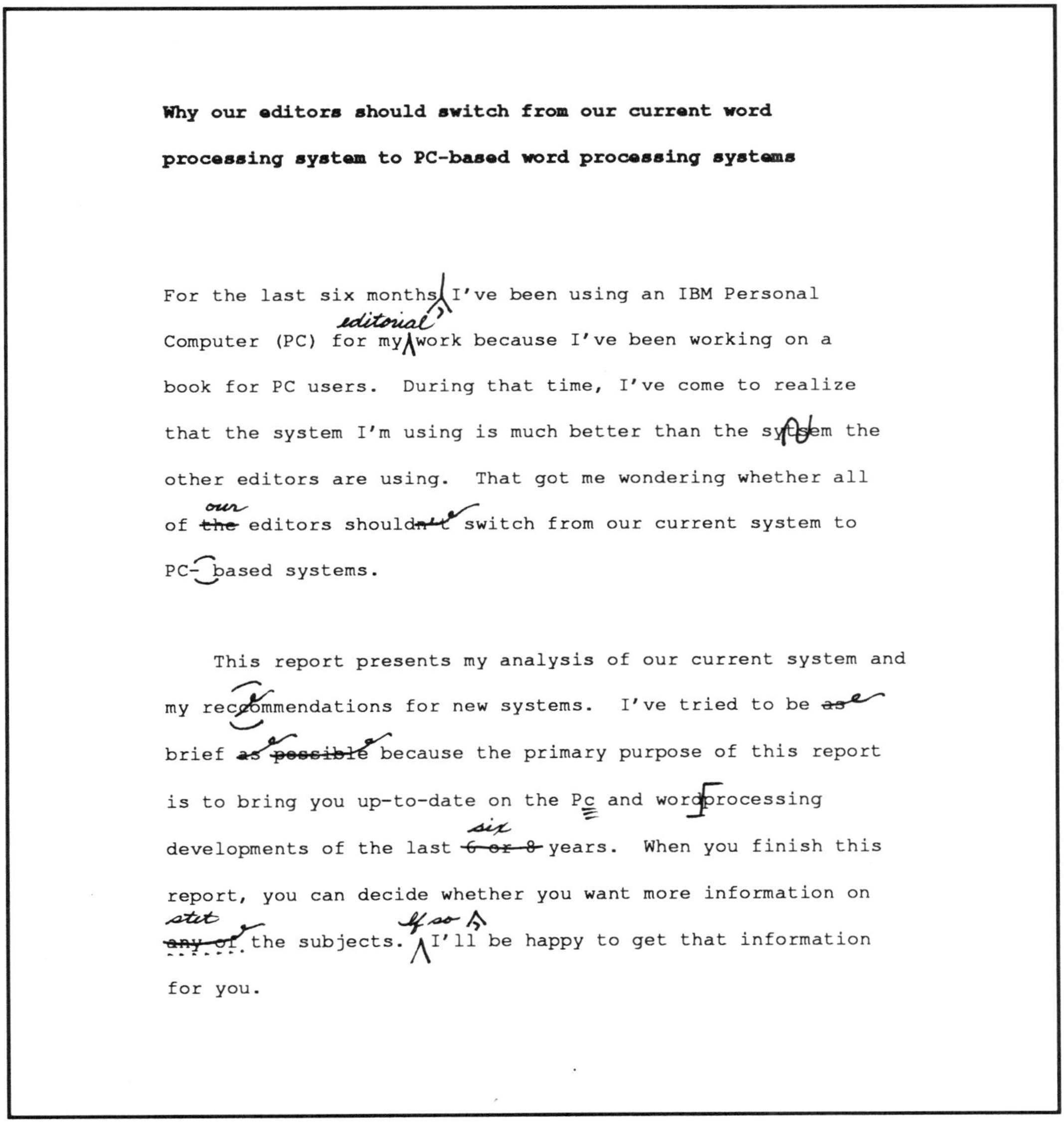

How to revise a first draft

> **Why our editors should switch from our current word processing system to PC-based word processing systems**
>
> For the last six months, I've been using an IBM Personal Computer (PC) for my *editorial* work because I've been working on a book for PC users. During that time, I've come to realize that the system I'm using is much better than the system the other editors are using. That got me wondering whether all of ~~the~~ *our* editors should switch from our current system to PC-based systems.
>
> This report presents my analysis of our current system and my recommendations for new systems. I've tried to be ~~as~~ brief ~~as possible~~ because the primary purpose of this report is to bring you up-to-date on the PC and word processing developments of the last ~~6 or 8~~ *six* years. When you finish this report, you can decide whether you want more information on ~~any of~~ the subjects. *If so,* I'll be happy to get that information for you.

Figure 6-6   Editing marks on a double-spaced draft of the PC recommendation

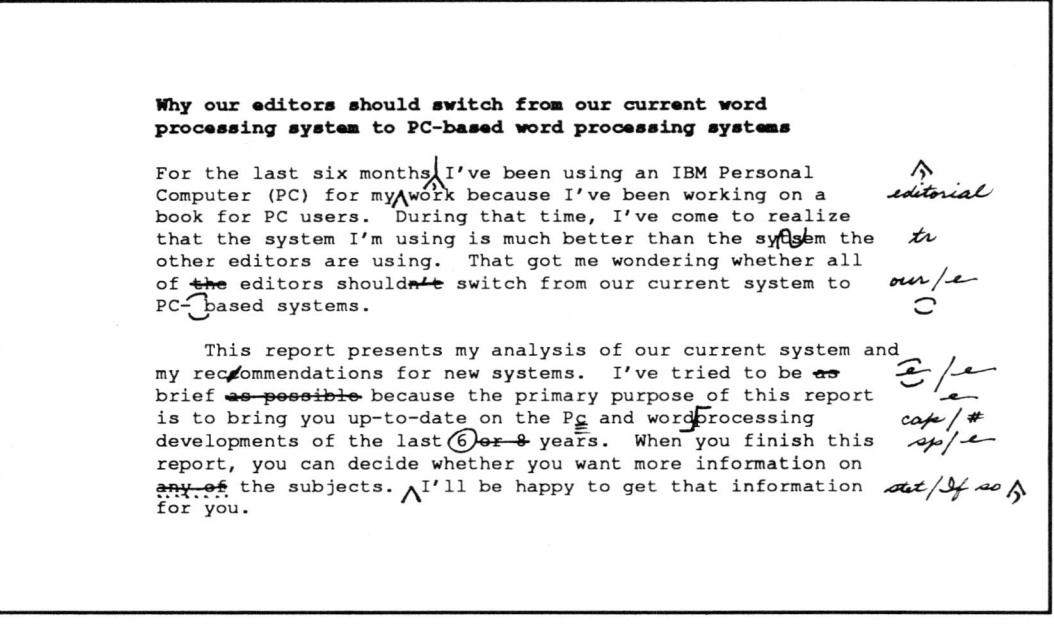

Figure 6-7 Editing marks on a single-spaced draft of the PC recommendation

corrected any misspellings, you can reprint the revised version of the draft.

4. If necessary, run your writing analyzer and revise based on its suggestions   If you have a writing analyzer on your system, you should run it after you've made your revisions. With some analyzers, you can wait to print your revised document until after you've used your writing analyzer, but it's usually more efficient to print the revised document first. Then, if the writing analyzer recommends changes you agree with, you can mark these changes on the printed draft before you make them.

As I said in chapter 1, though, you probably won't need to use your writing analyzer for long. After you've used one for a few months, you will learn to avoid making the types of mistakes the analyzer is programmed to identify. Also, you will write at an acceptable readability level. When you reach this point, you can stop using your writing analyzer.

How to revise a first draft

Symbol	Symbol Extension	Meaning	Example
ℓ		Delete	This is an example. It should be self-explanatory.
∧		Insert	This is *just* an example. It should be self-explanatory.
.....	stet	Let it stand	This is an example. It should be self-explanatory.
∽	tr	Transpose letters or words	This only is an example. It should be self-explanatory.
(loop arrow)		Move words	This is an example. It should be self-explanatory.
≡	cap	Capitalize	This is an example. it should be self-explanatory.
/	lc	Use lowercase	This is an Example. It should be self-explanatory.
¶		Start paragraph	This is an example. It should be self-explanatory.
no ¶		No paragraph	This is an example. no ¶ It should be self-explanatory.
―――	ital	Italicize	This is an *example*. It should be self-explanatory.
﹏﹏	bf	Use boldface	This is an **example**. It should be self-explanatory.
⌒		Close up	This is an example. It should be self-explanatory.
⌐		Insert space	This is anexample. It should be self-explanatory.
ẽ		Delete and close up	This is an exammple. It should be self-explanatory.
⋏		Insert punctuation	This is Johns example it should be self-explanatory.

Figure 6-8 Basic editing and proofing marks (part 1 of 2)

Symbol	Extension	Symbol Meaning	Example
][	ctr	Center	]This is an example.[
||		Align	This is an example. It should be self-explanatory.
]		Move right	This is an example. It should be self-explanatory.
[		Move left	This is an example. It should be self-explanatory.
⌒		Same line	This is an example.⌐ ⌐It should be self-explanatory.
⊂		Run over	This example is self-ex- planatory.
⊃		Turn back	This example is self-explana- tory.
○	sp	Spell out or vice versa	He was over six ft. tall.
⌒	wf	Wrong font	This is an example. It should be self-explanatory.
G?		Grammatical error?	He weren't to be denied. G?
F?		Factual error?	Sales increased 37.2 percent so far this year. F?
Any question or remark		Any question or remark	Under no circumstances will we accept their conditions. Are you sure?

Figure 6-8 Basic editing and proofing marks (part 2 of 2)

Four major guidelines for editing a draft

When you edit your draft, you try to improve your sentences by using all of your writing skills. The most important writing skills are presented in section 3 of this book (chapters 8 through 13). These

Symbol	Special Character
#	Space
⊙	Period
⨀	Colon
∧	Comma
∧	Semicolon
∨	Apostrophe
∨	Quotation mark
=	Hyphen
1/m	Dash
?	Question mark
!	Exclamation mark
( )	Parentheses
[ ]	Brackets
∧	Subscripted number
∨	Superscripted number

Figure 6-9 Editing symbols for spaces and punctuation marks

skills include everything from developing your paragraphs fully to putting commas after introductory clauses and phrases.

When you're learning to write, it's difficult to remember all of the principles and guidelines you've been taught. So let me give you four major guidelines you can concentrate on as you edit. While you're learning, you may want to edit your draft four different times, once for each of these guidelines. As you become more competent, though, you can edit for all four at once.

Edit for readability Chapter 9 shows you how to write readable sentences, and chapter 12 shows you how to use certain kinds of sentence structures to improve the readability of your writing. If your sentences aren't written at an acceptable level of readability, your writing isn't going to be effective no matter how well you do all of the other steps in the 12-step writing procedure. So when you edit for readability, you make sure that your writing is at an acceptable reading grade level.

Edit for continuity   Chapter 10 shows you how you can improve your writing by providing continuity between your paragraphs and sentences. In fact, showing the transitions between your paragraphs and sentences is one of the marks of a professional writer and one of the skills most amateur writers are missing. When you edit for continuity, you try to show these transitions.

Edit for tone   Chapter 11 shows you how to write with an effective tone. It shows you how to write with a positive attitude and a conversational style. It shows you how to write with your reader in mind. And it shows you how to avoid offending people with sexist language. As you edit, you should apply the skills of chapter 11 so you achieve an effective tone.

Edit for grammar   Chapter 12 introduces you to the punctuation required by various sentence structures, and chapter 13 shows you how to improve your grammar. Since punctuation and grammatical errors are signs of an uneducated writer, you should edit your document thoroughly to remove these errors.

Other ideas that will help you edit and revise

If you've mastered the skills in section 3 of this book, you shouldn't have much trouble editing your drafts. But let me give you a few more ideas that will help you.

When to edit and revise on your PC   If you make too many editorial marks on a single paragraph, they become difficult to follow. Then, it's often best to stop editing the paragraph and to mark it so you'll know that you need to edit and revise it on your PC. When you revise your draft using your PC later on, you can make extensive revisions to the marked paragraphs or you can completely rewrite them.

When to prepare a third draft   In general, your goal should be to prepare only three drafts of a document: the first draft, the second draft, and the final draft. However, the more editing you do on your first draft, the more likely it is that you can significantly improve your second draft by further editing. So if your first draft is heavily marked, you should probably edit the second draft too. In other words, you should develop a third draft by repeating this eleventh step before you go on to the next step.

When to stop editing   To some extent, you can improve a draft each time you edit it. If you've edited once, why not edit a second time? If you've edited twice, why not edit a third time? Doesn't the document keep getting better?

In business, though, too much editing is impractical. So you have to know when to stop. To help you make this decision, here's a test question: Is my document effective in its present form? As soon as you're confident that it is, stop editing.

Discussion

To edit well, you must master all of the skills presented in section 3 of this book. If these skills are new to you, you won't become a competent editor without working hard at it. The more you write and edit, the more competent you'll become.

Terms

editing
editing marks
special characters
revising

Objectives

1. Describe the procedure for editing and revising a draft.

2. Describe the four major guidelines that you should concentrate on when you edit.

3. After you've done the first ten steps for a document, edit and revise it.

Step 12: Proofread and correct the second draft

When you finish editing and revising your document, you should feel confident that it will be effective. Although you may occasionally need to do a third draft, you'll usually stop editing and revising at the second draft. Then, in step 12, all you have to do is proofread that draft and correct any errors you find. This is a trivial step that shouldn't take long to do. After you make the corrections or determine that your draft doesn't have any errors, it becomes your finished copy, or *final draft*.

The procedure for proofreading and correcting a draft

Figure 6-10 presents the simple procedure for proofreading and correcting a second draft. First, you proofread it. Then, if you find any mistakes, you correct them.

1. Proofread the draft When you *proofread*, or just *proof*, a document, you read it. However, you read it more slowly for proofing than you would for comprehension. If your normal reading speed is 600 words per minute, you should proof at a rate of perhaps 200 words per minute. If you find an error, you mark it using the same editing marks you use when you edit. Of course, you proof the visual aids as well as the text during this step. So if you find any mistakes in the visual aids, you mark them too.

During this step, you should only try to find errors. In particular, you should be looking for spelling and typographical errors. Remember that you've already revised for readability, continuity, tone, and grammar, so you don't want to repeat that effort now. You just want to be sure that your final draft is error-free.

2. Correct the draft Once you've marked the errors, you make the changes. When you use word processing for the text, this is a trivial step, so your final draft should be error-free. However, you should check the corrections to make sure you did them right.

Discussion

This is a trivial step, but a necessary one. If a reader sees a few spelling or typographical errors in the first page or two of one of your documents, it may reduce the effectiveness of your entire document.

How to revise a first draft 175

The procedure for proofreading and correcting the second draft

1. Proofread the draft.
2. Correct the draft.

Figure 6-10 The procedure for proofreading and correcting a draft

So give your documents every chance for success by carefully proofing them during this last step of the 12-step writing procedure.

Terms

final draft
proofread
proof

Objectives

1. Describe the procedure for proofreading and correcting a draft.

2. After you've done the first eleven steps for a document, proofread and correct it.

Heading plan for chapter 7

The procedure for developing a multi-unit document
1. Define the job
2. Get the information you need
3. Select the content
4. Plan the table of contents
5. Develop each unit using the 12-step writing procedure
6. Proofread the entire document

Some examples of contents problems

A table of contents that is too diverse for its audience

A table of contents with titles that aren't meaningful

A table of contents with an ineffective structure

A table of contents with units that aren't independent

Discussion

Chapter 7

Six steps for developing a multi-unit document

If you can develop a one-unit document using the 12-step writing procedure, you can develop a multi-unit document like a six-unit report or a four-unit proposal. After you decide what units your document is going to contain, you develop one unit at a time. As a result, developing a six-unit document is much like developing six one-unit documents.

The procedure for developing a multi-unit document

Figure 7-1 presents a general procedure for developing a multi-unit document. As you can see, you start by defining the job, getting the information you need, and selecting the contents for the document. That's what you do when you develop a one-unit document.

Then, you plan the table of contents for the document. Once you have the table of contents, you develop each of its units using the 12-step writing procedure. When you have a final draft for **each** of the units, you proofread the entire document to make sure it's consistent from the first unit to the last.

1. Define the job When you define the job for a multi-unit document, you start by defining your audience and purposes. Once you've done that, you usually know whether or not your document is going to require more than one unit. For instance, you've been assigned to rewrite your company's procedures manual. You're going to write a lengthy sales proposal with detailed explanations of three system alternatives. Or you've been doing an extensive study of administra-

---

The procedure for developing a multi-unit document

1. Define the job.
2. Get the information you need.
3. Select the content.
4. Plan the table of contents.
5. Develop each unit using the 12-step writing procedure.
6. Proofread the entire document.

Figure 7-1   The procedure for developing a multi-unit document

tive operations for the last two months, and now you're going to present your analysis of five operational areas.

After you've defined your audience and purposes, you consider alternatives to the document you envision. Should you write one large procedures manual or a few smaller, more specific ones? Should you write one long sales proposal or one for each system option and present them with a cover letter? Should you write one report on operations or a separate report for each operational area? Often, a change in the packaging of your document can make a dramatic improvement in its effectiveness or in your efficiency as you develop it.

If a multi-unit document is going to take months to develop, you should also make sure that it's worth developing. Will anybody actually read or use the document you're considering? Will the cost of its development ever be justified by the benefits it delivers? If you look through the bookshelves of most companies, large and small, you'll find at least one company-developed manual that is covered by dust indicating that no one ever uses it.

2. Get the information you need   When you get the information for a multi-unit document, you do it just as you would for a single-unit document. There's just more information to get. As a result, you shouldn't feel that you have to get all the information you need for writing every unit within the document. Just get as much information as you need to plan the document. You can get more information when you develop each of the units within your document.

3. Select the content   When you select the content for a multi-unit document, you do it just as you would for a single-unit document.

However, you work at a higher level of information. You think more in terms of topics and subtopics, and less in terms of ideas and thoughts. You know you can get the detailed information for each of your topics and subtopics later on.

Sometimes, you don't know whether your document is going to require more than one unit until you select the content. But as you develop your contents list, you realize (1) that you're dealing with more information than you usually put in a one-unit document, and (2) that the information can be divided into two or more independent subjects. Then, it becomes clear that your document should be divided into units.

4. Plan the table of contents   The *table of contents* (or just *contents*) of a multi-unit document is the list of units in the front of the document. Figure 7-2, for example, presents the table of contents for a procedures manual.

When you develop a multi-unit document, you develop a table of contents for it in this fourth step of the procedure. In general, you should use a word processor instead of an outline processor for this, because a word processor lets you format your contents just the way you want.

In a book, each unit is called a chapter. In a procedures manual, each unit is likely to be called a section. In an instructional manual, the units are often called modules. In this book, though, we use the term *unit* to refer to any of these divisions.

The word *unit* implies that each chapter, section, or module should deal with only *one* subject. That in turn means that each unit should be largely independent of the other units. Although you can't design your units so they're completely independent, you should design them with the goal of independence in mind. The more independent your units are, the easier it is to develop them.

When you plan the table of contents for a document, you do it in much the same way you develop a heading plan for a one-unit document. First, you group the content items on your contents list into units, and you give each unit a title. Next, you arrange the unit titles in a logical sequence for presentation. When you do this, you can use the same organizational methods you use for planning topics and subtopics. Then, when you're satisfied with the structure of your table of contents, you rewrite the unit titles so they're meaningful to your readers. If possible, your unit titles should also promise a benefit, and they should be written with consistent language structures.

```
Contents for a manual on office procedures

1.  How to use this manual
2.  How to open and sort the mail
3.  How to process orders
4.  How to process payments
5.  How to handle customer inquiries
6.  How to handle customer complaints
7.  How to process vendor invoices
8.  How to handle vendor correspondence
```

Figure 7-2   An effective table of contents for a procedures manual

To see an example, look again at the table of contents for a manual on office procedures shown in figure 7-2. It has functional organization. After the introductory unit, each unit title describes one office function. As a result, each unit is largely independent of the other units.

Figure 7-3 shows the table of contents for a multi-unit report or proposal. It is presented in a logical sequence that isn't based on any one organizational method. If each of the units were just a page or two, this document could be a one-unit document composed of six topics. However, if one or more of the topics are extensive, it's often best to present a report or proposal like this as a multi-unit document. Then, it's easier for the readers to refer to the document later on.

If you're developing a document with many units, you should consider adding another level of structure to your table of contents. To do this, you group the units into larger divisions. For instance, figure 7-4 presents the table of contents for a book on PCs that one of our authors is developing right now. Here, the 20 chapters are grouped into six parts. This helps the reader see how the chapters are related. For ease of use, this book is designed so the reader can skip to the chapters in any one of the last five parts after reading the chapters in the first part.

5. Develop each unit using the 12-step writing procedure

Once you've established the table of contents for a multi-unit document, you develop each of the units using the 12-step writing procedure. If, for example, you've designed a four-unit document, you can start by doing the 12 steps for unit 1. In step 1 for unit 1, you won't

```
Contents for a multi-unit report

1.  Introduction
2.  An analysis of the existing system
3.  Proposal 1:  Some cost-effective modifications
4.  Proposal 2:  A proven replacement system
5.  Proposal 3:  A state-of-the-art replacement system
6.  Recommendations
```

Figure 7-3   An effective table of contents for a multi-unit report

need to define the audience because you've already done that, but you can define specific objectives for the unit if they're not apparent. In step 2, you can get more information for the unit if you need it. In step 3, you select the content for just the unit you're working on. Then, in steps 4 through 12, you plan, write, and revise the unit so you end up with a final draft for it. After you finish unit 1, you develop the next unit using the 12-step procedure, and you continue in this way until you have final drafts for all of the units.

If you've designed your units so they're as independent as possible, you don't have to develop them in sequence. Often, in fact, you shouldn't develop your units in sequence because that isn't the most efficient way to develop them. If, for example, you were developing the units in figure 7-3, you would probably develop unit 2 first, then units 3 through 5 in whatever sequence you felt most comfortable with, then unit 6, and unit 1 last. If you were developing the units in figure 7-2, you could develop them in whatever sequence you wanted to since each one represents an independent function.

6. Proofread the entire document   When you have final drafts for all of the units in a document, you proofread the entire document. That way you can make sure that all of the units are coordinated. If one unit refers to a figure in another unit, you can check to make sure that the reference is correct. If one unit promises that something will be explained in another unit, you can check to make sure that it is. Because you try to plan your units so they're as independent as possible, you shouldn't have many problems like this, but a final proofreading will make sure there aren't any.

```
Contents for Get Control of Your PC! by Doug Lowe

Part 1        The least you need to know about DOS

Chapter 1     DOS fundamentals
Chapter 2     Ten DOS commands every PC user should know
Chapter 3     How to make DOS easier to use

Part 2        Organizing your data

Chapter 4     How to organize the directories on your hard disk
Chapter 5     How to keep track of your files
Chapter 6     How to manage diskette files

Part 3        Protecting your data

Chapter 7     How to back up your data
Chapter 8     Other ways to protect your data

Part 4        Making your software work for you

Chapter 9     How to select the right software
Chapter 10    How to install your programs
Chapter 11    How to master your software
Chapter 12    How to make your programs work together

Part 5        Making your PC faster and better

Chapter 13    How to make your PC faster without adding hardware
Chapter 14    How to add new equipment and devices to your PC
Chapter 15    How to install a new version of DOS
Chapter 16    How to make your computers work together

Part 6        Living with your PC

Chapter 17    How to buy hardware, software, and supplies
Chapter 18    How to set up your computer work area
Chapter 19    How to get help
Chapter 20    What to do if your computer breaks

Appendix A    How to obtain software recommended in this book
Appendix B    The Get Control of Your PC! program diskette
```

Figure 7-4 An effective table of contents for a book that is divided into sections

```
Contents for an advertising agency's operations manual
    1.  Introduction
    2.  The services we provide
    3.  Marketing our services
    4.  Our competition
    5.  Competitive factors
    6.  Servicing accounts
    7.  Forms, systems, records, and files
    8.  Credit and collections
    9.  Managing your time
   10.  Technical compendium for production services
```

Figure 7-5 A table of contents that is too diverse for its audience

Some examples of contents problems

In case it isn't obvious, the most critical part of the procedure in figure 7-1 is item 4. If you can plan an effective table of contents, you should be able to develop an effective multi-unit document. But if your table of contents is ineffective, it reduces the effectiveness of your entire document no matter how good the individual units are. To show you what I mean, I'll give you four examples of contents problems.

A table of contents that is too diverse for its audience Figure 7-5 illustrates a table of contents that isn't appropriate for any one audience. Some of the content is for the marketing staff. Some is for the administrative staff. And so on. Here, the problem goes back to the first part of the procedure, defining the job. The author probably should have developed one manual for each of the different audiences.

A table of contents with titles that aren't meaningful Figure 7-6 illustrates a table of contents for a book on game theory with titles that aren't meaningful. Or, more accurately, the titles aren't meaningful to the intended readers. Here, the author is a technical person, but he's written a book for business people. As a result, the titles should be stated in terms that business people can understand. It would also help if the titles promised a benefit, because not many business people are going to be interested in game theory unless they can see how they're going to profit from it.

```
Contents for a book on game theory for businessmen
    Chapter 1      Games of one person
    Chapter 2      Finite, zero-sum games of perfect information (two
                   persons)
    Chapter 3      General, zero-sum games of perfect information (two
                   persons)
    Chapter 4      Non-zero-sum games (two persons)
    Chapter 5      N-person games
```

Figure 7-6 A table of contents that is meaningful to the author, but not to the reader

A table of contents with an ineffective structure Figure 7-7 shows the table of contents for a request for proposal that we received from a Fortune 500 company. The first unit tells you what it is that the company wants you to do. The other 15 units present information related to the company's bureaucratic procedures, and these units don't seem to be in any logical sequence at all. Can you believe that "general provisions" is unit 7 between "gifts" and "freedom to provide services"? To improve this table of contents, you could group the units into sections and rearrange the units. Perhaps you could also combine some of the smaller units so there would be fewer units overall. At the least, the table of contents should indicate which units describe the work to be done and which present auxiliary information.

A table of contents with units that aren't independent Most writers instinctively plan units that are reasonably independent of the other units. But not all do. Figure 7-8, for example, presents the table of contents for a book on MS DOS. Here, there are two chapters each on batch files, menu systems, and macro processors. Worse, unrelated chapters separate each pair of related chapters. When the relationships between units are strong, though, your document becomes more difficult to write. It also becomes more difficult to read, understand, and refer to.

Discussion

When you develop a multi-unit document, you work from the top down until you have an effective table of contents. This table of contents should present independent units with meaningful titles in a

Six steps for developing a multi-unit document 185

```
Contents for a request for proposal

 1. Scope of work
 2. Substantiation of charges
 3. Confidential information
 4. Disclosure and rights
 5. Warranty
 6. Gifts
 7. General provisions
 8. Freedom to provide services
 9. Termination
10. Sole agreement
11. Insurance
12. Damages
13. Equal Employment Opportunity
14. Occupational Safety and Health Act
15. Contractor's agreement with its employees
16. Subcontracts
```

Figure 7-7   A table of contents with an ineffective structure

```
Contents for an advanced book on MS DOS

Chapter 1      The PC machine
Chapter 2      Simple batch files
Chapter 3      RAM disks
Chapter 4      Macro processors
Chapter 5      Designing an interactive menu system
Chapter 6      Controlling your monitor
Chapter 7      Controlling your printer
Chapter 8      More about batch files
Chapter 9      Your own menu system
Chapter 10     Macro processors and your own executive system
```

Figure 7-8   A table of contents with units that aren't independent

logical sequence. After that, it's just a question of perseverance as you develop each of the units within the document.

Terms

table of contents
contents
unit

Objectives

1. Describe the six steps in the procedure for developing a multi-unit document.

2. Given a writing assignment that requires the development of a multi-unit document, plan the table of contents for it.

Section 3

The essential language skills for business and technical writers

This section presents essential language skills that many business and technical writers don't have. In contrast to the way you've been taught these skills in the past, though, this section presents them in a top-down sequence that moves from the most important to the least important skills. If you master all of the skills of this section, you'll see obvious improvements in your writing.

Heading plan for chapter 8

The principles of paragraphing

    Principle 1: Put one and only one idea in each paragraph

    Principle 2: Develop the idea of each paragraph fully

    Principle 3: Start each paragraph with a sentence that gives the idea of the paragraph or a sentence that provides a transition from the previous paragraph

How to write special kinds of paragraphs

    Paragraphs that introduce topics, subtopics, and other paragraphs

    Paragraphs that present dialogue

    Paragraphs that present numbered lists

    Paragraphs that present unnumbered lists

Three more ideas about paragraphing

    How to plan the paragraphs you're going to write

    The effect of paragraph length on reading ease

    Four ways to organize paragraphs

Two examples of paragraphing problems

    Example 1: A paragraph with more than one idea

    Example 2: Poorly developed paragraphs that don't present useful information

Discussion

Chapter 8

How to write effective paragraphs

When you write the first draft of a document, you should concentrate on writing effective paragraphs. Sure, you write one word at a time, and a group of words makes up one sentence. But paragraphs are the critical units of writing. If a document contains effective paragraphs, it will most likely be effective.

In this chapter, I'll start by presenting the three main principles for effective paragraphing. Next, I'll show you how to write some special kinds of paragraphs. Then, I'll present some ideas that are related to effective paragraphing, and I'll illustrate some common paragraphing problems.

When you finish this chapter, you'll be able to write effective paragraphs. That means you'll have mastered one of the most important skills for effective writing. Then, the other chapters in this section will show you how to improve the sentences you write within your paragraphs.

The principles of paragraphing

There are three principles you need to follow if you want to write effective paragraphs. Although they are simple principles, most business writers disobey all three of them.

To illustrate these principles, I'm going to use six paragraphs on word processing. These paragraphs are shown in figure 8-1. As you can see, the six paragraphs are from a topic called "The Benefits of Word Processing."

Principle 1: Put one and only one idea in each paragraph If you were to create a paragraph analysis for the paragraphs in figure 8-1, you would come up with a list like the one in figure 8-2. This

> **The Benefits of Word Processing**
>
> In simplest terms, the benefits of any word processing package are (1) improved writing productivity and (2) improved writing effectiveness. Perhaps these benefits are obvious, but, in case they're not, let me describe them in more detail.
>
> Word processing helps you increase your productivity in at least three ways. First, you can enter the first draft of a document into a word processing system at least 30 percent faster than you can type it. As you create the first draft, you can correct your typing errors as you go, so the printed draft will have fewer errors than it would have had if you typed it.
>
> Second, word processing dramatically improves revision speed because you only have to make the changes, insertions, and deletions that you require. You don't have to retype the entire document. When I wrote chapter 1, for example, it took me about eight hours to enter the first draft. However, it took me less than one hour to revise the draft after I had edited it, even though I made some extensive changes.
>
> Third, word processing improves your productivity because it reduces the need for proofing. When someone makes word processing changes for you, you only have to proof the changes. In contrast, when someone retypes a document for you, you should proof the entire document because new errors may have been introduced by the typing process.
>
> Although improved productivity is an important benefit of word processing, improved writing effectiveness may be more important. First, because revisions are easy to make on a word processing system, you won't hesitate to make any revisions that will improve a document. In contrast, you hesitate to make even minor revisions to a document when you know that someone will have to retype the entire document if you do. Second, because you only have to proof the changed areas of a revised document, there's less chance that an error will slip by you.
>
> Beyond this, word processing helps you improve your writing in subtle ways. If you do your own entry work, you can change a sentence, decide you liked it better the way it was, and restore the first version with just a keystroke or two. You can move a paragraph or group of paragraphs from one portion of a document to another to see how that works with just a few keystrokes. You can copy paragraphs that you used successfully in other documents into the document you're working on and revise them so they're appropriate for your new purpose. Until you've used word processing for a while, it may be hard for you to understand how these capabilities will improve your writing, but they will...and the improvements are often dramatic.

Figure 8-1   Six paragraphs from a topic on word processing

The ideas presented in the word processing topic

1. Introduction: Word processing improves your writing productivity and your writing effectiveness.
2. Word processing increases your typing speed.
3. Word processing increases your revision speed.
4. Word processing reduces the need for proofing.
5. Word processing improves writing effectiveness because you can revise your documents more easily.
6. Word processing improves writing effectiveness in other ways that you have to experience to appreciate.

Figure 8-2 The main idea in each paragraph presented in figure 8-1

shows that each paragraph contains one and only one idea. The first paragraph introduces the two main benefits of word processing: improved productivity and writing effectiveness. Paragraphs 2 through 4 show three ways word processing helps you increase your productivity. Paragraphs 5 and 6 show how word processing can help you improve your writing effectiveness.

Business writers frequently disobey this first principle by writing paragraphs that contain two or more ideas. This makes their writing difficult to read and understand. It also indicates that they don't have a clear view of what their ideas are.

Sometimes, though, it's difficult to say where one idea ends and another starts. For instance, you might feel that the six paragraphs in figure 8-1 should be written as the three paragraphs in figure 8-3. Here, the first paragraph introduces the two main benefits of word processing. The second paragraph shows how word processing helps you increase your productivity. The third paragraph shows how word processing helps you improve your writing effectiveness.

As an editor, I would say that the paragraphs in both figure 8-1 and in figure 8-3 are acceptable because you can interpret the content as either six or three ideas. However, I prefer the paragraphing in figure 8-1 because it's easier to read. This shows that sometimes paragraphing can be a matter of personal preference.

The Benefits of Word Processing

In simplest terms, the benefits of any word processing package are (1) improved writing productivity and (2) improved writing effectiveness. Perhaps these benefits are obvious, but, in case they're not, let me describe them in more detail.

Word processing helps you increase your productivity in at least three ways. First, you can enter the first draft of a document into a word processing system at least 30 percent faster than you can type it. As you create the first draft, you can correct your typing errors as you go, so the printed draft will have fewer errors than it would have had if you typed it. Second, word processing dramatically improves revision speed because you only have to make the changes, insertions, and deletions that you require. You don't have to retype the entire document. When I wrote chapter 1, for example, it took me about eight hours to enter the first draft. However, it took me less than one hour to revise the draft after I had edited it, even though I made some extensive changes. Third, word processing improves your productivity because it reduces the need for proofing. When someone makes word processing changes for you, you only have to proof the changes. In contrast, when someone retypes a document for you, you should proof the entire document because new errors may have been introduced by the typing process.

Although improved productivity is an important benefit of word processing, improved writing effectiveness may be more important. First, because revisions are easy to make on a word processing system, you won't hesitate to make any revisions that will improve a document. In contrast, you hesitate to make even minor revisions to a document when you know that someone will have to retype the entire document if you do. Second, because you only have to proof the changed areas of a revised document, there's less chance that an error will slip by you. Beyond this, word processing helps you improve your writing in subtle ways. If you do your own entry work, you can change a sentence, decide you liked it better the way it was, and restore the first version with just a keystroke or two. You can move a paragraph or group of paragraphs from one portion of a document to another to see how that works with just a few keystrokes. You can copy paragraphs that you used successfully in other documents into the document you're working on and revise them so they're appropriate for your new purpose. Until you've used word processing for a while, it may be hard for you to understand how these capabilities will improve your writing, but they will...and the improvements are often dramatic.

Figure 8-3   The six paragraphs of figure 8-1 rewritten as three paragraphs

Although some paragraphing decisions are arbitrary, you can be sure that you'll understand what I mean by "one idea per paragraph" by the time you complete this chapter. As a result, you'll know when one paragraph should end and another should begin. You'll also be able to write paragraphs that are appropriate in length and content for the audience you're trying to reach.

If you read other books on writing, you'll discover that some define a paragraph as a group of sentences that present a *single point*, some as a group of sentences that present a *single thought*, and some as a group of sentences that present a *single subject*. However, all of the books agree on the principle that each paragraph should contain only one idea, point, thought, or subject. Since most books use the term *idea* for what it is that a paragraph expresses, I'm going to use that term throughout this book.

Principle 2: Develop the idea of each paragraph fully When I talk about developing an idea or a paragraph fully, I mean to present enough supporting detail to get the idea of the paragraph across to the reader. In other words, you must support your generalizations, statements, and ideas with facts, anecdotes, and examples.

Here again, amateur writers frequently disobey this principle. For instance, an amateur might write the six paragraphs in figure 8-1 as shown in figure 8-4. If you compare the two versions of this topic on word processing, I hope you'll agree that the one in figure 8-1 is more convincing. Why? Because *the paragraphs are developed fully*. To say it another way, because *the generalizations are supported by specifics*. To say it a third way, because *the statements are supported by facts*.

To illustrate this point, read the third paragraph in figure 8-4. Do you believe the statement it makes, that word processing dramatically improves revision speed? Are you convinced by it? Now, read the third paragraph in figure 8-1. It not only explains how word processing helps you increase revision speed, it also gives an actual example of the times required to create and revise a document. This paragraph is convincing because its idea is developed fully.

As a rule of thumb, all your paragraphs should contain three sentences or more. I will present a few exceptions to this rule in a moment, but otherwise this is a good rule. If you frequently write paragraphs with fewer than three sentences, that's a strong indication that you're not developing your ideas fully.

The Benefits of Word Processing

In simplest terms, the benefits of any word processing package are improved writing productivity and effectiveness. That's why word processing is so much better than typewriting.

Word processing helps you increase your productivity in at least three ways. First, you can enter the first draft of a document into a word processing system faster than you can type it. That's an important improvement.

Second, word processing dramatically improves revision speed. That's an even more important improvement.

Third, word processing improves your productivity because it reduces the need for proofing. This is less important.

Although improved productivity is an important benefit of word processing, improved writing effectiveness may be more important. This results because it's easier to change your documents.

Word processing also helps you improve your writing in other ways. Some of these ways are hard to appreciate until you've used word processing for a while.

Figure 8-4   Six paragraphs on word processing that aren't fully developed

Because amateur writers seem to sense that paragraphs should contain more than a sentence or two, they often write paragraphs like this:

> Word processing can increase a writer's productivity. In general, word processing is much better than typing. If you have a choice between word processing and typing, by all means choose word processing. Word processing offers a major improvement in clerical efficiency.

Here, it looks at first glance as though the paragraph is fully developed because the paragraph consists of four sentences. But the last three sentences don't say anything that the first sentence didn't already say. So guard against this type of superficial writing. If you have the facts, develop your paragraphs fully by letting the facts speak for themselves.

> **The first sentences of**
> **the six word processing paragraphs in figure 8-1**
>
> 1. In simplest terms, the benefits of any word processing package are (1) improved writing productivity and (2) improved writing effectiveness.
>
> 2. Word processing helps you increase your productivity in at least three ways.
>
> 3. Second, word processing dramatically improves revision speed because you only have to make the changes, insertions, and deletions that you require.
>
> 4. Third, word processing improves your productivity because it reduces the need for proofing.
>
> 5. Although improved productivity is an important benefit of word processing, improved writing effectiveness may be more important.
>
> 6. Beyond this, word processing helps you improve your writing in subtle ways.

Figure 8-5   The first sentences of the paragraphs presented in figure 8-1

Principle 3: Start each paragraph with a sentence that gives the idea of the paragraph or a sentence that provides a transition from the previous paragraph   If you review the paragraphs in figure 8-1, you'll see that they start with the sentences shown in figure 8-5. Here, the first paragraph starts with a sentence that gives its idea, and the second paragraph starts with a sentence that provides a transition from the first paragraph. The third and fourth paragraphs start with sentences that present their ideas. Then, the fifth and sixth paragraphs start with sentences that not only provide transitions but also present their ideas. In summary, three of the paragraphs start with sentences that give their ideas, one starts with a sentence that provides a transition, and two start with sentences that both provide transitions and give their ideas.

One way to obey this third principle is to start each paragraph with a sentence that gives its idea. For instance, figure 8-6 shows how the first two paragraphs of figure 8-1 can be rewritten as three paragraphs that start with sentences that give the ideas of the paragraphs. If you write this way, you're obeying some advice that you may have been taught in grade school. That is (1) that the *topic sentence* in each paragraph is the one that gives the idea of the para-

> **The Benefits of Word Processing**
>
> **In simplest terms, the benefits of any word processing package are (1) improved writing productivity and (2) improved writing effectiveness.** Perhaps these benefits are obvious, but, in case they're not, let me describe them in more detail.
>
> **Word processing helps you increase your productivity in at least three ways.** It will help you increase entry speed, increase revision speed, and decrease the time you spend proofing.
>
> **First, you can enter the first draft of a document into a word processing system at least 30 percent faster than you can type it.** As you create the first draft, you can correct your typing errors as you go, so the printed draft will have fewer errors than it would have had if you typed it.

Figure 8-6 The first two paragraphs in the topic on word processing after they have been revised into three paragraphs with the topic sentence first in each paragraph

graph, and (2) that you should start every paragraph with a topic sentence.

In practice, though, you can't always start your paragraphs with topic sentences. Often, business ideas are so complex that it's difficult to express them in a single sentence. Then, the best you can do is to start your paragraph with a sentence that *suggests* the idea you're trying to get across. You use the other sentences in the paragraph to develop the idea suggested by your opening sentence.

Also, if you start every paragraph with a topic sentence, you may be omitting some of the transitions that make your writing easier to read and understand. For instance, the first sentence in the second paragraph in figure 8-1 provides a transition from the first paragraph. Then, the second sentence of the second paragraph gives the idea of the paragraph. If I had omitted the first sentence, you would have had a harder time following the sequence of my ideas.

For those reasons, you shouldn't worry about starting each paragraph with a topic sentence. Instead, you should be content to start each paragraph with a sentence that either (1) presents or suggests the idea of the paragraph or (2) provides a transition from the previous paragraph. Sometimes, your starting sentences will do both.

How to write special kinds of paragraphs

Now, I'll show you how to write some special kinds of paragraphs. In particular, I'll show you how to write introductory paragraphs, paragraphs that present dialogue, and paragraphs that present lists.

Paragraphs that introduce topics, subtopics, and other paragraphs   Earlier in this chapter, I told you to watch for paragraphs with fewer than three sentences. I want you to know now that this doesn't necessarily apply to introductory paragraphs. It's still a good rule to remember, but if you see no reason for developing an introductory paragraph beyond one or two sentences, that's acceptable.

When you write an introductory paragraph, you think more in terms of purpose than main idea. In general, the purpose of an introductory paragraph is to introduce topics, subtopics, or a series of paragraphs. For instance, the purpose of the first paragraph in figure 8-1 is to introduce the next five paragraphs. Although this paragraph contains only two sentences, it prepares the reader for the paragraphs that follow. As a result, it is an acceptable paragraph.

Similarly, the first paragraph in figure 8-7 introduces three topics or subtopics that are identified by headings. It simply points to the headings that follow so readers can see where they are being led. This introductory paragraph contains only two sentences, and the idea of the paragraph is actually developed by the three topics that follow.

If you're writing a paragraph that introduces a series of ideas, you can include the first idea of the series in the paragraph. For instance, the second paragraph in figure 8-1 introduces three ways that word processing helps you increase productivity, and it also presents the first one. However, you can also introduce a series with an introductory paragraph that stands alone as in figure 8-6. Perhaps this second way is more in keeping with the principles of paragraphing, but either way is acceptable.

Paragraphs that present dialogue   You probably have been taught that you should start a new paragraph each time the speaker changes when you present dialogue. This is illustrated by the first example in figure 8-8. Fiction writers normally obey this rule.

For business writing, though, it's often acceptable and even appropriate to compress dialogue into a single paragraph as long as it all relates to the single idea you're trying to present. The second example in figure 8-8 shows what I mean. Here, the point of the para-

---

> The three types of software that all managers should be trained to use are: word processing software, electronic spreadsheet software, and business graphics software. I will introduce each of these now.
>
> **Word processing software**
>
> This is the most important type of software for business writers. It can . . .
>
> **Electronic spreadsheet software**
>
> Spreadsheet software is also important for business writers. It is . . .
>
> **Business graphics software**
>
> As business graphics software improves, business writers are using it with greater frequency. Today, it is . . .

Figure 8-7 A paragraph that introduces three subtopics

---

graph is that the employee was unnecessarily defensive about his education, and the dialogue serves to establish that point.

Paragraphs that present numbered lists *Numbered lists* are common in business documents. "There are four reasons why we should reject the Webster proposal." "There are three steps you must take to start this machine." And so on. When you use a numbered list, it's easy to refer to reason 4, for example, or step 3, so your writing has a structure that's easy to follow.

Figure 8-9 illustrates four ways to handle numbered lists. Often, as in the first example, the best way to present the items in a list is to present them as complete sentences using the connecting words *first, second,* and so on. If each item in the list requires more than a sentence, you can treat each item as a separate paragraph. This is illustrated by the second, third, and fourth paragraphs in figure 8-1.

If you want to draw attention to the items in a list, you can set them off from the paragraph as shown in the third and fourth examples in figure 8-9. That way your readers can quickly refer to the

How to write effective paragraphs

Dialogue as presented in fiction

When I felt that my guest was comfortable, I got to the point of our meeting. I explained that I was trying to get background for some advertising literature about him. Then, I said, "How about starting with some biographical data."

My guest replied, "To begin with, I didn't go to college."

Surprised that he would start with such a negative statement, I asked, "Do you think that has limited your advancement in business?"

He replied, "No, not at all."

Isn't it curious how people give themselves away?

Dialogue as it may be presented in business writing

When I felt that my guest was comfortable, I got to the point of our meeting. I explained that I was trying to get background for some advertising literature about him. Then, I said, "How about starting with some biographical data." To my surprise, my guest replied, "To begin with, I didn't go to college." Then, when I asked whether he thought that had limited his advancement, he replied, "No, not at all." Isn't it curious how people give themselves away?

Figure 8-8   Two ways to present dialogue in business documents

numbered items later on. Lists like these are often used in letters and memos.

When you use numbered lists, be sure to punctuate them correctly. When you use an embedded list with numbers in parentheses, use semicolons to separate the items if the items are full sentences or if any of the items contain commas. Otherwise, use commas to separate the items, as shown in the second example in figure 8-9.

If the items in a set-off list are complete sentences, use a period at the end of each item as in the fourth example in figure 8-9. If they're not complete sentences, do not use periods as in the third example. If the items in a list are mixed (some are complete sentences, some aren't), use a period at the end of each item.

An embedded list with full sentences

In summary, word processing can improve your productivity in at least three ways. First, it can increase your typing speed. Second, it can increase your revision speed. Third, it can reduce the amount of time you spend proofing. In addition, word processing can provide other benefits such as spelling verification and repeat letter typing.

An embedded list with numbered phrases

In summary, word processing can improve your productivity by: (1) increasing your typing speed, (2) increasing your revision speed, and (3) reducing the amount of time you spend proofing. In addition, word processing can provide other benefits such as spelling verification and repeat letter typing.

A set-off list with items that are phrases

In summary, word processing can improve your productivity by:

1. Increasing your typing speed
2. Increasing your revision speed
3. Reducing the amount of time you spend proofing

In addition, word processing can provide other benefits such as spelling verification and repeat letter typing.

A set-off list with items that are full sentences

In summary, word processing can improve your productivity in three ways:

1. It can increase your typing speed.
2. It can increase your revision speed.
3. It can reduce the amount of time you spend proofing.

In addition, word processing can provide other benefits such as spelling verification and repeat letter typing.

Figure 8-9 Four ways to present numbered lists

Although there are times when mixed items can't be avoided, you should try to make the items in your lists as parallel in structure as possible. For instance, you shouldn't create a list like this:

1. By increasing your typing speed.
2. It can increase your revision speed.
3. By helping you to reduce proofing time.

In this case, it's easy to rewrite the items so they're parallel in structure as in the fourth example in figure 8-9. Then, the items won't be mixed, and the list will be easier to read.

Because business writers use numbered lists so frequently, you must be careful to make sure all your lists are sensible. So often, I come upon lists that are illogical or foolish. For example, look at the list in figure 8-10. Here, the author tried to list all of the ways you can start writing a document. But the list is so long and the items are so cryptic that the list is overwhelming. Also, there's considerable overlap and duplication in the list items. Aren't "illustration" and "example" the same? How do "scope" and "point of view" differ? Finally, what good does it do to include an item like "miscellaneous"? Too many lists end with an item like this in an attempt to include everything. In effect, the item says "everything not accounted for by the previous list items."

So here's my advice on using lists. First, watch out for lists that consist of more than six or seven items. After that many items, a reader's mind starts to wander so it's tempting to skip the list altogether. Second, make sure all of the items in the list pertain to the purpose of the list. Third, combine duplicates and eliminate overlap in the list. If you do these three things and if you use the formats shown in figure 8-9, you'll use numbered lists effectively.

Paragraphs that present unnumbered lists Obviously, an *unnumbered list* is a list that isn't numbered. Although unnumbered lists aren't used as frequently as numbered lists in business writing, there are times when unnumbered lists are useful. In particular, unnumbered lists are useful in advertisements and other marketing documents.

Figure 8-11 shows two examples of unnumbered lists. Since the punctuation rules for unnumbered lists are the same as those for numbered lists, the embedded items in the first example in figure 8-11 are separated by semicolons. The set-off items in the second example end in periods.

> Because starting can be difficult, I am now going to present 19 ways to start a document. They are as follows:
>
> 1. Summary
> 2. Scope
> 3. Point of view
> 4. Specific details
> 5. Purpose
> 6. Plan of development
> 7. Problem
> 8. Background
> 9. Quotation
> 10. Question
> 11. Interest
> 12. Comparison
> 13. Definition and classification
> 14. Illustration
> 15. Action
> 16. Forecast
> 17. Humor
> 18. Example
> 19. Miscellaneous
>
> When you're through with this chapter, you can use this list to help you get started.

Figure 8-10 A list that is too cumbersome to be useful

When you use an unnumbered list, you imply to some extent that the order of items isn't sequential. In other words, you're *not* listing the four steps of a procedure or the five benefits of something in order of importance. Nevertheless, the sequence of items in an unnumbered list should be as logical as possible. If, for example, you're listing benefits, you should list the items in the sequence that you think represents their decreasing order of importance, even if this order is debatable. If you're listing tasks, you should list them in sequence as they are usually done. Occasionally, it makes sense to list items in increasing order of importance. And sometimes, the sequence just doesn't seem to matter. Whenever possible, though, put your numbered and unnumbered lists in a sequence that makes sense.

> **An embedded list**
>
> To get the most from your microcomputer, you must do three things: learn to type well; use the computer system for most of your writing tasks; and enter your own data and text into the system. If you do all three, the microcomputer will have a dramatic effect on your writing. If you don't, you will miss some of the most important benefits of microcomputing.
>
> **A set-off list with items that are highlighted by asterisks**
>
> To get the most from your microcomputer you must do three things:
>
> * Learn to type well.
> * Use the computer system for most of your writing tasks.
> * Enter your own data and text into the system.
>
> If you do all three, the microcomputer will have a dramatic effect on your writing. If you don't, you will miss some of the most important benefits of microcomputing.

Figure 8-11 Two ways to present unnumbered lists

Three more ideas about paragraphing

If you apply the ideas you've learned so far in this chapter, you'll write effective paragraphs. But here are three more ideas that may help you write more effective paragraphs.

How to plan the paragraphs you're going to write   As I explained in chapters 2 and 4, I recommend that you list the ideas of the paragraphs you intend to write before you start to write them. We call this listing of paragraphs a *paragraph plan*. For instance, figure 8-12 presents two paragraph plans for a topic on the benefits of word processing. The first plan consists of three paragraphs; the second plan consists of seven. Either plan is acceptable; it depends on your definitions of audience and purpose.

Now that you know the principles of paragraphing, you should be able to develop effective paragraph plans using handwriting, word processing, or an outline processor. Because a paragraph plan is a working paper that you will throw away when your document is finished, the paragraph descriptions only have to be meaningful to

Plan 1

1. Introduction
2. Increased productivity
3. Improved writing effectiveness

Plan 2

1. Introduction to increased productivity
2. Increased entry speed
3. Increased revision speed
4. Reduced proofing
5. Introduction to improved effectiveness
6. Benefits related to increased productivity
7. Other less obvious benefits

Figure 8-12 Two paragraph plans for a topic on the benefits of word processing

you. As long as they indicate the main ideas or purposes of the paragraphs you intend to write, they will be a useful guide for your writing.

The effect of paragraph length on reading ease Look back to figure 8-3. It presents the six paragraphs of figure 8-1 as three paragraphs. The problem is that the three paragraphs in figure 8-3 aren't as easy to read as the six paragraphs in figure 8-1. Clearly, there's a relationship between paragraph length and reading ease: When paragraphs are too long, they're difficult to read.

As a rule of thumb for business writing, I recommend that you watch out for paragraphs that consist of more than seven sentences or more than 15 printed lines. On that basis, you should consider rewriting two of the three paragraphs in figure 8-3. You can usually rewrite a long paragraph into two or more paragraphs without violating the principles of paragraphing. This is illustrated by the paragraphs in figure 8-1. You just divide one large paragraph idea into its components.

If that rule of thumb seems too arbitrary, here's the advice of E. B. White and William Strunk, Jr. as taken from their classic book on writing called *The Elements of Style*. They say that good paragraphing "calls for a good eye as well as a logical mind." So when you see a single paragraph that's a half-page long, let your eye tell you that you should divide it into two or more paragraphs.

Four ways to organize paragraphs   In general, you can organize a paragraph in four different ways. These methods of organization are illustrated in figure 8-13. After I describe these methods, I'll explain why it doesn't help your writing much to know what they are.

The first method of organization is called the *order of support*. In this case, you present an idea or statement in the first sentence of a paragraph, and you use the other sentences in the paragraph to support it. This organization is the one you should use most of the time for business writing.

The second method of organization is called the *order of climax*. Here, you start the paragraph by presenting the facts or supporting details. You end the paragraph by summarizing or drawing a conclusion. You should use this structure infrequently so it has additional impact when you do use it.

The third and fourth organizations are called *narrative* and *description*. A narrative paragraph tells about something that has happened. A descriptive paragraph describes some person, place, or thing. If you're like most business writers, you won't write many narrative or descriptive paragraphs.

I've presented these organizational methods because you'll often find them in other books on writing. However, they're not that useful for two reasons. First, they don't provide for all types of paragraphs. Second, you don't think about them when you're writing. For instance, you don't think to yourself: Should I write a narrative paragraph or a paragraph organized by order of climax? Instead, you concentrate on the idea you're trying to present in the paragraph. If you do, you'll write paragraphs using each organizational method, and you'll write paragraphs that combine two or more of the methods. This will happen naturally.

Two examples of paragraphing problems

I hope by now you have a good idea of what you should be trying to do when you write paragraphs. But perhaps two examples of poor paragraphing will help refine your thinking.

Order of support

Word processing can help you double your writing productivity. It can increase your basic typing speed by 30 percent or more. It can improve your efficiency when revising. And it can reduce the amount of proofing you have to do as you go from the first draft of a document to the final draft.

Order of climax

Word processing differs substantially from typing. By using word processing, you can increase your basic typing speed by 30 percent or more. You can improve your efficiency when revising a manuscript by 100 percent or more. And you can reduce the amount of proofing you have to do as you go from the first draft of a document to the final draft. In short, word processing can help you double your writing productivity.

Narrative

Before I tell you more about word processing, let me reminisce a bit. When I first got into the publishing industry some 20 years ago, all of the staff writers were given IBM Selectric typewriters. Most of us were excited to get what was then the most advanced typewriter ever created. But not our editor-in-chief. He had a manual (yes, manual) typewriter that he had been using for years, and he didn't see how a Selectric could improve his performance.

Description

A small word processing system usually consists of four components. The television-like screen is called a *monitor*; it displays the data that has been entered into the system. The data is entered into the system through the *keyboard*, which is right in front of the monitor. The keyboard is like a typewriter keyboard, but it includes some functional control keys, and it may include a ten-key entry pad for numeric data. To the left or the right of the keyboard and monitor, you'll find a *printer*. The printer prints the data that has been entered into the system whenever the operator wants to print it. The fourth component of the system is the *electronics unit*. It is the box-like unit that you may find under the monitor, on the side of the desk, or standing on its side on the floor.

Figure 8-13 Four ways to organize paragraphs

> Many managers have suggested that zero-base budgeting be renamed "zero-base planning" or "zero-base planning and budgeting" because the process requires effective planning and immediately shows up any lack of planning. The planning and budgeting process can be contrasted as follows: *Planning* identifies the *output* required; *budgeting* identifies the *input* required. Planning is more general than budgeting. Planning establishes programs, sets goals and objectives, and makes basic policy decisions for the organization as a whole. Budgeting analyzes in detail the many functions or activities that the organization must perform to implement each program, analyzes the alternatives within each activity to achieve the end product desired, and identifies the trade-offs between partial or complete achievement of the established goals and the associated costs. The relationship between planning and budgeting is dynamic because the resources required to achieve the desired goals are not unlimited. Therefore, we must determine whether achieving the last 10% of each goal requires 25% of the cost, or vice versa; whether we can achieve each goal; and whether we must eliminate and/or reduce some goals. If we fixed our goals, the zero-base budgeting process would be a suboptimization tool, telling us how best to achieve the given results. However, the realistic requirement to modify goals based on a cost/benefit analysis makes the zero-base budgeting process both a suboptimization and total-optimization tool.

Figure 8-14   A paragraph with more than one idea

Example 1: A paragraph with more than one idea   Figure 8-14 is a typical paragraph that presents more than one idea. It appears to me that the writer started out to explain how planning and budgeting are related, but got sidetracked somewhere along the way. By the end of the paragraph, he's talking about suboptimization and total-optimization tools.

If I were to rewrite this paragraph, I would divide it into at least three paragraphs: one on planning, one on budgeting, and one on the relationships between the two. To be sure, the paragraph in figure 8-14 has other problems that make it ineffective. But if it were rewritten so the principles of paragraphing were followed, most of those problems would go away.

One result of having more than one idea in a paragraph is that the ideas are usually not developed well. For instance, I don't think the ideas about planning and budgeting are supported adequately in figure 8-14. And I have no idea what an optimization tool is, let alone a suboptimization tool. If these ideas were presented in separate paragraphs, I think this lack of support would be obvious.

Example 2: Poorly developed paragraphs that don't present useful information   Figure 8-15 presents a topic that contains six poorly developed paragraphs. This is typical of much of the writing in business.

To me, the problem with this writing is that it doesn't tell me anything. Although the study is about teachers and professors, most of the facts are true for any profession: salaries are important; salaries are going up; there are regional variations in salaries; and benefits are going up too. When you're presenting data like this, you have an obligation to show what its significance is. How do the salaries compare with those in other fields? Why does it matter that more teachers than professors have second incomes? Without this kind of supporting detail, you have an empty presentation that could be presented more effectively in a series of charts.

When you analyze your paragraphs using the procedure that I presented in chapter 6, you should make sure not only that each paragraph has an idea, but also that each idea is worth presenting. For instance, the main idea in the first paragraph is something like: salaries are important. But isn't that obvious? Wouldn't it be better to combine the ideas of the first two paragraphs in an opening paragraph like this:

> In the teaching profession, salaries help hire and hold competent people just as in any other profession. As a result, I'm pleased to report that salaries have been going up over the last ten years. The average salary for teachers in public schools has gone up 80% in this period. The average for college professors has gone up 76%. And the average for college instructors has gone up 67%.

Although this still doesn't say that much, it's at least an acceptable beginning for the topic.

When you find that your paragraphs don't present useful ideas or that they aren't fully developed, you may conclude that you need to do more research. In fact, the problem with much business and technical writing is that the writers don't know enough about their subjects. If that's your problem, you should get the specific information you need so you can write effective paragraphs. Sometimes, though, you

How to write effective paragraphs

> Salary, probably more than any other factor, determines the relative strength or weakness of any occupational group to attract and hold competent persons. The financial reward offered to members of the teaching profession is thus a critical issue.
>
> During the ten year period, the mean annual salary of the instructional staff in public schools increased 80%. The median salary for full professors increased 76%. College instructors showed the smallest increase, 67%.
>
> Regional differences in mean salaries paid are still very marked, varying as much as $4,000. The mean salary of the instructional staff in public schools in the East South Central and West South Central is the lowest. The Pacific region is the highest, followed by the Middle Atlantic region.
>
> A higher percentage of teachers have second incomes. The chief source of supplementary income is additional teaching in summer sessions and tutoring.
>
> In addition to rising salaries, benefits are rising. Some types of benefits offered are life insurance, health and accident insurance, and sabbatical leaves.
>
> According to the Census Bureau, the higher the grade or college year a woman is teaching, the more likely she is to be single. The level of teaching does not seem to affect the marital status of men significantly.

Figure 8-15 Poorly developed paragraphs that don't present useful information

already have the information you need; you just haven't obeyed the principles of paragraphing.

Discussion

Figure 8-16 presents the principles and rules of thumb for effective paragraphing. If you follow these recommendations, you should be able to write effective paragraphs. But the sentences within your paragraphs may be awkward, wordy, and hard to read. If they are, your paragraphs will be less effective than they should be. That's why the next chapter will show you how to write effective sentences that are easy to read.

The principles of paragraphing

1. Put one and only one idea in each paragraph.
2. Develop the idea of each paragraph fully.
3. Start each paragraph with a sentence that gives the idea of the paragraph or a sentence that provides a transition from the previous paragraph.

Rules of thumb

1. If your paragraphs don't contain three or more sentences, it's a sign that they aren't fully developed. Exceptions: paragraphs that introduce topics, subtopics, or other paragraphs.
2. If your paragraphs are more than seven sentences or 15 typewritten lines long, it's a sign that they should be presented as two or more paragraphs. Otherwise, the paragraph length may affect readability.

Figure 8-16 A summary of the principles and rules of thumb for effective paragraphing

Terms

topic sentence
numbered list
unnumbered list
order of support
order of climax
narrative paragraph
descriptive paragraph

Objectives

1. List the principles of paragraphing.

2. Write paragraphs that adhere to the principles of paragraphing and rules of thumb presented in this chapter.

Heading plan for chapter 9

The least you should know about readability measurement
- The Flesch Readability Formula
- The Gunning Fog Index
- How to measure readability with your PC
- The limitations of readability measures
- An appropriate reading level for business documents

Four guidelines for shortening your sentences
- Put one and only one thought in each sentence
- Use the simple expression
- Use fewer adjectives and adverbs
- Remove unnecessary words

Four guidelines for simplifying your words
- Use common words whenever possible
- Avoid words with prefixes and suffixes
- Avoid technical terms and jargon
- Avoid elegant variation

Five guidelines for expressing your exact meaning
- Be specific
- Use the active voice
- Avoid figurative language
- Avoid trite expressions
- Avoid nouns used as adjectives

Discussion

Chapter 9

How to write readable sentences

If you want your documents to be effective, you must select useful content, organize it well, and present it in a series of fully developed paragraphs. Within those paragraphs, though, you must make sure that your sentences are written at a reading level that is appropriate for your audience.

To illustrate this point, figure 9-1 presents three writing samples. If you read them, you'll discover that the reading level increases in difficulty from the first sample to the third. The first sample was taken from a classic book on writing; it is easy to read. The other samples were taken from actual business documents. In my opinion, they are too difficult to read for their intended audiences. As a result, they aren't effective.

When you write a business document, reading ease is an important consideration. This factor is often referred to as the *readability* of a document. The easier a document is to read, the better its readability.

In this chapter, I'll show you how to improve the readability of your writing. First, I'll tell you what you need to know about readability measurement. Then, I'll present some guidelines for improving the readability of your writing. When you finish this chapter, you should be able to write sentences at a reading level that is appropriate for any of your intended audiences.

**The least you should know
about readability measurement**

In 1946, Rudolf Flesch wrote *The Art of Plain Talk*. In this book, Mr. Flesch analyzed the business writing of the time and pointed out why most business documents were so hard to read and understand. He also identified the factors that affect reading ease, and he offered a formula for measuring the readability of a document. In a 1949 book called *The Art of Readable Writing*, Mr. Flesch presented a revised formula for measuring readability that he felt was easier to use than his original formula.

During the last 40 years, Rudolf Flesch's ideas have had a significant influence on business writing. As a result, most memos and letters are easier to read and understand today than they were 30 years ago. For example, few correspondents today write: "Enclosed please find the check in the amount of $220.50 as per our telephone conversation of Wednesday, March 23." A modern correspondent says something like: "Here's the check I promised you."

Today, if you want to measure the readability of your writing, you can do so in several ways. For instance, you can still use the original Flesch formula. Or, you can use any one of several other readability formulas that are in common use. If you use a PC for your writing, you can quickly measure readability by using one of the writing analysis programs available for your system.

No matter how you measure readability, you should realize that the primary factors that affect it are (1) sentence length and (2) word difficulty. If you shorten your sentences and simplify your words, the readability of your writing improves. And vice versa. That's what Mr. Flesch said back in the 1940s, and that's still true today.

To give you a better understanding of readability, I'm now going to present two readability formulas in more detail: the original Flesch Readability Formula and the Gunning Fog Index. Next, I'll describe two writing analyzers that measure readability on a PC. Then, I'll present some of the limitations of readability measurement. I'll finish by recommending an appropriate reading level for your business documents.

The Flesch Readability Formula   Figure 9-2 presents the 10 steps of the Flesch Readability Formula. Although we don't recommend that you use this formula, I thought you should be familiar with it anyway. In step 1, you select one or more 100-word samples from the document you're going to analyze. You do this no matter

How to write readable sentences

Sample 1: From *The Art of Readable Writing* by Rudolf Flesch

What it all comes down to is this. Good openings and endings don't just happen. And you can't produce them by applying mechanical rules either. The best way to convey your ideas to a reader is to plan carefully the beginning, middle, and end—sounding the main theme at the beginning, echoing it at the end, and developing it by natural steps in the middle. This is the point at which most textbooks go into pages and pages on how to make an outline, laying down rules and formulas and whatnot. I don't think anybody has ever profited from these rules. Usually they deal with Roman numerals and lowercase letters rather than writing.

Sample 2: From a police department manual on report writing

For all other witnesses, including the victim, be cautious about reporting direct quotes and minute details of their statements. At trial, you will not be able to testify as to what a witness told you (hearsay), except for limited purposes, such as impeachment. If your report shows the victim said something that conflicts with his testimony, you may be called as a *defense* witness to prove that a prosecution witness made a "prior inconsistent statement." Therefore, you should be very sure you are correctly attributing a precise detail to the *right* witness— double check it with the witness before leaving the scene, and be sure your notes are clear.

Sample 3: From a curriculum recommendation in computer information systems

The curriculum guidelines have implications primarily for four-year undergraduate programs commonly offered through schools of business or through applied computer science programs that require a concentration of business courses in support of the computer-oriented courses of study. The recommendations also apply to two-year community college data processing programs where transfer credit towards CIS programs is offered. The guidelines recognize the need for articulation between these two-and four-year programs as well as the value of having terminal degree programs at both levels.

Figure 9-1 Writing samples at three levels of readability

How to use the Flesch Readability Formula

1. Select one or more random samples of at least 100 words from the document.

2. Count the number of words in each sample. Contractions and hyphenated words count as one word. Count numbers and letters as one word too. For instance, 27,419 counts as one word and C.O.D. counts as one word.

3. Count the number of sentences in each sample. Try to count units of thoughts rather than sentences marked off by periods. Sometimes, for example, units of thought are marked off by semicolons or colons. However, a compound sentence joined by a conjunction like *and* or *but* counts as one sentence.

4. Count the number of syllables in each sample. Count the syllables as you pronounce the words when reading aloud, not necessarily as they are spelled. Do this for letters, numbers, and symbols also.

5. Calculate the average sentence length in each sample. To do this, divide the number of words in the sample by the number of sentences.

6. Calculate the average number of syllables per hundred words. To do this, divide the number of syllables by the number of words in the sample and multiply by 100.

7. Multiply the average sentence length, from step 5, by 1.015.

8. Multiply the number of syllables per hundred words, from step 6, by .846.

9. Add the numbers you got in steps 7 and 8. Write down the total: _____

10. Subtract this total from 206.835:

	206.835
Total from step 9	− _____

The difference is your reading-ease
score. It should be a number between
0 and 100.   _____

Figure 9-2   How to use the Flesch Readability Formula

what formula you're going to use. In steps 2 through 4, you count the words, sentences, and syllables in each sample. In steps 5 through 10, you perform the calculations that lead you to the "reading ease" score for each sample. This score should range from a low of zero, which means the sample is extremely difficult to read, to a high of 100, which means the sample is extremely easy to read.

If you apply this formula to a sample from your own writing, you'll discover that it is both difficult and time-consuming to use. You also have to wonder about the constants that the formula uses: 1.015, .846, and 206.835. Can readability really be measured precisely down to three decimal places? Nevertheless, this formula was a starting point for the measurement of readability.

If you look ahead to figure 9-4, you'll find the reading-ease scores for the three writing samples in figure 9-1. As you would expect, the first sample had the highest score at 64, the third sample had the lowest score at 13, and the second sample scored in between the two at 45. You can see, then, that this formula does lead to scores that reflect the relative reading ease of typical business documents.

The Gunning Fog Index   If you want to measure the readability of your writing and you have to do it by hand, I recommend that you use the Gunning Fog Index. It's somewhat easier to use than the Flesch formula, and it gives you a score, or index, that reflects a grade level in school. As a result, you can more easily relate the score to your intended audience.

Figure 9-3 presents the seven steps for calculating the Gunning Fog Index. In steps 1 through 3, you select a sample and count the words and sentences. In step 4, you count the number of difficult words (those of three syllables or more), but you don't count capitalized words, compound words, or verbs that have three syllables because of *ed* or *es* endings. Then, in steps 5 through 7, you perform the calculations that lead you to the Gunning Fog Index for each sample.

In figure 9-4, you can see the indexes for the writing samples in figure 9-1. The first sample has an index of 12, which means it is written at a twelfth grade reading level. In contrast, the second sample has an index of 17 (first year of graduate school), and the third sample has an index of 21 (last year of a doctoral program?). This shows that the Gunning Fog Index correlates fairly well with the Flesch reading ease scores for these samples. Sample 1 is clearly the easiest one to read; sample 3 is clearly the most difficult one to read; and sample 2 is somewhere in between.

How to use the Gunning Fog Index

1. Select one or more random samples of at least 100 words from the document.

2. Count the number of words in each sample.

3. Count the number of sentences in each sample.

4. Count the number of difficult words in each sample. Words of three syllables or more are counted as difficult words. But don't count (1) words that are capitalized, (2) compound words that are made up of easy words like *timekeeper*, and (3) verbs that are made into three syllables by adding *ed* or *es* as in *dictated* or *successes*.

5. Calculate the average number of words per sentence in each sample. To do this, divide the number of words by the number of sentences.

6. Calculate the percentage of difficult words in each sample. To do this, divide the number of difficult words by the number of words and multiply by 100.

7. Calculate the grade level at which the writing is easily read. To do this, add the factors you derived in steps 5 and 6 and multiply by .4.

Figure 9-3 How to calculate the Gunning Fog Index

How to measure readability with your PC When you use a PC for your writing, you can quickly and easily measure the readability of a writing sample or a complete document. To do so, you run one of the programs for writing analysis. On my system, for example, I have two writing analyzers: *RightWriter* and *Grammatik III*. When run on the three writing samples in figure 9-1, these programs calculated the *reading grade levels* (*RGLs*) shown in figure 9-4.

Both of these programs use one of the Flesch-Kincaid formulas to calculate the reading grade level of a document. This formula is used by many government agencies. For instance, the Department of Defense requires its use by all contractors that produce manuals for the armed services.

Grammatik III also calculates two other readability scores. It calculates a "Flesch reading ease" score based upon the Flesch Readability Formula of figure 9-2. These scores are still used by the insur-

	RightWriter Flesch-Kincaid RGL	Grammatik III Flesch-Kincaid RGL	Grammatik III Gunning Fog Index	Grammatik III Reading Ease Score
Sample 1	8.56	9	12	64
Sample 2	13.51	14	17	45
Sample 3	17.53	18	21	13

Figure 9-4 Readability scores for the three writing samples in figure 9-1

ance industry to rate the readability of insurance policies. In addition, *Grammatik III* calculates a Gunning Fog Index based on the formula in 9-3.

The limitations of readability measures Whenever you measure the readability of a document, you should realize the limitations of these measures. Yes, they give you an indication of how readable a document is, but you've got to keep these scores in perspective. In particular, you should realize that the scores are affected by the formulas used, the way sentences are counted, the way word difficulty is measured, and the writing samples used. But let me explain.

First, readability scores always depend on how the scores are calculated. If, for example, you refer to the grade level scores in figure 9-4, you can see that the scores for sample 1 range from grade 8.56 to grade 12. Similarly, the RGLs for sample 2 range from 13.51 to 17.

Second, the rules for determining sentence length are somewhat arbitrary. For instance, these words are counted as one sentence by both the *RightWriter* and *Grammatik III* programs:

The members of the committee reviewed the three systems;
then, they made a decision.

But the same words are counted as two sentences if they're written this way:

The members of the committee reviewed the three systems.
Then, they made a decision.

That means that all you have to do to improve your readability scores when you're using either of these programs is to stop using semicolons. But that won't necessarily improve the actual readability of your writing.

Third, the rules for determining word difficulty are imprecise. For instance, the Flesch Readability Formula bases word difficulty on the average number of syllables per hundred words, while the Gunning Fog Index bases it on the number of words that contain three syllables or more. Yet, neither of these measures is an accurate representation of word difficulty. Sometimes shorter words are more difficult than their longer synonyms.

Fourth, the writing samples you use can have a dramatic effect on readability scores. For instance, we once sampled the third and fourth paragraphs from every other chapter of five business books to see what results we would get. Within a single book, it was common to see a variation of two or three grade levels from one sample to another. You should keep this in mind when you let a computer program calculate a score for an entire document. If, for example, the overall grade level score for a 15-page report is 12, individual paragraphs within the document may range from grades 9 through 15.

Because readability scores are so inexact, you should realize that a score of 8.56 doesn't mean that the writing is exactly at grade level 8.56. Similarly, you shouldn't think that a document with a score of 8.56 is one grade level easier to read than a document with a score of 9.74. Instead, you should treat a score of 8.56 as one that indicates a reading level ranging from grade 7 through 10, and perhaps even from grade 6 through 11. As a result, some parts of a document with a score of 8.56 will be easier to read than some parts of those in a document with a score of 9.74, and some parts will be harder to read.

Beyond these measurement limitations, many people criticize the concept of readability because readability scores can't insure comprehension. Way back in 1955, for example, one study showed only an 8 percent improvement in reader comprehension when a manual was rewritten from an RGL of 16 to an RGL of 12, and no further improvement when it was rewritten down to an RGL of 8. Since then, many other studies have shown that readability scores correlate poorly with reader comprehension.

No matter what the limitations, though, you can't afford to disregard the concepts of readability. Obviously, your writing can be superficial, unorganized, and ineffective, no matter what its RGL is. That's why the chapters in section 2 emphasize analysis and planning. On the other hand, if its RGL is too high, your writing can be ineffective even if it presents the right information in a well-organized manner.

An appropriate reading level for business documents For most business documents, we recommend an overall reading level of tenth grade or below. If you write a document at the tenth-grade level, individual paragraphs within the document may range in reading level from seventh grade to the first year of college. So if your writing scores much above the tenth-grade level, it becomes difficult to read even for good readers.

When I rated some writing samples from best-selling business books, I found that scores ranging from grade 11 to 15 were typical. That seems reasonable because the average reader for these books has had some college and is often a college graduate. But when I rated samples from ten business documents, I found scores ranging from grade 11.2 to 26.8. Yes, 26.8. And scores between 16 and 20 were common. With scores like that, it's not hard to explain why most business documents are ineffective.

In case you're interested, the overall reading grade level for each of the chapters in this book is tenth grade or below as measured by *RightWriter*. This chapter has an RGL of 8.51. And the two paragraphs before this one have an RGL of 8.06.

Four guidelines for shortening your sentences

One of the factors in all readability formulas is sentence length. As a result, if you shorten your sentences, your readability scores will improve. Here, then, are four guidelines that will help you write shorter, more readable sentences.

Put one and only one thought in each sentence Remember the first principle of paragraphing? It is to put one and only one idea in each paragraph. When a paragraph contains more than one idea, it becomes more difficult to read and understand.

The same principle applies to sentences. When a sentence contains more than one *thought*, it becomes more difficult to read and understand. Apparently, the mind works best when it tries to understand only one thought at a time. And the pauses that your readers take at the ends of your sentences allow them to accurately receive your thoughts. That's why the most important guideline for improving readability is to put one and only one thought in each sentence.

Figure 9-5 illustrates what I mean by putting one and only one thought in each sentence. In each of the three examples, the original sentence contained two or more thoughts. When I rewrote each one, I converted the original sentence into three new sentences that contained only one thought each.

As I rewrote the examples in figure 9-5, I reduced the average sentence length in each example by more than 50 percent. This in turn improved the readability scores dramatically. For instance, the original sentence in example 1 had an RGL of 15.02 as calculated by *RightWriter*, but the three-sentence revision has an RGL of 6.53.

As you write sentences with only one thought in each, you sometimes ask yourself where one thought ends and another begins. But this is often debatable. As a result, you should use your eye for making these decisions as well as your mind. When one of your sentences becomes four or more typewritten lines long, you should divide the thought you're trying to express into two or more thoughts. Then, you put each thought in a single sentence.

Use the simple expression   Expressions like "in regard to your letter of," "enclosed please find," and "in the event of" are carried over from the formal days of business. But they no longer fit our style of living. Today, we still want to be courteous, but in an efficient, straightforward manner.

Figure 9-6 lists some wordy expressions along with simpler ones. If you use the simpler expressions, you'll make an immediate improvement in your writing. Whenever you choose a simple expression instead of a wordy one, you shorten your sentence and improve its readability.

To illustrate, the first example in figure 9-7 presents a sentence that uses a wordy expression. By substituting *since* for *due to the fact that*, sentence length is reduced by four words with no loss in meaning. This in turn reduced the RGL by about one grade level.

Use fewer adjectives and adverbs   Most business writers use too many adjectives and adverbs. In other words, they try to get their ideas across with modifiers when they should use nouns and verbs that create images in the reader's mind.

The second example in figure 9-7 illustrates this problem. By deleting six adjectives and adverbs, I have improved the readability of the sentence with no loss in meaning. In this case, the six adjectives and adverbs can simply be deleted because they don't enrich the thought of the sentence. To remove the adjectives and adverbs in

Put one and only one thought in each sentence

Example 1
RGL=15.02

Our new agency program, which has the support of all branch managers and which will be the basis for all sales activities in the coming year, represents a much-needed change in our policies.

Improvement
RGL=6.53

Our new agency program represents a much-needed change in our policies. It provides the basis for all of our sales activities in the coming year. And all of our branch managers support it.

Example 2
RGL=18.44

Because the discussion (one that was more a clash of personalities than an expression of ideas) lasted almost an hour without accomplishing anything, I suggest that you attend our next meeting to help resolve the conflict.

Improvement
RGL=9.26

In my opinion, the discussion was more a clash of personalities than an expression of ideas. As a result, it lasted almost an hour without accomplishing anything. That's why I suggest that you attend our next meeting to help resolve the conflict.

Example 3
RGL=28.13

Citing changes that would affect the auto insurance business, she pointed out that the California legislature is challenging companies which sell automobile insurance on a discriminating basis with discrimination being defined more broadly to include not only class and race, but also driver occupation and location within a particular geographic district.

Improvement
RGL=14.88

She started out by citing changes that would affect the auto insurance business. In particular, she pointed out that the California legislature is challenging companies which sell automobile insurance on a discriminating basis. When she defined discrimination, she said it included not only a person's class and race, but also his occupation and location within a particular geographic district.

Figure 9-5 The most important guideline for shortening your sentences

The wordy expression	The simple expression
pertaining to in reference to in regard to	about
enclosed please find	here is
in the event of	if
in the vicinity of	near
at this point in time	now
call your attention to	point out
bring to your attention	remind
due to the fact that	since
we would like to ask that you	please
be of assistance to	help
in order to	to
for the reason that	because
in lieu of	instead of
prior to	before
subsequent to	after
check in the amount of	check for

Figure 9-6   Some commonly used expressions and their simpler alternatives

> **Use the simple expression**
>
> **Original**
> RGL=10.78
> I'm sorry, but we can't allow the 2 percent discount you took due to the fact that we didn't receive your payment within 30 days from the invoice date.
>
> **Improvement**
> RGL=9.74
> I'm sorry, but we can't allow the 2 percent discount you took since we didn't receive your payment within 30 days from the invoice date.
>
> **Use fewer adjectives and adverbs**
>
> **Original**
> RGL=16.88
> I am actively working with several of our leading producers to develop more specific information about the failure of our highly regarded agency program.
>
> **Improvement**
> RGL=13.06
> I am working with several of our producers to develop information about the failure of our agency program.
>
> **Remove unnecessary words**
>
> **Original**
> RGL=14.42
> As this report shows, our salesmen have dealt with the matter of competing products in many creative and original ways in many different environments.
>
> **Improvement**
> RGL=8.35
> As this report shows, our salesmen have dealt with competing products in many creative ways.

Figure 9-7 Three more guidelines for shortening your sentences

other sentences, though, you may have to rewrite the sentences using nouns and verbs rather than adjectives and adverbs.

In general, business writers tend to overuse adverbs more than adjectives. For instance, I've received many letters like this during the last 15 years:

> We *sincerely* enjoyed meeting with you yesterday. We were *tremendously* impressed by your organization. And we *eagerly* await a response to our offer.

Here, the writer wants the adverbs to do the work for him. But the message would be just as strong without the adverbs:

We enjoyed meeting with you yesterday. We were impressed by your organization. And we await a response to our offer.

In fact, this message seems to be more sincere without the adverbs.

To cut down your use of adjectives and adverbs, just ask yourself whether each one is necessary. In general, you'll find that most adverbs are unnecessary because they don't add to the meanings of your sentences. You'll also find that many of your adjectives are unnecessary.

Remove unnecessary words   Grammarians refer to the unnecessary words in a sentence as *deadwood*. As I've just shown you, adjectives and adverbs are often deadwood. If you remove all of the deadwood in a sentence, the sentence has to be easier to read and understand because you make every word count.

Unfortunately, you would think that many business writers are getting paid by the word. For instance, look at the third example in figure 9-7. This is a sentence taken from an actual business document. To improve its readability, I simply removed all of the words that didn't add to the meaning of the sentence. Instead of a 24-word sentence, I ended up with a 15-word sentence that clearly expresses its thought.

In this example, the phrase, *the matter of*, adds nothing to the meaning of the sentence. But what about *and original*? In my opinion, *original* is the same as *creative* so you can use one word or the other, but there's no point in using both. As for the phrase *in many different environments*, this too is unnecessary. If the salesmen have sold their products in many creative ways, we can assume they've sold their products in many different environments.

To remove deadwood, you ask yourself whether each word and phrase in a sentence is necessary. Does it add to the meaning of your thought? If it doesn't, strike it out. The more words and phrases you remove, the shorter your sentences become and the easier they are to read.

Four guidelines for simplifying your words

The second factor in all readability formulas is word difficulty. As a result, if you simplify your words, your readability scores will improve. Here, then, are four guidelines for simplifying your words.

Use common words whenever possible It's clear to me that some people like complexity. In my business experience, the number of people who complicate things far outnumber those who simplify them. And the words they use tend to indicate which category they belong in.

When I write, I always try to use common, everyday words that my audience will understand. For instance, I write that I will "do" something rather than "perform" it. I "finish" something rather than "finalize" it. I "say" something rather than "articulate" it.

But the common word isn't always the shortest word. And sometimes it's simpler to use a phrase than a single word. For example, I say I will "illustrate" something rather than "depict" it. And I talk about "sentence structure," not "syntax."

The first example in figure 9-8 shows how easy it is to simplify your words by using common words whenever possible. Here, I just substituted *use* for *utilize* and *sent* for *submitted*. When I did this, I reduced the number of syllables in the sentence by four and thus improved its readability.

Avoid words with prefixes and suffixes Words like *indispensable* and *prefabrication* are made up of root words plus prefixes and suffixes. For instance, *indispensable* is based on the root word *dispense*, and *prefabrication* is based on the root word *fabric*. When you avoid words that have prefixes or suffixes, you are forced to use simpler, more common words in their place. As a result, your writing becomes easier to read.

To some extent, this guideline for simplifying your words is the same as the first one I gave you, because it forces you to use common words. However, this guideline expands on the first one because it asks you to avoid words with prefixes and suffixes even if they are common words. In general, words with prefixes and suffixes are more difficult to understand than those without because the prefixes and suffixes change the meanings of the root words.

In particular, you should look out for prefixes like *pre*, *re*, or *de*, and suffixes like *able*, *ation*, *ality*, *ability*, *ousness*, and *ization*. That's why I normally say *easier to read*, not *more readable*, and that's why I

Use common words

Original
RGL=5.81

I don't think we can utilize the product you submitted to us.

Improvement
RGL=1.87

I don't think we can use the product you sent to us.

Avoid words with prefixes and suffixes

Original
RGL=13.44

A study done by the purchasing department gives an indication that our expenses for office supplies are reducible by as much as 15 percent.

Improvement
RGL=11.85

A study done by the purchasing department indicates that we can reduce our expenses for office supplies by as much as 15 percent.

Avoid technical terms and jargon

Original
RGL=12.77

Our word processing package offers as much functionality as any competing package, and it's user friendly.

Improvement
RGL=9.79

Our word processing package offers all the functions of any competing package, and it's as easy to use.

Avoid elegant variation

Original
RGL=8.99

We just finished analyzing the study done by the purchasing department, and we don't agree with it. To start, the report presents some facts that are questionable. In addition, the document's analysis of the facts is illogical.

Improvement
RGL=8.43

We just finished analyzing the study done by the purchasing department, and we don't agree with it. To start, this study presents some facts that are questionable. In addition, its analysis of the facts is illogical.

Figure 9-8 Four guidelines for simplifying your words

normally avoid using a word like *readability*. In this book, though, I use the terms *readable* and *readability* because they are common writing terms and I thought you should know them.

The second example in figure 9-8 shows how this guideline can help you simplify your words. When I revised the original sentence, I first identified *indication* and *reducible* as two words that contain prefixes and suffixes. Then, I rewrote the sentence so I wouldn't have to use those words. When I did, I not only simplified the word usage, I also shortened the sentence by four words.

Avoid technical terms and jargon   As you write and edit, you should adapt your words to your readers' knowledge. In particular, you should avoid technical terms and jargon when you're writing for non-technical readers. Make sure you use words your readers understand.

To illustrate, the original sentence in the third example in figure 9-8 uses terms that aren't appropriate for a reader who isn't familiar with the jargon of the PC industry. Although the terms *functionality* and *user friendly* are commonly used in that industry, they mean little to someone who's unfamiliar with them. When I rewrote the sentence without the jargon, the RGL improved by almost three grade levels.

Of course, you can't avoid complicated or uncommon words when you write about some of the more technical business subjects. For instance, accounting has a language of its own. So do education, computing, and finance. But even when you write using the specialized vocabularies of your field, don't overdo it. In particular, you should try to keep the technical jargon to a minimum because it tends to be so imprecise. For instance, the term *user friendly* means easy-to-use. But does it also mean easy-to-learn? Does it also mean that entry mistakes will be easy to correct when you use the software? Instead of assuming that your readers will understand the implications, avoid the jargon and explain what you mean.

Avoid elegant variation   The term *elegant variation* was first used in H. W. Fowler's reference book, *Modern English Usage*. This refers to the practice of varying a word for the sake of variation. This often shows up when people write dialogue. Although *said* is the best verb for this purpose, they vary it elegantly like this:

> When I presented our offer, he flatly *said*, "I'm not interested." I *insisted*, "Well, maybe we can improve our offer." He finished the conversation when he *grunted*, "There's absolutely no way we can get together."

Although an occasional *replied* or *responded* is okay, there's no need for this type of variation. It can only reduce readability.

The original paragraph in the fourth example in figure 9-8 gives another example of elegant variation. It uses the words *study*, *report*, and *document* to refer to the report in question. However, this variation can only cause confusion. Is the report the same as the study, and is the document the same as the report?

The best way to avoid elegant variation is to use pointers or pronouns. You'll learn how to use them in the next chapter, and that's what I used when I rewrote the paragraph in the fourth example in figure 9-8. However, if pointers or pronouns don't work, it's better to repeat the original word than to vary the word. That may not show up in your readability score, but it will improve readability.

Five guidelines for expressing your exact meaning

One of the limitations of readability measurement is that you can write documents that score well even though they don't say what you mean. As a result, it's not enough to shorten your sentences and simplify your words. You must also write in a way that accurately expresses your ideas and thoughts. Here, then, are five guidelines that will help you express your exact meaning.

Be specific In the chapter on writing paragraphs, I told you that you should support your generalizations with specifics. That means some of the sentences within each paragraph should present the facts that support the idea of the paragraph. When you present those facts, you should be as specific as possible.

But business people often seem reluctant to be specific. "Our sales are increasing" is specific...to some extent. "Our sales have increased by 35 percent" is more specific. "Our sales have increased by 35 percent when compared with sales last year at this time" is specific enough to be useful. Do you see the improvement? If your

---

A paragraph that perhaps draws the wrong conclusion because it hasn't been specific

As I see it, the morale in the administrative department is at an all-time low. Absenteeism is high; turnover is high; and productivity is low. We must do something and do it soon.

The paragraph rewritten so it presents the facts

I think we might have some morale problems in the administrative department. Absenteeism has increased from 3.2 percent last year to 3.4 percent this year. Turnover has increased from 12.0 percent to 13.1 percent. On the other hand, productivity in terms of cost per thousand orders has stayed about the same. Do you think this is worth looking into?

Figure 9-9 Be specific

sentences leave the reader wondering, you're not being specific enough.

When we don't use specifics, we confuse our readers and even ourselves. We need facts to help us order our world. Several years ago, for example, our administrative manager told me we were getting "all sorts of complaints" about billing problems. Since we had just installed a new computer system, she assumed there was something wrong with its programs.

Before I could help, I needed more information. So I asked her to tell me how many bills we had issued since the system was installed and how many complaints we had received. In addition, I asked her to get copies of the bills and correspondence related to the complaints. As it turned out, we had issued around 5,000 bills since we installed the new system, and we had received only seven complaints. Of these, only two were related to programming. Somehow "all sorts of complaints" didn't seem to be the right description once we knew the facts.

Figure 9-9 shows how being specific can help you say what you mean. In the improved version, the writer gives the facts he omitted in the original version. By being specific, his conclusion seems to have changed.

When you make an effort to be specific, you often find that your view of a situation changes. For instance, when you start to write a report, you sometimes think you have a clear idea of what your conclusions are going to be. But when you assemble the facts for the report, your ideas change. Maybe the problem isn't as bad as you thought it was. Maybe sales aren't as good as you thought they were. By finding and presenting the facts, your analysis improves and your ideas become more convincing.

Use the active voice   Do you know the difference between active voice and passive voice? In *active voice*, you say:

I wrote a report.

In *passive voice*, you say:

A report was written by me.

In active voice, people do things. In passive voice, things get done. Because readers like to read about people doing things, the active voice is generally more interesting than the passive voice. In addition, it clearly shows who did what.

Figure 9-10 presents a typical business paragraph that uses the passive voice. As a result, no one is doing anything. In the rewritten version, customers are complaining, salesmen are losing sales, and so on. By using the active voice, the rewritten version is not only more readable but also more accurate.

Unfortunately, I've more than once heard business people defend the passive voice on the grounds that it allows them to be "objective." By using the passive voice, they can make statements like

Mr. Clark's employment was terminated today.

rather than

I fired Mr. Clark today.

or

Mr. Clark quit today.

> **A paragraph that overuses the passive voice**
>
> Apparently, problems are associated with our new product. Many complaints about it are being received and business is being lost every day. As a result, its sales are not affected by our recent increase in its commission percent.
>
> **The paragraph rewritten in the active voice**
>
> Apparently, we have some problems with our new product. Each day, dozens of customers call to complain about it. And our salespeople say they are losing sales with it. As a result, they won't try to sell this product even though we've increased the commission on it.

Figure 9-10 Use the active voice

Supposedly, when you use the passive voice, you leave your feelings out of it. But you also avoid facing the facts, often misleading yourself and your company. In this case, the man either quit or was fired, and the difference should matter.

Other people defend the passive voice on the grounds that it sounds so harsh when you say things like "I fired him." They argue that the passive voice helps you soften your statements. Although that can be true, you can also do this in the active voice. And you can do so more directly and more honestly than you can in the passive voice. Here, for example, is the first paragraph of a "termination review" written in the active voice:

> I fired Mr. Clark today, and I'm sick about it. He is a pleasant man and a competent man. But he simply refused to apply his talents to our objectives. After six months, I just had to give up on him. Is it possible that we overlooked something when we hired him?

Would you call this writing "harsh"?

My point is that you can use the active voice in most of your sentences when you write business documents. The passive voice can't be justified by the claims that it lets you write more objectively or that it softens your statements.

That doesn't mean, however, that you should never use the passive voice because there are times when you will either want to use it or have to use it. Occasionally, you may want to use the passive voice to put the emphasis on the thing being done. For instance, this sentence emphasizes the product rather than the inventor:

This product was invented in 1973.

At other times, you will be forced to use the passive voice to avoid naming the person doing the thing. If, for example, you don't know who invented the product, the sentence above will get your thought across without identifying the inventor.

Whenever possible, though, you should avoid the passive voice because it too often disguises your meaning. In general, the more you use the passive voice, the less exact your meaning will be. When you use the active voice, it helps you to express and know the truth.

Avoid figurative language   When you use a *figure of speech*, you try to express your meaning by relating what you're talking about to something that is familiar to your reader. For example, "fresh as a daisy" is a figure of speech that means something like "very fresh." And "dumb as a post" is a figure of speech that means something like "very dumb."

When you use *figurative language*, you use language that makes use of figures of speech. Some examples follow:

The discussion came to a head.

We don't want to leave a stone unturned as we search for a solution.

Our game plan for the marketing department is ready, and I'm tossing the ball to our sales manager.

Many people in business enjoy using figurative language, and many of their figures of speech are related to sports.

But now, I'm going to recommend that you avoid figurative language in your writing. Although this type of language is sometimes acceptable in speech, it doesn't seem to serve its purpose in business or technical writing for two reasons. First, figures of speech tend to be too general or imprecise. For instance, "game plan" refers to an offensive or defensive plan for one football game. So does a

---

A paragraph that uses figurative language

Today, microcomputers are readily available, but a software vacuum exists and it will mushroom in the years ahead. Our company will puncture that vacuum and aid the revolution away from manuals, meetings, and memos.

The paragraph rewritten so it doesn't use figurative language

Today, microcomputers are readily available, but instructional software isn't. In the years ahead, we expect the demand for instructional software to increase. Our goals are (1) to provide the instructional software that the industry demands and (2) to move training away from manuals, meetings, and memos and towards computer based instruction.

Figure 9-11   Avoid figurative language

marketing game plan refer to a plan for just one week, one month, or what? For one department, one region, or what? The term isn't precise because businesses don't plan games.

Second, figures of speech rarely help clarify anything. In fact, they usually tend to confuse. Why? Because the reader has to interpret how the figure of speech relates to the topic under discussion. Is the relationship close or distant? Is the relationship true in all aspects or only in a couple? Too often, the use of figurative speech creates as many questions as it answers.

In a book on PCs, for example, I came upon this figure of speech about operating systems:

> An operating system plays a role something like a symphony conductor.... The players in the orchestra and their instruments represent the hardware. The experience and skill of the conductor represent the software. The score represents an application program.

Does this tell you anything about operating systems? Even if the analogy is a good one, it doesn't enhance my knowledge. Besides that, I'm not quite sure what a *score* is, so I can't understand how that relates to an application program.

Figure 9-11 presents a figure of speech taken from a business proposal that was designed to raise one million dollars in venture capital for a startup company. Here, the writer relates their product plans to a vacuum and also to a revolutionary force. Worse, the way the writer relates their goals to a vacuum is completely illogical. How does a vacuum mushroom and how do you puncture a vacuum? In the rewritten version, the meaning is apparent without the use of any figurative references...and there's no chance for confusion.

How far should you go toward avoiding figurative speech? I recommend that you avoid all uses of figurative speech, even common ones, because they always seem to interfere with clarity. By avoiding figurative language, you will be able to express your exact meaning.

Avoid trite expressions   *Trite* means overused. When words are used in the same combinations again and again, they become trite. They become so common to the ear that the reader says "I've heard that before" and doesn't pay attention. For instance, "aggressive salesman," "dynamic industry," and "viable project" are all trite expressions because those adjectives and those nouns are so frequently used together.

If you avoid trite expressions like these, you'll start to say what you mean. In addition, you may find that your language will become more specific. Instead of talking about "aggressive salesmen," maybe you'll start talking about salesmen who aren't afraid to make cold calls. Instead of "dynamic industries," maybe you'll start talking about industries that are growing at a rate of 15 percent or more annually. Instead of "viable projects," maybe you'll start talking about projects with a 70 percent chance of success. When you avoid trite language, the precision of your language has to improve.

Figure 9-12 gives an example of a trite expression taken from a sales letter. In this case, the trite expression is "tailored to your needs," which is also a figure of speech. In fact, many trite expressions are figures of speech.

The improvement in figure 9-12 is my attempt to show what "tailored to your needs" might mean if it were expressed in specific language. As far as I know, insurance programs usually consist of standard contracts plus one or more standard riders. But if some company can actually tailor a contract for you, they should take the time to explain how. So if it were possible, wouldn't the improved version be a more effective sales story than the original?

The point of this example is that trite expressions aren't specific, interesting, or effective. That's why you should avoid them. If you take pride in your writing, you should do your best to create expressions that express your exact meaning.

How to write readable sentences

A sentence that uses a trite expression

Our insurance programs are tailored to your needs.

The sentence rewritten so it doesn't use trite expressions

With the help of our underwriting department, we are able to select paragraphs from a contract library. We then assemble these paragraphs so your insurance contract will do just what you want it to do. In all, 13,457,221 different combinations are possible using the paragraphs now in the library. And this library will grow as conditions change. Can any other insurance company offer you this degree of customization?

Figure 9-12 Avoid trite expressions

Avoid nouns used as adjectives Business writers frequently use nouns as adjectives. For instance, I recently came across the phrase "management development seminar" in a marketing letter. Although *management* and *development* are normally nouns, they are used as adjectives in this phrase. In other words, the phrase is supposed to mean something like a "seminar for the development of managers."

When you use too many nouns as adjectives, your sentences become more difficult to read for two reasons. First, because your readers expect nouns to be used as nouns, they have to interpret them in a new way when they're used as adjectives. Second, a phrase that contains nouns used as adjectives usually isn't as precise as it should be. For instance, I can't say for sure what the phrase "management development seminar" is supposed to mean. Is it a seminar for old managers on how to develop new managers, or is it a seminar that is designed to teach management skills to new or developing managers?

Figure 9-13 shows what can happen when too many nouns are used as adjectives. Here, the original version uses five nouns as adjectives in a single sentence. In my opinion, the terms *business administration core content curriculum* and *competency development* are not only difficult to read, but downright foolish. When I rewrote the original sentence, I left one noun as an adjective: the *core* in the term *core content*, since this term is commonly used in academic circles. But I removed the other nouns used as adjectives. As a result, the readability of the sentence has improved, and its meaning is clearer.

A sentence that uses five different nouns as adjectives

The focus of the business administration core content curriculum is competency development in management and accounting.

The sentence rewritten so it uses only one noun as an adjective

The purpose of the core content in our curriculum is to develop competency in management and accounting.

Figure 9-13 Avoid nouns used as adjectives

If you watch out for the use of nouns as adjectives, you can avoid them and thus improve your writing. Don't hesitate to use common terms that use nouns as adjectives such as *computer program*. But don't create new uses of nouns as adjectives. The less you use nouns as adjectives, the more exactly you'll express your meanings.

Discussion

During the last 40 years, Rudolf Flesch's books and formulas have changed the style of business writing. Today, when you read a business letter that consists of short sentences and familiar words, you have evidence of that change.

Does that mean most business documents are written at satisfactory reading levels? Unfortunately, it does not. It seems, in fact, that many people in business enjoy writing at reading grade levels that are far too high for their intended audiences. They write as if they've never heard about Rudolf Flesch or readability measurement. And most of them haven't.

If you doubt this, look at figure 9-14. Here, I've changed the names of the firms and products involved, but I can tell you that this is the first page of an executive report prepared by one of the eight largest accounting firms in America. The client that received this report is a large company in the computer industry. Since the project that the executive report summarizes probably cost tens of thousands of dollars, you would think the report would be well written. But look at it. When measured by *RightWriter*, its reading grade level is 15.4.

How to write readable sentences   239

> This is a synopsis of how Megatech computers were noted to benefit several of HighTech Computer, Inc.'s (HighTech) business customers. The synopsis was developed from Grim Bosworth Dross & Co.'s interim report entitled "Megatech Benefits Study" of May 29, 1987, which contains a number of detailed business case studies that highlight operational business benefits that have been derived from the Megatech. These case studies, developed from an ongoing survey of certain major HighTech accounts, uncover and highlight business benefits that Megatech has brought to common business activities and functions. Tactical and strategic benefits reported from highly respected enterprises were documented to develop a business-oriented rationale for justifying introduction of technology to operations. Productivity, quality, efficiency, and effectiveness concepts are used frequently throughout the report to highlight Megatech's benefits. Technical computing aspects of Megatech's design (e.g., hardware configurations, system design, and compatibility features) were not the focus of this study, and therefore comparisons with technical features or timings of competing technology have not been included in this report.
>
> Grim Bosworth utilizes a study approach it developed and named "80-20 IA" (Internal Analysis) methodology. The methodology uses Pareto's principle, focusing on the 20 percent of the critical work efforts in a company that produce 80 percent of the enterprise's strategic value. The first step of the 80-20 IA work plan used in this study was to conduct directional interviews with management to identify the 20 percent of functional activities accounting for 80 percent of the organization's value and management's attention, as well as those areas where improvements from the Megatech were deemed most beneficial. Before and after process flow diagrams that depict how the Megatech has improved an organization's operation were developed and verified through interviews with users and their managers. Then structured group discussions were conducted. The groups were made up of experienced Megatech users who are considered by management to be among their best employees.
>
> The "80-20 IA" approach is a structured case study methodology. The case studies cited in this report were purposely selected to learn about the benefits of Megatech in organizations that are skilled at making good use of Megatech technology. The users' reports are based on their recollections and available records, and represent their best subjective estimates of times and costs associated with their work. Through extensive use of multiple measures of costs and benefits, the methodology can look for consistency across measures to gain confidence in the results.

Figure 9-14   The first page of an executive summary prepared by one of the Big 8 accounting firms

Four guidelines for shortening your sentences

1. Put one and only one thought in each sentence.
2. Use the simple expression.
3. Use fewer adjectives and adverbs.
4. Remove unnecessary words.

Four guidelines for simplifying your words

1. Use common words whenever possible.
2. Avoid words with prefixes and suffixes.
3. Avoid technical terms and jargon.
4. Avoid elegant variation.

Five guidelines for expressing your exact meaning

1. Be specific.
2. Use the active voice.
3. Avoid figurative language.
4. Avoid trite expressions.
5. Avoid nouns used as adjectives.

Figure 9-15 A summary of the guidelines for shortening your sentences, simplifying your words, and expressing your exact meaning

Worse, the report is so imprecise that I'm not at all sure it says anything of significance.

If you want to become an effective writer, you can't overlook the importance of readability. And you can't overlook the need to express your exact meanings. That's why this chapter gives you four guidelines for shortening your sentences and four for simplifying your words. Once you master these guidelines, your readability scores will improve. Then, you can concentrate on the five guidelines that will help you express your exact meanings. As a reference, figure 9-15 summarizes the 13 guidelines presented in this chapter.

If you use a writing analyzer on a PC, it will give you some recommendations that can help you apply some of the guidelines in figure

9-15. For instance, *RightWriter* identifies long sentences, sentences that use the passive voice, and an occasional word that isn't necessary. *Grammatik III* identifies the use of the passive voice, vague adverbs, wordy phrases, and trite phrases. If you make the changes suggested by either of these analyzers, you will improve the readability of your writing. However, because *Grammatik III* identifies more writing weaknesses than *RightWriter*, it is the more helpful program of the two.

On the other hand, no writing analyzer will help you apply all of the guidelines in figure 9-15. That's why you need to master them. Once you start using all of these guidelines, your writing will quickly improve.

Terms

readability	active voice
reading grade level	passive voice
RGL	figure of speech
deadwood	figurative language
elegant variation	trite

Objectives

1. Calculate the reading grade level of any one of your documents by using a writing analyzer on your PC.

2. Describe three limitations of readability measurement.

3. Describe four guidelines for shortening your sentences.

4. Describe four guidelines for simplifying your words.

5. Describe five guidelines for expressing your exact meaning.

6. Given a writing sample, rewrite it so the reading grade level is 10 or below as measured by a writing analyzer on a PC.

Heading plan for chapter 10

Three ways to provide paragraph continuity
- Subject or word repetition
- Pronouns and pointers
- Connecting words

Four ways to provide sentence continuity
- Subject or word repetition
- Pronouns and pointers
- Connecting words
- Parallel sentence structures

An example of writing with inadequate continuity

Discussion

Chapter 10

How to provide continuity in your writing

Although readability scores give you a good indication of how readable your writing is, there is more to readability than short sentences and common words. To write well, you must provide continuity between your paragraphs and between your sentences. To say it another way, you must show the relationships between your ideas and between your thoughts.

To illustrate, figure 10-1 presents the topic on word processing that I originally presented in chapter 8. However, in this version, I have removed most of the words and phrases that provide continuity between the paragraphs and between the sentences. If you take the time to read this version, you'll see that it presents the same ideas and facts as the earlier version. But as you read, you get the uneasy feeling that you don't know where all the facts are taking you.

Providing continuity is important because it makes your writing easier to understand. If your writing doesn't provide continuity, your readers must figure out the relationships between your ideas and thoughts for themselves. That's why the word processing topic in figure 10-1 is more difficult to understand than the earlier version, even though its RGL is lower (9.59) than the RGL of the earlier version (10.43).

If your content is complex and your writing doesn't provide continuity, some of your readers will be unwilling or unable to see the relationships between your ideas and thoughts. If they can't see these relationships, they won't get your messages at all. That's why this skill is so important for business and technical writing. In general, the more complex your content is, the more important it is that you provide continuity in your writing.

> **The Benefits of Word Processing**
>
> In simplest terms, the benefits of any word processing package are improved writing productivity and improved writing effectiveness. Now let me describe the benefits in more detail.
>
> You can enter the first draft of a document into a word processing system at least 30 percent faster than you can type it. Because you can correct your entry errors as you go, the printed draft will have fewer errors.
>
> You can improve revision speed because you only have to make the changes, insertions, and deletions that you require. You don't have to retype the entire document. When I wrote chapter 1, it took me about eight hours to enter the first draft. It took me less than one hour to revise, even though I made some extensive changes.
>
> When someone makes word processing changes for you, you only have to proof the changes. When someone retypes a document for you, you should proof the entire document because new errors may have been introduced by the typing process.
>
> Because revising is easy, you won't hesitate to make any revisions that will improve a document. You hesitate to make even minor revisions to a document when you know that someone will have to retype the entire document if you do. Because you only have to proof the changed areas, there's less chance that an error will slip by you.
>
> If you do your own entry work, you can change a sentence, decide you liked it better the way it was, and restore the first version with just a keystroke or two. You can move a paragraph or group of paragraphs from one portion of a document to another to see how that works with just a few keystrokes. You can copy paragraphs that you used successfully in other documents into the document you're working on and revise them so they're appropriate for your new purpose. It may be hard for you to understand how the capabilities will improve your writing, but the improvements are often dramatic.

Figure 10-1 The topic on word processing without the language that provides paragraph and sentence continuity

In this chapter, I'll show you how to provide continuity in your writing. First, I'll show you how to provide continuity from one paragraph to the next. Then, I'll show you how to provide continuity from one sentence to the next.

Three ways to provide paragraph continuity

When you end one paragraph and start another, you end one idea and start another. As a result, it's important that you start each paragraph by showing the reader how the paragraph is going to relate to the preceding paragraph or to the topic you're presenting. To some extent, you do this when you obey the third principle of paragraphing: Start each paragraph with the main idea of the paragraph or with a transition from the previous paragraph. However, there's more to providing continuity than that.

When you provide continuity between your paragraphs, you can refer to it as *paragraph continuity*, or *paragraph linkage*. You can also think of it as providing transitions between paragraphs, or *paragraph transitions*. To provide these transitions, you can use (1) subject and word repetition, (2) pronouns and pointers, and (3) connecting words. To illustrate these techniques, the original version of the word processing topic is reprinted in figure 10-2. This time, the words that provide continuity between the paragraphs are boldfaced.

Subject or word repetition   If you read the first sentences of the six paragraphs in figure 10-2, you can see that all six say something about the subject of the topic, *word processing*. By repeating the subject of the topic, the writer shows how the paragraph relates to the topic at hand. That's how *subject repetition* or *word repetition* provides continuity from one paragraph to another.

The word that's repeated doesn't always have to be the subject of the topic. For instance, in the second and fourth paragraphs in figure 10-2, the first sentences both use the word *productivity*. Because this word is mentioned in the first paragraph, the reader should realize that while the first paragraph introduced the subject of productivity, the second and fourth paragraphs treat it in more detail. In this way, word repetition helps the reader see the relationships between the paragraphs.

Pronouns and pointers   When there is a close relationship between one paragraph and one or more preceding paragraphs, you can provide continuity by using a pronoun or pointer word in the first sentence of a paragraph. The *pointer word*, or just *pointer*, points at a word or idea in a previous paragraph so the reader can see the relationship between the paragraphs.

Pronouns that are commonly used as pointers are *he, she, it,* and *they*. The possessive forms of these pronouns are *his, her, its,* and

The Benefits of Word Processing

In simplest terms, the benefits of any word processing package are (1) improved writing productivity and (2) improved writing effectiveness. Perhaps these benefits are obvious, but, in case they're not, let me describe them in more detail.

Word processing helps you increase your **productivity** in at least three ways. First, you can enter the first draft of a document into a word processing system at least 30 percent faster than you can type it. As you create the first draft, you can correct your typing errors as you go, so the printed draft will have fewer errors than it would have had if you typed it.

Second, word processing dramatically improves revision speed because you only have to make the changes, insertions, and deletions that you require. You don't have to retype the entire document. When I wrote chapter 1, for example, it took me about eight hours to enter the first draft. However, it took me less than one hour to revise the draft after I had edited it, even though I made some extensive changes.

Third, word processing improves your **productivity** because it reduces the need for proofing. When someone makes word processing changes for you, you only have to proof the changes. In contrast, when someone retypes a document for you, you should proof the entire document because new errors may have been introduced by the typing process.

Although improved **productivity** is an important benefit of **word processing**, improved writing effectiveness may be more important. First, because revisions are easy to make on a word processing system, you won't hesitate to make any revisions that will improve a document. In contrast, you hesitate to make even minor revisions to a document when you know that someone will have to retype the entire document if you do. Second, because you only have to proof the changed areas of a revised document, there's less chance that an error will slip by you.

Beyond this, word processing helps you improve your writing in subtle ways. If you do your own entry work, you can change a sentence, decide you liked it better the way it was, and restore the first version with just a keystroke or two. You can move a paragraph or group of paragraphs from one portion of a document to another to see how that works with just a few keystrokes. You can copy paragraphs that you used successfully in other documents into the document you're working on and revise them so they're appropriate for your new purpose. Until you've used word processing for a while, it may be hard for you to understand how these capabilities will improve your writing, but they will...and the improvements are often dramatic.

Figure 10-2 Using word repetition, pointers, and connecting words to provide paragraph continuity

their. If, for example, one paragraph describes a man and his company, the first sentence of the next paragraph may provide a transition by using pronouns as follows:

> Although **he** sold **his** company before it ever became successful, Bill Azores is still recognized as a pioneer in the electronics field.

Here, the pronouns *he* and *his* point to words in the previous paragraph.

Other commonly used pointer words are *this, that, such, these,* and *those*. In figure 10-2, for example, you can see the word *this* used in the first sentence in the sixth paragraph. Here, the word *this* points to the idea discussed in the previous paragraph so the relationship between the two paragraphs is obvious.

When you use pronouns and pointer words, you must write your sentences so there's no mistaking what the pointer words refer to. I'll show you how to do this in chapter 13. In general, though, you should write your sentences so nothing comes between the pointer word and the word it refers to that could be mistaken for the word it refers to. If there's a chance for misunderstanding, you should provide the transition in some other way. You'll see more examples of the correct use of pointer words in just a moment when I show you how to provide continuity between sentences.

Connecting words The English language has dozens of *connecting words*, or *connectives*, that can help you achieve continuity in your writing. Figure 10-3 lists some of them. Since you undoubtedly use many of these connectives already, you should have no problem learning how to use them to provide continuity between paragraphs.

The paragraphs in figure 10-2 use two connecting words to provide continuity. The third paragraph starts with the word *second*, so you know the preceding paragraph must have presented the first point. The fourth paragraph starts with the word *third*, so you know the preceding paragraph must have presented the second point. In addition, the last paragraph starts with the words *beyond this*, which can be thought of as a connective that contains a pointer.

If you review some typical business documents, you will probably discover frequent use of connecting words. After all, business decisions are supposed to be reasonable and logical, so it's natural to use a language of *therefores, howevers,* and *furthermores*. But watch out

Purpose	Connecting Words
To restate an idea	in other words
To present another idea	and besides also in addition furthermore moreover
To present a contrasting idea	but however on the other hand nevertheless in contrast still
To present an example	for example for instance to illustrate
To present an idea that follows logically	so as a result therefore consequently accordingly
To present a summary	in short in brief to sum up in summary
To arrange ideas in sequence	first second next then finally

Figure 10-3 Common connecting words (part 1 of 2)

Purpose	Connecting Words
To arrange ideas in time	meanwhile
	next
	then
	afterwards
	later
	before
To arrange ideas in space	above
	below
	to the left
	to the right
	beyond

Figure 10-3 Common connecting words (part 2 of 2)

for misusing or overusing connecting words. This can make the logic of your argument seem artificial.

Four ways to provide sentence continuity

When you write a paragraph, you want it to be a cohesive unit built around the idea of the paragraph. That means each sentence within the paragraph should relate to the idea of the paragraph. That also means there should be continuity from one sentence to another within the paragraph. When you provide this continuity, you can refer to it as *sentence continuity*, or *sentence linkage*. You can also think of it as providing *sentence transitions*.

As you might guess, you achieve sentence continuity in much the same way that you achieve paragraph continuity. You use subject and word repetition, pronouns and pointers, and connecting words. In addition, you can achieve continuity within a paragraph by writing sentences that are parallel in structure.

To illustrate, the six paragraphs on word processing are printed again in figure 10-4. This time all the words that provide continuity between the sentences are boldfaced, but the words that provide continuity between paragraphs are not.

The Benefits of Word Processing

In simplest terms, the benefits of any word processing package are (1) improved writing productivity and (2) improved writing effectiveness. Perhaps **these** benefits are obvious, but, in case **they**'re not, let me describe **them** in more detail.

Word processing helps you increase your productivity in at least three ways. **First**, you can enter the **first draft** of a document into a word processing system at least 30 percent faster than you can type it. As you create the **first draft**, you can correct your typing errors as you go, so the printed draft will have fewer errors than it would have had if you typed it.

Second, word processing dramatically improves revision speed because **you** only **have** to make the changes, insertions, and deletions that you require. **You** don't **have** to retype the entire document. When I wrote chapter 1, **for example**, it took me about eight hours to enter the first draft. **However**, it took me less than one hour to revise the draft after I had edited it, even though I made some extensive changes.

Third, **word processing** improves your productivity because it reduces the need for proofing. When someone makes **word processing** changes for you, you only have to **proof** the changes. **In contrast**, when someone retypes a document for you, you should **proof** the entire document because new errors may have been introduced by the typing process.

Although improved productivity is an important benefit of word processing, improved writing effectiveness may be more important. **First**, because revisions are easy to make on a word processing system, you won't hesitate to make any revisions that will improve a document. **In contrast**, you hesitate to make even minor revisions to a document when you know that someone will have to retype the entire document if you do. **Second**, because you only have to proof the changed areas of a revised document, there's less chance that an error will slip by you.

Beyond this, word processing helps you improve your writing in subtle ways. If you do your own entry work, **you can** change a sentence, decide you liked it better the way it was, and restore the first version with just a keystroke or two. **You can** move a paragraph or group of paragraphs from one portion of a document to another to see how that works with just a few keystrokes. **You can** copy paragraphs that you used successfully in other documents into the document you're working on and revise them so they're appropriate for your new purpose. **Until** you've used word processing for a while, it may be hard for you to understand how these capabilities will improve your writing, but they will...and the improvements are often dramatic.

Figure 10-4 Using word repetition, pronouns, pointers, connecting words, and parallel sentence structures to provide sentence continuity

Subject or word repetition   If you read the second and third sentences in the second paragraph in figure 10-4, you can see that the term *first draft* is repeated. Similarly, the term *word processing* is used in both the first and second sentences of the fourth paragraph. This repetition helps provide continuity between the sentences. Don't overdo the repetition, though, because it can make your writing seem cumbersome.

Pronouns and pointers   The first paragraph in figure 10-4 uses two pronouns and a pointer to achieve continuity between sentences. The words *they* and *them* are pronouns that refer to the benefits of word processing. The word *these* is a pointer word that refers to the benefits listed in the previous sentence.

If you review the writing in magazine articles and books, you'll discover extensive use of pronouns and pointers. They make your writing more fluid. In contrast, the writing in most business documents doesn't make adequate use of pronouns and pointers. As a result, you can make a quick improvement in your writing by using pronouns and pointers with clear references.

Connecting words   In figure 10-4, you can see the connecting words *first, second, for example, however, in contrast* (twice), and *until*. Since there are 21 sentences in these six paragraphs, that means one out of every three sentences uses connecting words to provide continuity between sentences. In addition, three of the first sentences in the paragraphs use connecting words to provide continuity between paragraphs. That shows how important connecting words can be for providing continuity between sentences and paragraphs.

Parallel sentence structures   The paragraph in figure 10-5 is built around *parallel sentence structures* that start with the words *it can*. As a result, the continuity is obvious to the reader. Note, however, that this wouldn't be effective if the pronoun *it* weren't used. The repetition of the term *word processing* would be deadly.

The sixth paragraph in figure 10-4 also illustrates parallel sentence structures. Here, the second, third, and fourth sentences all contain structures starting with *you can*. To a lesser extent, the third paragraph also uses parallel sentence structures in its first and second sentences based on the words *you have*.

Obviously, you can use parallel sentence structures only in certain types of paragraphs. So I shouldn't have to caution you about

> I don't want to overstate the benefits of word processing, but its benefits are impressive. **It can** increase your typing speed by 30 percent or more. **It can** increase your revision speed by 100 percent or more. **It can** reduce the amount of proofing you do by 70 percent or more. And **it can** improve the quality of your writing.

Figure 10-5 A paragraph that uses parallel structures to provide sentence continuity

overusing them. When an entire paragraph is built around parallel sentence structures as in figure 10-5, it draws attention and gives special emphasis to the idea of the paragraph.

An example of writing with inadequate continuity

Figure 10-6 shows an example of writing taken from a government manual on buying small computers. It is quite wordy so its RGL is 14.82. It also has a couple of paragraphing problems. Perhaps its worst problem, though, is its failure to show the relationships between its ideas and thoughts.

In figure 10-6, I've boldfaced the words that provide what little continuity the topic has. As you can see, the writer has used only three connectives and one pointer word in the six paragraphs. He didn't provide any linkage between paragraphs, and he didn't use pronouns to show the relationships between sentences. Although the writer did use word repetition, you can see that this by itself doesn't provide much continuity. In fact, since the words the writer repeats are difficult ones, the word repetition tends to reduce readability more than it improves continuity. Fortunately, the writer used one heading and two subheadings in this topic so you can tell what each paragraph is supposed to be about. But I still have a hard time figuring out what the writer intends, even though I understand the intent of each sentence. The ideas and thoughts seem isolated from one another.

Unfortunately, this example is typical of most business and technical writing. Because the relationships between the ideas and thoughts are unclear, the overall message is unclear. If the writer had taken the time to show these relationships, his writing would be easier to read and understand.

Analyzing costs and benefits

The **acquisition** process should not be an obstacle to effective use of PCs. Recent changes to the **acquisition** regulations make clear that the degree of analysis and documentation supporting an **acquisition** should match the size and complexity of the need. **Therefore**, one to three pages should normally be sufficient to document the need and obtain approval for a single PC or a small number of low-cost PCs and associated software.

Before writing a **justification** for acquiring PC equipment, one should determine the method of showing that the benefits of end user computing outweigh the costs. **This justification** may be based on either increased **efficiency** or improved **effectiveness** (or a combination of the two). If the improvements in either **efficiency** or **effectiveness** are not explained, the **justification** probably will be challenged.

Efficiency justifications **Efficiency** justifications compare costs under existing conditions with the costs of buying and using PCs. Improvements are procedural but products are essentially unchanged. Some examples of new PC capabilities used to improve **efficiency** are electronic spreadsheets, word processing, graphics for reporting, data base management, and project management.

Compare the cost of current procedures with the costs of buying and using PCs to determine whether the bottom line is advantageous over the life of the PC systems. Remember that for low-cost PCs, the comparison should be simple and straightforward.

Effectiveness justifications Increased **effectiveness** means a better accomplishment of the overall mission. Improvements usually depend upon adding PC capabilities to support new products, new functions, better decisions, or better management. Some examples of new PC capabilities that might increase office **effectiveness** are project management, economic modeling, document retrieval, statistical analysis, and access to government or public data bases through telephone lines.

The performance of managers and professionals cannot be easily quantified. **Therefore**, the efficiency justification may not address critical issues because of a lack of measurement data. The **effectiveness** approach may meet resistance due to the subjectivity of the benefits anticipated. **Furthermore**, since **effectiveness** improvements tend to confront basic assumptions, they may be more controversial. Despite resistance to subjectivity and basic change, **effectiveness** improvements are often more significant to the overall organization than efficiency improvements.

Figure 10-6   A topic with inadequate paragraph and sentence continuity

Discussion

When you try to show your reader the relationships between your ideas and paragraphs, you improve your own understanding of your subject. That's the hidden benefit you get by providing continuity in your writing. Then, because you understand your own ideas better, you can transmit your ideas to your readers better. That's why this skill is so important to business and technical writers.

You should realize, though, that you don't have to worry about paragraph or sentence continuity as you write the first draft of a document. Instead, you should concentrate on the ideas you're presenting. Later on, when you edit your writing, you can decide whether or not your writing has adequate continuity. If it doesn't, you can revise your paragraphs and sentences so they provide the necessary transitions.

As you become more skilled at writing, you'll try to provide continuity as you write your first drafts. You'll visualize your readers, and you'll try to help them understand your writing by showing them all the relationships between your ideas and thoughts. When you're able to do that, you'll know that you've reached a new level of writing competence.

Terms

paragraph continuity	pronoun
paragraph linkage	connecting word
paragraph transition	connective
subject repetition	sentence continuity
word repetition	sentence linkage
pointer word	sentence transition
pointer	parallel sentence structures

Objectives

1. Describe three ways to provide paragraph continuity.

2. Describe four ways to provide sentence continuity.

3. Given a writing sample, rewrite it so it provides both paragraph and sentence continuity.

Heading plan for chapter 11

Tone and style in business writing
- The elements of tone
- The elements of style
- An effective tone and style for business writing
- Your own tone and style

Three guidelines for improving the tone of your writing
- Write with a *you* attitude
- Write with a positive attitude
- Write with a conversational style

Ten guidelines for improving the style of your writing
- Write about people doing things
- Use quotations
- Use an occasional question
- Use *I*, *we*, and *you*
- Use the other pronouns and pointer words
- Use *that*, not *which*
- Remove unnecessary *thats*
- Use more contractions
- Avoid constructions such as *he/she* and *and/or*
- Use an occasional sentence fragment

Three guidelines for avoiding sexist language
- Write with a *you* language, not a *he* or *she* language
- Use plurals when describing the actions of men and women
- Avoid sexist words and terms

Discussion

Chapter 11

How to write
with an effective tone and style

If you write readable sentences within fully developed paragraphs and you provide paragraph and sentence continuity, your writing should be effective. However, it may not be if the tone of your writing isn't effective. That's why you should be aware of your tone whenever you write. To a lesser extent, you should also be aware of your style. If your writing has an appropriate tone and style, it is more likely to be effective.

In this chapter, I'll show you three ways to improve your tone and ten ways to improve your style. Then, I'll show you how to write without using sexist language because language like that has a negative effect on both your tone and your style. If you apply the guidelines of this chapter to your writing, you should develop an effective tone and style.

Tone and style in business writing

Before I can show you how to improve your tone and style, you have to know what the elements of tone and style are. After I present these, I'll describe a tone and style that I think is appropriate for most business writing.

The elements of tone   *Tone* refers to the attitudes that your writing reveals. Your tone may reveal your attitudes about your audience or your attitudes about your subject. For instance, you may have a hostile attitude toward your audience or a negative attitude about your subject. Or, you may have a sympathetic attitude toward your audience or an enthusiastic attitude about your subject.

To illustrate the effect tone can have on your writing, figure 11-1 presents five paragraphs taken from letters. Since all five letters were sent to me, I can tell you how I interpreted the tone in each of these paragraphs. Although your interpretation of the tone in these paragraphs may differ from mine, these examples will give you some idea of how tone varies from one document to another.

Example 1 was taken from a letter written by a person who decided *not* to invest in my company. I think its tone is friendly, sincere, sympathetic, and positive. The writer made me feel as though my business idea had a reasonable chance for success, even though he didn't want to invest in it.

Example 2 was taken from a marketing letter written by a person I didn't know. Its purpose was to get me to advertise our products in a certain trade magazine. I think the writer's tone is positive, confident, and enthusiastic. As a result, I read the articles that the writer enclosed.

Example 3 was taken from a followup letter for a marketing research project. I think its tone is a bit arrogant and irritating. It sounds as if the author thinks his research project is more important than my time. I didn't complete his followup questionnaire.

Example 4 was taken from a sales letter written by a person who wanted to develop training materials for us. I think its tone is presumptuous and a bit pompous. I also doubt that anyone who writes like that could develop effective training materials. That's why I replied that I wasn't interested in their services.

Example 5 was taken from a letter issued from the credit-processing department within a bank. I think its tone is unfriendly, negative, and irritating, even though it includes a *thank you* and a *please*. You have to wonder whether the people in the credit-processing department know that the bank spends thousands of dollars each year trying to get people to apply for credit.

If you try to identify the elements of tone, you can see that they include the ideas and thoughts that a writer expresses. For instance, this sentence definitely sets the tone in example 3 in figure 11-1:

Since you didn't reply, I suppose you didn't think it was worth your time.

However, the elements of tone also include language elements like word choices and sentence structures. That's why the tones in examples 4 and 5 are irritating. If the language is so complicated that the

Example 1: From a potential investor's letter

   Thanks for offering me the chance to invest in your company, and thanks for sending me your business prospectus. I reviewed your plan at length, and I think you have a lot going for you. Unfortunately, it's not the right investment for me.

Example 2: From an advertising salesman's letter

   I found some interesting articles in *High Tech Marketing* concerning direct marketing and I thought I'd share them with you. The findings from their research support what I've been saying all these months. We are involved in a great, growing segment of marketing!

Example 3: From a marketing research letter

   About three weeks ago I wrote you asking you to complete a questionnaire about your computer system and the software you use. Since you didn't reply, I suppose you didn't feel it was worth your time. Fair enough. That's why I'm enclosing a shortened form of the questionnaire this time.

Example 4: From a training company's sales letter

   The purpose of this letter is to ask where, within your organization, it is appropriate for our company to introduce its capability and services. We are developers of customized data processing training materials and end-user oriented explanatory materials. We have particular expertise in developing practical and easy to understand self-study materials for user education.

Example 5: From a bank's credit-processing letter

   Thank you for your recent application to open a credit account. However, in order to make the necessary verification of your stated income, please furnish us within thirty (30) days from the date of this letter, with complete copies of your Federal and State income tax returns for the past three (3) years, including all schedules, W-2 forms, 1099 forms and other attachments. Please do not send us your personal copies, as this information will not be returned to you.

Figure 11-1   Five examples of tone in business writing

reading grade level is much above 12, the tone is likely to be too formal and impersonal for most business documents.

The elements of style *Style* refers to the way something is written, as distinguished from its content. As a result, the elements of style include your headings and subheadings, your visual aids, the effectiveness of your paragraphs, the readability of your sentences, your diction, and your grammar. Another element of style is your tone. In short, everything you do in your writing is an element of the stylistic impression that it creates.

Figure 11-2 presents four examples of style taken from successful books. As you move from example 1 to example 4, the styles range from informal to formal, from conversational to academic, and from personal to impersonal. The reading grade levels in these four examples are 4.99, 11.08, 6.62, and 18.24. Because these examples are taken from books, the tones aren't that obvious, but I think the writers of examples 2 and 3 are both confident and enthusiastic about their subjects. In contrast, I think the tone in example 1 is overly personal and a bit insincere, while the tone in example 4 is too academic for business writing. Here, you can see that tone is an important element of style.

An effective tone and style for business writing When you write in business, you want your documents to achieve their intended purposes. As a result, you want to write with a tone and style that is effective for your business purposes. Although this will vary somewhat from one document to another, you should try to develop a general tone and style you can use for all business writing. Then, you can adjust this tone and style for special circumstances.

What are the characteristics of an effective tone for business writing? Since your writing tone reveals your personality, you can think of tone characteristics in the same way that you think of personality characteristics. So the same characteristics you admire in a person's personality are the ones you should try to present in the tone of your writing. That's why you should strive for a tone that is friendly and courteous rather than unfriendly or discourteous; one that is positive and encouraging rather than negative or discouraging; one that is understanding and sympathetic rather than closed-minded or callous. If your writing establishes a tone that is friendly, positive, and understanding, it should be effective for any business document. And that's going to be true whether the message you have to present is pleasant or unpleasant.

Example 1: From *The Great Brain Robbery* by Ray Considine and Murray Raphel

Nearly 10,000 firms go out of business every year in the United States.
So how come you're still around?
And will you be here next year when the mortality roll is called on that great Dun and Bradstreet in the sky?

Example 2: From *Why Johnny Still Can't Read* by Rudolf Flesch

There's little doubt that we'll soon have doctors who can't easily read medical journals, lawyers who have difficulty researching a case, scientists who stumble through their professional literature. In the 1990s we'll have to import top professionals from abroad. We'll join the ranks of such undereducated Third World countries as the Ivory Coast, Saudi Arabia, and Zambia. And there'll be few, if any, Nobel Prize winners who learned to read in an American school.

Example 3: From *Managing for Results* by Peter Drucker

Today's job takes all the executive's time, as a rule; yet it is seldom done well. Few managers are greatly impressed with their own performance in the immediate tasks. They feel themselves caught in a "rat race," and managed by whatever the mailboy dumps into their "in" tray. They know that crash programs which attempt to "solve" this or that particular "urgent" problem rarely achieve right and lasting results. And yet, they rush from one crash program to the next. Worse still, they know that the same problems recur again and again, no matter how many times they are "solved."

Example 4: From *Future Shock* by Alvin Toffler

To understand what is happening to us as we move into the age of super-industrialism, we must analyze the processes of acceleration and confront the concept of transience. If acceleration is a new social force, transience is its psychological counterpart, and without an understanding of the role it plays in contemporary human behavior, all our theories of personality, all our psychology, must remain pre-modern. Psychology without the concept of transience cannot take account of precisely those phenomena that are peculiarly contemporary.

Figure 11-2 Four examples of style in business writing

I think examples 1 and 2 in figure 11-1 have effective tones for business writing. Example 3 has a tone that is too irritating to be completely effective. And examples 4 and 5 are so poorly written that the tones are ineffective. Note in the first example that the tone is friendly, positive, and understanding, even though the message is an unpleasant one.

But what about the characteristics of an effective style for business writing? Since the elements of style include all of the writing elements, styles can range considerably and still be effective. In general, though, an effective style for business writing is one that no one notices. As a result, the style doesn't interfere with the meaning or purpose of a document. A document with an effective style is characterized by words such as *well organized, convincing,* and *clearly understandable.* A document with an ineffective style is characterized by words such as *unorganized, wordy,* and *illogical.*

Examples 2 and 3 in figure 11-2 illustrate effective styles for business writing. They are easy to read, to the point, and convincing, and they have a pleasant, earnest tone. On the other hand, I think the style in example 1 is too informal and cute for most business documents; its style is more appropriate for advertisements. And I think the style in example 4 is too formal, wordy, and academic for most business documents; its style is more appropriate for a thesis.

Your own tone and style   If you do everything this book recommends, you will learn to write effectively. As part of that, you will also develop your own tone and style.

Your tone will be your own because your writing will reflect your personality. If you're happy about something, your writing will show it. If you're disappointed, discouraged, or outraged about something, your writing will show that too. I just recommend that you express your attitudes with a tone that is as friendly, positive, and understanding as is reasonable for the circumstances.

Your style will be your own because you are the one who selects the content, organizes it, and writes it. You decide what's important. You interpret the information. You decide what details to use to convince your readers. You choose your words and sentence structures. In short, you develop your own writing style by applying your own experience, wisdom, and personality to the methods, techniques, and guidelines this book presents.

Three guidelines for improving the tone of your writing

When I described an effective tone for business writing, I said that it should be friendly, positive, and understanding. Friendly because you don't gain anything by being unfriendly in business. Positive because you don't accomplish anything by being negative. And understanding because your writing isn't likely to be effective if you don't understand your reader. The three guidelines that follow will help you achieve a tone that is friendly, positive, and understanding.

Write with a *you* attitude   When you write with a *you* attitude, you try to understand the other person's point of view. If you're trying to sell something, you try to understand why the other person may or may not want to buy your product. If you're trying to explain why you're not going to hire someone, you try to understand the disappointment of the person you're turning down. If you're trying to get information from someone, you try to understand why the person may or may not be willing to give you the information.

Figure 11-3 shows how writing with a *you* attitude can affect the tone of your writing. Here, the original paragraph has a *we* attitude as it describes what the business associates program did with the money it collected in the previous year. In this paragraph, the pronoun *you* is never used. In contrast, the revised paragraph briefly tells what the program did with the money it collected. Then, it shows how those activities relate to the reader. As a result, the revised paragraph has a *you* attitude even though it uses the word *we* four times and *you* only twice.

When you write with a *you* attitude, you turn the emphasis away from yourself and toward your audience. As figure 11-3 shows, that implies a way of thinking as well as a way of writing. When you write with this attitude, you avoid the impersonal impression so many business documents convey and you hold your reader's interest. Besides that, your writing usually has a tone that is friendly and understanding.

Write with a positive attitude   In any business, you frequently have to do negative things like turning down credit applications, returning damaged goods, and reprimanding employees. But that doesn't mean you have to do them with a negative attitude. Instead, you should look at such tasks with a positive attitude, and your writing should reflect this attitude.

From a letter written with a *me* attitude

Our business associates program had a great year last year with 44 firms contributing $1000 or more to our educational programs. These funds allowed us to recruit quality faculty, further faculty research, support paper presentations at national professional meetings, keep faculty current on up-to-date business education and innovative instructional methods, and provide a quality education for our students in days of financial cutbacks of State funds. If we are to continue in our quest for excellence, we will need even more support next year.

The same paragraph written with a *you* attitude

When we asked for your help last year, you helped us. In return, we did our best to train the young people who will become the business managers of the future. We hope, of course, that some of these young people will become valued members of your company. And we hope that you will continue to support us in our quest for excellence.

Figure 11-3   Write with a *you* attitude

To see an illustration of negative and positive writing, look at the example in figure 11-4. The original paragraph was taken from an actual credit-processing letter. In fact, it was taken from the same letter that example 5 in figure 11-1 was taken from. But as negative as the tone of that letter was, the company approved my application when I sent them what they requested. So why did the letter have to be so negative?

The rewritten paragraph in figure 11-4 takes a more positive approach to credit processing. It says that the applicant's credit will be approved if he can provide documents that support the claims on the application. That's positive, isn't it? It never says that the applicant's credit request will be denied if they don't hear from him within 30 days. Instead, it says they'll assume the applicant is no longer interested in getting a credit card from them.

If you look for it, you can usually find a positive way to approach any business problem. You're sorry that you aren't going to place an order with a company, but you hope you can do business with them in the future. You're sorry that you're not interested in publishing

> **From a letter written with a negative attitude**
>
> If we do not receive this requested/required information within thirty (30) days from the date of this letter, your application for credit will be declined. If you provide us with this requested information within the thirty (30) day period, we will be able to proceed with an evaluation of your application.
>
> **The same paragraph written with a positive attitude**
>
> Please send us the items we've requested as soon as possible so we can continue processing your credit application. If these items support the data on your application, you should receive your credit card within 15 days from the time we get the items. If we don't hear from you within 30 days, we'll assume that you're no longer interested in getting a credit card from us.

Figure 11-4 Write with a positive attitude

someone's manuscript, but some other publisher probably will be. You're sorry to report that an employee's work is unsatisfactory, but you believe the employee has some aptitude that could be used effectively in another position. When you look for it, you can usually find a positive side to an issue so you can write with a positive attitude.

Write with a conversational style If you write with a conversational style, your writing will be easier to read because it will use common words and manageable sentence structures. It will also have a friendly tone. Years ago, people deliberately wrote in a formal style that didn't resemble conversation in any way. But today, most businesses recommend a conversational style for letters, memos, reports, and most other documents.

For some reason, though, many people don't write with a conversational style. Perhaps they think it's more businesslike to write in a formal and impersonal style. Perhaps they don't realize that their formal and impersonal tone and style decreases the effectiveness of their writing.

Figure 11-5 shows how a conversational style can improve the tone of your writing. In the original paragraph, the writer used words and phrases that she would never have used in conversation such as

> **From a letter written in a stilted, formal style**
>
> I certainly appreciate your time during our last conversation, referencing off-site storage for your vital records. Sounds as if effective contingency planning has been initiated by your company and our safe-deposit program would intensify the disaster recovery aspect. Pursuant to our discussion, at your request, find enclosed the information currently available for the program.
>
> **The same paragraph written in a conversational style**
>
> Thanks for talking with me last week about off-site storage for your vital records. It sounds as though you already have an effective contingency plan for disasters. But I think our safe-deposit program could make it even better. That's why I'm enclosing information about our program.

Figure 11-5 Write with a conversational style

"referencing off-site storage," "has been initiated," and "pursuant to our discussion." I know the writer wouldn't have used these phrases because I talked with her on the phone two days before I received her letter. In the rewritten paragraph, I used phrases and sentence structures like the ones she used in our telephone conversation.

The rewritten paragraph in figure 11-5 shows that a conversational style isn't the same as conversation. Instead, it should be improved conversation. To write with a conversational style, you write the way you talk, but you improve it by following the guidelines I've given you for writing effective paragraphs and readable sentences. As a result, your writing should be more fluid, more logical, and more precise than your conversation.

Ten guidelines for improving the style of your writing

The three guidelines I've just given you are important ones. Since they will help you improve the tone of your writing, they will also help you improve your style.

But your style is dependent on all of the elements of writing. So now, I'm going to present ten guidelines for improving your style. These guidelines are summarized in figure 11-6. No one of these guidelines is that important, but each one will contribute to an improved style. Each one will also contribute to an improved tone.

Write about people doing things   People like to read about people doing things. That's why novels are best sellers. But so many business documents don't talk at all about people doing things. Sales are down, salaries are up, and our operations have improved. But who's doing what in the company?

To apply this guideline, you do more than just remove the passive voice from your writing. You make a conscious effort to write about people doing things. If you walk through your company, you'll see active people everywhere. People are making products, performing services, typing letters, developing programs, conducting meetings, taking orders, collecting money, and hiring other people. So start writing about them whenever it seems appropriate.

Example 1 in figure 11-6 shows how this guideline can improve the style of your writing. The improved version is more interesting than the original. It is also more specific.

Use quotations   People like to hear what other people say. So use quotations whenever they can help you present an idea. It doesn't matter whether or not you use quotation marks as long as the reader can tell that you're quoting directly.

Example 2 in figure 11-6 shows how quotations can improve your style. The improved version is more interesting than the original. And it's more accurate.

Use an occasional question   When you talk with people, you ask questions to get information, feedback, and confirmation. So you should feel free to ask an occasional question in your writing too. This can make your writing more personal.

Example 3 in figure 11-6 shows one way to use a question. This is particularly useful when you write letters, but it can also be useful in any kind of business document. Have you noticed the questions I've asked throughout this text?

Use *I*, *we*, and *you*   I've already advised you to write with a *you* attitude. Now, I'm specifically advising you to use the pronouns *I*, *we*, and *you*.

Example 4 in figure 11-6 shows how these words can make a difference. In the original version, the writer sends his organization's thanks to the reader's company. But isn't this really a letter from one person to another? If so, the improved version is more direct, readable, and friendly.

As simple as this guideline is, many business writers refuse to use the words *I* and *we*. I guess they want to be impersonal, even though that doesn't lead to an effective tone and style. If they do use one of these words, they usually use *we* as in this example:

> We're sorry, but we have decided that we're not interested in publishing your manuscript.

Here, the use of the word *we* implies that the decision was made by more than one person. But too often, people use the word *we* to avoid taking the responsibility for what they've done by themselves. My advice is to use *I* if you're speaking for yourself and you're responsible for the action. Use *we* only if you're speaking for a group, a department, or the entire company.

Use the other pronouns and pointer words In chapter 10, I recommended that you use pronouns and pointer words to show the relationships between your paragraphs and sentences. When you do this, you also improve the tone and style of your writing. So, in addition to *I*, *we*, and *you*, remember to use the other pronouns such as *he, she, they, it, him, her, them, your, our, their*, and *its*. Remember also to use pointer words such as *this, that, these*, and *those*.

Example 5 in figure 11-6 shows how the use of pronouns and pointer words can improve your style. Here, the improved version uses the pronoun *our* three times and the pointer word *this* once.

Use *that*, not *which* This is another one of Rudolf Flesch's suggestions for business writing. Quite simply, he recommends that we replace *which*es with *that*s. He says you should go on a *which* hunt. He thinks *which* is a formal word so this simple change will improve the tone of your writing.

Does it work? I'll let you decide. In example 6 in figure 11-6, I replaced the *which*es with *that*s. I think it improved the tone and style of the sentence.

The only time you shouldn't replace *which* with *that* is when the *which* introduces a non-restrictive clause. For instance, the *which* in this sentence shouldn't be replaced by *that*:

> The home office, which is located in Virginia, will be moved to Kentucky.

1. Write about people doing things.

Original Apparently, our Des Moines office has discovered the secret of selling our new software package, even though it isn't supposed to be competitive.

Improvement Bill Brisbane in our Des Moines office sold 21 copies of our new software package in just one week, even though everyone else says that our package isn't competitive.

2. Use quotations.

Original He wasn't interested in our offer.

Improvement He said, "Your offer isn't even competitive."

3. Use an occasional question directed to your reader.

Original If you have any questions or comments, please don't hesitate to call or write.

Improvement Do you have any questions or comments? If so, please call or write.

4. Use *I*, *we*, and *you*.

Original This letter is just to express our appreciation for the excellent service given by your organization in helping us implement the best possible safety program for our employees.

Improvement I just want to thank you for the help you gave us when we implemented our new safety program.

5. Use the other pronouns and pointer words.

Original The products of the BMA organization are excellent. The BMA service is excellent too. Thus, continued growth for the entire organization is a reasonable prediction.

Improvement Our products are excellent, and so are our services. This should lead to continued growth for our entire organization.

Figurre 11-6 Ten guidelines for improving your style (part 1 of 2)

6. Use *that*, not *which*.

Original The products which are most in demand are the ones which we continually run out of.

Improvement The products that are most in demand are the ones that we continually run out of.

7. Remove unnecessary *thats*.

Original The products that are most in demand are the ones that we continually run out of.

Improvement The products that are most in demand are the ones we continually run out of.

8. Use more contractions.

Original I am sorry, but I cannot accept your offer. Although your services are acceptable, they do not seem to be competitively priced.

Improvement I'm sorry, but I can't accept your offer. Although your services are acceptable, they don't seem to be competitively priced.

9. Avoid constructions such as *he/she* and *and/or*.

Original A known commercial interest means that the subject is already commonly taught/bought for management/salesmanship development.

Improvement A known commercial interest means that companies are already buying and teaching the subject for the development of managers and sales representatives.

10. Use an occasional sentence fragment.

Original Why do we have the best service in the industry? We're the best because we try the hardest.

Improvement Why do we have the best service in the industry? Because we try the hardest.

Figure 11-6 Ten guidelines for improving your style (part 2 of 2)

If you don't understand this, you will after you read the next chapter. I'll also explain why you should avoid clauses like this so all your writing should be as *which*less as possible.

Remove unnecessary *thats* After you substitute *that*s for *which*es, you should ask yourself whether the *that*s can be removed. Frequently, they can because they don't contribute to the clarity of your sentences. Then, deleting them improves the readability, tone, and style of your writing. This is another Flesch suggestion.

Example 7 in figure 11-6 illustrates the use of this guideline. Here, I decided the first *that* was necessary, but the second one wasn't. To decide whether a *that* can be removed, all you have to do is read the sentence without the *that*. If it sounds better and the meaning of the sentence isn't changed, remove the *that*.

Use more contractions If you use more contractions, the tone and style of your writing will improve. In particular, Rudolf Flesch says you should try to use contractions like *didn't* and *can't* because they soften the tone of the word *not*.

Does this suggestion work? Read example 8 in figure 11-6 and decide for yourself. In my opinion, the improved version is more friendly and personal than the original. So I use contractions whenever they seem appropriate.

Avoid constructions such as *he/she* and *and/or* Not too many people use constructions separated by slashes. But those who do seriously damage the tone and style of their writing. That's why we recommend that you avoid these constructions always...no exceptions. No *he/she*, no *and/or*, and no *it/its*.

Example 9 in figure 11-6 shows how your writing improves when you avoid these constructions. Even though the improved version is longer than the original, it's easier to read. It also has a better tone and style.

Use an occasional sentence fragment A *sentence fragment* is a phrase that is written as though it's a complete sentence even though it isn't. But you probably know that already because you've been taught for years to avoid using sentence fragments. Nevertheless, an occasional sentence fragment in business writing can improve the readability and style of your writing.

Of course, I don't mean that you should use sentence fragments without knowing that you're using them. If you use a sentence fragment, you should do so deliberately. For instance, one good use of sentence fragments is for answering questions as in example 10 in figure 11-6. If you don't use a sentence fragment for the answer, you just make your writing more difficult to read.

Occasionally, you can also use sentence fragments for emphasis:

> We have five reasons for turning down your proposal. Good reasons.

Here, "Good reasons" is an obvious sentence fragment.

When you use a sentence fragment, you should keep it short so your readers can tell at a glance that it is a fragment. If a fragment is too long, your readers will keep looking for the subject and verb of your sentence without ever finding them. Then, they may have to re-read the fragment to get its meaning. This, of course, reduces the readability of your writing and defeats the purpose of the fragment.

Incidentally, some people consider sentences starting with *and*, *but*, or *so* to be sentence fragments. For instance, the third sentence in the sequence that follows can be considered a sentence fragment:

> He was late to work three times this week. He left early twice. And his work is unsatisfactory.

By today's standards, though, "And his work is unsatisfactory" isn't a sentence fragment because you can think of it as a colloquial way of saying: "In addition, his work is unsatisfactory." Similarly, you can think of "But his work is excellent" as another way of saying: "However, his work is excellent." And you can think of "So we had to fire him" as another way of saying: "As a result, we had to fire him." Whether or not you consider them sentence fragments, these structures are commonly used in business writing today because they improve readability.

Three guidelines for avoiding sexist language

In the jargon of today, *sexist language* means language that makes an unnecessary and perhaps offensive gender reference. Your writing will not be as effective as it should be if it offends someone. So you should do your best to avoid language that could offend either men or women. The three guidelines that follow will help you do that.

Write with a *you* language, not a *he* or *she* language   One of the writing habits that offends some people is the constant use of the pronouns *he*, *him*, and *his* and the exclusion of the pronouns *she*, *her* and *hers*, even when the actions could be done by men or women. A variation of this habit is referring to managers, lawyers, and accountants with masculine pronouns and to receptionists, secretaries, and clerks with feminine pronouns.

The easiest way to correct this problem is to write with a *you* attitude as I explained earlier. That will lead you to a *you* language instead of a *he* or *she* language.

This guideline is illustrated by example 1 in figure 11-7. In the original version, the clerical worker is obviously a woman. In the improved version, the writer talks directly to the reader with a *you* language.

Use plurals when describing the actions of men and women
A second way to correct the masculine or feminine tone in your writing is to use plurals when describing actions that could be done by men or women. This forces you to use plural pronouns. And plural pronouns like *they* and *them* don't indicate gender.

This guideline is illustrated by example 2 in figure 11-7. The improved version doesn't differ much from the original, but it avoids sexist language. As a result, it applies more accurately to any caller.

Avoid sexist words and terms   Certain terms and phrases are carryovers from the days when all managers and sales reps were men. These terms include words like *businessman* and *salesman*. However, these terms can all be replaced by words like *manager*, *client*, or *sales representative* without sacrificing meaning.

Other terms and phrases seem to suggest a built-in prejudice. For instance, some people refer to the "girls in the office," even though the office workers are middle-aged women. Some people use terms like "female lawyer" instead of just *lawyer*, perhaps implying that a female lawyer is unusual or less qualified. And some use terms like "male nurse" instead of just *nurse*, perhaps implying that the gender of the nurse is what's important.

To avoid sexist language, you should replace any terms or phrases that might be offensive with acceptable ones. This is illustrated by example 3 in figure 11-7. In this case, I just replaced the reference to *girls* with a reference to *someone*. If you're sensitive to the feelings and concerns of others, this type of editing is easy to do, so you shouldn't have any trouble with sexist terms and phrases.

---

1. Write with a *you* language, not a *he* or *she* language.

Original   When a terminal user analyzes information for her manager, she starts by getting and entering his password so the billing will be correct.

Improvement   If you are going to analyze information for your manager, start by getting the manager's password so the billing will be correct.

2. Use plurals when describing the actions of men and women.

Original   When a customer calls for information about his account, he should be able to get it while he's still on the phone.

Improvement   When customers call for information about their accounts, they should be able to get it while they're still on the phone.

3. Avoid sexist terms and phrases.

Original   If you have a problem with your billing code, please see one of the girls in the administrative department.

Improvement   If you have a problem with your billing code, please see someone in the administrative department.

Figure 11-7   Three guidelines for avoiding sexist language

Discussion

Tone is frequently a problem in business writing. Refusal letters are unnecessarily negative. Collection letters are unnecessarily threatening. Sales letters are insincere. Reports and proposals are pompous. And so on. Sometimes, the tone is just a bit unsatisfactory; sometimes it completely defeats the purpose of a document.

To see an example of ineffective tone, look at the letter in figure 11-8. It was sent to me by a prospective author who wanted my company to review his manuscript for possible publication. Due to its tone, though, the letter put me in a negative frame of mind from the

How to write with an effective tone and style

Dear Mr. Murach:

We have had numerous inquiries from publishers about the book we are writing entitled: <u>Microcomputer Management: A Pragmatic Approach.</u> Before committing ourselves to just any publisher, we wanted your company's consideration.

Our book will have a strong demand, due to the many disciplines that will have a need to teach the use of microcomputers. Colleges and universities are starting to offer courses that address this area, but the major problem is that they are lacking adequate texts. The only texts to date that we have found take either a systems analysis or a classical management approach, neither of which adequately addresses the total concept. Our text will pragmatically address the comprehensive nature of this task. My co-author and myself both have had extensive experience with microcomputer management and can give to the book a reality that theorists don't grasp.

Because of our educational orientation, we would like to see our book published by a company with a good share of the educational market place.

We have included the preface, outline, and our personal resumes. We would be open to hearing any consideration that your company would care to offer in terms of:

- -Publishing schedule
- -Current market share and orientation
- -Author rights, fees, and royalties
- -Copy of your standard contract

We would like your response within four weeks.

Thank you for your time and consideration of our proposal for a text.

                    Sincerely,

Figure 11-8 A typical business letter that would benefit from an improved tone and style

start. Although we still reviewed the book, we decided that we weren't interested in publishing it. I don't know if the author ever got his book published, but it wouldn't surprise me if he didn't. Too often, problems with tone indicate problems with perspective.

Of course, if you don't write readable sentences and effective paragraphs, any concerns about tone and style are irrelevant. If you don't write sentences at an acceptable level of readability, the only tone your writing will have will be an ineffective one. If you don't write fully developed paragraphs in a logical sequence of presentation, your style will be ineffective and that's all anyone will remember about it. In other words, none of the guidelines in this chapter can help you if you write unreadable sentences and ineffective paragraphs.

On the other hand, if you're already writing effective paragraphs and readable sentences, the guidelines in this chapter will help you improve your writing effectiveness. These guidelines are summarized in figure 11-9. By improving your tone and style, you'll get your message across to more of your readers. You'll be the one who writes the letters, memos, and reports people enjoy reading.

Incidentally, a writing analyzer will help you apply only a few of the guidelines in figure 11-9. For instance, when I ran *Grammatik III* on the letter in figure 11-8, it recommended that I change some of the "pompous" words like *numerous*, *concept*, and *orientation*, but it was unable to make other recommendations that would improve the tone of this letter. Similarly, *Grammatik III* will identify some uses of sexist language, but not all. For the most part, then, you must master and apply the guidelines in figure 11-9 without much help from a writing analyzer.

On the other hand, you can use your word processor to help you search for *which*es, *that*s, and masculine pronouns such as *he*, *him*, and *his*. As the word processor locates each one, you can decide whether to change it, delete it, or leave it alone. This should take only a few minutes as part of the editing and revision step, so it's usually worth doing.

If you want to read a delightful book on writing that supports and enhances the guidelines of this chapter, let me recommend one. It is called *On Business Communications*; it was written by Rudolf Flesch; and it's available in paperback. Although you can read it in just a few hours, it may change your writing style forever.

Three guidelines for improving the tone of your writing

1. Write with a *you* attitude.
2. Write with a positive attitude.
3. Write with a conversational style.

Ten guidelines for improving the style of your writing

1. Write about people doing things.
2. Use quotations.
3. Use an occasional question.
4. Use *I*, *we*, and *you*.
5. Use other pronouns and pointer words.
6. Use *that*, not *which*.
7. Remove unnecessary *thats*.
8. Use more contractions.
9. Avoid constructions such as *he/she* and *and/or*.
10. Use an occasional sentence fragment.

Three guidelines for avoiding sexist language

1. Write with a *you* language, not a *he* or *she* language.
2. Use plurals when describing the actions of men and women.
3. Avoid sexist words and terms.

Figure 11-9   A summary of the guidelines for improving the tone and style of your writing

Terms

tone
style
sentence fragment
sexist language

Objectives

1. Distinguish between tone and style.

2. Describe the characteristics of an effective tone for business writing.

3. Describe three guidelines for improving the tone of your writing.

4. Describe seven of the ten guidelines for improving the style of your writing.

5. Describe three guidelines for avoiding sexist language.

6. Given a writing sample, rewrite it to improve its tone and style and to remove any sexist language.

Heading plan for chapter 12

Clauses and phrases

The four basic sentence structures for business writing

- The simple sentence without introductory or concluding phrases
- The compound sentence
- The complex sentence with an introductory adverbial clause
- The complex sentence with a concluding adverbial clause

Three ways to expand the basic sentence structures

- Use introductory words and phrases
- Use noun clauses
- Use restrictive adjective clauses

Three ways to simplify your sentences

- Avoid participial phrases
- Avoid non-restrictive clauses and phrases
- Avoid lengthy parentheticals

Three guidelines for improving your sentence structures

- Limit the complexity of your sentence structures
- Show relationships by using complex sentences with adverbial clauses
- Avoid a series of sentences starting with the subjects

Discussion

Chapter 12

How to write
with manageable sentence structures

All too frequently, business and technical writers use sentence structures that are either too simple or too complicated for their purposes. That's why most writers can improve their writing by becoming more aware of the structures they use. Then, they can control those structures. Although this chapter may tell you far more about sentence structures than you ever wanted to know, it can also help you make an obvious improvement in your writing.

To start, I'll explain how clauses are different from phrases and show you some of the basic types of both. Next, I'm going to introduce you to the four basic sentence structures that I recommend for business and technical writing. Then, I'll show you three ways to expand these structures, and three ways to simplify them. With this as background, I'll give you three guidelines for improving your sentence structures.

If you have problems with grammar and punctuation, this chapter will show you how to reduce your grammatical problems by controlling your sentence structures. In particular, if you use the sentence structures I recommend and punctuate them as shown, you'll make fewer grammatical errors. You'll also find that you'll write more easily.

In this chapter, I'm assuming you already know what *subjects*, *verbs*, *nouns*, *adjectives*, and *adverbs* are. When I describe the structures and guidelines for writing effective sentences, I'll use these terms and I'll also present more grammatical terminology. For instance, I'll present *adverbial clauses* so I can show you how they can be used to show relationships. Similarly, I'll present *non-restrictive clauses* so I can advise you to avoid them. If you already know this terminology, it should be easy for you to understand the ideas presented in this chapter. If you don't, you'll be getting a quick course in terminology as you learn how to improve your sentence structures.

Clauses and phrases

Before I can present the four basic sentence structures I recommend for business writing, you need to know the difference between a clause and a phrase and you need to know the basic types of clauses and phrases. After I present this information, I'll show you how it applies to the four sentence structures.

A *clause* is a group of words that contains a subject and a verb. In figure 12-1, for example, you can see some typical clauses. These clauses are divided into two types: independent clauses and dependent clauses.

An *independent*, or *main*, *clause* is a clause that makes sense by itself. As you can see in figure 12-1, each *simple sentence* or *complex sentence* contains one independent clause. However, a *compound sentence* contains two or more independent clauses.

A *dependent*, or *subordinate*, *clause* is a clause that doesn't express a complete thought. For example, "when I interviewed him" is a subordinate clause. It doesn't mean anything until you add an independent clause to it as in this sentence:

When I interviewed him, Mr. Clark was open and friendly.

In figure 12-1, you can see dependent clauses used as adverbs, nouns, and adjectives. As a result, these clauses are referred to as adverbial, noun, and adjective clauses.

In contrast to a clause, a *phrase* is group of words that functions as a unit within a sentence, within a clause, or within another phrase. For instance, figure 12-2 shows five types of phrases used within a single sentence. The essential difference between a clause and a phrase is that a clause must contain a subject and a verb, but a phrase doesn't have to.

The four basic sentence structures for business writing

There are two common mistakes business writers make in choosing sentence structures, and both of them can reduce the effectiveness of your writing. The first is to use only simple sentence structures in an effort to be clear and direct. Unfortunately, when you repeat the same

How to write with manageable sentence structures 283

Independent clauses

In a simple sentence

The committee reviewed three systems.

Mr. Clark is an open, friendly man.

In a compound sentence

The members of the committee reviewed three systems, and they selected the first one.

Mr. Clark is an open, friendly man, but he isn't overly friendly.

In a complex sentence

After the members of the committee reviewed the three systems, they selected the first one.

I recommend that we hire Mr. Clark, if we can meet his salary expectations.

Dependent clauses

Adverbial clauses

After the members of the committee reviewed the three systems, they selected the first one.

I recommend that we hire Mr. Clark, if we can meet his salary expectations.

Noun clauses

The members of the committee said that they preferred the first system.

Mr. Clark seemed to have a good sense of what was appropriate during the interview.

Adjective clauses

The members of the committee that reviewed the three systems selected the first one.

I prefer Mr. Clark, who is open and friendly, to the others.

Figure 12-1 Independent and dependent clauses

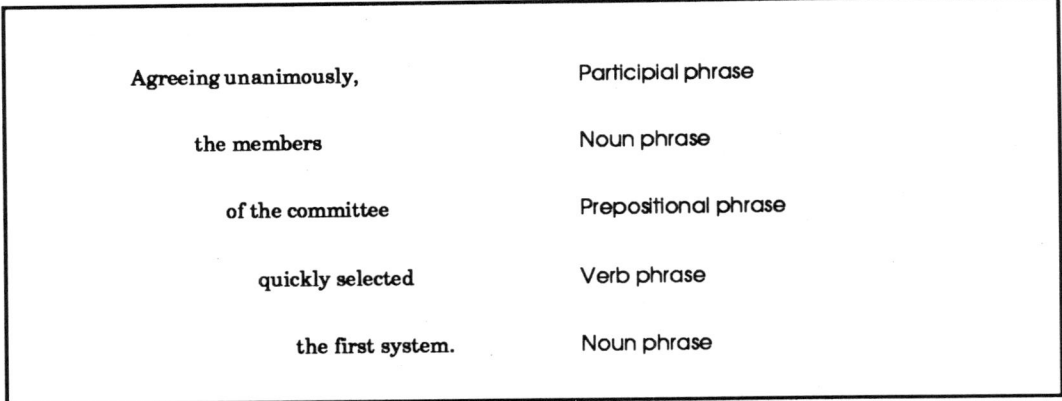

Figure 12-2 Phrases

sentence structure many times, your writing may be clear, but it may also be monotonous and uninteresting. Another problem with using only simple sentence structures is that it limits your ability to show relationships between sentences.

Another common mistake in business writing is using complicated sentence structures you don't understand. Then, it's easy to become confused because your writing is awkward or unclear, and you don't know how to improve it. Since each type of sentence structure has its own rules of punctuation and grammar, there are more opportunities for errors when you use more types.

Although there are many kinds of sentence structures, you can write almost anything with only four basic types. I'm going to tell you about these four types and explain how you can use them to make your writing varied and interesting. If you understand these four basic sentence structures, you'll be able to use them to write with confidence and accuracy.

The simple sentence without introductory or concluding phrases Using traditional terminology, a *simple sentence* is a sentence that consists of one independent clause. In its simplest form, a simple sentence is a sentence that contains one subject and one verb such as

Bill Miller started the company.

However, a simple sentence can also have a *compound subject* as in this sentence:

Bill Miller and *John Walsh* started the company.

Or, it can have a *compound verb* as in this sentence:

Bill Miller *started* the company and *made* it prosper.

In fact, it can have both a compound subject and a compound verb as in this sentence:

Bill Miller and *John Walsh started* the company and *made* it prosper.

A simple sentence can also contain introductory or concluding phrases (but not clauses). For instance, the simple sentence that follows contains both an introductory and a concluding phrase:

After analyzing many aspects of the direct mail industry, Bill Miller and John Walsh decided to start with products designed for children.

Here, the introductory phrase is "after analyzing many aspects of the direct mail industry," and the concluding phrase is "designed for children."

The first basic sentence structure I recommend is the simple sentence without any introductory or concluding phrases. This is illustrated by the two examples in figure 12-3. Most of the time, you should also try to use the normal subject-verb order when you write a sentence in this structure. That means you should start your sentence with the subject and follow it with a verb in the active voice.

The problem with simple sentences is that they don't show relationships well. To show them, you have to start your simple sentences with connecting words like *however*, *meanwhile*, and *nevertheless*. As a result, you can often show relationships more effectively with complex sentences than you can with simple sentences. More about this in a moment.

The compound sentence A *compound sentence* consists of two or more independent clauses usually joined by a *coordinating conjunction* like the ones listed in figure 12-4. The most common conjunctions

The simple sentence without introductory or concluding phrases

Basic form	Subject followed by verb and its supporting elements.
Examples	The committee reviewed three systems. Mr. Clark is an open, friendly man.

The compound sentence

Basic forms	Main-clause, conjunction main-clause. Main-clause; main-clause.
Examples	The members of the committee reviewed three systems, and they selected the first one. Mr. Clark is an open, friendly man, but he isn't overly friendly. The members of the committee reviewed three systems; they selected the first one.

The complex sentence with an introductory adverbial clause

Basic form	Adverbial-clause, main-clause.
Examples	After the members of the committee reviewed the three systems, they selected the first one. Since Mr. Clark is open and friendly, I prefer him to the others.

The complex sentence with a concluding adverbial clause

Basic forms	Main-clause adverbial-clause. Main-clause, adverbial-clause.
Examples	The committee selected the first system because it satisfied all of their requirements. I recommend that we hire Mr. Clark, if we can meet his salary expectations.

Figure 12-3 The four basic sentence structures for business writing

are *and* and *but*, but other words such as *nor*, *or*, and *yet* can also be used as coordinating conjunctions. To some extent, a compound sentence implies that the clauses are approximately equal in importance.

In most cases, you punctuate a compound sentence with a comma after the first main clause and before the coordinating conjunction as shown in figure 12-3. However, you can also write a compound sentence without a conjunction. In this case, you use a semicolon to show that the clauses are connected, as in this example:

> Mr. Clark is open and friendly; he also has extensive experience in our field.

Obviously, then, a compound sentence like this can easily be written as two simple sentences. The only difference is in the punctuation.

When written with a semicolon or with *and* as the conjunction, the compound sentence has the same problem two simple sentences have. It doesn't show relationships well. Since you usually want to show some relationship between the clauses, you shouldn't use compound sentences like these very often.

On the other hand, a compound sentence joined by the word *but* does show a relationship. It shows that the second clause contrasts with the first clause. As a result, the *but* form of the compound sentence is useful in business writing.

The complex sentence with an introductory adverbial clause

Using traditional terminology, a *complex sentence* is one that contains one independent clause and one or more dependent clauses. When used as an adverb, a dependent clause is called an *adverbial clause*. A clause like this can modify a verb, an adjective, or an adverb, but it modifies a verb most of the time.

Adverbial clauses start with a connecting word called a *subordinating conjunction*. Some of these conjunctions are listed in figure 12-4. For instance, conjunctions like *because* and *since* introduce clauses that tell why. Conjunctions like *after*, *before*, *until*, *when*, and *while* introduce clauses that tell when. Conjunctions like *although*, *if*, *though*, and *unless* introduce clauses that present conditions.

To write effectively, you should start many of your sentences with adverbial clauses. That way, the subordinate clause enhances the

Coordinating conjunctions

and
but
or
nor
yet

Subordinating conjunctions used in adverbial clauses

after
although
as
as long as
because
before
if
since
so
though
until
unless
when
while

Relative pronouns used in noun and adjective clauses

that
what
which
who
whom
whose

Figure 12-4 Conjunctions and relative pronouns

meaning of the main clause because it shows a relationship. For instance,

> I prefer Mr. Clark to the other applicants. He is open and friendly.

doesn't show the relationship between the two sentences. But the adverbial clause in the sentence that follows makes the relationship obvious:

> Since Mr. Clark is so open and friendly, I prefer him to the other applicants.

Here, the adverbial clause answers the question *why*.
    Similarly, adverbial clauses that answer the question *when* are often most effective when they start a sentence. Then, the reader can place the statement in time before he reads the main clause. This is illustrated by this sentence:

> When I interviewed Mr. Clark, he was open and friendly.

Notice the difference when the adverbial clause follows the main clause as in this sentence:

> Mr. Clark was open and friendly when I interviewed him.

Here, the subordinate clause is anticlimactic.
    Finally, adverbial clauses that present conditions are often most effective when they start a sentence. This is illustrated by this sentence:

> If we hire him, he will cost us dearly.

Compare this with:

> He will cost us dearly if we hire him.

A sentence like this is often more effective when the adverbial clause is first because the main clause has more meaning if you know what the conditions are as you read it.
    To punctuate this kind of sentence, you put a comma after the introductory adverbial clause. This is illustrated by the examples in

figure 12-3. Although some books on writing say this comma is optional, I recommend that you always use it for business writing. Because it lets the reader know where the main clause starts, it makes the meaning clearer.

The complex sentence with a concluding adverbial clause If you look at the examples of this structure in figure 12-3, you can see that it's just like the preceding structure only the adverbial clause is last rather than first. In general, though, this structure isn't as effective as the one with the adverbial clause first. As a result, you shouldn't use it as often. It's also dangerous with long or complex sentences, because it lengthens your sentences even more and reduces readability.

When the adverbial clause is closely related to the main clause, you shouldn't use a comma to separate the clauses. But if the adverbial clause isn't closely related to the main clause, you should separate the clauses with a comma. For instance, a comma is appropriate in this sentence:

> The committee selected the first system, although I certainly don't agree with their decision.

Too often, writers use concluding adverbial clauses to add thoughts that deserve sentences of their own. The result is an awkward series of afterthoughts that is part of a *strung-along sentence*:

> The committee selected the first system, although I certainly don't agree with their decision because many people are unhappy that we didn't consider more possibilities.

So when you use a concluding adverbial clause, keep it simple and make sure it belongs in the same sentence as the first clause. That way, you will avoid writing strung-along sentences.

Three ways to expand the basic sentence structures

You can expand the four basic sentence structures I've just presented in many ways. Some of these are useful. Some interfere with clarity.

Figure 12-5 shows three acceptable ways to expand the basic sentence structures. As I present these, I'll tell you how and when to use them. I'll also show you how to punctuate them.

How to write with manageable sentence structures 291

Use introductory words and phrases

<u>Over a period of five months</u>, the committee reviewed three systems.

<u>During the interview</u>, Mr. Clark was open and friendly, but he seemed quite reserved after the interview.

<u>After a lengthy discussion</u>, the committee members selected the first system because it satisfied all of their requirements.

<u>Nevertheless</u>, because Mr. Clark is so open and friendly, I prefer him to the others.

Use noun clauses

The members of the committee said <u>that they preferred the first system</u>.

Mr. Clark seemed to have a good sense of <u>what was appropriate during the interview.</u>

Use restrictive adjective clauses

The members of the committee reviewed the three systems <u>that had been recommended to them.</u>

Mr. Clark is an open, friendly man <u>who should fit in well here.</u>

Figure 12-5   Three ways to expand the basic sentence structures

Use introductory words and phrases   An *introductory phrase* is one that starts a sentence. It comes before the first clause of the sentence. As you can see in figure 12-5, an introductory phrase can be used effectively in a simple sentence, a compound sentence, or a complex sentence.

The comma after an introductory word or phrase is optional, but I recommend that you use it for business writing. Then, the reader can easily tell where the first clause of the sentence begins. The longer the phrase is, the more useful the comma is.

Use noun clauses A *noun clause* is a subordinate clause that is used as a noun. In the first example in figure 12-5, the noun clause is used as the object of the verb *said*. It tells what was said. In the second example, the noun clause is used as the object of the preposition *of*.

Noun clauses are usually introduced by *relative pronouns* such as *that* or *what*. Some of these pronouns are listed in figure 12-4. In some cases, as in the second example in figure 12-5, the relative pronoun is the subject of the subordinate clause. (Remember that a clause contains a subject and a verb.)

You shouldn't have any trouble using noun clauses. No punctuation is needed for them because they don't interfere with the flow of a sentence. So use them whenever they contribute to the thought you're trying to express.

As I said in the last chapter, you should consider deleting the word *that* when it is used as the relative pronoun of a noun clause. If you do, it can give your writing a more informal tone and style. For instance:

They said they preferred the first system.

is equivalent to

They said that they preferred the first system.

However, the first sentence is slightly more conversational than the second sentence. Although you can't always delete the word *that* because its removal can make a sentence difficult to follow, you should remove it whenever you can.

Use restrictive adjective clauses An *adjective clause* is a clause that is used to modify a noun. These clauses are frequently introduced by relative pronouns like *who, whom, that,* or *which*. In the sentence that follows, the adjective clause modifies the word *man*, and it is introduced by the word *whom*:

We hired a man whom I met by accident.

Sometimes, the relative pronoun is omitted as in this sentence:

We hired a man I met by accident.

But this is still an adjective clause.

In grammatical terms, there are two types of adjective clauses: restrictive and non-restrictive. A *restrictive clause* is essential to the meaning of the sentence, while a non-restrictive clause isn't. In general, you should use restrictive adjective clauses whenever they are appropriate. They are easy to use, and they require no punctuation.

As I said in the last chapter, you should avoid using the relative pronoun *which* in restrictive adjective clauses. In its place, you should use the pronoun *that*. So instead of saying "the three systems which we recommended," you should say "the three systems that we recommended." This will give your writing a more informal tone and style.

Three ways to simplify your sentences

Now, I'm going to present three constructions you should avoid using when you write your sentences. They're troublesome because they can make your writing confusing and difficult to follow. These constructions are summarized in figure 12-6.

Avoid participial phrases   A *participial phrase* is a group of words controlled by a verb form called a *participle*. In the sentence that follows, the underlined words make up the participial phrase:

<u>Studying the report,</u> he noted several discrepancies.

Within this phrase, *studying* is the participle. You can recognize the participles in phrases like "swimming toward shore" and "studying the report" because the participles are verbs that end with *ing*. However, a participle doesn't function as a verb; it functions as an adjective.

Although participial phrases are quite common in business and academic writing, I recommend that you avoid them. Unlike a clause, a participial phrase doesn't have a subject, so you can't always tell who is doing the action implied by the participle. As a result, you can usually present the thought of a participial phrase more effectively with a clause, as in this example:

As he studied the report, he noted several discrepancies.

> **Avoid participial phrases**
>
> Original Combining both writing ability and technical expertise, the author of this report is well qualified to report on changes in our industry.
>
> Improvement Because the author has both writing ability and technical expertise, she is well qualified to report on changes in our industry.
>
> **Avoid non-restrictive clauses and phrases**
>
> Original Our new agency program, which has the support of all branch managers and which will be the basis for all sales activities in the coming year, represents a much-needed change in our policies.
>
> Improvement Our new agency program represents a much-needed change in our policies. All of our branch managers support this program. And it will be the basis for all of our sales activities in the coming year.
>
> **Avoid lengthy parentheticals**
>
> Original Because the discussion (one that was more a clash of personalities than an expression of ideas) lasted almost an hour without accomplishing anything, I suggest that you attend our next meeting to help resolve the conflict.
>
> Improvement In my opinion, the discussion was more a clash of personalities than an expression of ideas. As a result, it lasted almost an hour without accomplishing anything. I suggest, then, that you attend our next meeting to help resolve the conflict.

Figure 12-6 Three constructions to avoid

Here, nouns and verbs are doing the work so the language is more interesting.

Figure 12-6 presents another example of how the removal of a participial phrase can improve sentence clarity. If you study it, I think you'll get my point. I'm not saying that you shouldn't ever use a participial phrase, but you can usually find a more direct way to present your thought.

To check your writing, you can use the search function on your word processing system to find words ending in *ing*. As it locates each one, you can decide whether to change the word or leave it alone. Not all words ending in *ing* are participles, but you may discover you're using more of them than you thought.

Avoid non-restrictive clauses and phrases   A *non-restrictive clause* or *phrase* isn't essential to a sentence. As a result, it can be removed without changing the primary meaning of the sentence. For example, this sentence contains a non-restrictive phrase:

> Mr. Clark, a man whom I recommend hiring, has a pleasant personality.

Here, "a man whom I recommend hiring" is a non-restrictive phrase that contains an adjective clause.

One problem with a non-restrictive clause or phrase is that it interferes with the main thought of the sentence. The other problem is that the ideas presented in non-restrictive clauses or phrases don't get the emphasis they deserve. These problems are demonstrated by the example in figure 12-6. Here, the writer has used two non-restrictive clauses to modify the subject of the sentence. As a result, 22 words come between the subject and the verb. This, of course, makes the sentence difficult to read. In addition, the thoughts in the clauses don't get the emphasis they deserve. In the rewritten version, the writer presents these thoughts in separate sentences so there's no doubt about the importance of the new agency program.

To avoid problems like these, I recommend that you avoid non-restrictive clauses and phrases altogether. If the thought of a non-restrictive clause or phrase is worth presenting, it should be presented in an independent clause or in an adverbial clause that shows a relationship.

Avoid lengthy parentheticals   A *parenthetical* is a phrase or clause that interrupts the movement of a sentence. For instance, connecting words and phrases like *however* and *for instance* are often used as parentheticals as in this sentence:

> My choice, however, is the second system.

Here, the word *however* is a parenthetical.

If a parenthetical is short and clearly related to the context of the sentence, you set it off with commas. Obviously, it's okay to use parentheticals like this. They're only a minor interruption to the movement of a sentence, and they can help show relationships.

On the other hand, you should avoid lengthy parentheticals, particularly those that aren't closely related to the main thought of the sentence. If you use a lengthy parenthetical, it should be set off by parentheses as in this example:

> The report was poorly written (in fact, I had to pinch myself three times to keep from falling asleep as I read it), so I insisted that it be rewritten.

To improve readability, though, you should remove the parenthetical by rewriting the sentence as in this example:

> The report was poorly written. In fact, I had to pinch myself three times to keep from falling asleep as I read it. That's why I insisted that it be rewritten.

When you write the sentence this way, each sentence presents only one thought, and the punctuation is obvious.

Figure 12-6 gives another example of the use of parentheticals. Here, you can see that the parenthetical presents an important thought. When you give this thought its own sentence, clarity improves because the thought receives its proper emphasis. In addition, the rewritten version shows the relationship between this thought and the other thoughts of the original sentence.

Three guidelines for improving your sentence structures

Now that you know the four basic sentence structures, three ways to expand them, and three ways not to expand them, you can start thinking about how you can improve your own sentence structures. Here, then, are three guidelines to help you write better sentences.

Limit the complexity of your sentence structures   If you limit the complexity of your sentence structures, you also increase the readability of your writing. That's why I recommend that you use only the four basic sentence structures plus the three ways to expand them for almost all of the sentences you write. You can write anything using

How to write with manageable sentence structures 297

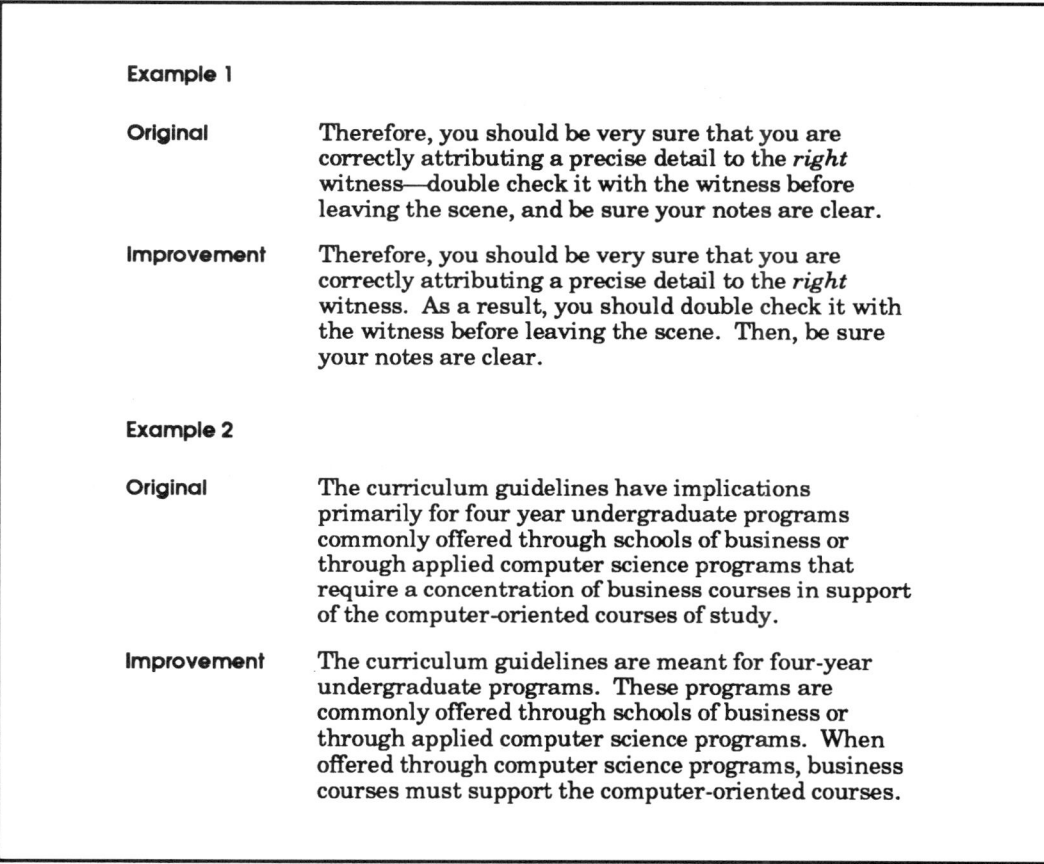

Figure 12-7 Limit the complexity of your sentences

these structures, and your readers will never notice how limited your sentence structures are. They'll just notice how easy it is to read your writing.

Figure 12-7 illustrates what I mean by limiting the complexity of your sentences. In example 1, the author presents three thoughts in a sentence that has an unnecessarily complicated structure. When I rewrote this sentence, I used three simple sentences with introductory words or phrases.

In example 2, the author really hasn't said much in his 39-word, strung-along sentence. But I think he's trying to identify the audience that his report is meant for. When I rewrote this sentence, I used two simple sentences followed by a complex sentence with an introductory adverbial clause. I'm not sure this rewriting expresses the intent of the author, but I hope you see the point I'm trying to make.

If you limit your sentence structures in this way, you also limit your problems with grammar and punctuation. That's why this guideline is particularly useful for those who aren't confident about their writing. Just punctuate the four basic sentences and the three expansions as shown in this chapter.

Show relationships by using complex sentences with adverbial clauses   Some business writers use simple sentences as frequently as possible because they think it will simplify their writing. The trouble is that you have to use connecting words to show the relationships between simple sentences. And even then, you can't always show the relationships you want to show. That's why you should use complex sentences with adverbial clauses more frequently.

Figure 12-8 shows how the use of complex sentences with adverbial clauses can help you show the relationships between your thoughts. This is particularly true when the relationships you're trying to express are complicated. That's why this structure is important for technical writers. In terms of readability scores, all three of the improved sentences in figure 12-8 score worse than the original sentences. But that just shows the limitations of readability measurement.

Avoid a series of sentences starting with the subjects   Unless you're deliberately using parallel sentence structures, a series of sentences starting with the subjects just doesn't read well. In editorial jargon, a series of sentences like that doesn't "flow." It has a deadening effect. It detracts from the interest of the thoughts. So you should do your best to avoid this writing flaw.

Figure 12-9 illustrates this problem and the solution. To correct the problem, all you have to do is start one of the sentences in the series with an introductory word, an introductory phrase, or an introductory adverbial clause. As you make this change, you can concentrate on showing relationships as well as making the writing flow.

Discussion

When I started writing as a professional, I tried to make extensive use of short, simple sentences, and I tried to avoid the use of complex sentences. I did this because I thought it would lead to a clear writing

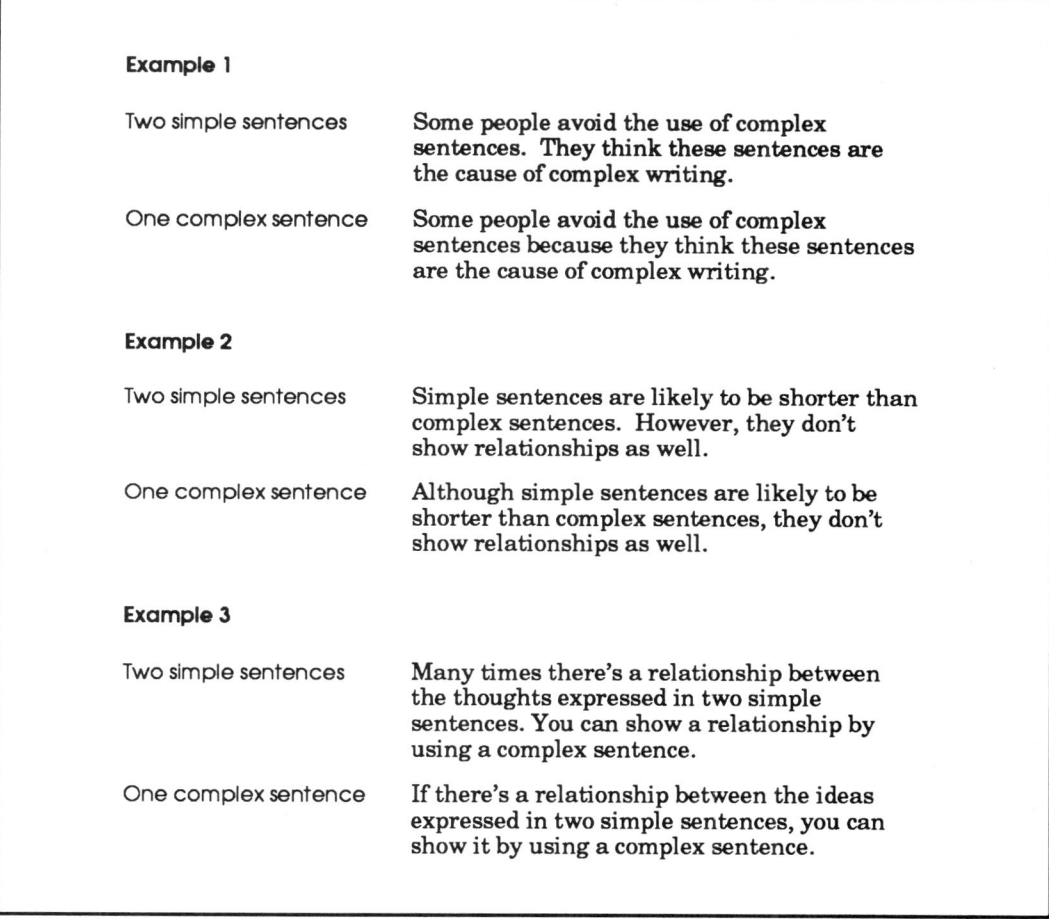

Figure 12-8 Show relationships by using complex sentences with adverbial clauses

style. But soon I realized that you can't show all the relationships you want to show if you restrict yourself in this way. I also realized that a complex sentence with either an introductory adverbial clause or a concluding adverbial clause is the most effective structure for showing the relationships between your thoughts.

Today, the majority of my sentences are still simple sentences. But I use complex sentences with adverbial clauses whenever they help me show a relationship. I also use introductory phrases with many of my simple sentences because these phrases help me show

---

Original

One writing problem is starting each sentence with the subject. The writing seems to bog down after two or three sentences like that in a row. It seems to have a deadening effect. This is an easy problem to correct. You start one of the sentences with an introductory phrase or clause.

Improvement

One writing problem is starting each sentence with the subject. After two or three sentences in a row like that, the writing seems to bog down. It seems to have a deadening effect. Fortunately, this is an easy problem to correct. Whenever you recognize it, you start one of the sentences with an introductory word, phrase, or clause.

Figure 12-9 Avoid a series of sentences starting with the subjects

relationships. If you were to study the sentence structures I use, you would find that I use the four basic structures in figure 12-3 with just the three extensions in figure 12-5 almost all the time.

If you want to become an effective business or technical writer, I recommend that you use a limited number of sentence structures too. If you do, you'll be able to master the structures that you use. Then, you'll have fewer grammatical problems and you'll write more easily. You'll also keep your writing at an acceptable reading level.

Terms

clause
independent clause
main clause
dependent clause
subordinate clause
phrase
simple sentence
compound subject
compound verb

compound sentence
coordinating conjunction
complex sentence
adverbial clause
subordinating conjunction
strung-along sentence
introductory phrase
noun clause
relative pronoun
adjective clause
restrictive clause
participial phrase
participle
non-restrictive clause
non-restrictive phrase
parenthetical

Objectives

1. List and describe the four basic sentence structures I recommend for business writing.

2. List and describe the three ways I recommend for expanding the basic sentence structures.

3. Explain why you should avoid using participial phrases, non-restrictive clauses and phrases, and lengthy parentheticals.

4. List and describe the three guidelines for improving your sentence structures.

5. Given a writing sample, rewrite it so the sentence structures are consistent with the guidelines given in this chapter.

Heading plan for chapter 13

Six fundamental rules of grammar
- Use complete sentences
- Make sure each verb agrees with its subject
- Make sure each pronoun reference is clear and that each pronoun agrees with its antecedent
- Make sure your verb forms are simple and consistent
- Make sure your modifiers clearly relate to the words they modify
- Keep your parallel constructions parallel

How to use the most common punctuation symbols
- Commas
- Other punctuation symbols
- Capitalization
- Underlining or italics

The elements of good diction
- The right word choices
- Correct spelling
- Correct pronunciation

How to improve your grammar and diction
- Build a library for business writers
- Set up a 30-day plan to improve your grammar
- Set up a 30-day plan to improve your diction

Discussion

Chapter 13

How to write
with correct grammar and diction

You don't learn to write well just by learning grammar, punctuation, and diction. No, your writing can be poor even though your grammar, punctuation, and diction are perfect. That's why this is the last chapter in the section on writing skills.

On the other hand, you can't write well without an adequate mastery of grammar, punctuation, and diction. Although business people are generally tolerant of minor errors, there are limits that you can't go beyond. If you make too many errors, your readers will be distracted from the content and logic of your writing. That in turn will reduce the effectiveness of your writing.

That's why this chapter introduces the grammar, punctuation, and diction skills you need for effective business writing. Although this chapter isn't designed to teach you all the skills you need to master, it will show you how to avoid many of the common errors business writers make. This chapter will also make you aware of any shortcomings you have and show you how to overcome them.

Like the last chapter, this chapter assumes you already know what *subjects*, *verbs*, *nouns*, *adjectives*, and *adverbs* are. It also assumes you've read chapter 12 and learned its terminology. From that base, this chapter introduces you to the most important applications of grammar and punctuation in business writing. Then, it shows you the importance of correct diction. Last, in case you're not satisfied with your own mastery of grammar and diction, this chapter shows you how you can improve it once and for all.

Before I start, I want to remind you that you'll have fewer problems with grammar and punctuation if you improve the readability of your sentences. In particular, you'll have fewer problems if you limit the complexity of your sentence structures as I explained in the last chapter. If you keep your sentence structures simple, it's easier to identify sentence fragments, incorrect subject and verb agreement, unclear pronoun references, and so on. It's also easier to correctly use commas and other punctuation symbols.

Six fundamental rules of grammar

Grammar consists of rules that provide the logic that clarifies the meaning in your writing. If you don't follow these rules, your readers will have difficulty understanding your writing. In addition, they may assume you're uneducated, so they will discredit the content and logic of your writing.

Since most business people have little training in writing, they tend to be quite tolerant of minor grammatical errors. For instance, the letter in figure 13-1 contains at least three of them. Yet, it is used by a marketing subsidiary of a Fortune 500 company as the standard cover letter for the presentation of price quotations on copiers. Although this letter is ineffective for many reasons, one of these reasons is that the grammar is below acceptable standards for business writing.

Can you find and correct the grammatical errors in this letter? If not, you need to work on your grammatical skills. The topics that follow present some of the more important skills you need to master for most business writing.

Use complete sentences   Since grade school, you've most likely been taught to write complete sentences and to avoid incomplete sentences, or *sentence fragments*. As a result, you already know how to recognize fragments and revise them so they're complete sentences. However, some people don't know how to do that, and some people use sentence fragments deliberately when they shouldn't.

Figure 13-2 presents two examples of sentence fragments I took from recent business letters. In the first example, I'm sure the fragment was unintentional because it becomes a complete sentence if you replace the *and* with a comma. In the second example, I know the writer used the fragment deliberately because he used that stylistic device several other times in the two-page letter. However, the fragment in the example is too long to be effective. After you read the entire fragment looking for the verb without finding it, you have to re-read the fragment to get what little meaning it contains.

```
Dear :

Thank you for giving us at Nationwide Business Systems, Inc.
the opportunity to be of service to your organization.

Based upon your needs, attached will be found the pricing
information pertinent to the equipment and accessories that
we discussed.

Nationwide Business Systems, as a direct retail owned
subsidiary of Nationwide Corporation is in a position to
fulfill the needs of your company, not only today, but also
as your needs grow.

Nationwide has established a valued reputation for more than
50 years, and over 2-1/2 decades of experience in the
photocopying industry.  Our professional sales staff, timely
and effective servicing, and our dedicated administrative
support are only a few highlights of our success.

Should you have any questions, please do not hesitate to
give us a call.

Cordially,
```

Figure 13-1 A standard sales letter used by a marketing subsidiary of a Fortune 500 company

As I suggested in chapter 11, an occasional sentence fragment can improve your tone and style. But you must use fragments deliberately and with clear purpose. Two effective uses of them are (1) to answer your own question and (2) to add emphasis to a thought. Whenever you use a sentence fragment, you should keep it short so your readers can tell at a glance that it is a deliberate sentence fragment.

Make sure each verb agrees with its subject   To write grammatically, you must make each verb agree with its subject in number. That means singular subjects take singular verb forms; plural subjects take plural verb forms.

Figure 13-3 summarizes the most commonly used rules of subject and verb agreement. Most business writers seem to know these rules, but they occasionally fail to apply them, perhaps due to careless proofreading. Take a minute now to study these rules and make sure you know them.

An unintentional sentence fragment

Wrong: On May 8 when you first sent us your check and I returned the check with a letter stating the amount was incorrect. Now I'm returning your check again.

Right: On May 8, when you first sent us your check, I returned it with a letter explaining the amount was incorrect. Now, I'm returning your check again for the same reason.

A deliberate, but ineffective, sentence fragment

Wrong: The most important aspect of a career with us is the company behind you. You'll be part of a financial services leader with assets of over $130 billion. A company with such an outstanding reputation for financial security and service that it's recognized by most American consumers.

Right: The most important aspect of a career with us is the company behind you. If you join us, you'll be part of a company with $130 billion in assets and an outstanding reputation for customer service.

Figure 13-2 Use complete sentences

Make sure each pronoun reference is clear and that each pronoun agrees with its antecedent If your grade school and high school teachers told you to avoid using pronouns, they probably did so because many students misuse pronouns. To use them correctly, you must make sure that each pronoun clearly refers to the noun it represents. This noun is called the *antecedent* of the pronoun. You must also make sure that each pronoun agrees with its antecedent in gender and number.

Figure 13-4 shows some typical problems business writers have with pronouns. To make your references clear, you must make sure that only one noun qualifies as a possible antecedent for each pronoun. To make your pronouns agree with their antecedents, you must know what the antecedent is and whether it is singular or plural. This often goes back to knowing the rules for subject and verb agreement.

> 1. **Make sure the verb agrees with the subject; don't be confused by the object of a preposition or an expletive such as *there*.**
>
> Wrong: *One* of every five new books *are* successful.
> Right: *One* of every five new books *is* successful.
>
> Wrong: There's two *products* in our new line.
> Right: There *are* two *products* in our new line.
>
> 2. **Compound subjects connected by *and* take plural verbs no matter how many words come between them.**
>
> Wrong: Our *plant* on the north end of Chicago *and* our *factory* on the river in Ohio still *produces* all of our products.
> Right: Our *plant* on the north end of Chicago *and* our *factory* on the river in Ohio still *produce* all of our products.
>
> 3. **Take the number of a compound subject connected by *or* or *nor* from the second-named noun or pronoun.**
>
> Wrong: Either Jake or *Tom have* to make the trip.
> Right: Either Jake or *Tom has* to make the trip.
>
> Wrong: Neither you nor your two *trainees is going*.
> Right: Neither you nor your two *trainees are going*.
>
> 4. **Treat most collective nouns as singular.**
>
> Wrong: Your entire *staff have been invited* to the meeting.
> Right: Your entire *staff has been invited* to the meeting.

Figure 13-3   Make sure each verb agrees with its subject (part 1 of 2)

Make sure your verb forms are simple and consistent   Figure 13-5 presents some typical problems with verb consistency. In the first example, the writer changed from the present to the future tense although both clauses are talking about events that take place at the same time. In the second example, the writer first used a past tense

5. **When the subject is a collective noun used with a plural noun in a prepositional phrase, make the verb singular if it describes the actions of the group as a unit. Make it plural if it describes their actions as individuals.**

Wrong: A *delegation* of undergraduates *are* presenting the award.
Right: A *delegation* of undergraduates *is* presenting the award.

Wrong: The *majority* of students polled *doesn't* want a dress code.
Right: The *majority* of students polled *don't* want a dress code.

6. **Treat company names as singular unless they sound as if they're plural.**

Wrong: *Mike Murach & Associates, Inc. have* their own staff of writers.
Right: *Mike Murach & Associates, Inc. has* its own staff of writers.
Right: *The System Associates accept* your terms.

7. **Treat indefinite pronouns such as *anybody* and *everybody* as singular.**

Wrong: *Everybody* leaving the seminar sessions *need* passes.
Right: *Everybody* leaving the seminar sessions *needs* a pass.

8. **Make the verb in an adjective clause agree with the noun that the relative pronoun refers to.**

Wrong: We have *problems* with equipment that's hard to solve.
Right: We have *problems* with equipment that *are* hard to solve.

9. **For a fraction, make the verb agree with the noun that follows.**

Wrong: Two-thirds of the *rent are* due today.
Right: Two-thirds of the *rent is* due today.

Figure 13-3 Make sure each verb agrees with its subject (part 2 of 2)

Unclear pronoun references

Wrong: After the managers and staff members had met, they felt they had been thwarted.

Right: After *their* meeting with management, the staff *members* felt *they* had been thwarted.

Wrong: Michael discussed the problem with David and told him it was his responsibility.

Right: Michael discussed the problem with *David* and made *him* responsible for its solution.

Lack of number agreement between pronouns and antecedents

Wrong: *Each* of the managers brought *their* portfolios.

Right: *Each* of the managers brought *her* portfolio.

Wrong: Either Doug or Steve should be responsible for the plan, and they should have full power to implement it as they see fit.

Right: Either *Doug* or *Steve* should be responsible for the plan, and *he* should have full power to implement it as *he* sees fit.

Figure 13-4 Make sure each pronoun reference is clear and that each pronoun agrees with its antecedent

verb with an infinitive ("to walk") and then used a clumsy verb form with three auxiliary words ("would have been").

If you're like most business writers, you don't know the difference between the indicative and the subjunctive mood. You also may not know the difference between simple tenses and perfect tenses. However, you do know the differences between *present tense, past tense,* and *future tense.* And you probably could correct the examples in figure 13-5 without any further training.

With that in mind, I don't think it's appropriate to try to teach you the intricacies of tense and mood. You should realize, though, that you should keep your verb forms consistent and logical. If you're talking about events in the past, you can write in the past tense. If you're talking about events in the future, you can use the future tense. And if you're talking about ideas and opinions, you can often use just the present tense.

Inconsistent tenses

Wrong: When I *walk* into the office each Monday morning, the staff members *will be talking* about what they did during the weekend.

Right: When I *walk* into the office each Monday morning, the staff members *are talking* about what they did during the weekend.

Awkward and inconsistent forms

Wrong: When I *used to walk* into the office Monday morning, the staff members always *would have been talking* about what they did during the weekend.

Right: When I *walked* into the office Monday morning, the staff members *were* always *talking* about what they did during the weekend.

Figure 13-5 Make sure your verb forms are simple and consistent

Beyond this, you should keep your verb forms as simple as possible. This helps you keep them consistent. For most business writing, you can get by with just the simple forms of the past (he *walked*), present (he *walks*), and future (he *will walk*) tenses. If you find yourself using perfect tenses (he *had walked*, he *has walked*, and he *will have walked*), try to rewrite your sentences using the simple tenses. When you find yourself in a maze of *would have*s, *could have had*s, and *should have*s, it's time to revise for clarity.

Make sure your modifiers clearly relate to the words they modify This principle is pretty obvious. If you want your language to be understandable, your readers must be able to tell what your phrases, adverbs, and adjectives relate to. To say it another way, they must be able to tell what your modifiers modify.

Figure 13-6 presents three common problems with modifiers. The first is called a *dangling modifier*. This is often a phrase at the start or end of a sentence that could be applied to more than one noun in the sentence. In the first example, the phrase "without adequate training" could modify "word processing system" or "your productivity

> **Dangling modifiers**
>
> Wrong: Without adequate training, this word processing system can't solve your productivity problems.
>
> Right: Unless your staff has adequate training, this word processing system can't solve your productivity problems.
>
> Wrong: Based upon your needs, we're sending the pricing information for the equipment we discussed.
>
> Right: Here is the pricing information for the equipment that we agreed is appropriate for your needs.
>
> **Misplaced adverbs**
>
> Wrong: He answered all the questions asked by the staff members patiently.
>
> Right: He patiently answered all the questions asked by the staff members.
>
> **Misplaced prepositional phrases**
>
> Wrong: I am looking for a job with salary and benefits that are appropriate for my education and experience with room for professional growth.
>
> Right: I am looking for a job that provides fair compensation and an opportunity for professional growth.

Figure 13-6 Make sure your modifiers clearly relate to the words they modify

problems." Neither makes sense. In the second example, the phrase "based upon your needs" doesn't seem to apply to any of the words in the sentence.

The second problem in figure 13-6 involves a misplaced adverb, and the third problem involves a misplaced prepositional phrase. The general rule for the placement of modifiers is to put them as close as possible to the words they modify. Then, the relationships are more likely to be clear.

Items in a series

Wrong: You can count on our professional staff, effective servicing, and our trained administrative support.

Right: You can count on our professional staff, our effective service, and our trained administrative support.

Right: You can count on our professional staff, effective service, and trained administrative support.

Phrases or clauses within a sentence

Wrong: We have a valued reputation of more than 50 years, and over 2-1/2 decades of experience in the photocopier industry.

Right: We've been in business for more than 50 years, and we've been in the photocopier industry for more than 25 years.

Right: We have a valued reputation of more than 50 years and experience in the photocopier industry of more than 25 years.

Figure 13-7 Keep your parallel constructions parallel

Keep your parallel constructions parallel If you're using parallel constructions, you should try to keep them as consistent as possible. Otherwise, your readers won't see the relationships you're trying to show.

Figure 13-7 shows two problems caused by a lack of consistency. In the first example, the three items in the series don't have quite the same structure. As a result, the rewritten sentences are easier to read than the original one. In the second example, the lack of consistency makes the simple thought of the sentence difficult to follow.

How to use the most common punctuation symbols

Punctuation is the use of symbols that guide your readers through your words and sentences. These symbols tell your readers when to pause, what items to group together, and where sentences begin and end. Punctuation includes the use of commas and other punctuation symbols, the use of capital letters, and the use of underlining or italics.

If you understand grammar, there's nothing difficult about punctuation. You just memorize the rules for using the symbols, and you use them. The topics that follow present most of the punctuation rules you need for business writing.

Commas   Figure 13-8 presents 12 acceptable uses for the comma. It includes almost all the uses you'll require in business writing. If you use commas as shown in the examples, you shouldn't have any more trouble with comma use.

In recent years, many people have relaxed the rules about the use of commas and have adopted an *open system* of punctuation. However, I don't think that's appropriate for business and technical writing. As a result, the summary in figure 13-8 presents a more traditional list of comma uses that make up a *closed system* of punctuation. For instance, although some business writers omit the comma after an introductory word, phrase, or clause, this comma frequently improves readability. As a result, the summary in figure 13-8 indicates that you should use this comma. Similarly, although some business writers omit the comma before the last item in a series, this comma frequently improves readability. So the summary indicates that you should use it too.

One common punctuation problem in business writing is the use of a comma where one doesn't belong. This just confuses the reader. For instance, the first sentence in the fourth paragraph in figure 13-1 has an unnecessary comma that makes the sentence more difficult to read. So use a comma only if it fits one of the uses summarized in figure 13-8. If you think you need a comma to prevent misreading, rewrite your sentence so you don't need the comma.

Other punctuation symbols   Figure 13-9 summarizes the use of other punctuation symbols like the semicolon and colon. It includes almost all the uses of the other punctuation symbols that you'll require in business writing. If you use the symbols as shown in this summary, you shouldn't have any problems with them.

Although you may have forgotten some of them, you should be familiar with the punctuation uses shown in figure 13-9. The one exception may be the use of the hyphen to prevent confusion when using adjectives. Because business writers frequently use nouns as adjectives, this use of hyphens can improve readability. For instance,

1. **To separate independent clauses in a compound sentence**

   Wrong: Tom conducted the interview and he made the selection.
   Right: Tom conducted the interview, and he made the selection.

2. **After an introductory word or phrase**

   Wrong: Whoever wins our support will go to the new president.
   Right: Whoever wins, our support will go to the new president.

   Wrong: However we didn't agree on the final decision.
   Right: However, we didn't agree on the final decision.

3. **After an introductory clause**

   Wrong: Because he was the chairman I asked others to make the decision.
   Right: Because he was the chairman, I asked others to make the decision.

4. **To separate items in a series**

   Wrong: Our distribution department is now divided into pickup, warehousing, accounting and delivery.
   Right: Our distribution department is now divided into pickup, warehousing, accounting, and delivery.

5. **To separate two or more preceding adjectives that each modify the noun**

   Wrong: A shy quiet soft-spoken person would not be right for this job.
   Right: A shy, quiet, soft-spoken person would not be right for this job.

   Note: But don't separate the last adjective when it's considered part of the noun.

   Wrong: My grandmother is a healthy, active, senior citizen.
   Right: My grandmother is a healthy, active senior citizen.

Figure 13-8 Comma use (part 1 of 2)

6. **To set off direct quotations**

Wrong: He said "Don't take another step."
Right: He said, "Don't take another step."

7. **To set off non-restrictive phrases and clauses**

Wrong: Mr. Clark who is about 35 years old made a good impression.
Right: Mr. Clark, who is about 35 years old, made a good impression.

8. **To set off parentheticals that mildly interrupt the thought of a sentence**

Wrong: In my opinion though it is wrong.
Right: In my opinion, though, it is wrong.

9. **To set off contrasting phrases**

Wrong: He selected the standard not the innovative approach.
Right: He selected the standard, not the innovative, approach.

10. **To set off words like Jr., Sr., and Inc.**

Wrong: William Styles Jr.
Right: William Styles, Jr.

11. **To set off the years within dates**

Wrong: He arrived on August 31, 1988 and stayed for months.
Right: He arrived on August 31, 1988, and stayed for months.

12. **To separate the parts of an address or location**

Wrong: She lives at 2019 Erie Street Racine Wisconsin.
Right: She lives at 2019 Erie Street, Racine, Wisconsin.

Figure 13-8 Comma use (part 2 of 2)

the term *PC-based word processing system* is easier to read than *PC based word processing system*.

Note in figure 13-9 that I don't recommend the use of dashes and exclamation points. In practice, most dashes serve to replace the functions of colons and parentheses, so you can easily get along without them. Also, a dash is typed as two hyphens on a typewriter or word processor, so it is an imprecise symbol.

As for exclamation points, they're frequently the mark of an ineffective writer. If you want to exclaim, do it with your words, thoughts, and ideas. Don't do it artificially with an exclamation point (!) or, worse, several of them (!!!).

Capitalization Figure 13-10 summarizes the uses of capital letters in business writing. The primary use, of course, is for *proper nouns*; that is, nouns that identify a specific person, place, or thing. If you don't know whether a noun is a proper noun, just look it up in the dictionary to see whether it is capitalized.

Except for the uses in figure 13-10, the trend is to use fewer capital letters in business writing. For instance, as I suggested in chapter 6, you only have to capitalize the first letter of report titles, headings, and subheadings, not the first letter of all the main words in them. By using fewer capital letters, you improve readability because most people can read lowercase letters more easily than capitals.

Underlining or italics Figure 13-11 summarizes the use of underlining or italics in business writing. When you use word processing, you can use either one, but you'll probably choose the one that's easier to use on your system. When a document is typeset or produced on a desktop publishing system, though, underlines are usually treated as italics.

Note that figure 13-11 does not suggest that you use underlining or italics for emphasis. When you write effectively, you let your words show what you want to emphasize. Nevertheless, I frequently get business letters with every third sentence underlined for emphasis. The writers don't seem to know that when you emphasize too much, you emphasize nothing.

Semicolon

1. **To separate closely related, independent clauses not joined by a coordinating conjunction**

Wrong: Tom conducted the interview, then, he made the selection.
Right: Tom conducted the interview; then, he made the selection.

Wrong: We had assumed the product would appeal most to single mothers, however, our market research doesn't support that assumption.
Right: We had assumed the product would appeal most to single mothers; however, our market research doesn't support that assumption.

2. **To separate items in a series when the items contain commas or when the items are complete sentences**

Wrong: He had lived in Miami, Florida, Ada, Ohio, and Ames, Iowa.
Right: He had lived in Miami, Florida; Ada, Ohio; and Ames, Iowa.

Wrong: The steps are: (1) Type A, (2) Press ENTER, and (3) Log off.
Right: The steps are: (1) Type A; (2) Press ENTER; and (3) Log off.

Colon

To introduce a question, phrase, quotation, or items in a series

Wrong: The question is would you do it over again?
Right: The question is: Would you do it over again?

Wrong: She had three outstanding qualities, intelligence, confidence, and determination.
Right: She had three outstanding qualities: intelligence, confidence, and determination.

Wrong: The company had one goal - to be an industry leader.
Right: The company had one goal: to be an industry leader.

Figure 13-9 Other punctuation (part 1 of 5)

Parentheses

To set off parentheticals that break away from the main structure of a sentence

Wrong: Although we had almost unanimous agreement, mine was the only dissenting vote, I don't think the new plan will be popular.

Right: Although we had almost unanimous agreement (mine was the only dissenting vote), I don't think the new plan will be popular.

Quotation marks

1. **To identify direct quotations**

Wrong: Though planning is basic, she said, each phase is vital.
Right: "Though planning is basic," she said, "each phase is vital."

2. **To set off the title of a news story, magazine article, or chapter within a book**

Wrong: She had just read an article called The Art of Delegation.
Right: She had just read an article called "The Art of Delegation."

3. **To indicate you are using certain words as irony or slang**

Wrong: His smart business involved both unethical and illegal practices.
Right: His "smart business" involved both unethical and illegal practices.

Wrong: When I asked for an earlier delivery date, the sales rep suggested that I cool it.
Right: When I asked for an earlier delivery date, the sales rep suggested that I "cool it."

Figure 13-9 Other punctuation (part 2 of 5)

How to write with correct grammar and diction

Apostrophes

1. **To indicate missing letters within contractions**

But don't use an apostrophe to make a noun plural.

Wrong: I cant sell these product's at a discount.
Right: I can't sell these products at a discount.

And don't use an apostrophe when *its* is a possessive pronoun.

Wrong: I like the report, but I dont like it's title.
Right: I like the report, but I don't like its title.

2. **To create possessives**

Use *'s* after all singular nouns or names and after plural nouns that don't end in *s*. Use only an apostrophe after plurals ending in *s*.

Wrong: She criticized Mrs. Smiths report, Mr. Mills' ideas, the repair mens' fees, and 15 worker's suggestions.
Right: She criticized Mrs. Smith's report, Mr. Mills's ideas, the repair men's fees, and 15 workers' suggestions.

Hyphens

1. **To avoid repeated letters when you add prefixes**

Wrong: She reevaluated her decision.
Right: She re-evaluated her decision.

2. **To join the parts of some compound words**

Wrong: This is the most up to date version.
Right: This is the most up-to-date version.

3. **To prevent confusion when using adjectives**

Wrong: He gave a talk on how computer aided instruction works.
Right: He gave a talk on how computer-aided instruction works.

Figure 13-9 Other punctuation (part 3 of 5)

4. **To mean *from* and *to*, indicating a range of numbers or dates**

Wrong: The course will run from Sept. 15-28 and from Oct. 10-23.
Right: The course will run Sept. 15-28 and Oct. 10-23.

Periods

1. **To signal the end of a sentence**

Wrong: Thank you for the information - I'll be in town next week and maybe we can get together for lunch - I have lots of news about our relocation!
Right: Thank you for the information. I'll be in town next week, so let's get together for lunch. I have lots of news to tell you about our relocation.

2. **To identify abbreviations, but not common business abbreviations like IBM or FCC**

Wrong: He reported to Mrs Andrews.
Right: He reported to Mrs. Andrews.

Wrong: She worked for N.B.C.
Right: She worked for NBC.

Question marks

To identify direct questions

Wrong: Don't you agree this is the best solution.
Right: Don't you agree this is the best solution?

Wrong: "Will you be there," he asked?
Right: "Will you be there?" he asked.

Figure 13-9 Other punctuation (part 4 of 5)

Ellipses

To identify omitted parts of quotations

Wrong: The report says, "It became clear to us that she was completely unaware of any impropriety."

Right: The report says, "It became clear to us . . . that she was completely unaware of any impropriety."

Wrong: Remember the author's warning, "Ask not for whom the bell tolls."

Right: Remember the author's warning, "Ask not for whom the bell tolls. . . . "

Dashes

In business writing, don't use dashes to indicate a sudden break or shift in thought. Instead, rewrite your sentence so the break or shift occurs between sentences.

Wrong: First, I want you to see what the problem is—no, better yet—see if they can handle it themselves.

Right: First, I want you to see what the problem is. Better yet, let them handle it themselves.

Exclamation points

To punctuate words that are used only as interjections

Wrong: I think we've succeeded with our report! The boss had only one thing to say: Hallelujah!!

Right: I think we've succeeded with our report. The boss had only one thing to say: Hallelujah!

Figure 13-9 Other punctuation (part 5 of 5)

> **For proper nouns**
>
> | | |
> |---|---|
> | Pepsi Cola | Queen Victoria |
> | Waldorf Hotel | St. Agnes Hospital |
> | Monday | September |
> | Times Square | Maple Street |
> | Yellowstone Park | Mary Jackson |
> | Revolutionary War | Magna Carta |
> | Old Testament | the Almighty |
> | Neptune | Australia |
>
> **For names derived from proper nouns**
>
> | | |
> |---|---|
> | an American | British hospitality |
> | Spanish history | a Virginian |
>
> **For points of the compass when they refer to parts of the country**
>
> | | |
> |---|---|
> | the West | the Northeast |
>
> **For the first word and every important word in the titles of books, magazines, articles, etc.**
>
> *The Wall Street Journal*
> *The Search for Excellence*
> The chapter called "The Art of Delegation"

Figure 13-10 Capitalization

The elements of good diction

Diction refers to your choice of words when you write or speak. If your words precisely express your meanings and attitudes, you have good diction.

Although many business writers have better than average vocabularies, they don't always use good diction. The critical factor is

How to write with correct grammar and diction

For the titles of books, newspapers, magazines, and journals

Wrong: He was reading "Business Week."
Right: He was reading *Business Week*.

For letters used as letters and words used as words

Wrong: Don't pronounce the "t" in the word often.
Right: Don't pronounce the *t* in the word *often*.

Wrong: Business people like to use a language of howevers and therefores.
Right: Business people like to use a language of *however*s and *therefore*s.

To introduce a new term or a key term

Wrong: We call this document a heading plan.
Right: We call this document a *heading plan*.

For foreign words and phrases

Wrong: This type of ad hoc reasoning is irrelevant.
Right: This type of *ad hoc* reasoning is irrelevant.

Don't use underlining or italics for emphasis. Write your sentences so your emphasis is clear without using underlining or italics.

Wrong: We *have* to get this done by *Friday*, because it's really *important* to our company.
Right: If our proposal isn't done by Friday's deadline, we'll lose the account.

Figure 13-11 Underlining or italics

choosing the right word at the right time. Beyond that, you must spell your words right and pronounce them right.

The right word choices   To use the right word, you have to avoid jargon and use words that are appropriate for your readers. I explained that in chapter 9. You must also avoid general words and try to find the words that express your exact meanings.

If your vocabulary is limited, you won't always be able to choose the right word. But at least you can be sure that you use your words correctly. And yet, many business writers confuse and misuse words. For instance, the letter in figure 13-1 misuses at least one word.

To test your diction, figure 13-12 presents a short list of words that are frequently misused in business. Do you have any problems with these? Do you know, for example, that *reticent* means silent and that *reluctant* means unwilling? Do you know that *farther* should be used when you're talking about distances and *further* should be used when you're talking about movement in an abstract sense? I took this list from a much longer list of words that are frequently misused in business, so you can see how common diction problems are.

Incidentally, a thesaurus is of limited value when it comes to improving your diction. Although an on-line thesaurus may help you when you just can't think of the right word, it doesn't explain the word distinctions that help you select the right word. For that, you need a dictionary. Remember, then, that the goal in diction isn't to use a wider variety of words; the goal is to use the right word at the right time.

Correct spelling   The most glaring errors in business documents are often misspellings. If you misspell a word in a memo to your boss, the misspelling is liable to be noticed before anything else. Nevertheless, misspellings are quite common in business letters. Last week, for example, I received a letter that used the word *guarantee* spelled right three times and wrong three times ("gurantee"). That could have resulted from poor proofing, but two other words in the letter were also misspelled.

If you have a spelling checker on your PC, you should be able to catch most of your spelling errors with it. For instance, all five of the misspellings in the letter I just mentioned would have been caught by a spelling checker. As I explained in chapter 1, though, you can't depend on a spelling checker to catch all misspellings. To make sure you've spelled all your words right, you have to be a good proofreader and you have to know when to look up a word in your dictionary.

Figure 13-13 presents a short list of frequently misspelled words. If you have trouble with any of these, you know you have some work to do to improve your spelling. You can start by getting a book that lists frequently misspelled words so you can study them and identify

```
about-around
adapt-adopt
affect-effect

allusion-illusion
amount-number
complement-compliment

continual-continuous
disinterested-uninterested
famous-notorious

farther-further
fewer-less
good-well

ingenious-ingenuous
liable-likely
persecute-prosecute

principal-principle
reluctant-reticent
stationary-stationery
```

Figure 13-12 Some frequently confused and misused words

the words you don't know. Then, whenever you're in doubt about a word, you must look it up in your dictionary.

Correct pronunciation   I know this book is about writing, but I can't mention diction without talking about pronunciation. If some of the most glaring errors in a business document are spelling errors, the most glaring errors in speech are pronunciation errors. When a speaker pronounces *perspiration* as PRESpiration or *irreparable* as irrePARable, it is likely to distract the listeners and reduce the effectiveness of the speaker's message.

To avoid pronunciation errors, you must look up any words you're not sure of in your dictionary. If you hear a word pronounced in more than one way, look the word up to learn which way is correct. Unless

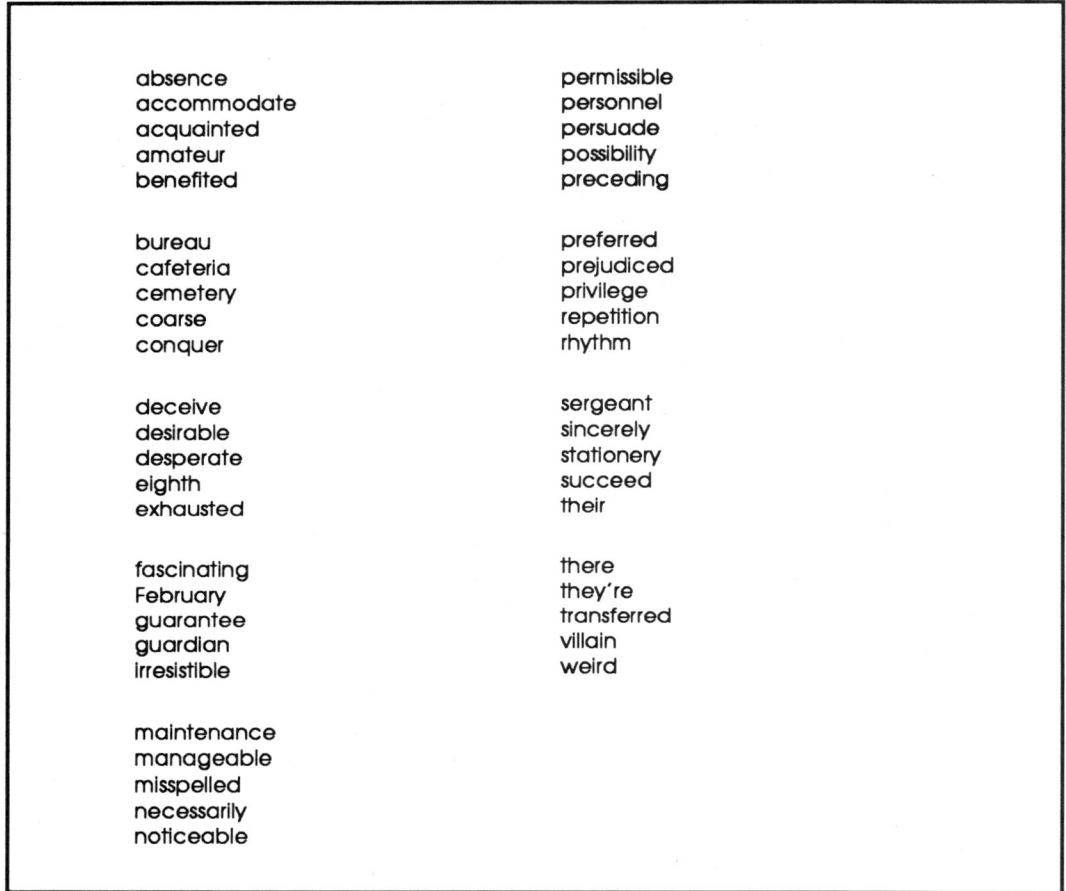

Figure 13-13 Some frequently misspelled words

you're sure about a word's pronunciation, you dare not use it in the presence of your business associates.

How to improve your grammar and diction

Most business writers would do well to improve their grammar and diction. That's why one of the purposes of this chapter is to shake your confidence in your grammar and diction. If you didn't know everything presented in the figures in this chapter, you should spend some time to improve your skills. And if you couldn't understand some of the figures at all because your background in grammar is inadequate, you've got some hard work to do on your own.

What can you do? I recommend that you start by developing your own library of books for writing. You'll use these for both study and reference. Beyond that, I recommend that you actively study both grammar and diction.

Build a library for business writers Figure 13-14 gives you some ideas for your own writing library. A dictionary is the first item on the list and the most important reference you will have. A good dictionary explains the differences between words so you can use the right one. It also shows you correct spellings and pronunciations. No writer can get by effectively without a good dictionary. In contrast, I didn't even include a thesaurus on this list, although I do think that an on-line thesaurus is worth having. A thesaurus helps the most when you already know the exact meanings of words, but need something to remind you of the choices.

The second group in figure 13-14 contains grammar and usage books. Books like these will give you information about grammar, punctuation, and diction. Although all of them have something to offer, no one book seems to present everything you need to know. That's why you should have more than one book like this.

The third group in figure 13-14 contains books on writing. These books give you many ideas about writing that couldn't possibly have been included in this book. They include ideas on writing methods and skills as well as ideas on grammar and diction. And several of them are written with an upbeat style that makes them fun to read.

The fourth group in figure 13-14 contains books that are fun to read if you enjoy language. However, these books will also help you improve your writing because they force you to think more carefully about the language you use every day.

Set up a 30-day plan to improve your grammar If you acquire a library like the one suggested in figure 13-14, the next step is to use it. Unfortunately, most people don't like the study of grammar, so they use their grammar books only when they want to look something up. But this habit allows them to continue making grammatical mistakes because they don't look up the faults they're unaware of.

What I suggest, then, is that you set up a rigid schedule for learning. If, for example, you get a book like *Essentials of English Grammar*, you should read it from cover to cover. To do this, set aside an hour or so each morning or each evening. Promise yourself that you'll cover a certain number of pages each day so you'll finish the book in 30 days. At the end of that time, your grammar skills will have improved so much that they'll be better than those of most business writers. Repeat this with another book or two, and your skills will soon be better than those of your boss, your company's president, and the tens of thousands of other business writers who are too complacent to learn their own language.

Set up a 30-day plan to improve your diction It's more difficult to improve your diction than your grammar. But you can do it. All it takes is work.

To improve your diction, you have to start caring more about words. Whenever you hear a word you're not sure of, write it down. Whenever you read a word you're not sure of, circle it. If you think you know what a word means, that's not good enough. To use words well, you have to be sure that you know exactly what they mean.

Next, write each word you need to learn on the front of a 3-by-5 card. Then, look up each word in your dictionary and write its definition on the back of the card. If the word is difficult to pronounce, write its pronunciation key underneath its definition. As you write the definition, try to include the distinctions that make it different from comparable words. What, for example, is the distinction between *continuous* and *continual*? If you're able to record the distinctions, you'll be able to use the word properly later on.

After you've created these cards, study them. Keep going over them, day after day, until you've mastered them. Make sure you master the distinctions so you'll be able to use the words that express your exact intentions. Make sure you master the pronunciations so you can use the words in your conversations.

If you spend one hour a day studying words, you'll be amazed at your progress. In about 30 days, you'll be using many words correctly for the first time. And you'll be surprised to find how many people use words incorrectly. In addition, you'll find that you're hearing and reading fewer and fewer words you don't know.

Discussion

Theoretically, a writing analyzer or grammar checker on a PC should be able to detect most of your grammatical errors. However, the analyzers of today can't do that. When it comes to grammar checking, they are extremely limited. And if an analyzer does find an error, you

For primary reference

A good dictionary like *Webster's Seventh New Collegiate Dictionary*.

For self-directed study and secondary reference

L. Sue Baugh. *Essentials of English Grammar*. Passport Books, 1989.

Rudolf Flesch and A. H. Lass. *A New Guide to Better Writing*. Warner Books, 1982.

Rudolf Flesch. *The ABC of Style*. Harper & Row, 1980.

Vincent F. Hopper, et al. *The Pocket Guide to Grammar*. Barron's Educational Series, Inc., 1984.

For one-time reading and occasional reference

Theodore M. Bernstein. *The Careful Writer*. Atheneum, 1965.

Rudolf Flesch. *How to Write, Speak, and Think More Effectively*. Signet Books, 1946.

Rudolf Flesch. *On Business Communication (or How to Say What You Mean in Plain English)*. Barnes & Noble Books, 1974.

William Strunk, Jr. and E. B. White. *The Elements of Style*. MacMillan Publishing Company, 1972.

For fun as well as enlightenment

Theodore M. Bernstein. *Miss Thistlebottom's Hobgoblins (The Careful Writer's Guide to the Taboos, Bugbears, and Outmoded Rules of English Usage)*. Simon and Schuster, Inc., 1971.

Edwin Newman. *Strictly Speaking*. Warner Books, 1974.

Edwin Newman. *A Civil Tongue*. Warner Books, 1976.

Figure 13-14 A library for a business writer

still have to know enough grammar to recognize what's wrong and correct it.

That's why you should do whatever it takes to improve your grammar and diction. As I've tried to show you, it shouldn't take more than an hour or two a day for a few months. But that work should pay for itself many times over during the rest of your business career.

Terms

grammar
sentence fragment
antecedent
present tense
past tense
future tense

dangling modifier
punctuation
open system of punctuation
closed system of punctuation
proper noun
diction

Objectives

1. Apply the grammatical principles of this chapter to all your writing.

2. Apply the punctuation rules of this chapter to all your writing.

3. Develop a plan to improve your grammar and diction and then follow it.

Section 4

Practical presentation skills for PC users

This section shows you how to prepare a document for presentation after you've finished writing it. Chapter 14 shows you efficient techniques for presenting your documents when you use word processing. Chapter 15 shows you how to present your document when you use desktop publishing. Since you can't use desktop publishing effectively unless you know something about typography and graphics design, chapter 15 emphasizes those features.

Heading plan for chapter 14

Presentation guidelines for five types of documents

    Letters

    Informal memos, reports, and proposals

    Formal reports and proposals

    Bound reports, proposals, and manuals

    Newsletters

General guidelines for all word processing presentations

    Use standard presentation formats

    Watch your pagination

    Don't indent the first paragraph after a heading or subheading

    Avoid vertical and horizontal rules when you create tables

    Avoid justified text

    Limit the number of type variations you use

Discussion

Chapter 14

How to use word processing to present your documents

When you finish the last step of the 12-step writing procedure I recommend in this book, you have a final draft of a document. Often, this draft is suitable for delivery to your intended readers. Then, you make as many copies of your document as you need and distribute them to the right people.

Sometimes, though, you will want to improve the appearance of your final draft before you distribute it. For instance, you may want to put a title page on the front of a report, include a table of contents with the report, or change the size of the type that is used for the headings and subheadings. We refer to this type of enhancement as the *presentation* of a document.

Today, a word processing package gives you many presentation options. For instance, my word processor lets me lay out pages using two or more columns, like newspaper columns. It lets me put illustrations in ruled boxes within the text pages. It lets me create page headings and footers in a wide variety of styles. And it lets me use the several different sizes and styles of type that are available on my printer. In fact, my word processor provides many of the features of desktop publishing software.

Unfortunately, you can't take advantage of many of the advanced presentation features of a word processing package unless your PC has a laser printer. If, for example, you want to put boxes around your figures but your system doesn't have a laser printer, the lines around your boxes probably won't be sharp. Similarly, you won't be able to print the wide variety of type sizes and styles that your word processor supports.

In this chapter, I'll give you some guidelines for presenting a document when you use a typical word processor without a laser printer. First, I'll give you specific guidelines for presenting some common business documents. Then, I'll give you general guidelines for all word processing presentations. In the next chapter, I'll show you how you can improve your presentations by using desktop publishing.

Presentation guidelines for five types of documents

To a large extent, the presentation of a document depends on its type. For instance, the way you present a memo to your boss is quite different from the way you present an extensive proposal to a prospective customer. So here are some guidelines for presenting five types of documents.

Letters The most important guideline for presenting letters is that they should look as if they're typewritten. That way they look more personal, and marketing studies have shown that personal letters get better results than mass letters. As a result, you shouldn't use fancy typefaces, varied type sizes, or justification (a feature that lines up the text straight at the right margin as well as the left).

Another way to make your letters look more friendly, informal, and readable is to indent the paragraphs. This is of minor importance, but at least a few studies have shown that a simple thing like that can improve marketing results. Although most companies have a standard format for letters, that format shouldn't stop you from indenting your paragraphs.

Informal memos, reports, and proposals When you're writing a memo, report, or proposal for someone you work with, your document can usually be presented in an informal style. That means you don't have to use any of the presentation features of word processing.

In our company, for example, we present informal reports in the form shown in appendix A. Here, the title is on the first page of the report with no title page and no table of contents preceding it. On each page of the report, you can see a standard page heading, called a *header*, that includes the date and page number. Note, however, that we don't use *footers*. All of the headings and subheadings of the report are in boldface starting at the left margin. Because the report uses underlining instead of italics, no special typefaces are used within the text at all. At the end of the report, you can find the four figures that are referred to in the text with one illustration on each page. We use this presentation style for all informal reports because it helps our writers create effective presentations quickly.

If you look closely at the report in appendix A, you can see that it doesn't include the author's name because we normally include a cover memo with an informal report. The cover memo identifies the author as well as those who will receive the report. A cover memo or letter also gives you a chance to introduce a report or proposal in a slightly more personal style than you would use in the document itself. If you don't use a cover memo or letter, you should include the author's name in the page header or present it right after the document title.

If you're developing a long report or proposal, you may want to add a combined title page and table of contents to your document. Figure 14-1, for example, shows a front page I could have used for the report in appendix A. This gives the title, author's name, report contents, and a list of the figures used in the report. Using *Word-Perfect*, I identified the headings, subheadings, and figure legends that would be used in the table of contents as I created the report. Then, I used a word processing function to generate a contents and figures list in about five seconds after I completed the final draft.

Formal reports and proposals If you're writing a report for someone you don't know, either within your own company or in another company, your writing style should be more formal. But this doesn't mean you need to spend a long time preparing your document for presentation.

For most formal documents, you should include some sort of title page, table of contents, and figures list. But often, a combination page like the one in figure 14-1 is all you need. You don't need one title page, one contents page, and one figures page. Most of the time, these extra pages just waste paper.

Today, an *executive summary* is a common feature of most formal documents. This type of summary gives the main ideas of a report or proposal in just a page or two so busy decision makers don't have to read the details if they don't want to. For instance, figure 14-2 is an executive summary for the report in appendix A. You create a summary like this after you finish the final draft of the document itself. Then, the executive summary becomes the first page of your report, and you include it in the table of contents.

On a modern PC, the printer is likely to offer several type styles and sizes, so you may want to spend a few minutes trying to improve the type of a formal document. For instance, figure 14-3 shows the

```
Why our editors should switch
from our current word processing system
to PC-based word processing systems

by Mike Murach

What's wrong with our word processing system ................   1

What's right about PC-based word processing ................   2
        Improved system speed ....................................   2
        Improved functions .......................................   2
        Improved monitors and printers ...........................   3

PC software that can make an editor's job easier ............   3
        Spreadsheet software .....................................   3
        Writing analyzers ........................................   4
        Graphics software ........................................   4
        Desktop publishing .......................................   4

The benefits of a PC-based system ...........................   4
        Improved editorial productivity ..........................   4
        Improved editorial quality ...............................   5
        Adaptability to future systems ...........................   5

The costs of a PC-based system ..............................   6
        Hardware costs ...........................................   6
        Software costs ...........................................   6
        Training costs ...........................................   6

Cost/benefit analysis .......................................   7

Recommendations .............................................   7
        What hardware should we buy? .............................   7
        What software should we buy ..............................   7
        How and when should we convert? ..........................   8

Conclusion ..................................................   8


        Figure 1    The summary page from RightWriter when run on the
                    first draft of this report .......................  10

        Figure 2    The benefits of a PC-based system ................  11

        Figure 3    Typical costs for a PC-based system ..............  12

        Figure 4    Payback and return-on-investment (ROI)
                    possibilities based on productivity improvements
                    only .............................................  13
```

Figure 14-1   A combined title and contents page for the PC recommendation in appendix A

How to use word processing to present your documents   337

Executive summary

This report recommends that our editors switch from our current word processing system to PC-based word processing systems. If we make this switch, we have the potential to increase editorial productivity by 20 percent or more. In addition, this switch will help us improve the quality of our editorial work.

The cost of one PC-based system

Figure 3 summarizes the costs of a typical PC-based system. If you include just the hardware and the software, the total cost for each system is around $3600. In addition, we can expect about one week's training time for each editor. As a result, the total cost for each system including the training time is around $4200.

The payback and return-on-investment

Figure 4 shows the payback period and return-on-investment (ROI) for each system based on three levels of productivity improvements. If we experience the improvements I think are possible (20 percent or more), the payback period is just 1.4 years and the ROI is 71.4 percent.

Conclusion

I think we should make the switch to PC-based systems as soon as possible. Because each system is independent, we can install one or two at a time so our editors can switch over to their new systems after they have finished one project and before they start the next one. At that rate, all our editors will switch to the new systems within six months. If cash is a problem, we can slow this installment schedule down. But the sooner we get started with the first new systems, the better off we'll be.

Figure 14-2   An executive summary for the PC recommendation

first page of the report in appendix A with some enlarged type used for the title and headings. If your word processor provides a "style sheets" feature, you can make changes like this quite easily by changing the type specifications for each heading level and reprinting the document. Unless your system has a laser printer, though, the type styles and sizes are usually limited. In general, I don't think type changes like these improve the effectiveness of a document, but your audience may like them.

**Why our editors should switch
from our current word processing system
to PC-based word processing systems**

For the last six months, I've been using an IBM Personal Computer (PC) for my editorial work because I've been working on a book for PC users. During that time, I've come to realize that the system I'm using is much better than the system the other editors are using. That got me wondering whether all of our editors should switch from our current system to PC-based systems.

This report presents my analysis of our current system and my recommendations for new systems. I've tried to be brief because the primary purpose of this report is to bring you up-to-date on the PC and word processing developments of the last six years. When you finish this report, you can decide whether you want more information on any of the subjects. If so, I'll be happy to get that information for you.

What's wrong with our word processing system

We installed our current system in 1982. It is a minicomputer system with one terminal (keyboard and monitor) for each person in the editorial department. The nine people in this department share the one printer that is located in the department. They also share the minicomputer and its disk drives with 15 other users of the system in the administrative and marketing departments.

Because this is a shared system, the editors experience frequent delays when they use the word processing software. This is particularly true between 10 A.M. and 3 P.M. when the system receives its heaviest use. Our editors also experience delays when they go from one function like editing to another function like printing. Because the word processing software consists of several programs rather than just one large program, the system must load the next program to be processed when a user changes functions. The delays occur while a program is being loaded.

Because the word processing software for this system was developed in the 1970s, it is dated. Although most of our editors don't realize it, our current word processing system just doesn't compare with a modern word processing package. In particular, it is inefficient when it comes to some of the time-consuming functions like paginating and checking spelling. Although our software was at one time the best word processing software in the industry, it is no longer a competitive product.

Figure 14-3 Varied type sizes used on the first page of the PC recommendation

If you want to improve your page headers, you can do so quite easily using word processing as illustrated by the header in figure 14-4. Here, I've dropped the date and file name (PCREC) from the page header, and I've added a short report title to it. I've also put a line under the header to separate it from the body of the text. You can also include footers in formal documents, but this just complicates your presentation, so I don't recommend using them.

Because some word processors make it relatively easy for you to create boxes within the text and insert figures within them, it's tempting to do this for a formal report or proposal. For instance, figure 14-4 shows one page of the PC recommendation with a boxed figure. However, inserting figures into the text like this can be quite time consuming, and it usually doesn't improve the effectiveness of a document. That's why I don't recommend doing this. When you put the figures at the back of a document with one figure on each page, your readers can usually review them more easily than when they're boxed and inserted into the body of the report.

In summary, you shouldn't go to extremes just because you're presenting a formal report or proposal. Remember that the success of your document is going to depend primarily on the effectiveness of your writing, not on your document's appearance. If you can make some presentation improvements in just a few minutes, as you can on most PCs today, that's usually justifiable. But don't spend more time on presentation than it's worth.

Bound reports, proposals, and manuals When you create bound reports, proposals, or manuals, you use a formal style and present the pages as I've just described. If the pages are going to be printed on both sides, though, you should have both a left and a right page header. That way, the page numbers will be on the outside of the pages and your readers can find the pages they're looking for more easily.

If your document consists of more than one unit or if it's long, you may want to box the figures. But this depends on your audience. If, for example, you're presenting a manual for use by your office staff, it may be more practical to present the figures for each unit at the end of the unit.

Because the binding takes up some of the space on the insides of your pages, you must be sure to leave adequate inside margins for your pages. If, for example, you're using a 3-ring binder to bind an 8-1/2 by 11-inch manual, an inside margin of an inch is adequate, but an inch and one-quarter is even better. Because most word processors

```
Why we should switch to PCs                                          4


             <<** SUMMARY **>>
        OVERALL CRITIQUE FOR: d:\wp\bc\pcrec1

     READABILITY INDEX: 9.81
     Readers need a 10th grade level of education to understand.

         Total Number of Words in Document:3592
         Total Number of Words within Sentences:3590
         Total Number of Sentences: 185
         Total Number of Syllables:5465

         STRENGTH INDEX: 0.31
     The writing can be made more direct by using:
                     - the active voice
                     - shorter sentences
                     - less wordy phrases
                     - fewer weak phrases

         DESCRIPTIVE INDEX: 0.61
     The use of adjectives and adverbs is in the normal range.

         JARGON INDEX: 0.00

         SENTENCE STRUCTURE RECOMMENDATIONS:
               1. Most sentences contain multiple clauses.
                  Try to use more simple sentences.
              14. Consider using more predicate verbs.
```

Figure 1 The summary page from RightWriter when run on the first draft of this report

Graphics software   Some graphics programs let you create many different kinds of charts such as organization charts, bar charts, pie charts, and line charts. Other graphics programs let you create illustrations. Although I don't think the charting programs are going to be much use to us, they may come in handy for an occasional presentation to the marketing department. On the other hand, the drawing programs would let us create finished illustrations instead of the rough drawings that we pass on to the production department now. This would eliminate a lot of editorial proofing, and it would simplify the job of the production department.

Desktop publishing   We've all read a lot about desktop publishing in the last six months, and there's no doubt now that it's here to stay (see the supplementary section in the August issue of <u>Info-Systems</u>). That means that we'll eventually be doing some of our production work using desktop publishing. Although this work will probably be done in the production department, some of it may be done in the editorial department. That's why we should start learning more about it. If we all have PC ATs, of course, we'll be able to run desktop publishing software on our own systems.

Figure 14-4 A page with an enhanced header and a boxed figure

don't provide for different margins on left and right pages, set both margins the same on each page.

Newsletters As I've just explained, you should use a limited number of presentation features for most of your documents. For documents like monthly newsletters, though, you can be more creative. For instance, figure 14-5 shows the word processing presentation we use for our monthly newsletter. As you can see, it uses special type in the heading and two columns for the text. Once you set up the format for a document like this, you can use it quite efficiently.

If you go much beyond this level of presentation, you're usually limited by your software and your printer. So the next step is desktop publishing with a laser printer. If, for example, you want to develop customer newsletters or marketing brochures on your PC, you're probably ready for desktop publishing. In the next chapter, I'll show you when and how to use it.

General guidelines for all word processing presentations

Now that I've given you some specific guidelines for presenting several types of documents, let me give you some general guidelines that apply to all word processing presentations. These will help you make effective presentations as efficiently as possible.

Use standard presentation formats If you've ever experimented with the presentation features of a modern word processor, you know that using them can take a lot of time. That's why you should use standard presentation formats whenever possible. Once you've developed these formats, you can easily reuse them whenever they apply.

To start, you should have standard formats for letters, memos, reports, and proposals. These formats should specify what the headers should include, what type styles and sizes to use, how title and contents pages should look, and so on. Then, you can incorporate these formats into prototype documents or macro functions on your word processor so you'll always use the same formats. If everyone in your company uses the same formats, the writers won't have to worry about presentation details. They can concentrate on their writing instead.

MMA Newsletter

February Recap   March 4, 1989

New people Chanci Little and Kate Marshall started working in the administrative department on March 1. Chanci is a Fresno native who went to Clovis High School. Kate is from Australia. Both are young and charming, and we hope they're with us a long time.

New management In preparation for Becky's leave of absence, Lisa will be the acting administrative manager from now until Becky returns. So please see her if you have any administrative problems.

VSE JCL revision The revision of VSE JCL is now in our warehouse. Also, our announcement of it to our customers should be in the mail today.

Write Better with a PC Steve produced this entire book in one week...incredible. Now, we've proofed it, and he has made the corrections to the page proofs. Next week, the index. Then, off to the printer so we should have it in our warehouse sometime in April. Meanwhile, Judy has prepared the direct marketing piece that announces this product to our customers.

Revision of VSAM for the COBOL Programmer At last, we seem to have this project under control. Sheila is doing the editing, and the project is moving along nicely. With luck, we'll have it into production by March 17, but at the latest by the 24th, so our current off press prediction is July 1.

VM/CMS REXX Anne is making good progress on this manuscript with eight chapters done. She expects to complete it by April 1. If so, we should have it into production by May 15 so our current off press prediction is August 15.

Get Control of your PC Since Doug has taken over marketing management, he's been struggling to finish the last 5% of this book. To help him reduce his workload, he will submit a rougher manuscript to us than normal, so Rebecca and I will be doing more editing than normal. However, this may make it possible for us to get the book into production by May 1 so we can get it off press by August 1.

New projects Tim and Pat are now free to start working on their next projects so we'll be trying to refine the plans for their projects during the next two weeks.

Writing class Starting March 14, Becky, Steve Ehlers, Lisa, Cris, and Georgia will be taking a writing class given by Professor Mike. They already write well, but this class will help them refine their skills.

Minireels During February, we started preparing minireels on the Wang tape drive instead of the IBM drive. This has simplified the procedure so we can now prepare a minireel in one minute instead of ten. We made this switch knowing that we'll be getting rid of our IBM 4300 system in May.

Figure 14-5 The first page of a newsletter with some special presentation features

Watch your pagination A *widow* in publishing terminology is a line that contains only one word. This happens when the last word of a paragraph happens to be on a line by itself. Traditionally, publishers have avoided widows, even though studies have shown that widows make blocks of text easier to read.

Today, some word processors have features that automatically prevent "widows" and "orphans". In this case, however, *widow* refers to the first line of a paragraph that falls on the last line of a page, and *orphan* refers to the last line of a paragraph that falls on the first line of a page. If your word processor has a feature that prevents widows and orphans, we recommend using it because it makes your text easier to read.

You should also watch out for headings or subheadings that fall at the end of a page due to automatic pagination. When this happens, you should force a page break so the heading will appear on the same page as the text that follows it.

Don't indent the first paragraph after a heading or subheading One of the traditional rules of graphics design is that you shouldn't indent the first paragraph after a heading. The reason is that the heading and paragraph make a more cohesive visual block without the indentation. I've followed this guideline throughout this book and in the report in appendix A.

Avoid vertical and horizontal rules when you create tables In general, you don't need vertical or horizontal *rules*, or lines, when you create tables like the one in figure 14-6. When you use rules, it takes you longer to create a table, but the information usually isn't any clearer. That's why you should avoid using rules unless the table is confusing without them.

Avoid justified text One of the presentation features of most word processors today is *justification*. This means that the word processor can automatically align both the left and right sides of a block of text. When text is aligned on both sides, it is referred to as *justified text*. If text is aligned at the left side only, it is referred to as *ragged right*. These options are illustrated in figure 14-7.

Although many people like to use justification for their word processing presentations, ragged-right documents are easier to read than justified documents for two reasons. First, the spacing between the words in ragged-right text is uniform. Second, no words have to be split and hyphenated at the ends of lines when you use ragged

A table without rules

Software type		Some useful products	Common uses
1	Word processing	WordPerfect Word PFS: Professional Write	Plan your writing Create visual aids Write the first draft Revise your drafts
2	Spelling checker	A WordPerfect feature A Word feature Pop-up products	Check the spelling of a word, page, or document
3	On-line thesaurus	A WordPerfect feature A Word feature Pop-up products	Find the appropriate word
4	Writing analyzer	RightWriter Grammatik III	Check for writing and grammatical problems
5	Electronic spreadsheet	Lotus 1-2-3 Quattro	Organize information Analyze information
6	Business graphics	A Quattro feature Harvard Graphics	Create visual aids

The same table with rules

Software type		Some useful products	Common uses
1	Word processing	WordPerfect Word PFS: Professional Write	Plan your writing Create visual aids Write the first draft Revise your drafts
2	Spelling checker	A WordPerfect feature A Word feature Pop-up products	Check the spelling of a word, page, or document
3	On-line thesaurus	A WordPerfect feature A Word feature Pop-up products	Find the appropriate word
4	Writing analyzer	RightWriter Grammatik III	Check for writing and grammatical problems
5	Electronic spreadsheet	Lotus 1-2-3 Quattro	Organize information Analyze information
6	Business graphics	A Quattro feature Harvard Graphics	Create visual aids

Figure 14-6 Avoid vertical and horizontal rules when you create tables

---

Justified text

For the last six months, I've been using an IBM Personal Computer (PC) for my editorial work because I've been working on a book for PC users. During that time, I've come to realize that the system I'm using is much better than the system the other editors are using. That got me wondering whether all of our editors should switch from our current system to PC-based systems.

This report presents my analysis of our current system and my recommendations for new systems. I've tried to be brief because the primary purpose of this report is to bring you up-to-date on the PC and word processing developments of the last six years. When you finish this report, you can decide whether you want more information on any of the subjects. If so, I'll be happy to get that information for you.

Ragged-right text

For the last six months, I've been using an IBM Personal Computer (PC) for my editorial work because I've been working on a book for PC users. During that time, I've come to realize that the system I'm using is much better than the system the other editors are using. That got me wondering whether all of our editors should switch from our current system to PC-based systems.

This report presents my analysis of our current system and my recommendations for new systems. I've tried to be brief because the primary purpose of this report is to bring you up-to-date on the PC and word processing developments of the last six years. When you finish this report, you can decide whether you want more information on any of the subjects. If so, I'll be happy to get that information for you.

Figure 14-7 Avoid justified text

right. As a result, I don't recommend right justification for word processing presentations.

If you like justification so much that you want to continue using it for reports and proposals, at least drop it for letters. Remember that letters are most effective when they look personal, and justification takes away the personal look.

Limit the number of type variations you use   When you use too many type faces, styles, and sizes in a single document, the document gets a cluttered look. That's why you should limit yourself to just a few variations for each document. Furthermore, some typefaces, styles, and sizes are more effective than others, so you should use only the most effective combinations in all your documents.

In general, you can get by with just one type size if you use it in regular, boldface, and italic styles. In our company, for example, we use 12-pitch type for all text with 12-pitch boldface type for all headings and subheadings. Instead of italics, we use underlining, so we actually use only one type size and two type styles for all of our work. Although that may be more limited than it needs to be, we don't believe it reduces our effectiveness in any way, and we know it provides for maximum presentation efficiency.

Discussion

I guess it's obvious by now that I don't think you should spend much time on your word processing presentations. If you use standard formats and features for your documents, you can prepare an attractive presentation in just a few minutes for a typical document. That frees you to concentrate on the content and quality of your writing. Then, if you need a more professional presentation, you can consider the use of desktop publishing.

Terms

presentation	orphan
header	rule
footer	justification
executive summary	justified text
widow	ragged right

Objectives

1. Describe the presentation guidelines for each of the five types of documents presented in this chapter.

2. Describe the six general guidelines for all word processing presentations.

Heading plan for chapter 15

When to use desktop publishing
- The costs of desktop publishing
- The benefits of desktop publishing
- Who should do the desktop publishing

Typographic features
- Type families, type styles, and typefaces
- Serif and sans serif type families
- Type size, fonts, line length, and leading
- Justification
- Hyphenation
- Headings and subheadings
- The number of typographic variations

Design features
- Trim size
- Margins
- Headers and footers
- Figures and legends
- Two-column pages
- Title pages, contents pages, unit openers, appendixes, and indexes
- The number of design elements on each page

General guidelines for desktop publishing presentations
- Use standard presentation formats
- Don't start a new design from scratch
- Don't insist that all figures be developed on the PC

Discussion

Chapter 15

When and how to use desktop publishing to present your documents

If you're already using desktop publishing, you're probably familiar with most of what's in this chapter. Nevertheless, this chapter should give you at least a few ideas that will help you present your documents more effectively. You should realize from the start, though, that this chapter was designed for those who are new to desktop publishing.

If you aren't already using desktop publishing, this chapter may help you avoid some serious mistakes because desktop publishing isn't right for everybody. That's why I'll start by explaining when you should use desktop publishing. To help you understand more completely, I'll present its costs as well as its benefits. Then, you can decide whether you should use it for some of your projects. If you decide you should, you'll also have to choose between having someone else do the desktop publishing and doing it yourself. So I'll finish this topic by giving you some ideas about that.

Because you need some background in typography and design before you can use desktop publishing, I'll continue by presenting that information. Then, I'll give you some general guidelines that apply to all desktop publishing presentations. When you finish this chapter, you should not only know whether you want to use desktop publishing, you should also have the background you need for learning how to use it effectively.

As you read this chapter, you should realize that some of the advanced word processing packages provide desktop publishing features. As a result, you can get started in desktop publishing by using these features. To make efficient use of them, though, your system requires a laser printer. You also need to understand most of the desktop publishing concepts presented in this chapter. In general, everything this chapter says about desktop publishing software also applies to the desktop publishing features of word processing.

When to use desktop publishing

At a recent publishing seminar, the instructor estimated that nearly 50 percent of all desktop publishing projects in 1987 failed. Although that estimate may be high, it's clear today that many desktop publishing projects do fail. It's also clear that they fail because of false expectations. In practice, desktop publishing isn't nearly as inexpensive or as easy to use as its promoters would have you believe.

The costs of desktop publishing   Figure 15-1 lists some typical costs of desktop publishing. These include the one-time costs of hardware, software, and training. But they also include the production cost for each document.

Today, the hardware for desktop publishing should include a fast processor, plenty of hard disk storage, and a laser printer. It may also include a large-screen monitor so you can see the page layouts more easily before you print them. If you buy a complete system, the total cost can be $10,000 or more.

The software costs include the cost of the desktop publishing software. They also include the cost of any graphics software you'll need for the illustrations within your documents. Remember from chapter 1 that it's most convenient if all the figures for a desktop publishing presentation are created on the PC. That's why you usually need some new graphics software for your desktop publishing system. As a result, the total cost for software can easily exceed $1000.

The hidden cost of desktop publishing is training. And the lack of training is one of the primary reasons so many desktop publishing projects fail. Although you may think you can learn to use desktop publishing as easily as you learned to use word processing, it's much more complicated than that. As a result, you may not be able to learn how to use it from books and manuals alone. To get the most from desktop publishing, you may need to take one or more courses on its use. Without help, you may not even be able to get your system working the way you want it to.

To complicate the training problem, you need to know something about typography and graphic design before you can use desktop publishing well. This chapter will introduce you to these subjects, but

One-time costs

Hardware costs

A faster processor
More disk storage
An improved monitor
A laser printer

Software costs

Desktop publishing software
Graphics software

Training costs

Software training
Graphics training

The production cost for each document

The production cost is the cost of producing each document when using desktop publishing. This includes the cost of the operator's time as well as the cost of any production materials. The production cost is based on the size and complexity of a document.

The benefits

Improved appearance
Improved readability
Reduced copying or printing costs

Figure 15-1 The costs and benefits of desktop publishing

you may want to spend another week or two studying them on your own. And you may want to attend a course or two on graphics.

Once you purchase the hardware and software for your system and learn how to use it, you have the continuing costs of production. In the publishing industry, the term *production* refers to the conversion of a document from its final draft to its final presentation form, so I'll use that term throughout this chapter. If, for example, you decide you want to produce a 10-page proposal using desktop publishing instead of word processing, it can easily take two or three hours of production work to get the proposal in the form you want.

The benefits of desktop publishing Improved document appearance, improved readability, and reduced copying or printing costs are the three main benefits of desktop publishing. These are listed in figure 15-1.

To illustrate these benefits, appendix B shows the PC recommendation of appendix A after I had it produced using desktop publishing. First, as you can see, desktop publishing has improved the appearance of this report. In particular, it looks shorter and easier to read than the word processing version. Second, the desktop publishing text actually is easier to read than the word processing version. Third, the desktop publishing report is 10 pages long, but the word processing version is 13 pages long so it will be less expensive to make copies of the desktop publishing presentation.

If you use desktop publishing effectively, you should get all three of these benefits for every document you produce. However, these benefits may not compensate for the production costs, let alone the one-time costs of a desktop publishing system. For instance, it took three and one-half hours to produce the PC recommendation in the form shown in appendix B, even though this is a relatively simple presentation that was done by a person who uses desktop publishing every day. If you assume the cost for this work is $30 per hour, the total production cost is $105 plus the cost of any materials used for the document.

That's why it's hard to justify a desktop publishing presentation for this document. Although its appearance and readability are definitely improved by desktop publishing, the intended reader most likely would also read the report and get its message from a word processing presentation. As a result, these benefits can't be translated into dollars. Similarly, the reduced reproduction cost is a trivial benefit because this report is intended for only one reader. If you assume a copying cost of 10 cents per page, this benefit translates into a value of 30 cents.

On the other hand, these benefits can more than compensate for the production costs of some documents. If improved appearance means that your document will be read when it would be ignored otherwise, this benefit can insure the effectiveness of your document. That's why it often pays to present proposals and other marketing documents using desktop publishing. Similarly, if improved readability gets people to read long documents like manuals and books in their entirety, this can be a valuable benefit. Finally, reduced copying or printing costs is an important benefit for long documents. If, for example, desktop publishing lets you trim a 300-page manual down to 200 pages, you can cut your printing costs by 33 percent. Then, if the printing cost for 1000 copies would have been $6000, your cost will be reduced to $4000, a savings of $2000.

I hope this information helps you decide whether desktop publishing is right for your projects. Because it's hard to place a value on benefits like improved appearance and readability, it's easiest to justify a desktop publishing system based on reduced reproduction or printing costs. However, you can't overlook the other benefits. For some documents, appearance means the difference between success and failure.

Who should do the desktop publishing   If you decide that desktop publishing is right for some of your projects, the next question is: Who should do the desktop publishing? Or, more specifically: Should writers do their own desktop publishing?

For our first desktop publishing project, one of our writers not only wrote *The CICS Programmer's Desk Reference*, but he also did all the desktop publishing for the 500-page book. But that didn't work out too well. As the project wore on, we learned that writing and desktop publishing require two different sets of skills. That's why it makes sense for two different people to do them. Then, the writer can concentrate on writing, and the desktop publishing specialist can concentrate on desktop publishing. As a result, both people can work as efficiently as possible. Today, this conclusion is shared by most people who have tried it both ways.

Unfortunately, you can't always afford to have a desktop publishing specialist produce your documents. As a result, you may have to do your own desktop publishing. In this case, you should still separate writing from desktop publishing. First, you should write your document. Then, you should produce it.

Typographic features

Before you can do your own desktop publishing, you must know something about typography. At the least, you should be familiar with terms like *font*, *point*, and *leading*. In this topic, I'll introduce you to the most important typographic features and terms used in desktop publishing.

Before I introduce these terms, however, I want you to realize that they are not used consistently from one desktop publishing program to another. Although these terms have specific meanings in the publishing industry, they have frequently been misused by program developers. That's why a term like *typeface* may refer to one thing on one desktop publishing system and another thing on another desktop publishing system. Fortunately, it's not that hard to figure out how each program uses these terms, so you shouldn't be confused as long as you're aware of the problem. With that in mind, I'll now present the typographic terms as they have traditionally been used.

Type families, type styles, and typefaces Thousands of different *type families* are in use in the printing industry today, and hundreds of these are available on desktop publishing systems. Figure 15-2, for example, illustrates five common type families for use with desktop publishing. Here, *Times* is the name of one type family, and *Helvetica* is the name of another.

Figure 15-2 also shows four *type styles* for the Times type family. They are *regular* (sometimes referred to as *Roman*, or *book*), *italic*, *boldface* (or *bold*), and *boldface italic* (or *bold italic*). On a desktop publishing system, most type families are available in each of these four styles. For instance, you can set the text of a document in Times Roman and the headings in Times Bold. Traditional typesetting systems may also include other type styles for some type families. For instance, the styles for the ITC Bookman family include light, light italic, medium, medium italic, demibold, demibold italic, bold, and bold italic.

Traditionally, the term *typeface* has referred to a type family. In desktop publishing literature, however, the term is often used to refer to a specific type style within a type family. As a result, Times Bold is one typeface, and Times Italic is another typeface. In this chapter, I use the term *typeface* in its desktop publishing sense so it refers to a style within a family.

Five type families

This is Times:
ABCDEFGHIJKLMNOPQRSTUVWXYZabcdefghijklmnopqrstuvwxyz0123456789

This is New Century Schoolbook:
ABCDEFGHIJKLMNOPQRSTUVWXYZabcdefghijklmnopqrstuvwxyz0123456789

This is ITC Bookman:
ABCDEFGHIJKLMNOPQRSTUVWXYZabcdefghijklmnopqrstuvwxyz0123456789

This is ITC Avant Garde:
ABCDEFGHIJKLMNOPQRSTUVWXYZabcdefghijklmnopqrstuvwxyz0123456789

This is Helvetica:
ABCDEFGHIJKLMNOPQRSTUVWXYZabcdefghijklmnopqrstuvwxyz0123456789

Four type styles

This is regular (also known as Roman or book).
This is italic.
This is boldface (or bold).
This is boldface italic (or bold italic).

Ten typefaces

This is Times Roman.
This is Times Italic.
This is New Century Schoolbook Regular.
This is New Century Schoolbook Bold.
This is ITC Bookman Light.
This is ITC Bookman Medium.

This is ITC Avant Garde Book (or Regular).
This is ITC Avant Garde Italic.
This is Helvetica Light.
This is Helvetica Light Italic.

Figure 15-2 Type families, type styles, and typefaces

A typeface with serifs

This is set in Palatino Roman. It has serifs, so it is appropriate for body text. If you want to use it for headings and subheadings too, you can use its boldface style.

A sans serif typeface

This is set in Helvetica. It is a sans serif typeface that can be used for headings and subheadings, for headers and footers, for type within figures, and for legends. However, you shouldn't use it for body text because it is more difficult to read than a typeface with serifs.

Figure 15-3 Serif and sans serif typefaces

Serif and sans serif type families A *serif* is a horizontal line on the bottom or top of a vertical line in a character such as an *l* or an *m*. Some type families have serifs and some don't. The ones that don't are referred to as *sans serif* type families. In figure 15-2, for example, ITC Avant Garde and Helvetica are sans serif type families; the other three type families have serifs.

In general, sans serif typefaces are more difficult to read than typefaces with serifs as illustrated in figure 15-3. That's why you shouldn't use sans serif typefaces for the body text of your documents. However, sans serif typefaces are easy enough to read when they are set in short lines or large sizes. As a result, they can provide a useful contrast to the text when they are used for titles, page headers, the text within figures, or figure legends.

Type size, fonts, line length, and leading *Type size* is measured in *points* with 72 points to the inch. Figure 15-4 illustrates type sizes from 6 to 14 points, but desktop publishing systems can produce type that ranges in size from 6 to 72 points. Type size is measured from the bottom of a letter like a lowercase *p* or *y* to the top of a letter like a lowercase *b* or *d*.

When you select a type size, you must consider the reading ability of your readers. For the text in most business documents, 9- or 10-point type is an appropriate size. But you may want to increase the size if your readers have impaired vision or if they don't read well.

Type sizes

This is 6-point type.

This is 8-point type.

This is 10-point type.

This is 12-point type.

This is 14-point type.

Line lengths

This is 10-point type set with a line length that is too long for efficient reading. Its line length is the equivalent of about three alphabets. Although the line length won't bother you too much if you're only reading a line or two, the length is unacceptable for blocks of text.

This is 10-point type set with a line length that is acceptable for most business documents. Its line length is the equivalent of about two and one-half alphabets.

This is 10-point type set with a line length that is acceptable for most business documents. Its line length is the equivalent of about two alphabets.

Leading

This is 10-point type set with a line length that is acceptable for most business documents. Its line length is the equivalent of about two and one-half alphabets. However, this example has zero points of leading so its readability can be improved.

This is 10-point type set with a line length that is acceptable for most business documents. Its line length is the equivalent of about two and one-half alphabets. Since this example has one point of leading, it is quite easy to read.

This is 10-point type set with a line length that is acceptable for most business documents. Its line length is the equivalent of about two and one-half alphabets. Although this example has two points of leading, I don't think it's any easier to read than the example with one-point leading.

Figure 15-4 Type size, line length, and leading

For headings, you can go up to 12 points or more, and for text within figures you can go down to 8 points. In general, however, you shouldn't go below 8-point type if you want your type to be readable.

When you specify the typeface and a type size for a block of text, you have specified its *font*. For instance, 10-point Times Roman is one font; 11-point Times Roman is another; and 11-point Times Italic is a third. I mention this term because you will often see it in desktop publishing literature.

Type size is obviously an important factor for the readability of text, but so is the *line length*. In fact, many studies have shown that long lines of text have a negative effect on both reading speed and comprehension. The longer a line is, the more often your eyes must refocus and blink during the reading of a line. In addition, you lose time as your eyes travel back to the start of the next line. When a line is too long, you also have more difficulty finding the next line.

How long is too long? That depends to some extent on the type size. But at a normal reading distance of about 16 inches, the line length should be no more than 5 inches with a maximum of 70 characters per line. According to a rule of thumb based on type size, you should make a line no more than two and one-half times the length of the lowercase alphabet. This is an important typographic consideration that many desktop publishers ignore. You can see examples of various line lengths in figure 15-4.

One other factor that affects readability is leading. *Leading* (pronounced *ledding*) is the extra space between lines of type, and it is measured in points. Figure 15-4, for example, shows blocks of type with zero, one, and two points leading. In other words, the 10-point type is set on lines that are 10, 11, and 12 points high. As you can see, the text with one point of leading is easier to read than the unleaded text. However, the text with two-point leading isn't much easier to read than the text with one-point leading. In fact, too much leading decreases readability.

In general, you decide how much leading you should use for a block of type based on the typeface, type size, and line length. If the type is large or the line is long, you need more leading than you would otherwise. This will help the reader distinguish between the lines. For 8- or 9-point type, you should use from zero to two points of leading, depending on the line length. For 10- or 11-point type, you should use from one to three points of leading. And for 12- to 14-point type, you should use from two to four points of leading. Within these guidelines, you select the amount of leading that looks best with the typeface you're using.

In the publishing industry, line length is usually measured in *picas*, and one pica is one-sixth of an inch. So when you hear a type specification, you may hear something like "10-point Times Roman with two points leading on a 30-pica line." Or you may hear a specification in an abbreviated form such as "9/10 ITC Bookman Light on a 24-pica line." This means 9-point ITC Bookman Light type on a 10-point line (one-point leading) that is 24 picas long.

Justification   In chapter 14, I explained the difference between *justified text* and *ragged-right text*. I also explained that ragged-right text is easier to read than justified text when it's produced by a word processing system. Ragged-right text is also easier to read when it's produced by a desktop publishing system, as illustrated in figure 15-5. Nevertheless, it's okay to use justified text on a desktop publishing system because you don't get the uneven spacing between words in a line that you do with word processing.

Why would you use justified text when you know ragged right is easier to read? First, because justified text lets you get more words on each page. Second, because some people associate justified text with high-quality typesetting. If they see ragged-right text, they associate it with the less expensive typesetting methods of the past. So if you want to keep your document as short as possible or if you want to make sure that people perceive it as a high-quality presentation, you probably should use justified text.

Hyphenation   One reason ragged-right text is easier to read than justified text is that ragged-right doesn't require as much hyphenation at the ends of lines. As a general rule, you should hyphenate a word in a ragged-right text block only if each portion of the hyphenated word contains four letters or more. That means only a few words on each page should require hyphenation. In contrast, you may have to hyphenate many words in a page of justified text if you want to avoid some large spaces between words.

When you use ragged-right text on a desktop publishing system, you should make sure that you don't get more hyphenation than you want. For instance, the automatic hyphenation feature on some systems gives you almost as many hyphenated words with ragged-right text as it does with justified text. Since this defeats the purpose of ragged-right text, you usually should turn the automatic hyphenation feature off when you use ragged-right text.

Justified text

For the last six months, I've been using an IBM Personal Computer (PC) for my editorial work because I've been working on a book for PC users. During that time, I've come to realize that the system I'm using is much better than the system the other editors are using. That got me wondering whether all of our editors should switch from our current system to PC-based systems.

This report presents my analysis of our current system and my recommendations for new systems. I've tried to be brief because the primary purpose of this report is to bring you up-to-date on the PC and word processing developments of the last six years. When you finish this report, you can decide whether you want more information on any of the subjects. If so, I'll be happy to get that information for you.

Ragged-right text

For the last six months, I've been using an IBM Personal Computer (PC) for my editorial work because I've been working on a book for PC users. During that time, I've come to realize that the system I'm using is much better than the system the other editors are using. That got me wondering whether all of our editors should switch from our current system to PC-based systems.

This report presents my analysis of our current system and my recommendations for new systems. I've tried to be brief because the primary purpose of this report is to bring you up-to-date on the PC and word processing developments of the last six years. When you finish this report, you can decide whether you want more information on any of the subjects. If so, I'll be happy to get that information for you.

Figure 15-5 Justified and ragged-right text

Headings and subheadings When you choose fonts for your headings and subheadings, you want to make sure that your readers can easily distinguish between the levels of headings you've used. To do this, you can use techniques like centering level-1 headings and starting level-2 headings at the left margin. You can also use different type sizes or styles for different heading levels as illustrated in figure 15-6. Here, the headings are in 12-point Palatino Bold; the subheadings are in 10-point Palatino Bold Italic. Although it's simple to distinguish between heading levels when you use desktop publishing, many people don't do it effectively.

Why our editors should switch to PC-based systems 2

Because this is a shared system, the editors experience frequent delays when they use the word processing software. This is particularly true between 10 A.M. and 3 P.M. when the system receives its heaviest use. Our editors also experience delays when they go from one function like editing to another function like printing. Because the word processing software consists of several programs rather than just one large program, the system must load the next program to be processed when a user changes functions. The delays occur while a program is being loaded.

Because the word processing software for this system was developed in the 1970s, it is dated. Although most of our editors don't realize it, our current word processing system just doesn't compare with a modern word processing package. In particular, it is inefficient when it comes to some of the time-consuming functions like paginating and checking spelling. Although our software was at one time the best word processing software in the industry, it is no longer a competitive product.

What's right about PC-based word processing

When I talk about PC-based word processing, I'm talking about word processing that runs on an IBM PC or an IBM clone. To get the features that I'm about to describe, you need a powerful PC such as an IBM AT. You also need a hard disk. Once you have a system like this, you can buy any one of several word processing packages that will outperform our current word processing software. Two of the packages that would provide the features that we want are *WordPerfect* and *Word*, but there are several others that would do the job too. When you use one of these packages on an IBM AT, you will notice three major types of improvements.

Improved system speed

Word processing on an IBM AT will improve an editor's speed by eliminating the delays that are common to our current system. Because an AT system is a one-user system that is faster internally than our current multi-user system, you won't notice any delays as functions are executed. Also, because a modern word processing package is one, large program, there are no delays between functions while a program is being loaded into storage. The result is that you work with little or no waiting for the system or program to complete its work.

When you want to print on an IBM AT when using *WordPerfect*, you can start the function and continue working on the document that is printing. You don't have to wait for the printer to finish printing. This too

Figure 15-6 Headings and subheadings that show their levels

When you design your headings, you should avoid capitalization as much as possible. Remember that people find it easier to read lowercase letters than to read capitals, so the most readable headings are those with only the first letter capitalized. That's why, as you think of ways to distinguish your heading levels, you should avoid capitalizing all the letters in a heading.

The number of typographic variations If you use too many typefaces or sizes, the pages in your documents start to look cluttered. So if you want your document to look attractive and tasteful, you should limit the number of typographic variations you use. Many new desktop publishers reveal their lack of experience and judgment by trying to use as many different fonts as possible.

As a starting point, you can use one type family with serifs in its regular style for the body text (for example, 9-point Times Roman with two points leading). For figure legends, you can use that same type family in its boldface style (for example, 9-point Times Bold). For headings and subheadings, you can use that same type family in its boldface or boldface italic style, perhaps in sizes that are somewhat larger than the text (for example, 11-point Times Bold and 11-point Times Bold Italic). Then, for page headers, footers, and figures, you can use a second type family, perhaps a sans serif family. By changing its style and size, you can provide variety within all these components.

To see how we've limited the typographic variations in this book, take a moment to study it. Although this 400-page book is more complicated than most of the documents you'll ever produce using desktop publishing, you'll see that it contains only seven type fonts: 10-point New Century Schoolbook Regular for the text; 12-point New Century Schoolbook Bold for headings; 8-point New Century Schoolbook Bold and Regular for the figure legends; 8-point ITC Avant Garde Book for the page heading and some of the figures; 12-point ITC Avant Garde Bold for the page numbers; and 8-point Courier for figures that represent word processing documents.

Design features

Before you can do your own desktop publishing, you must also understand something about page and document design. In this topic, I'll present the most important design features you'll use in desktop publishing.

Trim size   The *trim size* is the physical size of the document you're producing. For instance, most of the documents and manuals in business have a trim size of 8-1/2 by 11. This size makes them easy to photocopy on any copying machine.

If you're going to have your document printed by a printing press, you may want to consider a more economical trim size. For instance, 5-1/2 by 8-1/2 is an economical trim size for some printing presses. Similarly, we chose a trim size of 7-3/8 by 9-1/2 for this book because it was an economical size for the press we used. Before you decide on a trim size, you may want to talk with your printer to make sure it's going to be economical.

Margins   *Margins* have several purposes. First, they provide a border around the text area of a document. Second, they provide for the printing and binding requirements of a document. Third, they improve the readability of a document by adding white space.

Figure 15-7, for example, shows typical margins for the lefthand pages of a bound document with a trim size of 8-1/2 by 11. To get the margins for the righthand pages, you use a mirror image of the page that's illustrated. In the publishing industry, margins (like line lengths) are usually measured in picas, and one pica is equivalent to 12 points. In this example, the *gutter margin* is six picas (one inch), the *head margin* is four picas, and the *foot margin* is five picas. Note, however, that the outside margin for the page header is four picas, but the *trim margin* is 11 picas.

In general, the trick in margin design is reaching an appropriate balance between white space and content. Because white space improves the appearance of a document, you don't want to be stingy with your margins. On the other hand, you don't want your gutter margin to be too large because too much white space between two pages can be distracting. Similarly, you don't want to make your head, foot, and side margins too large because that reduces the space you can use for your text and figures, which in turn increases the number of pages in your document. An optical illusion on the page makes equal head and foot margins appear unequal. So if you want the contents of your pages to look centered, you have to use a head margin that's smaller than the foot margin.

Headers and footers   When you produce a desktop publishing document of more than one page, you can include a *header*, a *footer*, or both on each page. These are similar to headers or footers in word processing documents, but you have more typographic and design

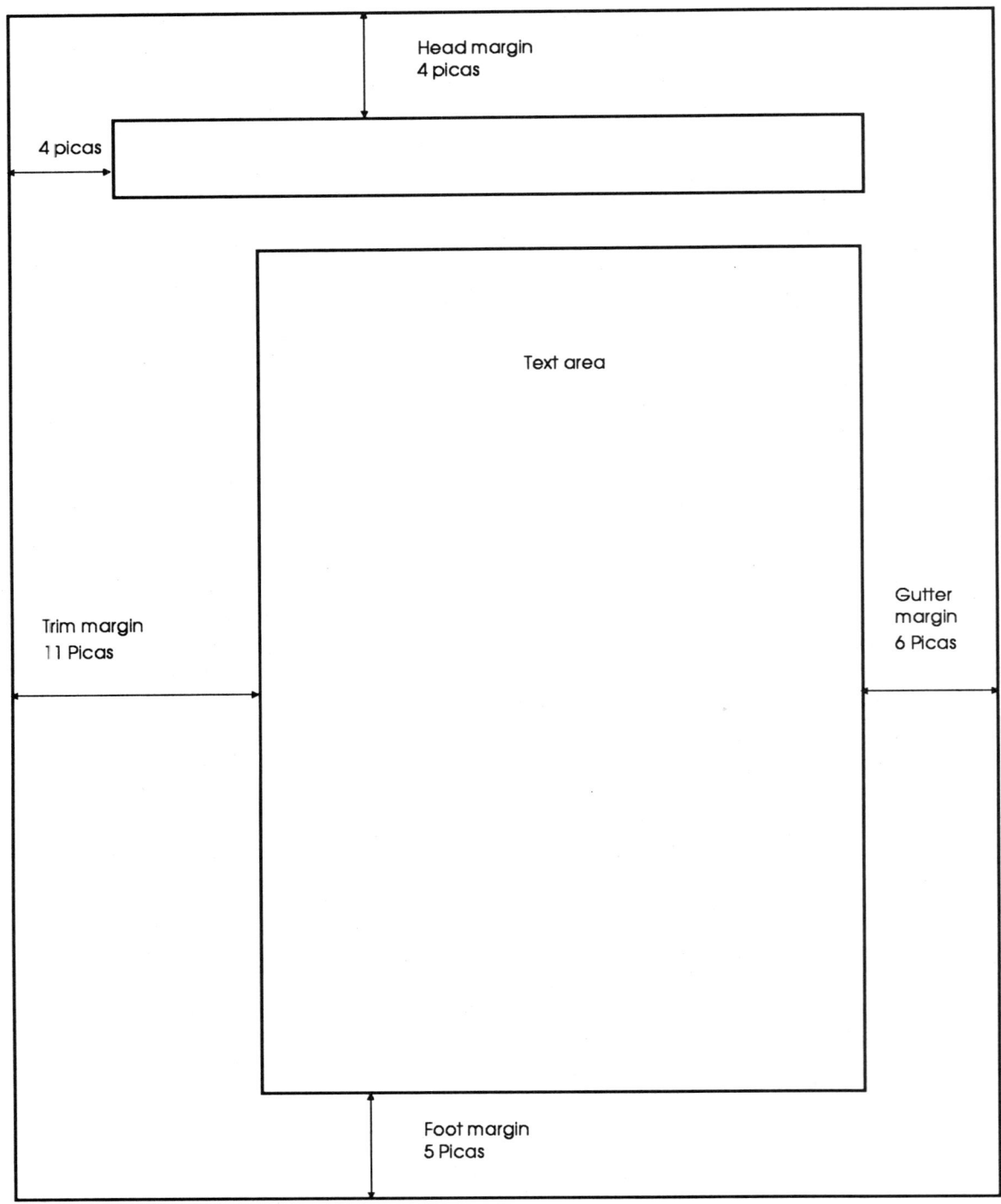

Figure 15-7 Typical margins for the left page in a bound document with a trim size of 8-1/2 by 11

options. If, for example, you study the headers in this book, you can see that the header text (called the *running head*) is set in 8-point ITC Avant Garde Book, and the page number (called a *folio*) is set in 12-point ITC Avant Garde Bold. The entire header is separated from the text by a *rule* that is three points thick and has three picas of white space beneath it. The header on each left page identifies the chapter by number; the header on each right page identifies the chapter by shortened name.

If you study the headers in appendix B, you can see that the running head and folio are printed below a 3-point rule at the top of each page. To separate the header from the text, the designer has used 18 points of white space. Because this is a one-unit document, the running head is a shortened version of the report title. For simplicity, the designer has used a footer on only the first page of the document.

If you look at the headers and footers in other books and documents, you can see many other design variations. To be effective, a header should present useful information in a readable font. If the pages are going to be used for reference, the folios need to be conspicuous and they need to be placed at the outer edges of the pages. In addition, the headings should be clearly separated from the text. However, too much white space between header and text can create an unattractive gap.

For a simple, functional design, here's what I suggest. For headers, you can set the running heads in one sans serif font (for example, 9-point Helvetica Light) and your folios in a related font (for example, 12-point Helvetica Bold). To separate the headers from the text, you can use three picas of white space with no rule. As for footers, I recommend that you avoid them unless they serve some reference function.

Figures and legends If you study the figures in this book, you can see that they are boxed. In addition, a 6-point rule is used to separate the legend from the box. Then, an 18-point white space is used to separate the legend from the text. The legend is set in 8-point New Century Schoolbook starting at the left margin. That's one way of handling figures and legends.

If you page through other books, you can see that figures and legends can be handled in many different ways. When you use desktop publishing, though, it's easiest to box all of the figures. Then, you can set the legends in the same font as the body text with one pica between the figure box and the legend and two picas between the legend and any text below it.

When you use desktop publishing, you define the spaces for text, figures, and legends. Whenever possible, you should place your figures at the top of a page so any text on the page will be below it. This will improve the appearance of your pages. If two figures are related, you should place them on facing pages so your readers can study them without turning pages. As much as possible, you should try to lay out your document so each figure and the text that refers to it are on the same set of facing pages. Because you usually can't adhere to all of these guidelines at once, you have to make compromises as you lay out the pages of a document.

Two-column pages If one of your design goals is to reduce printing costs, you should consider laying out your pages with two columns of text per page. Then, you can get considerably more text on each page without going to a line length that reduces readability. For instance, figure 15-8 illustrates a two-column page for the PC recommendation. When the document is presented this way, it only requires seven pages instead of the ten in appendix B.

When you design a two-column page, you may want to use a smaller point size than you would otherwise. That way you'll have fewer problems with hyphenation (and you'll also get more text on each page). Also, you should realize that the amount of white space between the columns is critical. Too little makes the columns run together; too much creates a white space that is visually distracting. Last, you should make sure your columns aren't so narrow that they're difficult to read.

When you lay out two-column pages, you should try to place your figures above both columns of the text. If a figure is narrow, you can place it at the top of one of the outside text columns, but you should avoid placing it in an inside column. Because text appears to be heavier than figures, you should keep your figures at the top or at the outer edges of your pages.

Title pages, contents pages, unit openers, appendixes, and indexes Up to this point, I've been talking primarily about the design of the text pages within a document. In addition, you may want to include a *title page* or a *contents page* for any document that you produce with desktop publishing. If you're producing a multi-unit document, you will definitely want to include a title page and a contents page, and you will also need pages called *unit openers* that

Why our editors should switch to PC-based systems 5

Typical hardware costs		
An AT clone with color monitor and 40 megabyte hard disk	$2,500	
Printer	500	
	$3,000	
Typical software costs		
Word processing package	$ 400	
Spreadsheet software	100	
Writing analyzer	50	
	$ 550	
Typical training costs		
Training and reference materials	$ 50	
One week of $30,000 salary	600	
	$ 650	
Total cost		
Hardware	$3,000	
Software	550	
Training	650	
	$4,200	

Figure 3 Typical costs for a PC-based system

The costs of a PC-based system

Figure 3 summarizes the costs of a typical PC-based system. The numbers here are just approximations because I can't say right now exactly which system and which software products we should buy. Also, we may be able to get quantity discounts if we buy several systems at once.

Hardware costs I purchased my system, an AT clone, for around $2500. It is a powerful, high-speed system with a color monitor. If necessary, it can be expanded so it will run any software that we are likely to install in the future. I also purchased a printer for around $500; it is a major improvement over our current minicomputer printer. I would recommend a system like this for each person in the editorial department.

Software costs I think each person in the editorial department should have one of the most advanced word processing packages. I've been using one of the best, which cost around $400. I also think each editor should have a spreadsheet program and a writing analyzer. We can buy these for about $150 per editor. We may also want to buy one or more copies of a desktop publishing package so we can evaluate it and use it whenever it is appropriate.

Training costs Since our editors already know how to use a word processing system, it should be relatively easy for them to learn how to use the PC software that they will need. As a result, we shouldn't need to buy expensive training materials. The manuals that come with the software products are adequate for most training purposes. When

Figure 15-8 A page from the PC recommendation when the text is set in two columns

mark the start of each unit. In this book, for example, each section starts with a *section opener*, and each chapter starts with a *chapter opener*. At the end of a document, you may want to include one or more appendixes, and you may also want to include an index.

When you design a document, each type of page requires its own desktop publishing format. If, for example, you look at the title page, contents page, section openers, chapter openers, appendixes, and index for this book, you will see several different formats. In addition, the left and right pages for the body of the text can have their own formats.

When you design the special pages of a document, you try to make the design appropriate for the function. For instance, the design for a title page should clearly indicate the title, author, and any other identifying information. The design for a contents page should make it easy for your readers to preview what they're going to be reading about. The design for unit openers should help your readers find the beginnings of units. And so on.

I mention these special pages so you'll begin to see how involved desktop publishing can be. Even a simple document like the PC recommendation in appendix B requires three different page formats: a unit opener, a left text page, and a right text page. That's why it can easily take three or more hours to produce a simple document like the PC recommendation when you use desktop publishing.

The number of design elements on each page   Just as you should limit the number of typographic variations you use within a document, you should limit the number of design elements you use on each page. If you don't, your pages will appear to be complicated or cluttered. Then, your readers may be reluctant to read what you've written.

The traditional rule of design has been that each page should have a maximum of three or four design elements. For instance, the traditional advertisement has consisted of a headline, an illustration, a block of copy, and possibly a prominent trademark or logo. If you study this book, you can see that each text page has a maximum of three elements: a header, a figure and legend treated as one element, and a block of text. Similarly, the chapter opener page consists of only three elements: the chapter title and number, a block of text, and a footer.

Today, many technical books and manuals are designed with more than three or four elements on each page. For instance, many books about PC software have pages that include optional elements like boxed comments, sidebars, and icons. Although these elements are intended to make it easier for the readers to find what they're looking for and to learn what they're trying to learn, I question the effectiveness of these extra elements. As I see it, these extra elements indicate that the books weren't organized properly in the first place. Most of these books would look better if there were fewer design elements on each page. But most of them would be more effective only if they were reorganized and rewritten.

General guidelines for desktop publishing presentations

Now that you understand the typographic and design considerations for desktop publishing, you should realize that it's a lot more complicated than word processing. As a result, you must be as organized as possible when you use desktop publishing. With that in mind, here are three guidelines that will help you produce effective desktop publishing presentations as efficiently as possible.

Use standard presentation formats   It takes time to create desktop publishing formats. That's why you should use standard presentation formats whenever they apply. For instance, you should have standard formats for newsletters, proposals, and manuals. By using formats you've already established, you can save many hours of production time.

Don't start a new design from scratch   Occasionally, you'll want to produce a document that requires a design that's different from the ones you have standard formats for. Unless you're a graphics designer, though, you should never start a design from scratch. Instead, you should copy the designs of other documents. That way you can use desktop publishing without becoming a graphics designer.

After you find a design you like in an appropriate trim size, you can copy the margins, headers, typefaces, type sizes, and so on for each kind of page within the document. Occasionally, you will want to combine design features that you copy from two different documents. Once you have entered the new formats into your desktop publishing system, they become standard formats for subsequent documents.

You may also be able to use the standard formats that come with your desktop publishing software. For instance, *Ventura Publisher* comes with several standard formats (called *style sheets*). Or, you may be able to buy standard formats for your system. For instance, one company sells a diskette for *PageMaker* on an IBM PC that includes formats for documents like brochures, catalogs, and two-column newsletters. At a modest price, formats like these can quickly pay for themselves by reducing production costs.

Don't insist that all figures be developed on the PC   Before a figure can be printed as part of a desktop publishing presentation, it must be stored on the PC. That's why you normally use spreadsheet or graphics programs in conjunction with desktop publishing. Then, the text is prepared using word processing, and the figures are prepared using spreadsheet or graphics programs. All the desktop publishing software does is help you present the text and figures in the formats you've established.

As long as you can prepare the figures efficiently using spreadsheet or graphics software, it makes sense to develop them on your PC. That way, everything you need for producing a document is stored on the PC. However, you shouldn't take this to extremes. If, for example, it takes you an hour to prepare a conceptual drawing on your PC when you could do it in ten minutes by hand, you don't have to prepare it on the system. Instead, you can prepare a space for the figure using desktop publishing. Then, you can draw the figure to size and paste it in the space.

Figure 6-6 in this book is an example of a figure that would have been difficult to create using graphics software. That's why we put the editing marks on the word processing text by hand. Then, we reduced the size of the figure using photographic equipment, (though many copy machines can now reduce your originals), and we placed it in the space created for it by desktop publishing.

Discussion

I hope this chapter makes you think twice about using desktop publishing. If you're a writer, you should realize by now that desktop publishing requires a new set of skills. As a result, it can be time consuming and frustrating, and it can distract you so much that your writing will suffer. So if it makes sense to prepare some of your documents using desktop publishing, I hope it also makes sense for someone else to do the desktop publishing for you.

If you're a writer and you have to do your own desktop publishing, I hope this chapter has given you some ideas that will help you use desktop publishing more effectively. In particular, I hope you realize that it makes sense to keep your designs simple and to use standard formats. If you do, you'll be able to devote more time to your writing. Remember that the content and quality of your writing is far more important than any appearance you can create with desktop publishing.

Terms

production
type family
type style
regular style
Roman style
book style
italic style
boldface style
bold style
boldface italic style
bold italic style
typeface
serif
sans serif
type size
point
font
line length
leading
pica

justified text
ragged-right text
trim size
margin
gutter margin
head margin
foot margin
trim margin
header
footer
running head
folio
rule
title page
contents page
unit opener
section opener
chapter opener
style sheet

Objectives

1. Describe the costs and benefits of desktop publishing.

2. Describe the typographic factors you should consider when you select the fonts for a document.

3. Describe the design factors you should consider as you design the pages for a document.

4. Describe the three general guidelines for all desktop publishing presentations.

Appendix A

An effective report in word processing form

This report is an example of the informal presentation style we use in our company. Each page includes a header that contains the date, the file name, and the page number, but footers aren't used. The headings and subheadings are boldfaced, but no other special typefaces or presentation features are used. The figures are presented at the end of the text with one figure on each page. This informal style makes it easy for our writers to make effective word processing presentations in a minimum of time.

Why our editors should switch from our current word processing system to PC-based word processing systems

For the last six months, I've been using an IBM Personal Computer (PC) for my editorial work because I've been working on a book for PC users. During that time, I've come to realize that the system I'm using is much better than the system the other editors are using. That got me wondering whether all of our editors should switch from our current system to PC-based systems.

This report presents my analysis of our current system and my recommendations for new systems. I've tried to be brief because the primary purpose of this report is to bring you up-to-date on the PC and word processing developments of the last six years. When you finish this report, you can decide whether you want more information on any of the subjects. If so, I'll be happy to get that information for you.

What's wrong with our word processing system

We installed our current system in 1982. It is a minicomputer system with one terminal (keyboard and monitor) for each person in the editorial department. The nine people in this department share the one printer that is located in the department. They also share the minicomputer and its disk drives with 15 other users of the system in the administrative and marketing departments.

Because this is a shared system, the editors experience frequent delays when they use the word processing software. This is particularly true between 10 A.M. and 3 P.M. when the system receives its heaviest use. Our editors also experience delays when they go from one function like editing to another function like printing. Because the word processing software consists of several programs rather than just one large program, the system must load the next program to be processed when a user changes functions. The delays occur while a program is being loaded.

Because the word processing software for this system was developed in the 1970s, it is dated. Although most of our editors don't realize it, our current word processing system just doesn't compare with a modern word processing package. In particular, it is inefficient when it comes to some of the time-consuming functions like paginating and checking spelling. Although our software was at one time the best word processing software in the industry, it is no longer a competitive product.

What's right about PC-based word processing

When I talk about PC-based word processing, I'm talking about word processing that runs on an IBM PC or an IBM clone. To get the features that I'm about to describe, you need a powerful PC such as an IBM AT. You also need a hard disk. Once you have a system like this, you can buy any one of several word processing packages that will outperform our current word processing software. Two of the packages that would provide the features that we want are WordPerfect and Word, but there are several others that would do the job too. When you use one of these packages on an IBM AT, you will notice three major types of improvements.

Improved system speed   Word processing on an IBM AT will improve an editor's speed by eliminating the delays that are common to our current system. Because an AT system is a one-user system that is faster internally than our current multi-user system, you won't notice any delays as functions are executed. Also, because a modern word processing package is one, large program, there are no delays between functions while a program is being loaded into storage. The result is that you work with little or no waiting for the system or program to complete its work.

When you want to print on an IBM AT when using WordPerfect, you can start the function and continue working on the document that is printing. You don't have to wait for the printer to finish printing. This too speeds up an editor's work. In contrast, on our current system, you have to stop editing, wait for the system to load the printing program, and wait for the printing to finish before you can continue editing.

Improved functions   Besides the speed of the system, a modern word processing package provides new and improved functions. For instance, WordPerfect provides improved functions for searching and replacing characters, for boldfacing and underlining, and for creating and using macros. It also provides new functions for aligning characters on the right side of a page, for generating contents lists and indexes, and for handling footnotes. If you need some of these functions, they can make dramatic improvements in your productivity. But let me give you two more examples to show you what I mean.

Example 1:   On our current system, you paginate a document after you have finished editing it. Although the system automatically tells you where the bottom of a page should be, you have to okay the system's decision for each page manually. For a 20-page document, this function alone may take a minute or two. In contrast, WordPerfect continually repaginates without you knowing it. If you add a paragraph to page 1 of a 20-page document, all of the other pages are automatically repaginated.

Example 2: On our current system, you can correct the spelling of a document after you have finished editing it. But it is a separate procedure that can take 10 minutes or more for a 20-page document, depending on how many misspellings the document contains. Using <u>WordPerfect</u>, though, you can check the spelling of a word, a page, or the entire document at any time. On an IBM AT, the system will check all the words of a 20-page document in about 30 seconds. And when it finds a misspelling, it offers the most likely corrections to you so you don't have to figure them out or enter them yourself. As a result, you can correct all the misspellings in a 20-page document in just a couple of minutes.

Improved monitors and printers You're probably used to it by now, but the characters on your terminal screen and the characters printed by our editorial printer are difficult to read because they are made up of a limited number of dots. In contrast, the characters on the monitor of an IBM AT or those printed by a modern printer have many more dots per inch so they are easier to read. To illustrate, look closely at the printing in this report. If you compare it with the printed output from our current system, you'll see a noticeable difference. This difference means you'll have less eyestrain on a PC-based system, and that can mean fewer headaches.

A modern printer also does a better job of handling paper than our current printer can. For instance, my printer can handle continuous forms as well as cut forms, and it only takes a few seconds to switch from one to the other. When you use continuous forms, you can tear the last sheet you've just printed on a tear-off bar. And you don't waste one blank page each time you print. Using this printer, I can print my own letters and envelopes on letterhead paper so I don't require clerical assistance the way the other editors do.

PC software that can make an editor's job easier

If you just compare PC-based word processing to the word processing on our current system, you have to be impressed by the improvements of the last six or eight years. But there's more. If you use a PC-based system, you have access to several other programs that can make an editor's job easier. Now, I'll introduce a few of the most common ones in case you're not familiar with them.

Spreadsheet software I know you've used 1-2-3, so I won't try to describe what this type of software does. But have you considered how the editors could use this type of software to control their projects more effectively? I haven't actually tried it, but I think spreadsheet software could be valuable if used for project management.

Writing analyzers   Just as spelling checkers detect spelling errors, writing analyzers detect grammatical errors and other writing problems. They also measure readability. For instance, figure 1 presents the summary page from an analyzer called RightWriter after it has processed this report. As you can see, the readability score is 9.81. RightWriter analyzed this 3592-word report and calculated its readability score in less than a minute, so you can imagine how a product like this could help an editor work more efficiently and more effectively.

Graphics software   Some graphics programs let you create many different kinds of charts such as organization charts, bar charts, pie charts, and line charts. Other graphics programs let you create illustrations. Although I don't think the charting programs are going to be much use to us, they may come in handy for an occasional presentation to the marketing department. On the other hand, the drawing programs would let us create finished illustrations instead of the rough drawings that we pass on to the production department now. This would eliminate a lot of editorial proofing, and it would simplify the job of the production department.

Desktop publishing   We've all read a lot about desktop publishing in the last six months, and there's no doubt now that it's here to stay (see the supplementary section in the August issue of InfoSystems). That means that we'll eventually be doing some of our production work using desktop publishing. Although this work will probably be done in the production department, some of it may be done in the editorial department. That's why we should start learning more about it. If we all have PC ATs, of course, we'll be able to run desktop publishing software on our own systems.

The benefits of a PC-based system

Figure 2 summarizes the three primary benefits that we'll get if we switch to PC-based systems. The most important of these in terms of system justification is improved editorial productivity. But the others could be important too. As I present these, I'll try to give you some idea of what the value of these benefits might be.

Improved editorial productivity   Editors who use PC-based systems instead of our current system should improve their productivity due to the improvements in system speed and the improvements in word processing functions like pagination and checking spelling. However, the editors may also improve their productivity by using spreadsheet software for project management or writing analyzers for grammar checking.

How much will their productivity improve? That's impossible to say, and I doubt that doing a study of it will give us a clear answer to this question either. Speaking personally, though, I can say that my word processing productivity has improved by at least 10 percent since I've switched to <u>WordPerfect</u> on an IBM AT. In fact, I would say that it has increased by 20 percent or more. Now, when I help a colleague do something on our minicomputer system, I am frustrated by the continual delays and by the use of its cumbersome, inefficient functions. These inefficiencies never bothered me that much when I used the system, but now I've been spoiled by a system that's much faster so I realize how inefficient the old system is.

To put a dollar value on an increase in word processing productivity, I've assumed a base editorial salary of $30,000, and I've assumed that editors use word processing about one-half of their working hours. Using these numbers, a 5% increase in productivity leads to a value of $750 per year; 10% leads to a value of $1500 per year; and 20% leads to a value of $3000 per year. These calculations are summarized in figure 2.

Improved editorial quality   If you use a modern spelling checker and writing analyzer, the quality of your work has to improve. And if you work more efficiently, you'll have more time and energy to spend on the quality of your work. So there's no doubt that the quality of our work will improve if our editors switch to PC-based systems.

What is the value of this benefit? I leave that up to you. Fewer spelling errors and grammatical errors probably won't help us sell any one book. But an overall improvement in quality will help us establish a reputation that will sell more books in the future.

Adaptability to future systems   Creating and selling PC software is a highly competitive business. That's why word processing and other software products keep improving. In contrast, the software for minicomputers is relatively static. New product announcements are infrequent, and minicomputer software hasn't improved to near the extent that microcomputer software has improved in the last six years. I expect this to continue during the next decade. So if you want to be able to buy and use the most advanced software, you're going to have to use IBM PCs and PS/2s, not minicomputers.

To some extent, then, you can view a switch to PC-based systems as preparation for the future. By getting used to these systems now, we'll be ready for the improvements that we've come to expect in PC software: improvements in word processing, in writing analyzers, in graphics packages, and in desktop publishing. And each time we install one of these improved products, we'll be improving our editorial operations. Although this benefit probably doesn't have any value when we first switch to PC-based systems, it will save us money in the future and it will help us stay competitive.

The costs of a PC-based system

Figure 3 summarizes the costs of a typical PC-based system. The numbers here are just approximations because I can't say right now exactly which system and which software products we should buy. Also, we may be able to get quantity discounts if we buy several systems at once.

Hardware costs   I purchased my system, an AT clone, for around $2500. It is a powerful, high-speed system with a color monitor. If necessary, it can be expanded so it will run any software that we are likely to install in the future. I also purchased a printer for around $500; it is a major improvement over our current minicomputer printer. I would recommend a system like this for each person in the editorial department.

Software costs   I think each person in the editorial department should have one of the most advanced word processing packages. I've been using one of the best, which cost around $400. I also think each editor should have a spreadsheet program and a writing analyzer. We can buy these for about $150 per editor. We may also want to buy one or more copies of a desktop publishing package so we can evaluate it and use it whenever it is appropriate.

Training costs   Since our editors already know how to use a word processing system, it should be relatively easy for them to learn how to use the PC software that they will need. As a result, we shouldn't need to buy expensive training materials. The manuals that come with the software products are adequate for most training purposes. When they aren't, we should be able to buy books that will satisfy our training requirements. So a budget of about $50 for each editor should be adequate for training and reference materials.

   The more expensive part of the training budget is going to be the time lost while an editor learns how to use a new system and its software. Fortunately, I didn't find this lost time to be excessive. Although I was frustrated by my PC for the first two weeks or so, I estimate my total amount of lost time for training at about one full week. At an annual salary of $30,000, the cost of this lost time will be about $600 per editor.

Cost/benefit analysis

In figure 4, I have calculated the payback period in years and the return-on-investment (ROI) percent based on the costs and benefit values that I have already presented. These calculations use the benefit values for improved productivity only, because these values are the most predictable. At a 10 percent improvement in word processing productivity, the benefit value is $1500 for an editor who earns $30,000 per year, so the payback period is 2.8 years and the ROI is 35.7%. Because I think a 10 percent improvement is a conservative estimate of what the actual improvement will be, I'm confident that the actual payback period will be shorter and the ROI higher than these numbers indicate.

When we analyze costs and benefits, though, I don't think we should disregard the benefits of improved editorial quality and our adaptability to future systems. Although it may be hard to put a value on them, they are real benefits. Also, I haven't even mentioned the possible values of some intangible benefits like reduced eyestrain or the improved morale that our editors may experience when they use state-of-the-art systems. These benefits could lead to fewer sick days and reduced employee turnover. When you consider all of the possible benefits, I think it's clear that we should replace our minicomputer system with PC-based systems for all editors as soon as possible.

Recommendations

If you agree that we should get PC-based systems for all of our editors, there are still several questions to be answered. What hardware should we buy? What software should we buy? How should we handle the conversion? And when should each editor convert?

For now, let me give you some quick answers to these questions. Then, if you want more detail, I'll be happy to provide it.

What hardware should we buy? As I see it, what we want to buy today are clones of IBM ATs. To get the system speed that we want, we can't accept systems that are less powerful than ATs. But we don't have to buy the more expensive PS/2 systems because they don't offer anything that we need right now. Also, AT clones will run the OS/2 operating system when it becomes available and when we feel that it offers us some capability that we need.

What software should we buy? I don't think we can go wrong if we buy one of the best-selling word processing packages. I've been using WordPerfect so I'm probably biased in its favor, but I'm confident that it does everything our editors are used to doing and much more. Also, it consistently gets top ratings by the editors of the leading computer magazines.

If you want to consider other word processing packages, we can do that too. It's difficult to choose between two packages, though, if you haven't actually used them both for editorial work. That's why a detailed evaluation can be time consuming.

In addition to word processing, I think each editor should have one or more writing analyzers. So far, I've used <u>Grammatik II</u> and <u>RightWriter</u>, and both have some useful features. <u>I'm also evaluating another one right now</u>. These programs are relatively inexpensive, though, so the choice isn't that critical.

If any of our editors wants to try using spreadsheet software for project management, I think we should provide this software too. However, I don't think our editors will use this type of software much, so an inexpensive program should be adequate for their purposes. One such program is <u>VP Planner</u>.

As we get more experience with PC software, we can evaluate new products. Whenever we find a program that's useful, we can add it to an editor's system. If you look back to the cost summary in figure 3, you can see that the major costs for each editor are going to be for hardware, training, and the word processing software. As a result, we can add new software to an editor's system at a marginal cost.

How and when should we convert? If you're convinced that our editors should convert to AT systems, you may be asking yourself how and when we should do the conversion. Should all of the editors convert at once? Or, should we convert one or two editors at a time? Because it's easy to convert an editor from a terminal to a PC-based system, I think we can do this in many different ways. As a result, conversion shouldn't put an unnecessary strain on our editorial budget, and it shouldn't interfere with the completion of any of our projects.

My only recommendation is that our editors convert to the new systems after they complete one editorial project and before they start the next one. That way they can devote themselves to the training that is required for the new systems without having to worry about ongoing projects. After a few days of training, they can start work on their next projects knowing that their productivity will be down for the first few weeks that they use the new system, but after that it will be up.

Conclusion

Whether or not you decide that our editors should convert to PC-based systems, I thought you should be aware of the word processing and system improvements of the last six years. I remember you recalling how much your productivity improved when you switched from a typewriter to our current system back in 1982. Now, in 1988, I think you'll enjoy a similar improvement in productivity if you switch to a PC-based system. The improvement won't be quite as dramatic as your earlier one, but you'll probably remember it fondly for many years to come. That's why I think the sooner we all make the conversion to PC-based systems, the better off our editorial department will be.

```
                  <<** SUMMARY **>>

     OVERALL CRITIQUE FOR: d:\wp\bc\pcrec1

     READABILITY INDEX: 9.81
Readers need a 10th grade level of education to understand.

          Total Number of Words in Document:3592
          Total Number of Words within Sentences:3590
          Total Number of Sentences: 185
          Total Number of Syllables:5465

     STRENGTH INDEX: 0.31
The writing can be made more direct by using:
                    - the active voice
                    - shorter sentences
                    - less wordy phrases
                    - fewer weak phrases

     DESCRIPTIVE INDEX: 0.61
The use of adjectives and adverbs is in the normal range.

     JARGON INDEX: 0.00

     SENTENCE STRUCTURE RECOMMENDATIONS:
               1. Most sentences contain multiple clauses.
                  Try to use more simple sentences.
              14. Consider using more predicate verbs.
```

Figure 1 The summary page from RightWriter when run on the first draft of this report

Improved editorial productivity

Resulting from

Improved system speed
Improved word processing functions
Spreadsheet software for project management
Writing analyzers

Benefit value

Assuming that each editor uses word processing one-half of the time on the job:

> A 5% increase in word procesing productivity for an editor earning $30,000 per year means a benefit value of $750/year.
>
> A 10% increase means a benefit value of $1,500 per year.
>
> A 20% increase means a benefit value of $3,000 per year.

Improved editorial quality

Resulting from

Spelling checker
Writing analyzers

Benefit value

What is the value of fewer spelling and grammatical errors? What is the value of a manuscript that's easier to read?

Adaptability to future systems

Resulting from

Our experiences with current versions of word processing, analyzer, graphics, and desktop publishing software

Benefit value

This has no value in the short term, but it means we'll be able to save money by converting to improved versions of software products. And the improvements are going to come on PC-based systems.

Figure 2   The benefits of a PC-based system

Typical hardware costs

An AT clone with color monitor and 40 megabyte hard disk	$2,500
Printer	500
	$3,000

Typical software costs

Word processing package	$ 400
Spreadsheet software	100
Writing analyzer	50
	$ 550

Typical training costs

Training and reference materials	$ 50
One week of $30,000 salary	600
	$ 650

Total cost

Hardware	$3,000
Software	550
Training	650
	$4,200

Figure 3 Typical costs for a PC-based system

Productivity improvement = 5%

Payback

$4200 divided by $750 = 5.6 years

ROI

$750 divided by $4200 times 100 = 17.9%

Productivity improvement = 10%

Payback

$4200 divided by $1,500 = 2.8 years

ROI

$1,500 divided by $4200 times 100 = 35.7%

Productivity improvement = 20%

Payback

$4200 divided by $3,000 = 1.4 years

ROI

$3,000 divided by $4200 times 100 = 71.4%

Figure 4   Payback and return-on-investment (ROI) possibilities based on productivity improvements only

Appendix B

An effective report in desktop publishing form

This report is the PC recommendation of appendix A after it has been produced by a desktop publishing system. Although the report is shorter and easier to read in this form, it took our desktop publishing specialist more than three hours to produce it. Whenever you consider the use of desktop publishing, you must decide whether the production costs are justified by the benefits.

Why our editors should switch from our current word processing system to PC-based word processing systems

For the last six months, I've been using an IBM Personal Computer (PC) for my editorial work because I've been working on a book for PC users. During that time, I've come to realize that the system I'm using is much better than the system the other editors are using. That got me to wondering whether all of our editors should switch from our current system to PC-based systems

This report presents my analysis of our current system and my recommendations for new systems. I've tried to be brief because the primary purpose of this report is to bring you up-to-date on the PC and word processing developments of the last six years. When you finish this report, you can decide whether you want more information on any of the subjects. If so, I'll be happy to get that information for you.

What's wrong with our word processing system

We installed our current system in 1982. It is a minicomputer system with one terminal (keyboard and monitor) for each person in the editorial department. The nine people in this department share the one printer that is located in the department. They also share the minicomputer and its disk drives with 15 other users of the system in the administrative and marketing departments.

Because this is a shared system, the editors experience frequent delays when they use the word processing software. This is particularly true between 10 A.M. and 3 P.M. when the system receives its heaviest use. Our editors also experience delays when they go from one function like editing to another function like printing. Because the word processing software consists of several programs rather than just one large program, the system must load the next program to be processed when a user changes functions. The delays occur while a program is being loaded.

Because the word processing software for this system was developed in the 1970s, it is dated. Although most of our editors don't realize it, our current word processing system just doesn't compare with a modern word processing package. In particular, it is inefficient when it comes to some of the time-consuming functions like paginating and checking spelling. Although our software was at one time the best word processing software in the industry, it is no longer a competitive product.

What's right about PC-based word processing

When I talk about PC-based word processing, I'm talking about word processing that runs on an IBM PC or an IBM clone. To get the features that

I'm about to describe, you need a powerful PC such as an IBM AT. You also need a hard disk. Once you have a system like this, you can buy any one of several word processing packages that will outperform our current word processing software. Two of the packages that would provide the features that we want are *WordPerfect* and *Word*, but there are several others that would do the job too. When you use one of these packages on an IBM AT, you will notice three major types of improvements.

Improved system speed Word processing on an IBM AT will improve an editor's speed by eliminating the delays that are common to our current system. Because an AT system is a one-user system that is faster internally than our current multi-user system, you won't notice any delays as functions are executed. Also, because a modern word processing package is one, large program, there are no delays between functions while a program is being loaded into storage. The result is that you work with little or no waiting for the system or program to complete its work.

When you want to print on an IBM AT when using *WordPerfect*, you can start the function and continue working on the document that is printing. You don't have to wait for the printer to finish printing. This too speeds up an editor's work. In contrast, on our current system, you have to stop editing, wait for the system to load the printing program, and wait for the printing to finish before you can continue editing.

Improved functions Besides the speed of the system, a modern word processing package provides new and improved functions. For instance, *WordPerfect* provides improved functions for searching and replacing characters, for boldfacing and underlining, and for creating and using macros. It also provides new functions for aligning characters on the right side of a page, for generating contents lists and indexes, and for handling footnotes. If you need some of these functions, they can make dramatic improvements in your productivity. But let me give you two more examples to show you want I mean.

Example 1: On our current system, you paginate a document after you have finished editing it. Although the system automatically tells you where the bottom of a page should be, you have to okay the system's decision for each page manually. For a 20-page document, this function alone may take a minute or two. In contrast, *WordPerfect* continually repaginates without you knowing it. If you add a paragraph to page 1 of a 20-page document, all of the other pages are automatically repaginated.

Example 2: On our current system, you can correct the spelling of a document after you have finished editing it. But it is a separate procedure that can take 10 minutes or more for a 20-page document, depending on how many misspellings the document contains. Using *WordPerfect*, though, you can check the spelling of a word, a page, or the entire document at any time. On an IBM AT, the system will check all the words of a 20-page document in about 30 seconds. And when it finds a misspelling, it offers the most likely corrections to you so you don't have to figure them out or enter them yourself. As a result, you can correct all the misspellings in a 20-page document in just a couple of minutes.

Improved monitors and printers   You're probably used to it by now, but the characters on your terminal screen and the characters printed by our editorial printer are difficult to read because they are made up of a limited number of dots. In contrast, the characters on the monitor of an IBM AT or those printed by a modern printer have many more dots per inch so they are easier to read. To illustrate, look closely at the printing in this report. If you compare it with the printed output from our current system, you'll see a noticeable difference. This difference means you'll have less eyestrain on a PC-based system, and that can mean fewer headaches.

   A modern printer also does a better job of handling paper than our current printer can. For instance, my printer can handle continuous forms as well as cut forms, and it only takes a few seconds to switch from one to the other. When you use continuous forms, you can tear the last sheet you've just printed on a tear-off bar. And you don't waste one blank page each time you print. Using this printer, I can print my own letters and envelopes on letterhead paper so I don't require clerical assistance the way the other editors do.

PC software that can make an editor's job easier

If you just compare PC-based word processing to the word processing on our current system, you have to be impressed by the improvements of the last six or eight years. But there's more. If you use a PC-based system, you have access to several other programs that can make an editor's job easier. Now, I'll introduce a few of the most common ones in case you're not familiar with them.

Spreadsheet software   I know you've used 1-2-3, so I won't try to describe what this type of software does. But have you considered how the editors could use this type of software to control their projects more effectively? I haven't actually tried it, but I think spreadsheet software could be valuable if used for project management.

Writing analyzers   Just as spelling checkers detect spelling errors, writing analyzers detect grammatical errors and other writing problems. They also measure readability. For instance, figure 1 presents the summary page from an analyzer called *RightWriter* after it has processed this report. As you can see, the readability score is 9.81. *RightWriter* analyzed this 3592-word report and calculated its readability score in less than a minute, so you can imagine how a product like this could help an editor work more efficiently and more effectively.

Graphics software   Some graphics programs let you create many different kinds of charts such as organization charts, bar charts, pie charts, and line charts. Other graphics programs let you create illustrations. Although I don't think the charting programs are going to be much use to us, they may come in handy for an occasional presentation to the marketing department. On the other hand, the drawing programs would let us create finished illustrations instead of the rough drawings that we pass on to the production department

```
                  <<** SUMMARY **>>

     OVERALL CRITIQUE FOR: d:\wp\bc\pcrec1

     READABILITY INDEX: 9.81
     Readers need a 10th grade level of education to understand.

            Total Number of Words in Document:3592
            Total Number of Words within Sentences:3590
            Total Number of Sentences: 185
            Total Number of Syllables:5465

     STRENGTH INDEX: 0.31
     The writing can be made more direct by using:
                 - the active voice
                 - shorter sentences
                 - less wordy phrases
                 - fewer weak phrases

     DESCRIPTIVE INDEX: 0.61
     The use of adjectives and adverbs is in the normal range.

     JARGON INDEX: 0.00

SENTENCE STRUCTURE RECOMMENDATIONS:
     1. Most sentences contain multiple clauses.
        Try to use more simple sentences.
     14. Consider using more predicate verbs.
```

Figure 1 The summary page from RightWriter when run on the first draft of this report

now. This would eliminate a lot of editorial proofing, and it would simplify the job of the production department.

Desktop publishing We've all read a lot about desktop publishing in the last six months, and there's no doubt now that it's here to stay (see the supplementary section in the August issue of *InfoSystems*). That means that we'll eventually be doing some of our production work using desktop publishing. Although this work will probably be done in the production department, some of it may be done in the editorial department. That's why we should start learning more about it. If we all have PC ATs, of course, we'll be able to run desktop publishing software on our own systems.

The benefits of a PC-based system

Figure 2 summarizes the three primary benefits that we'll get if we switch to PC-based systems. The most important of these in terms of system justification is improved editorial productivity. But the others could be important too.

Why our editors should switch to PC-based systems

Improved editorial productivity

Resulting from

Improved system speed
Improved word processing functions
Spreadsheet software for project management
Writing analyzers

Benefit value

Assuming that each editor uses word processing one-half of the time on the job:

> A 5% increase in word processing productivity for an editor earning $30,000 per year means a benefit value of $750/year.
>
> A 10% increase means a benefit value of $1,500 per year.
>
> A 20% increase means a benefit value of $3,000 per year.

Improved editorial quality

Resulting from

Spelling checker
Writing analyzers

Benefit value

What is the value of fewer spelling and grammatical errors? What is the value of a manuscript that's easier to read?

Adaptability to future systems

Resulting from

Our experiences with current versions of word processing, analyzer, graphics, and desktop publishing software

Benefit value

This has no value in the short term, but it means we'll be able to save money by converting to improved versions of software products. And the improvements are going to come on PC-based systems.

Figure 2 The benefits of a PC-based system

As I present these, I'll try to give you some idea of what the value of these benefits might be.

Improved editorial productivity Editors who use PC-based systems instead of our current system should improve their productivity due to the improvements in system speed and the improvements in word processing functions like pagination and checking spelling. However, the editors may also improve their productivity by using spreadsheet software for project management or writing analyzers for grammar checking.

How much will their productivity improve? That's impossible to say, and I doubt that doing a study of it will give us a clear answer to this question either. Speaking personally, though, I can say that my word processing productivity has improved by at least 10 percent since I've switched to *WordPerfect* on an IBM AT. In fact, I would say that it has increased by 20 percent or more. Now, when I help a colleague do something on our minicomputer system, I am frustrated by the continual delays and by the use of its cumbersome, inefficient functions. These inefficiencies never bothered me that much when I used the system, but now I've been spoiled by a system that's much faster so I realize how inefficient the old system is.

To put a dollar value on an increase in word processing productivity, I've assumed a base editorial salary of $30,000, and I've assumed that editors use word processing about one-half of their working hours. Using these numbers, a 5% increase in productivity leads to a value of $750 per year; 10% leads to a value of $1500 per year; and 20% leads to a value of $3000 per year. These calculations are summarized in figure 2.

Improved editorial quality If you use a modern spelling checker and writing analyzer, the quality of your work has to improve. And if you work more efficiently, you'll have more time and energy to spend on the quality of your work. So there's no doubt that the quality of our work will improve if our editors switch to PC-based systems.

What is the value of this benefit? I leave that up to you. Fewer spelling errors and grammatical errors probably won't help us sell any one book. But an overall improvement in quality will help us establish a reputation that will sell more books in the future.

Adaptability to future systems Creating and selling PC software is a highly competitive business. That's why word processing and other software products keep improving. In contrast, the software for minicomputers is relatively static. New product announcements are infrequent, and minicomputer software hasn't improved to near the extent that microcomputer software has improved in the last six years. I expect this to continue during the next decade. So if you want to be able to buy and use the most advanced software, you're going to have to use IBM PCs and PS/2s, not minicomputers.

To some extent, then, you can view a switch to PC-based systems as preparation for the future. By getting used to these systems now, we'll be ready for the improvements that we've come to expect in PC software: improvements in word processing, in writing analyzers, in graphics packages, and in desktop publishing. And each time we install one of these improved products, we'll be improving our editorial operations. Although this benefit probably doesn't have any value when we first switch to PC-based systems, it will save us money in the future and it will help us stay competitive.

Why our editors should switch to PC-based systems

Typical hardware costs	
An AT clone with color monitor and 40 megabyte hard disk	$2,500
Printer	500
	$3,000
Typical software costs	
Word processing package	$ 400
Spreadsheet software	100
Writing analyzer	50
	$ 550
Typical training costs	
Training and reference materials	$ 50
One week of $30,000 salary	600
	$ 650
Total cost	
Hardware	$3,000
Software	550
Training	650
	$4,200

Figure 3 Typical costs for a PC-based system

The costs of a PC-based system

Figure 3 summarizes the costs of a typical PC-based system. The numbers here are just approximations because I can't say right now exactly which system and which software products we should buy. Also, we may be able to get quantity discounts if we buy several systems at once.

Hardware costs I purchased my system, an AT clone, for around $2500. It is a powerful, high-speed system with a color monitor. If necessary, it can be expanded so it will run any software that we are likely to install in the future. I also purchased a printer for around $500; it is a major improvement over our current minicomputer printer. I would recommend a system like this for each person in the editorial department.

Software costs I think each person in the editorial department should have one of the most advanced word processing packages. I've been using one of the best, which cost around $400. I also think each editor should have a spreadsheet program and a writing analyzer. We can buy these for about $150 per editor. We may also want to buy one or more copies of a desktop publishing package so we can evaluate it and use it whenever it is appropriate.

Training costs Since our editors already know how to use a word processing system, it should be relatively easy for them to learn how to use the PC software that they will need. As a result, we shouldn't need to buy expensive training materials. The manuals that come with the software products are adequate for most training purposes. When they aren't, we should be able to buy books that will satisfy our training requirements. So a budget of about $50 for each editor should be adequate for training and reference materials.

The more expensive part of the training budget is going to be the time lost while an editor learns how to use a new system and its software. Fortunately, I didn't find this lost time to be excessive. Although I was frustrated by my PC for the first two weeks or so, I estimate my total amount of lost time for training at about one full week. At an annual salary of $30,000, the cost of this lost time will be about $600 per editor.

Cost/benefit analysis

In figure 4, I have calculated the payback period in years and the return-on-investment (ROI) percent based on the costs and benefit values that I have already presented. These calculations use the benefit values for improved productivity only, because these values are the most predictable. At a 10 percent improvement in word processing productivity, the benefit value is $1500 for an editor who earns $30,000 per year, so the payback period is 2.8 years and the ROI is 35.7%. Because I think a 10 percent improvement is a conservative estimate of what the actual improvement will be, I'm confident that the actual payback period will be shorter and the ROI higher than these numbers indicate.

When we analyze costs and benefits, though, I don't think we should disregard the benefits of improved editorial quality and our adaptability to future systems. Although it may be hard to put a value on them, they are real benefits. Also, I haven't even mentioned the possible values of some intangible benefits like reduced eyestrain or the improved morale that our editors may experience when they use state-of-the-art systems. These benefits could lead to fewer sick days and reduced employee turnover. When you consider all of the possible benefits, I think it's clear that we should replace our minicomputer system with PC-based systems for all editors as soon as possible.

Recommendations

If you agree that we should get PC-based systems for all of our editors, there are still several questions to be answered. What hardware should we buy? What software should we buy? How should we handle the conversion? And when should each editor convert?

For now, let me give you some quick answers to these questions. Then, if you want more detail, I'll be happy to provide it.

Productivity improvement = 5%

Payback

$4200 divided by $750 = 5.6 years

ROI

$750 divided by $4200 times 100 = 17.9%

Productivity improvement = 10%

Payback

$4200 divided by $1,500 = 2.8 years

ROI

$1,500 divided by $4200 times 100 = 35.7%

Productivity improvement = 20%

Payback

$4200 divided by $3,000 = 1.4 years

ROI

$3,000 divided by $4200 times 100 = 71.4%

Figure 4 Payback and return-on-investment (ROI) possibilities based on productivity improvements only

What hardware should we buy? As I see it, what we want to buy today are clones of IBM ATs. To get the system speed that we want, we can't accept systems that are less powerful than ATs. But we don't have to buy the more expensive PS/2 systems because they don't offer anything that we need right now. Also, AT clones will run the OS/2 operating system when it becomes available and when we feel that it offers us some capability that we need.

What software should we buy? I don't think we can go wrong if we buy one of the best-selling word processing packages. I've been using *WordPerfect* so I'm probably biased in its favor, but I'm confident that it does everything our editors are used to doing and much more. Also, it consistently gets top ratings by the editors of the leading computer magazines.

If you want to consider other word processing packages, we can do that too. It's difficult to choose between two packages, though, if you haven't actually used them both for editorial work. That's why a detailed evaluation can be time consuming.

In addition to word processing, I think each editor should have one or more writing analyzers. So far, I've used *Grammatik II* and *RightWriter*, and both have some useful features. I'm also evaluating another one right now. These programs are relatively inexpensive, though, so the choice isn't that critical.

If any of our editors wants to try using spreadsheet software for project management, I think we should provide this software too. However, I don't think our editors will use this type of software much, so an inexpensive program should be adequate for their purposes. One such program is *VP Planner*.

As we get more experience with PC software, we can evaluate new products. Whenever we find a program that's useful, we can add it to an editor's system. If you look back to the cost summary in figure 3, you can see that the major costs for each editor are going to be for hardware, training, and the word processing software. As a result, we can add new software to an editor's system at a marginal cost.

How and when should we convert? If you're convinced that our editors should convert to AT systems, you may be asking yourself how and when we should do the conversion. Should all of the editors convert at once? Or, should we convert one or two editors at a time? Because it's easy to convert an editor from a terminal to a PC-based system, I think we can do this in many different ways. As a result, conversion shouldn't put an unnecessary strain on our editorial budget, and it shouldn't interfere with the completion of any of our projects.

My only recommendation is that our editors convert to the new systems after they complete one editorial project and before they start the next one. That way they can devote themselves to the training that is required for the new systems without having to worry about ongoing projects. After a few days of training, they can start work on their next projects knowing that their productivity will be down for the first few weeks that they use the new system, but after that it will be up.

Conclusion

Whether or not you decide that our editors should convert to PC-based systems, I thought you should be aware of the word processing and system improvements of the last six years. I remember you recalling how much your productivity improved when you switched from a typewriter to our current system back in 1982. Now, in 1988, I think you'll enjoy a similar improvement in productivity if you switch to a PC-based system. The improvement won't be quite as dramatic as your earlier one, but you'll probably remember it fondly for many years to come. That's why I think the sooner we all make the conversion to PC-based systems, the better off our editorial department will be.

Appendix C

Writing procedure summaries

The twelve steps for developing a unit

Analyze

1. Define the job.
2. Get the information you need.
3. Select the content.

Plan

4. Plan the topics and subtopics.
5. Plan the headings and subheadings.
6. Plan the visual aids.
7. Plan the paragraphs.

Write

8. Develop the visual aids.
9. Write the text.

Revise

10. Analyze and improve the structure of the first draft.
11. Edit and revise the first draft.
12. Proofread and correct the second draft.

Detailed procedures for the twelve steps
within the procedure for developing a unit

Step 1: Define the job.

1. Define the audience.
2. Define your purpose or purposes.
3. Consider alternatives to the document you're developing.

Step 2: Get the information you need.

This book assumes that you've already developed effective techniques for getting the information you need. However, you should be aware that spreadsheet software, outline processors, and database software can help you organize that information.

Step 3: Select the content.

1. Create a preliminary contents list.
2. Expand the contents list.
3. Select the final contents.

Step 4: Plan the topics and subtopics.

1. Group the contents into topics.
2. Arrange the topics into a reasonable presentation sequence.
3. If necessary, divide the topics into subtopics.
4. Try to develop alternative topic plans.
5. Select the best plan.

Step 5: Plan the headings and subheadings.

1. Rewrite your topic plan in language that is meaningful to your readers.
2. If necessary, improve the structure of your plan.

Step 6: Plan the visual aids.

1. Identify the visual aids that will improve the effectiveness of the topics and subtopics in your heading plan.

Writing procedures 401

2. Develop a legend list, rough drafts, or first drafts for the visual aids you've planned.

Step 7: Plan the paragraphs.

1. Expand your heading plan into a paragraph plan.
2. If necessary, check your final contents list against your paragraph plan to make sure your plan provides for all of the content items.

Step 8: Develop the visual aids.

For most of your documents, you will use PC software for developing the visual aids that you need. As a result, the procedures for developing these aids will vary from one software product to another.

Step 9: Write the text.

Chapters 8 through 13 in this book present the skills for effective writing. Once you have planned the paragraphs you're going to write (step 7), you use these skills to write the first draft of your document.

Step 10: Analyze and improve the structure of the first draft.

1. Develop a paragraph analysis.
2. Identify any structural problems.
3. Plan the structural improvements.
4. Revise the draft to correct its structural problems.

Step 11: Edit and revise the first draft.

1. Edit the draft.
2. Revise the draft.
3. Run your spelling checker and correct any misspellings.
4. If necessary, run your writing analyzer and revise based on its suggestions.

Step 12: Proofread and correct the second draft.

1. Proofread the draft.
2. Correct the draft.

The six steps for developing a multi-unit document
1. Define the job.
2. Get the information you need.
3. Select the content.
4. Plan the table of contents.
5. Develop each unit using the 12-step writing procedure.
6. Proofread the entire document.

Appendix D

Writing Guidelines

The principles of paragraphing

1. Put one and only one idea in each paragraph.
2. Develop the idea of each paragraph fully.
3. Start each paragraph with a sentence that gives the idea of the paragraph or a sentence that provides a transition from the previous paragraph.

Two rules of thumb for effective paragraphing

1. If your paragraphs don't contain three or more sentences, it's a sign that they aren't fully developed. Exceptions: paragraphs that introduce topics, subtopics, or other paragraphs.
2. If your paragraphs are more than seven sentences or 15 typewritten lines long, it's a sign that they should be presented as two or more paragraphs. Otherwise, the paragraph length may affect readability.

Four guidelines for shortening your sentences

1. Put one and only one thought in each sentence.
2. Use the simple expression.
3. Use fewer adjectives and adverbs.
4. Remove unnecessary words.

Four guidelines for simplifying your words

1. Use common words whenever possible.
2. Avoid words with prefixes and suffixes.
3. Avoid technical terms and jargon.
4. Avoid elegant variation.

Four guidelines for expressing your exact meaning

1. Be specific.
2. Use the active voice.
3. Avoid figurative language.
4. Avoid trite expressions.
5. Avoid nouns used as adjectives.

Three ways to provide paragraph continuity

1. Subject or word repetition
2. Pronouns and pointers
3. Connecting words

Four ways to provide sentence continuity

1. Subject or word repetition
2. Pronouns and pointers
3. Connecting words
4. Parallel sentence structures

Three guidelines for improving the tone of your writing

1. Write with a *you* attitude.
2. Write with a positive attitude.
3. Write with a conversational style.

Ten guidelines for improving the style of your writing

1. Write about people doing things.
2. Use quotations.
3. Use an occasional question.
4. Use *I, we,* and *you.*
5. Use other pronouns and pointer words.
6. Use *that,* not *which.*

7. Remove unnecessary *that*s.
8. Use more contractions.
9. Avoid constructions such as *he/she* and *and/or*.
10. Use an occasional sentence fragment.

Three guidelines for avoiding sexist language

1. Write with a *you* language, not a *he* or *she* language.
2. Use plurals when describing the actions of men and women.
3. Avoid sexist words and terms.

The four basic sentence structures for business writing

1. The simple sentence without introductory or concluding phrases
2. The compound sentence
3. The complex sentence with an introductory adverbial clause
4. The complex sentence with a concluding adverbial clause

Three ways to expand the basic sentence structures

1. Use introductory words and phrases.
2. Use noun clauses.
3. Use restrictive adjective clauses.

Three ways to simplify your sentences

1. Avoid participial phrases.
2. Avoid non-restrictive clauses and phrases.
3. Avoid lengthy parentheticals.

Three guidelines for improving your sentence structures

1. Limit the complexity of your sentence structures.
2. Show relationships by using complex sentences with adverbial clauses.
3. Avoid a series of sentences starting with the subjects.

Six fundamental rules of grammar

1. Use complete sentences.
2. Make sure each verb agrees with its subject.
3. Make sure each pronoun reference is clear and that each pronoun agrees with its antecedent.
4. Make sure your verb forms are simple and consistent.
5. Make sure your modifiers clearly relate to the words they modify.
6. Keep your parallel constructions parallel.

Index

Active voice, 232
Adjective clause, 292
Adverbial clause, 287
Analysis phase, 34, 49, 55
Antecedent, 306

Bar chart, 15
Bold italic style, 354
Bold style, 354
Boldface italic style, 354
Boldface style, 354
Book style, 354
Business graphics software, 12, 70

CAD program, 22
Capitalization, 316, 322
CD ROM, 25
Chapter opener, 368
Chronological organization, 94
Clause, 282
Clause, adjective, 292
Clause, adverbial, 287
Clause, dependent, 282
Clause, independent, 282
Clause, main, 282
Clause, non-restrictive, 295
Clause, restrictive, 293
Clause, subordinate, 282
Clip art, 15
Closed system of punctuation, 313
Complex sentence, 287
Compound sentence, 285
Compound subject, 285
Compound verb, 285
Computer aided design and drafting program, 22
Concluding headings, 110
Connecting word, 247
Connective, 247
Contents, 179
Contents list, 37, 77, 80
Contents list, final, 77, 128
Contents page, 366
Contents, preliminary, 73

Contents, selection, 73
Contents, table of, 179
Continuity, paragraph, 245
Continuity, sentence, 249
Coordinating conjunction, 285

Dangling modifier, 310
Database, 22
Database software, 22
Deadwood, 226
Decreasing order of importance, 92
Dependent clause, 282
Descriptive paragraph, 205
Desktop publishing, 17, 333, 349
Dialogue, 197
Diction, 322
Document, 34, 55, 177, 333, 350
Document, one-unit, 34, 177
Document, multi-unit, 34, 177
Draft, final, 45, 174
Draft, first, 41, 143, 157
Draft, second, 43, 45, 174
Draft, structure of a, 41, 158
Draw program, 22

Editing, 43, 165
Editing marks, 165
Electronic note pad, 19
Electronic spreadsheet software, 12, 70
Elegant variation, 229
Embedded list, 201
Executive summary, 335
Expanded contents list, 74

Familiar-to-unfamiliar organization, 93
Figurative language, 234
Figure, 125
Figure, inline, 152
Figure of speech, 234
Final contents list, 77, 128
Final draft, 45, 174
First draft, 41, 143, 157
Flesch Readability Formula, 214

Folio, 365
Font, 358
Foot margin, 363
Footer, 334, 363
Functional organization, 94
Future tense, 309

Geographical organization, 94
Grammar, 304
Grammar checker, 9
Gunning Fog Index, 217
Gutter margin, 363

Hardware, 3
Head margin, 363
Header, 334, 363
Heading plan, 37, 102, 107, 113
Headings, 101, 145
Headings, concluding, 110
Headings, introductory, 109
Headings, level-1, 149
Headings, level-2, 149
Headings, level-3, 151
Headings, run-in, 149
How-to organization, 94

Idea processor, 19
Illustration, 125
Increasing order of importance, 92
Independent clause, 282
Inline figure, 152
Inline visual aid, 152
Introductory headings, 109
Introductory phrase, 291
Italic style, 354
Italics, 316

Jargon, 229
Job definition, 35
Justification, 343
Justified text, 343, 359

Laser printer, 18
Leading, 358
Legend, 121
Legend list, 120

Level-1 heading, 149
Level-2 heading, 149
Level-3 heading, 151
Line chart, 15
Line length, 358
Linkage, paragraph, 245
Linkage, sentence, 249
List, contents, 37, 77, 80
List, embedded, 201
List, final contents, 77, 128
List, legend, 120
List, numbered, 198
List, preliminary contents, 73
List, sequenced topic, 87
List, topic, 86
List, unnumbered, 201

Main clause, 282
Margin, 363
Margin, foot, 363
Margin, gutter, 363
Margin, head, 363
Multi-unit document, 34, 177

Narrative paragraph, 205
Non-restrictive clause, 295
Non-restrictive phrase, 295
Noun clause, 292
Numbered list, 198

Object oriented drawing program, 21
On-line forum, 24
On-line information service, 24
On-line thesaurus, 8, 324
One-unit document, 34
Opener, chapter, 368
Opener, section, 368
Open system of punctuation, 313
Order of importance, decreasing, 92
Order of importance, increasing, 92
Order of interest, 92
Order of support, 205
Order of climax, 205
Organization, chronological, 94
Organization, familiar-to-unfamiliar, 93
Organization, functional, 94

Organization, geographical, 94
Organization, how-to, 94
Organization, paragraph, 205
Organization, procedural, 93
Organization, simple-to-complex, 93
Organization, traditional, 95
Organizational methods, 37, 92, 177, 205
Orphan, 343
Outline, 50
Outline processor, 19, 69, 78, 98

Paint program, 21
Paragraph analysis, 43, 158
Paragraph continuity, 245
Paragraph linkage, 245
Paragraph plan, 41, 127, 203
Paragraph organization, 205
Paragraph transition, 245
Parallel sentence structures, 251
Parenthetical, 295
Participial phrase, 293
Participle, 293
Passive voice, 232
Past tense, 309
PC, 3, 78
Personal computer, 3
Phrase, 282
Phrase, introductory, 291
Phrase, non-restrictive, 295
Phrase, participial, 293
Pica, 359
Pie chart, 14
Planning phase, 34, 49, 85
Point, 356
Pointer, 245
Pointer word, 245
Pop-up product, 8
Preliminary contents list, 73
Present tense, 309
Presentation, 333
Presentation sequences, 96
Presentation software, 19
Primary research, 66
Primary source, 66
Procedural organization, 93
Production, 352

Promising a benefit, 105
Pronoun, 245
Proof, 174, 324
Proofread, 174
Proper noun, 316
Punctuation, 312
Punctuation, closed system, 313
Punctuation, open system, 313

Ragged right, 343
Ragged-right text, 359
Readability, 10, 165, 171, 213
Reading grade level (RGL), 218
Regular style, 354
Relative pronoun, 292
Report titles, 108
Resolution, 18
Restrictive clause, 293
Revising, 43, 166
Revision phase, 34, 157
RGL (reading grade level), 218
Roman style, 354
Rule, 343, 365
Run-in heading, 149
Running head, 365

Sans serif, 356
Screenshow, 15
Second draft, 43, 45, 174
Secondary research, 67
Secondary source, 67
Section opener, 368
Sentence, complex, 287
Sentence, compound, 285
Sentence, simple, 284
Sentence, strung-along, 290
Sentence, topic, 195
Sentence continuity, 249
Sentence fragment, 271, 304
Sentence linkage, 249
Sentence transition, 249
Sequenced topic list, 87
Serif, 356
Sexist language, 272
Simple sentence, 284
Simple-to-complex organization, 93

Software, 3, 25, 78
Software, business graphics, 12, 70
Software, computer aided design and drafting (CAD), 22
Software, database, 22
Software, desktop publishing, 350
Software, electronic note pad, 19
Software, electronic spreadsheet, 12, 70
Software, object oriented drawing, 21
Software, on-line thesaurus, 8, 324
Software, presentation, 19
Software, word processing, 5, 19, 69, 78
Software, writing analyzer, 9, 168
Special characters, 165
Spelling checker, 7
Structure of a draft, 41, 158
Strung-along sentence, 290
Style, 260
Style, bold italic, 354
Style, bold, 354
Style, boldface italic, 354
Style, boldface, 354
Style, book, 354
Style, italic, 354
Style, regular, 354
Style, Roman, 354
Style, type, 354
Style sheet, 369
Subheading, 101, 145
Subject repetition, 245
Subordinate clause, 282
Subordinating conjunction, 287
Subtopic, 86

Table of contents, 179
Text, 41
Text, justified, 343, 359
Text, ragged-right, 359
Thesaurus, on-line, 8, 324
Three-level topic plan, 97
Title page, 366
Tone, 257
Topic, 86
Topic list, 86
Topic list, sequenced, 87
Topic name, 86

Topic plan, 37, 88, 102
Topic plan, three-level, 97
Topic sentence, 195
Traditional organization, 95
Transition, paragraph, 245
Transition, sentence, 249
Trim size, 363
Trite, 236
Type family, 354
Type size, 356
Type style, 354
Typeface, 354
Typography, 349

Underlining, 316
Unit, 179
Unit opener, 366
Unnumbered list, 201

Verb-subject agreement, 305
Visual aid, inline, 152
Visual aids, 39, 41, 118, 134

What-if analysis, 12
Widow, 343
Word processing, 5
Word processing package, 5
Word processor, 19, 69, 78
Word repetition, 245
Word wrap, 5
Writing analyzer, 9, 168
Writing phase, 34, 133

Comment/Order form

Your opinions count

I'm eager to hear what you think of *Write better with a PC*. So please send me any comments, criticisms, suggestions, or questions. If you find any errors in the book, typographical or otherwise, please point them out so we can correct them in the next printing. And if you'd like a response, be sure to fill in your name and address.

Mike Murach

Dear Mike: _____
_____
_____
_____
_____
_____
_____

Name _____
Company (if company address) _____
Address _____
City, state, zip _____
Daytime phone number (including area code) _____

☐ I want to order more copies of *Write better with a PC*. Please send me _____ copies at $19.95 each.

☐ Bill me for the books plus shipping and handling (and sales tax in California).

☐ Charge the books plus UPS shipping and handling (and sales tax in California) to my:

☐ MasterCard   ☐ VISA

Card number _____   Valid thru (mo/yr) _____
Signature _____

☐ I want to SAVE shipping and handling charges. Here's my check or money order for $_____. California residents, please add 6% sales tax to your total. (Offer valid in the U.S. only.)

To order more quickly,

Call toll free 1-800-221-5528
  (Weekdays, 9 to 4 Pacific Standard Time)
In California, call 1-800-221-5527
Fax: 1-209-275-9035

```
                                    ┃┃┃┃
```

BUSINESS REPLY MAIL
First Class   Permit No. 3063   Fresno, CA

POSTAGE WILL BE PAID BY ADDRESSEE

Mike Murach & Associates, Inc.
4697 West Jacquelyn Avenue
Fresno, CA 93722-9960

NO POSTAGE
NECESSARY
IF MAILED
IN THE
UNITED STATES

Comment/Order form

Your opinions count

I'm eager to hear what you think of *Write better with a PC*. So please send me any comments, criticisms, suggestions, or questions. If you find any errors in the book, typographical or otherwise, please point them out so we can correct them in the next printing. And if you'd like a response, be sure to fill in your name and address.

                                                                                    Mike Murach

Dear Mike: _____
_____
_____
_____
_____
_____
_____

Name _____
Company (if company address) _____
Address _____
City, state, zip _____
Daytime phone number (including area code) _____

☐ I want to order more copies of *Write better with a PC*. Please send me _____ copies at $19.95 each.

☐ Bill me for the books plus shipping and handling (and sales tax in California).

☐ Charge the books plus UPS shipping and handling (and sales tax in California) to my:

  ☐ MasterCard   ☐ VISA

  Card number _____ Valid thru (mo/yr) _____
  Signature _____

☐ I want to SAVE shipping and handling charges. Here's my check or money order for $_____. California residents, please add 6% sales tax to your total. (Offer valid in the U.S. only.)

To order more quickly,

Call toll free 1-800-221-5528
   (Weekdays, 9 to 4 Pacific Standard Time)

In California, call 1-800-221-5527

Fax: 1-209-275-9035

fold

BUSINESS REPLY MAIL
First Class   Permit No. 3063   Fresno, CA

POSTAGE WILL BE PAID BY ADDRESSEE

Mike Murach & Associates, Inc.

4697 West Jacquelyn Avenue
Fresno, CA 93722-9960

NO POSTAGE
NECESSARY
IF MAILED
IN THE
UNITED STATES

fold

Comment/Order form

Your opinions count

I'm eager to hear what you think of *Write better with a PC*. So please send me any comments, criticisms, suggestions, or questions. If you find any errors in the book, typographical or otherwise, please point them out so we can correct them in the next printing. And if you'd like a response, be sure to fill in your name and address.

Mike Murach

Dear Mike: _____
_____
_____
_____
_____
_____
_____

Name _____
Company (if company address) _____
Address _____
City, state, zip _____
Daytime phone number (including area code) _____

☐ I want to order more copies of *Write better with a PC*. Please send me _____ copies at $19.95 each.

☐ Bill me for the books plus shipping and handling (and sales tax in California).

☐ Charge the books plus UPS shipping and handling (and sales tax in California) to my:

    ☐ MasterCard   ☐ VISA

    Card number _____ Valid thru (mo/yr) _____
    Signature _____

☐ I want to SAVE shipping and handling charges. Here's my check or money order for $_____. California residents, please add 6% sales tax to your total. (Offer valid in the U.S. only.)

To order more quickly,

Call toll free 1-800-221-5528
    (Weekdays, 9 to 4 Pacific Standard Time)

In California, call 1-800-221-5527

Fax: 1-209-275-9035

BUSINESS REPLY MAIL
First Class   Permit No. 3063   Fresno, CA

POSTAGE WILL BE PAID BY ADDRESSEE

Mike Murach & Associates, Inc.

4697 West Jacquelyn Avenue
Fresno, CA 93722-9960

Comment/Order form

Your opinions count

I'm eager to hear what you think of *Write better with a PC*. So please send me any comments, criticisms, suggestions, or questions. If you find any errors in the book, typographical or otherwise, please point them out so we can correct them in the next printing. And if you'd like a response, be sure to fill in your name and address.

Mike Murach

Dear Mike: _____
_____
_____
_____
_____
_____
_____

Name _____
Company (if company address) _____
Address _____
City, state, zip _____
Daytime phone number (including area code) _____

☐ I want to order more copies of *Write better with a PC*. Please send me _____ copies at $19.95 each.

☐ Bill me for the books plus shipping and handling (and sales tax in California).

☐ Charge the books plus UPS shipping and handling (and sales tax in California) to my:

☐ MasterCard   ☐ VISA

Card number _____ Valid thru (mo/yr) _____
Signature _____

☐ I want to SAVE shipping and handling charges. Here's my check or money order for $_____. California residents, please add 6% sales tax to your total. (Offer valid in the U.S. only.)

To order more quickly,

Call toll free 1-800-221-5528
(Weekdays, 9 to 4 Pacific Standard Time)

In California, call 1-800-221-5527

Fax: 1-209-275-9035

BUSINESS REPLY MAIL
First Class   Permit No. 3063   Fresno, CA

POSTAGE WILL BE PAID BY ADDRESSEE

Mike Murach & Associates, Inc.

4697 West Jacquelyn Avenue
Fresno, CA 93722-9960